SYLVIA BROWNE:

Accepting the Psychic Torch

ALSO BY SYLVIA BROWNE

SYLVIA BROWNE:
Accepting the Psychic Torch

Sylvia Browne

HAY HOUSE, INC.

Carlsbad, California • New York City
London • Sydney • Johannesburg
Vancouver • Hong Kong • New Delhi

Published and distributed in the United States by: Hay House, Inc.: www.hayhouse .com • **Published and distributed in Australia by:** Hay House Australia Pty. Ltd.: www.hayhouse.com.au • **Published and distributed in the United Kingdom by:** Hay House UK, Ltd.: www.hayhouse.co.uk • **Published and distributed in the Republic of South Africa by:** Hay House SA (Pty), Ltd.: www.hayhouse.co.za • **Distributed in Canada by:** Raincoast: www.raincoast.com • **Published in India by:** Hay House Publishers India: www.hayhouse.co.in

Design: Tricia Breidenthal

Interior photos courtesy of the author

Library of Congress Control Number: 2009924441

ISBN: 978-1-4019-2042-5

12 11 10 09   4 3 2 1
1st edition, October 2009

Printed in the United States of America

To my beloved husband, Michael

✳ CONTENTS ✳

❖

ACCEPTING THE PSYCHIC TORCH

❖

(**Please note:** The three books contained in this volume were written at different points in Sylvia Browne's life, with many years passing between each work. Every effort has been made during the compiling process to ensure that all three books are as accurate as possible, yet in the end, Sylvia put each of them together *to the best of her recollection.*)

⇥ INTRODUCTION ⇤

This year (2009) I will be 73 years old. I have been doing readings for about 55 of those years and have met so many remarkable people during that time! In fact, I deeply desire to get back to doing those one-on-one readings—I miss that closeness—so I've decided to limit my travels.

As I embark upon my "farewell tour" of lecturing, I've been thinking about my life up to this point, including the wonderful adventures I've had and the incredible things I've learned. I thought that this would be the perfect time to release a volume containing my "life story" up until now: including my first book, *Adventures of a Psychic,* written so many years ago with my friend Antoinette May; and *If You Could See What I See,* the "sequel" of sorts that was penned by me alone. And as my faithful readers know, I've spoken countless times of the impact my grandmother Ada had on me, both as a psychic and a human being. I've often mentioned that I'd like to compile a book of her letters and inspirational sayings . . . and I've done so now. *Accepting the Psychic Torch* is both a tribute to this amazing woman (and I do indeed share many of her letters and sayings) and another chapter in the story of my life.

Please note that while I may not be traveling so much anymore, this doesn't mean that I'm going to stop being there for you. You all are so important to me, and I will continue researching, writing, and doing readings for you as long as I am able. After all, there is so much more I have left to do in order to keep that psychic torch lit, and I look forward to the journey.

May you enjoy the material within these pages!

— Sylvia Browne

Adventures

of a

PSYCHIC

PREFACE

I had many reasons for wanting this book written, but two of my primary goals deserve special mention. First of all, I wanted to give people an understanding of what a psychic is truly all about. Being psychic is a family pattern that includes my grandmother, Ada Coil; an uncle; and my youngest son, Christopher Dufresne. The genetic aspect is important, but it is not the truest measure of what being psychic really entails. The real issues revolve around our trials and tribulations, our heartaches and struggles, and the tempering of our souls to make us a vehicle for God.

Second, this is a story about a woman. One who is perhaps (is this a crime?) too giving, too naive, too understanding, and too selfless. Yet, this woman is very intelligent, a type of savant almost, as far as people's lives, truth, and spirituality are concerned. I also want to show that a religious or spiritual person is also very human, not saintly, and will experience the same hurts, deceptions, fears, and phobias as everyone else.

Psychics are really just human beings with a gift, which does not serve us personally very well. I have found, as I get older, that the gift is not for my benefit in any way, shape, or form. It is something to be given away. If psychics could benefit from their gift, they would simply win the big lotto and never do what they are supposed to do—help others.

My life reads like a struggle for survival, as do most lives. There are loves that went unrequited, challenges met, deceptions at the hands of friends, and people who hurt me. I think that my story is every man's story, it is every woman's story. I hope that it is a story of bravery, because I have certainly had to be courageous, strong, and sometimes, in the very bottom of my heart, very frightened, alone, and childlike.

Mine is a story of faith, a woman's faith in her God and her Goddess. I came here to herald the first wave of the Gnostic Way, which is the most ancient quest of man searching for truth and his own spirituality. Where Novus Spiritus (my Spiritual Church) goes from here is only known to God. As for me, I will always be helping people, always guiding as God sees fit. If I must do my work from the back of a goat cart, I will. My contract with God must be fulfilled.

You will see that this book is written with humor. You will see the friendship between Antoinette and me that spans more than 20 years. You will see the love and respect we have for each other; you will see that there are many things yet to come as surprises—not only for you, but even for me. Bear with me in this odyssey; bear with me in this journey. Understand and try to see beyond just the written word to the heart of the woman, the heart of the person, who possibly is too naive, too understanding, and too giving, but certainly has a lot of guts.

For all of you who toil in little dark corners, remember me sometimes, this girl from Missouri. I did not necessarily "make good," but I certainly gave it my all. I think that God simply wants us to give it our all, give it our best shot. So this is a book of friendship; this is a book about loyalty, pain, heartache, and challenges. It is everyone's story. Would I have changed any of it? I had to think hard on that, but I think not. Someone told me that I am a "karmic catharsis" for everyone, which seems to fit well. I know that we all learn by experiencing and watching how a life unfolds; I hope you enjoy mine, and can learn faster than I did.

God love you, I do....

— Sylvia Browne

INTRODUCTION

The first time I met Sylvia Browne—and her spirit guide, Francine—was at a séance in my living room. A small psychic research group gathered there on a weekly basis in the 1970s, an outgrowth of a parapsychology class that I was teaching at a nearby community college.

All of us—psychologists, lawyers, real estate appraisers, writers, editors, educators, and salespersons—were fascinated by the possibilities of this "new" science. All of us were eager to learn more about the other world of the paranormal; and, in so doing, learn more about ourselves.

We experimented with a variety of ESP tests and meditative techniques; we were regressed to past lives, had our auras photographed by Kirlian cameras, and observed spoon benders, healers, and plant communicators. Some of what we saw and did was impressive, some strained credulity.

In the fall of 1975, shortly after publication of an article I'd written for *Psychic* magazine, I received a telephone call. "The mediums that you wrote about were interesting," said the woman, a stranger, "but I know someone far more gifted. When you meet her—when you see what she can do—you'll want to write about *her*."

Perhaps my caller, too, was a little psychic.

Our group was excited about the prospects of a séance. Few had attended one. None of us had heard of Sylvia, and we had no idea what to expect. Envisioning a Madame Lazonga type with cape and turban, we were unprepared for the lively, down-to-earth woman who appeared with her then-husband, Dal.

Dal explained that Sylvia would be leaving her body while Francine, her spirit guide, entered it. "It's Francine, not Sylvia, who will be answering your questions."

"I've spent so much time out of my body waiting for Francine to get through talking that I began to hope that it might impede the aging process," Sylvia admitted.

"Has it?" we all wanted to know.

"Not a damn bit."

Sylvia lay down on the couch, a pillow under her head. "It's necessary to be very quiet as she goes under, but afterwards you can make as much noise as you like," Dal explained to us.

We sat silently, expectantly waiting for something to happen. At first nothing did. I studied the woman on the couch. She was lying absolutely still. As I watched, it seemed that slowly, almost imperceptibly, Sylvia's features began to change. Her face seemed broader, flatter, the large dark eyes less prominent; the eyelids now seemed slightly hooded.

"Francine's here with us now; she's inside Sylvia," Dal announced. "You can ask her anything you like."

When the others hesitated, I plunged in. Having just completed a book, I was curious about what my next project would be.

"It will be another book," Francine told me in the precise, almost stilted manner that I learned was characteristic of her. "You will be working on it very soon. You are going to take the back of a book—something that you have already written—and rearrange it with something new. What was the back will be the front. Something unused before will be part of a new book." (And that's exactly what happened.)

Suddenly there were many questions. Everyone had something to ask about health, about money, about career choices, about relationships—particularly about relationships.

"Will I *ever* get along with my mother?" a middle-aged woman asked.

"No, your mother will always be difficult," Francine replied. "She is a very critical woman. She gives you many mixed messages. Nothing you do satisfies her."

"Why, that's *my* mother you're talking about!" another woman exclaimed.

"No, it's mine," someone else said.

"Sounds more like mine," yet another voice insisted.

Soon everyone was laughing at the recognition of this common problem shared by so many—everyone, that is, but the woman on the couch, who remained silent, unperturbed. Francine didn't laugh; nor, of course, did Sylvia.

When the laughter finally stopped, the spirit guide continued. "It is best for you to keep in mind that tolerance for your mother's impossible demands will enable you to move toward your own perfection."

Later, when the séance was over and Sylvia had reappeared, I told her what had happened. "I miss everything," she lamented. "It must have been funny, but actually that description—it sounds like *my* mother."

That evening was the beginning of an enduring friendship. Sylvia's unique combination of humor, strength, courage, and insight has enriched my life in many ways—as has Francine's wisdom. I've spent a number of long nights with Sylvia in haunted houses, watching as she quite literally called forth the dead; I've observed her work with doctors and with the police. At the same time, the nature of my own work has brought me in contact with a number of gifted psychics.

There is no one that I trust and respect more than Sylvia Browne. Her story of triumph over adversity is truly inspiring. The wisdom that she has received from Francine brings meaning and order into the seeming random chaos of life. Francine's path is one of both compassion and ultimate transcendence. Anyone can follow that path; everyone can benefit from it.

— Antoinette May

(**Antoinette** is an author and journalist whose books include *Witness to War, Haunted Houses,* and *Wandering Ghosts of California.*)

CHAPTER ONE
People Are Talking

The capacity audience is restless, eager. This isn't just any TV show. These people seek more than entertainment. They want answers.

The excitement is palpable as the lights brighten, and the theme music goes on. The studio audience stomps and cheers without prompting as the ebullient host, Ross McGowan, announces, "Today we have with us the internationally known psychic, our own Sylvia Browne."

The rotating stage moves on cue, stopping with a sudden jerk to reveal a Junoesque woman with warm brown eyes that seem to dominate her entire face. There's a burst of spontaneous applause. In the trade, Sylvia Browne is known as "good TV" because the ratings invariably zoom when she appears.

Ann Fraser, the attractive blonde co-host, steps forward. Scanning the excited audience, she asks, "Is there anyone here who doesn't believe in psychics?"

A tall, dark man raises his hand defiantly. "There's some kind of dairy farm that you'll be going into," Sylvia tells him. "You have two sons, but are raising two other boys as well." Her smile broadens at the familiar look of astonishment. Then she adds, "You should check the transmission on your car and see a doctor about that left knee."

The man stares at her, surprise and confusion apparent on his face.

"Does any of this hit home?" Ann Fraser asks.

"I wish you'd go to someone else. This is kind of spooky," he answers.

"What do you mean 'spooky'?" Ann persists.

The man talks so softly that he has to be urged to speak up. "I just learned last night that I'd inherited a dairy farm. I took my car into the garage this morning and was told that the transmission's shot. My knee has been hurting a lot these days, an old football injury acting up. I have two sons and those other two boys—well, I'd rather not talk about them."

And so it goes for voyeurs at home as well as for the studio audience. People wave wildly for the microphone, eager to discuss their tangled love lives, their rare diseases, their finances, their neurotic families. Sylvia's mobile face plays at martyrdom, her eyes rolling comically. Her presence is large and maternal, her style fast and frequently profane. Even skeptics are drawn to her warmth and compassion.

An older, gray-haired woman stands, her arms almost hugging her chest. "Some of what you say seems kind of general to me," she accuses. "When you tell someone they're going to move—couldn't that apply to anyone in California?"

"Possibly," Sylvia concedes. "But suppose I say to you, 'You moved last month into a white stucco house with blue trim.' Is that general? Of course not. General is, 'You're moving from darkness into the light.'"

The woman's jaw drops. "You—you're right," she stammers. "I did move, that's my house."

"It was a good move," Sylvia assures her. "You're going to be happy there."

"One thing you can say," the woman concedes, "it's certainly good show biz."

"Yeah," Sylvia agrees. "There is a little entertainment in what I do, but most of it is 'heal fast and make well.' I'm a fast-food psychic. Fast food means you come in, you get what you need to get healed, and then you walk out the door. It's a kind of battlefield situation. Life is a kind of battlefield."

The audience oohs and aahs as the TV show continues, but this is the easy stuff. The information Sylvia divulges can be verified instantly. The real work comes when she goes into the future precognitively and talks about things that are beyond present awareness. The subjects shake their heads doubtfully. "Me, another baby! I'll be 45 in December. No way!" Or, "Move to Minnesota? You've got to be kidding. It wouldn't matter how good the job was." The verification will come later, sometimes much later. Sylvia will receive a call and be told, "Remember me, I was the one you said…well, I just wanted to tell you…"

The local CBS-TV show is aptly named *People Are Talking*. People *are* talking about Sylvia Browne. But more precisely, they come to talk about themselves—their hopes, their fears, sometimes even their secrets. It's not new. The questions asked of this modern seer are identical to those placed before the Delphic oracles thousands of years ago. Only the delivery system has changed.

A pretty red-haired woman stands up, waving eagerly at Sylvia. "I'd like to ask something for my girlfriend and myself," she says. "My friend's 30 and wants to get married. I'm a little younger; right now I'd be happy with a meaningful relationship. Do you see anyone coming into either of our lives?"

"Yes," Sylvia nods emphatically, "but you'll marry first."

"Ooh! Me first! Is it the guy I met on the cruise—blonde, a little taller than me?"

"No, hon, someone else. A big, tall guy, handsome."

"Mmmm, sounds good." The young woman sits down smiling happily.

"He sounds good to me, too," Sylvia says as her eyes brighten mischievously to the color of warm sherry.

The girl stands up again. "My friend—"

"Yes, hon, she'll marry too, but not for five years."

An older woman raises her hand timidly and then, encouraged by Sylvia, begins slowly, tentatively. "I lost a baby three years ago," she declares. "It was a crib death. Why did it happen?"

"The timing wasn't right for either of you. Who are we to question that? The entity came through briefly to help you with your spiritual perfection—someone who was close to you before. The two of you made an agreement to be together for just a little while."

"But I want another child. Will I ever—?"

"What day is it?"

"I think I could be...maybe..."

"That's what I'm saying. You're already there."

The woman virtually shrieks with happy excitement. The whole audience is clapping wildly. When the noise subsides, Sylvia informs her, "It'll be another boy."

Ann Fraser looks at Sylvia in surprise. "She didn't say the child was a boy."

Sylvia laughs. "She didn't have to—remember, I'm psychic."

Sylvia uses the same telepathic shorthand in the next question. "I was in a bad accident a year ago—" a short, stocky man begins. A medical problem is anticipated by everyone, but Sylvia knows better. Before he can frame his query, she has interrupted him. "Yes, you'll come out well on that," she predicts. When the man pauses in surprise, Sylvia encourages him. "Your lawsuit. You'll do very well. Don't change lawyers. The one you've got—the tall, bald guy—he's very good. Keep him."

Sylvia's manner is frequently flip, funny, often suggestive of a stand-up comic, but underlying it all is a warmth and compassion that draws skeptics and believers alike. Sylvia always speaks in specifics and shoots from the hip. Now looking about the studio, she spots a woman sitting on the aisle near the back. "You're concerned, aren't you? About something that may even approach blackmail," she suggests. "Don't pay it. None of what's happened is as it appears to you now. He's playing on your fears. Call him on it and he'll drop the whole business." The woman's face brightens. Her relief is obvious. "Thank you," she murmurs.

These are the happy, easy answers. The more traumatic ones are harder to deal with, especially on television. Often the messages Sylvia delivers are carefully couched. "I see two pregnancies this year," she tells a young woman who hopes to conceive a child. "Don't feel bad about the first. The second will be a girl—born early next spring." The word *miscarriage* isn't used.

But other times Sylvia is more direct. "That new red sports car you're so crazy about—get rid of it *right away*," she warns a glitzy brunette.

Eventually, there are questions about Sylvia herself. "It sounds like you believe in reincarnation," a man ventures.

"I don't believe," she answers. "I know. God is an equal-opportunity employer. Do you think He'd give us just one chance?"

"How long have you felt that way?"

"Always, I guess. When I was three, I'd insist that my father taste my food first. They tell me I'd sit very patiently watching him chew, waiting. When nothing happened, I'd dive in—I've always had quite an appetite. It must have been hard for me to wait, but I did. Apparently I had a strong memory of being poisoned in a past life and wasn't about to make that mistake again. Maybe I sensed even then that I had lots to accomplish this time around."

Most children are born with past-life recall, Sylvia believes, but they can't pass on the information available to them for lack of vocabulary. Impatient or skeptical parents compound the problem, so unfortunately much valuable information is lost forever because, as we grow older, we tend to forget.

"What's it like to be psychic?" a young man calls out from the back of the studio.

"What's it like *not* to be psychic?" she asks, shrugging. "I've always known things without being told. When I was only five or so, my father took me to the drugstore and sat me down in front of some picture books while he went off somewhere. Suddenly I had a very clear picture of him in my mind, talking on the phone. I could see the person he was talking to as well—a pretty blonde woman whom I didn't know. Poor Daddy! When I got home, I told the whole family all about it. The silence was deafening—at least while I was present. The next day Daddy started out the door with his fishing rod. What a little fink I was! 'He isn't really going fishing,' I told my mother. 'He's going on a trip with his girlfriend.' That afternoon my grandmother, who also had the gift, gave me a long lecture on psychic etiquette."

This was only the beginning of a rapidly unfolding drama, as some of the fans in the audience already know. "What about your spirit guide?" someone asks. The questioner is a scholarly looking woman in a far corner. "What about Francine?"

Even the regulars lean forward expectantly. For them it's a familiar but still fascinating story. "I was seven when Francine first appeared to me," Sylvia explains. "It seems that I was always able to hear messages that others couldn't, but they tended to be far off in the background, almost like a soft whisper that could be ignored. Francine was something else entirely. One night I was lying in bed playing with a flashlight when suddenly I saw this Indian woman.

"'Don't be afraid, Sylvia, I come from God,' she said. Don't be afraid! She was as close, as real, as—as—Ann Fraser," Sylvia insists, pointing to the woman sitting beside her. "And there she was standing right in the middle of my bedroom. I jumped up and ran out screaming. Fortunately—is there really such a thing as fortune or chance?—my psychic grandmother was staying with us. She was very ho-hum about it all. And that was reassuring to me. She explained that we all have spirit guides who are assigned to us as helpers. The only difference was that she and I could see ours."

Sylvia's guide is a South American Indian whose name in life was Iena. "That was a little too bizarre for a seven-year-old," Sylvia remembers. "I liked the name Francine, so that's what I rechristened my new friend. She didn't mind; in fact, she seemed to know exactly the sort of things that would appeal to me. I lost my fear of her completely when she taught me to play 'What are they saying downstairs?' You can imagine the stir that game created, but it was a nice stir. Francine, like Grandma, was and is the quintessence of psychic etiquette. In the beginning, she seemed very old to me—she was about 30, and there she remains."

It was difficult at first to accustom herself to Francine's thought patterns, Sylvia says. "She's so literal compared to us, I'm still sometimes surprised. For instance, if I were to ask her, 'Can you describe yourself?' Francine would just say, 'Yes,' and stop there. In reply to someone's question about a forthcoming holiday, she'll just say something like, 'I see you going to the high country to hook animals.' We'd interpret that as a fishing trip in the mountains."

Ross McGowan asks a question for the audience. "Don't you sometimes feel that what you tell people robs them of their free will?" he inquires.

Sylvia shakes her head. "Absolutely not. If I get it, you're supposed to know. I believe that what I receive comes from God, just as Francine told me long ago." She laughs good-naturedly. "I'd hate to think it was coming from me!"

Specifics are essential, she believes. "That's what mediumship is all about. I wouldn't be a professional if I told people all that Mickey Mouse stuff about going from darkness into the light. *Anybody* can say something like that, but what good does it do? You can't help someone without giving specific information. Francine comes through when I'm in the trance state and tells people about their soul work, what their mission in life is, their themes and patterns. I stay with the now, the gritty soap opera of life."

Sylvia is able to tune in to the "blueprint" within each of her clients. Although she prefers to do one-on-one predictions, she has acquired a national reputation for general-interest forecasts. "It's really no different," she tells the audience. "I just sit down and ask myself questions. What about the economy? What about the President's health? What about earthquakes? What about—"

"What about my report card?" a small boy cries out.

"Something's dragging and it's not P.E.," Sylvia warns him.

Though she has scant interest in sports, Sylvia is always in demand to predict winners. Her success rate here is amazing. "I don't think I was even aware of the Super Bowl until people began asking me about it," she admits. "Now I've picked the last five winners in a row. A few years back, I announced that the Oakland Raiders would be moving.

Then they did. People were outraged. You should have seen the letters I got. You'd have thought I did it myself." She shrugs her shoulders in a familiar gesture of resignation.

"But how do you do it?" Ann Fraser asks.

"I don't know," Sylvia confides. "I really don't. I just open myself up and it comes. I don't analyze. Like once I told a woman that she was going to start a worm farm. Yes, a worm farm! If I'd thought about that I wouldn't have said it, but I *didn't* think, I just opened my mouth and out it came—exactly what I was receiving. The woman wasn't surprised at all. 'Yeah,' she said, 'I always thought that would be an interesting way to make a living.'"

An older man rises to ask one last question. "What about *you*, Sylvia? What's in *your* future?"

Sylvia shakes her head, the honey blonde hair gleaming under the TV lights. "I never know. The gift isn't meant for the medium herself. If I weren't doing the right thing, it would all shut down. People ask me if I ever get bored answering the same old questions. The answer's no, I certainly don't. If it's important to you, it's important to me. People are funny, though. Once I told a man he'd be starting a new job on April 5th, and he called indignantly to tell me I was all wrong—it had been April 6th."

"But don't you *ever* see anything for yourself?" the questioner persists.

"Very rarely," she answers firmly, "and I'm glad it's that way." For an instant, Sylvia's face clouds as her thoughts turn unbidden to a tragic love affair long ago. There *had* been a warning.

Ross signals. It's commercial time. A brief windup and the show is over. Sylvia is smiling again at the audience as the revolving stage moves her backward into the shadows.

CHAPTER TWO
Francine's Friend

It was nearly midnight, and Sylvia Browne was on her way to the séance. As her car hugged the narrow, winding road that snaked its way along the craggy seacoast, she smiled wryly.

Did fiction strive to emulate truth, or was it actually the other way around? Tonight was the proverbial dark and stormy night. A few miles to the north, 12 people waited for her in a century-old farmhouse. She would be the 13th. There were some—certain San Francisco press members among them—who believed the house was haunted. How sensational—even terrifying—it all sounded! For Sylvia, it was neither. Fiction—truth? Truth—fiction?

The windshield wipers beat valiantly against the driving rain. Grateful for the presence of the man at the wheel beside her, Sylvia leaned back, eyes closed, thoughts wandering.

It had been an exhausting day, beginning with an early-morning distress call. A child was missing. Sylvia's psychic insights had scarcely enabled the San Jose Police Department to bring the mystery to a happy conclusion before another case developed—the unidentified body of a teenage girl.

Reluctantly, Sylvia had focused on the tragedy. In her mind's eye she "saw" a pretty blonde lying half-clothed and bleeding on the shoulder of a busy freeway. "Anderson," Sylvia had told the police officer. "Her last name's Anderson. Her first name begins with a *C*— Carol, maybe, no Carey—Carolyn. I'm not sure. But she knew the killer; she'd gotten into his car. He was angry, jealous. That's all I'm getting," she apologized. It had been enough. The case was well on the way to solution.

Then there'd been the regular scheduled readings. Eight clients that day in her Nirvana Foundation office. Some insights had been pleasant—the whereabouts of an heirloom ring pinpointed. Another had been humorous—the raging temperature of a canny but less than intellectual boy, explained by a hot-water faucet. Some after-school tutoring would take care of him. Sylvia sighed as she thought of another client, a woman whose illness was terminal. What could one offer her but honesty, compassion, and a faith in the continuity of the human spirit?

The ghost-chasing expedition that had brought Sylvia to this desolate strip of the northern California coast came into sharp perspective. There had been so much chatter about ghosts of late, so many macabre headlines, such a proliferation of films, both humorous and horrible. Surely no one could deny that the very mention of the word exerts a fascination.

Sylvia was well aware that this enterprise might amount to little more than a parlor game, yet there was always the chance that there was some substance to the strange set of circumstances that had resulted in her summons. She hoped the séance would be productive. Often they evoked startling revelations, but, she reminded herself, just as often they proved to be dull time-wasters. She smiled, recalling the numerous nights her tape recorders had picked up the very mortal snores of witnesses who'd grown weary waiting until nearly dawn for something to happen.

Whatever might occur that night, the facts of life and the anomaly of death were very clear to Sylvia. Long ago she'd discovered that people don't die at all. They only die to you. That was the sad part, the hard part, the lesson forced upon her when she was scarcely more than a toddler.

Today Sylvia Browne can truly say that her best and *closest* friend has long been "dead." It wasn't always so simple.

Does present-day truth lie hidden in the ancient traditions of the Old Ones? Perhaps. Sylvia Celeste Shoemaker was born October 19, 1936, in Kansas City, Missouri, at 2 P.M. sharp. Her arrival was like that of any other baby, except that she was born with a caul.

When wrapped about the head of a newborn infant, a caul—the inner fetal membrane—has for centuries signified the birth of a child with the "sight," that inner seeing, inner *knowing*, that distinguishes the psychic from all others.

Bill Shoemaker, Sylvia's father, who attended the birth, already had a psychic mother-in-law to contend with. Now here was another psychic in the family. When the caul was removed, yet another mystical portent was revealed. On the forehead of his baby daughter, centered just above her two great brown eyes, was a tiny drop of blood. It looked for all the world like the mysterious third eye—the all-seeing orb of the prophet.

Sylvia has come to believe that everyone is psychic, but most people remain unaware of their own extrasensory abilities. It's possible that the presence of a caul may be a reminder to those whose lives will require a greater use of their gift. For Sylvia, the ancient sign was prophetic. She seems never to have known what it was like *not* to be psychic.

The "signs" appeared very early. It would seem that she was being prepared for the extraordinary path ahead. Sylvia *knew* who was at the door—before the guest even knocked. Then when she was three, Bill's father died suddenly of a heart attack. Bill learned of the tragedy at work and came home to inform his wife, Celeste. Sylvia was standing in the doorway when he entered. "Grandpa's dead," she announced before her father had uttered a word.

A far happier pronouncement was Sylvia's prediction that a baby sister was joining them. "She'll come in three years—when I'm six," she announced. Sharon arrived one month short of her sister's sixth birthday. Sylvia hears these stories told and retold at family gatherings, but can only smile at the continuing sense of marvel. What did they expect of a child building psychic muscle?

A far more important event occurred when Sylvia was four. Early one morning, hearing her postman father depart for his early-morning mail route, Sylvia trotted into her parents' room and climbed into bed beside her mother. Suddenly, as the tiny child glanced randomly at the ceiling, it burst open before her eyes. High above her was a glorious sunrise, with streaks of cerise, gold, hot pink, and purple against the somber dawn. Soaring across this grand panorama was a flock of wild birds in a V-formation. A voice spoke with great clarity, *"Sylvia, you will never be as free as the birds you see."*

"Did you hear that?" she asked her mother in astonishment. "What happened to the ceiling? Do you see those birds?"

Celeste Shoemaker had seen nothing. As the daughter of a medium, she'd grown up in a home where visions were commonplace. Although not psychic herself, paranormal phenomena were nothing new to her. Celeste's attitude toward Sylvia's growing "strangeness" was one of mild annoyance. She didn't welcome more eccentricity in her life and would do nothing to encourage it in her daughter.

The ceiling looked exactly as it always had, Celeste assured Sylvia, and she attempted to divert the child's attention with talk of breakfast.

But Sylvia never forgot the experience. In later years, recalling the free-flowing momentum of the birds, the full realization of the message was revealed to her. The word *freedom* has many meanings to as many people, but psychics are the first to agree that they themselves have very little freedom indeed.

Sylvia believes that people chosen to be psychic must share their gift—at whatever cost to their own comfort or peace of mind. For some, perhaps, lifelong dedication comes easily, but for her, it has not. The suffering has often been intense—particularly when the "gift" has come into open conflict with her own desires.

The unwanted knowing began when Sylvia was five. The family was assembled for a Sunday gathering. Sylvia was seated beside her father listening halfheartedly to the adult chatter. Glancing absently at Great-Grandmother Hattie, who was seated across from her, she was horrified to see the woman's face begin to slowly melt. Her features were running like wax, slowly oozing downward until there was no face—only a skull.

Screaming her terror, the child turned only to confront the face of her other Great-Grandmother, Sarah. It, too, appeared to be melting—not as rapidly, but melting nevertheless. Frantically, Sylvia pulled at her father's arm, begging him to take her home. Outside, she attempted to explain to him the frightful thing she'd witnessed. "I saw their faces running," the little girl sobbed. He would not, could not, understand her.

Within ten days, Hattie Braun was dead. Four days later, Sarah Shoemaker's death followed. Sylvia began to see other melting faces, and each vision was invariably followed by death. Her fear and confusion led to feelings of guilt. Was she in some way responsible? Sylvia was miserable. Again and again she tried to explain these happenings to parents too involved in their own affairs to recognize the enormity of what the child was experiencing.

Bill Shoemaker was ambitious, determined to get ahead in the world. He was also a charmer who found little difficulty balancing a philandering nature with conventional family responsibilities. Celeste was challenged by a Don Juan husband seven years her junior, but she had determined to wait it out. "One day Bill will grow up," she often sighed. In the meantime, her method of dealing with problems was to pretend they didn't exist.

Sylvia would vividly recall her mother's response to anything remotely threatening. Celeste simply excused herself and slipped off to have a long soak in the bathtub. It was a family signal that she'd insulated herself from reality and was not to be disturbed. During those traumatic days of melting faces, Celeste took many baths while Bill indulged himself with a passing parade of pretty ladies.

Then one day Sylvia's maternal grandmother, Ada Coil, came to call. Seating herself beside the frightened child, who was daily growing more and more withdrawn, she pulled the now-sobbing girl into her lap and comforted her. When the tears had subsided, Ada began to question her granddaughter gently and with great care.

Once again, Sylvia attempted to describe what she'd seen—the running, oozing faces slipping slowly downward until nothing remained but a skull. "Am I killing them, Grandma?" the child asked, her voice little more than a whisper.

"No, dear, it's their time to go. You have nothing to do with it," the older woman assured her.

"Then it *is* real?"

"Very real."

"Do you see the melting faces, too?" Sylvia asked, leaning forward conspiratorially.

"Not the faces, but other things. I see much that others don't—just as you do. It's because we're psychic."

Five-year-old Sylvia didn't want to be psychic. It wasn't fun at all! Patiently, Ada explained that the gift of sight was theirs—want it or not. It was a kind of trust to be used for the benefit of others.

"But I don't *want* to see melting faces; I'm afraid of skulls," Sylvia said, beginning to cry again.

"Then ask God not to show them to you," Ada advised. "What you can't handle, pray to be relieved of."

The young Sylvia did a lot of praying. The hideous visions have never returned.

❈

Tall, stately, and dominant, Ada Coil was a true mentor, providing both practical solace for this world and a magic thread to guide Sylvia through the dark labyrinth of the other. A German from the noble Rhine family of von Banica, she had taken the name

Coil from her Irish husband. She was a devout Episcopalian, but always a pragmatist.

The Shoemaker family was divided. Bill was a Jew, Celeste an Episcopalian. Harmony was not the most notable household characteristic. Something had to be done about their daughter. Sylvia clearly needed stability and guidance. Ultimately, the idea of a convent emerged as a perfect solution. So at Grandma's urging, the Shoemakers became a Catholic family marching down the aisle to be baptized together, and that's exactly what happened.

Sylvia adapted quickly to Catholic teaching. She was particularly impressed by the nuns and strove to emulate them. Soon there was a makeshift altar in her bedroom, and for days at a time the child insisted on wearing a long black dress with a white tea towel pinned to it. No one was surprised when she announced that she wanted to be a nun.

Like Grandma Ada, the nuns appeared to Sylvia as islands of strength and clarity in a world that was becoming more and more complex. Bright, eager both to learn and to please, Sylvia found that school was easy, although other things were not. Her increasing psychic abilities were a burden from which she could never free herself, separating her from friends and parents alike. More than anything, the child wanted to be "normal."

She had begun to see "inside" her head, frequently experiencing an eerie montage of spirits and mortals, two distinct vibrations going on simultaneously. Often she would ask people—anyone who happened to be near—"Did you see that?" The answer was always no.

What a relief it was to her when Grandma Ada provided unexpected validation. It was after dinner one Sunday evening. Family members gathered in the Shoemaker living room had begun to speak of relatives who'd passed on. Sylvia was seated on the floor looking up at Ada when slowly the form of a man, standing at Grandma's shoulder, began to take shape. At first he was merely a filmy outline, but then he grew clearer and clearer until he was as distinct as Ada.

"Who's that man behind you, Grandma?" the child asked.

"Just Sylvia showing off" was the consensus of the group—except for Ada, who asked matter-of-factly, "What does he look like?"

"He's tall with reddish brown hair. He has a nice face with little wire glasses."

"Anything else?"

"Well, he's wearing a string around his neck with a horn on it."

"A horn?"

"Yes, he listens to people's chests with it."

"Could it be Jim?" Celeste ventured.

"Of course, it must be," Ada agreed. "You're looking at your Uncle Jim," she explained to Sylvia. "He died from the flu epidemic of 1918. He caught it from one of his patients."

That experience was a pleasant one, with Sylvia sitting on Ada's lap and hearing about the things that Uncle Jim had done as a child. But most of the time Sylvia was very much alone. She knew without being told that none of her friends experienced the struggles that frequently beset her; she could scarcely define them herself. In crowds, the child would suffer bouts of severe exhaustion that frequently led to depression. It was years before she would learn to "turn off" the disturbing incubi of those about her.

But those occasions weren't always burdensome or negative. Once, while attending a movie with her father, Sylvia suddenly began to hyperventilate. Both she and Bill were enjoying the comedy immensely, and the seven-year-old tried to overcome the sensation. But its intensity only increased. A sick dizziness swept over her. The panic was overwhelming. *Am I dying?* she thought wildly. "No," a voice inside replied, "someone else."

Frantically the frightened child tried to remain calm, tried to resist the waves of sickening panic. *Where is this coming from?* she asked herself.

Seemingly in answer, a picture flashed before her mind's eye, clear and bold as the one on the screen—her baby sister gasping for air.

"We've got to go," Sylvia whispered to her father. "There's something terribly the matter with Sharon. She can't breathe. She's turning blue."

"That's ridiculous," he chided her. "We just left Sharon an hour ago. She's fine."

But Sylvia, now desperately frightened, persisted. Sharon's life depended on Bill believing her. "Daddy, we have to go home *now*," she ended with a scream.

"You'd better know what you're talking about," Bill snapped, as the two of them picked their way between the seats of the darkened theater, stumbling over the feet of the annoyed spectators around them.

The ride home was an agony for Sylvia, who was now experiencing all of Sharon's symptoms. "Hurry, Daddy, hurry," she pleaded. Her lungs seemed to be bursting with the effort to breathe. Certain that her sister must be dying, she gasped frantically for air. It seemed an eternity had passed when the frightened child at last saw her house in the distance.

As their car turned into the drive, Celeste ran out sobbing. The phone was out of order. Sharon had become desperately ill with what turned out to be double pneumonia. Bill was just in time to rush the infant to the hospital.

Grateful as they were for this apparent miracle, it was obscured by Sylvia's eccentricity, which Bill and Celeste saw increasing every day. She wasn't an easy child for them to understand. Their lives were complicated enough without the aberration of the "strange" little creature who tuned in psychically to every family secret and insisted on pointing out ghosts.

Sylvia's double vision was becoming a nuisance. The otherworldly dimension that had crept unbidden into their life was a nighttime distraction. "It's like a parade of people walking back and forth in my room," she attempted to explain. "Give her a flashlight," Grandma Ada advised.

One night, a few months after the incident of Sharon's illness, Sylvia was shining the light along the wall. Suddenly, it began to expand until it filled the entire room. Out of nowhere a tall, dark-haired woman appeared. She smiled and said, "Dear Sylvia, don't be afraid, I come from God."

The words signaled yet another psychic "gift." Not even eight years old, Sylvia had become clairaudient. Now, besides seeing things that others didn't see, Sylvia heard voices they didn't hear.

It's true that—as in the vision of the free-flying birds—there had been auditory sensations almost like whispered thoughts. But these words were spoken clearly and directly into Sylvia's ears. Don't be afraid, indeed! The child fled, shrieking, from the room.

Ada Coil put her arms around the screaming child. "It's just a bad dream," she explained to Celeste and Bill, who regarded their daughter with bewildered dismay. Gently, she led Sylvia up the stairs to the guest room.

Between sobs that gradually turned to hiccups, the frightened little girl explained what had happened. "Oh, is that all? I've heard voices all my life," Ada reassured her. "You've just made contact with your spirit guide—someone like a guardian angel, a person who's there to help you. You can be happy—not frightened. Most people never meet their guides."

Dear Grandma, the pillar of Sylvia's family, of her entire world! If *she* heard voices, perhaps it was okay. Sylvia stopped crying and began to listen. The appearance of a spirit guide was the beginning of what was to become the strongest, most enduring relationship of her life. Yet in those early days, the friendship was an uneasy one. Often, when the now-familiar buzz and high-pitched whine started, signaling the beginning of a message, the child would panic, almost paralyzed by terror. At the same time, she was filled with curiosity and a sense of destiny.

Iena, Sylvia's guide, took a lot of getting used to. The name alone was a bit off-putting. At the time, Francine was Sylvia's favorite name ("Oh, Mom, if only you'd named me Francine instead of dumb old Sylvia"), so that's what the child rechristened her new companion. "Lots of children have made-up friends," Celeste and Bill, still resisting, reminded one another in the beginning. But as time passed and Francine's predictions, imparted to them by Sylvia, came true, they ruefully began to revise their opinions.

Sylvia saw no conflict between Francine's ever-increasing presence and the teachings of the nuns. Weren't they forever talking of guardian angels and messages from God? Maybe she wasn't so different, after all. The thought brought Sylvia some relief from her family's accelerating chaos.

Bill's fortunes were improving. From mailman, he'd progressed to jewelry salesman, then to employment with a major freight line, where he would eventually rise to vice president. He was sexually aggressive as well—warmly humorous, dashing, debonair, Bill had no difficulty finding partners. Again and again, the Shoemakers teetered on the brink of divorce.

During a brief period of unity, Bill and Celeste begged and borrowed their way into possession of a three-story Victorian mansion. The purchase was meant as a promise of a future of affluence and solidarity. The solidarity, however, was never to materialize.

After enduring the many moves linked with her father's financial successes and amatory weaknesses, Sylvia perceived the new home as a bastion. She loved it and knew in her heart that the house loved her as well. Running from room to room, she took a delighted inventory: an impressive entry with large walnut pillars and graceful stairway, an inviting living room accented by a tile fireplace, an elegant dining room with stained glass windows, a large, homey kitchen and butler's pantry, four large bedrooms, and finally, the promising mystery of an attic to explore.

The Shoemakers moved in—Bill and Celeste, Sylvia and Sharon. Happily for Sylvia, Grandma Ada came, too, and along with her came "Brother." Sylvia adored her uncle, a lifelong invalid. Despite a crippling birth defect accompanied by a form of vertigo that caused his head to be pulled to one side, Brother had a brilliant mind and a sweet and gentle disposition. Grandma cared for him lovingly and protectively; Sylvia kept him entertained with lively chatter. On one occasion, Brother may have saved his niece's life.

Sylvia had been sitting in the front yard when, for no apparent reason, she became aware of a sudden, anxious sensation. Today the psychic recognizes that visceral feeling as a warning of imminent danger. She stood still, puzzled, unsure of what to do next.

"Run!" a voice called out. Looking up, Sylvia saw Brother emerge from the house walking much faster than anyone thought he could. "Run, run, run!" he yelled to his niece.

Sylvia froze. Run where? What was happening? She sat motionless, literally paralyzed with fear. And then she saw what Brother had seen. It was a figure out of a nightmare. Racing toward her was a large woman with unkempt hair and wild black eyes. Her face, so pale that it appeared stark white, was contorted in an expression of pure hatred. It seemed to the terrified child that time had slowed almost to a standstill. This fearful creature was lumbering toward her in slow but inexorable motion.

"Run, Sylvia, run!"

Somehow, she never knew how, Sylvia moved out of the way just as frail, little Brother interposed himself and took the full brunt of the woman's crazed frenzy. She knocked him to the ground and was fiercely pummeling him with her fists when two more women who appeared at the sound of Sylvia's frightened screams managed to pull her away. The effort took all their combined strength.

Later it was learned that the attacker was the mentally disturbed daughter of a wealthy neighbor who kept her at home under the questionable protection of two psychiatric nurses, rather than institutionalize her.

Delightful as the house was, the family scene wasn't enough for Bill. Or perhaps it was too much. Whatever the cause, it wasn't long after the move that he became involved in yet another romance, this one more significant. A compromise was reached. Bill would remain married while settling his mistress into a comfortable apartment conveniently located six blocks from home.

Despite all the distractions, he remained a devoted father. Bill doted on Sylvia but set high standards for her. "Show them what you can do" was his favorite refrain. Fearful that she, like her mother, might lose the attention of this mercurial man, Sylvia was determined not to disappoint him. What if some random act on her part inadvertently drove her father away forever? She must never do anything to cause dissension; it was her duty to please everyone. The responsibility was overwhelming.

But her increasing acceptance of her psychic gifts compensated, and Sylvia's natural vivacity returned. Great things were expected of this quick, witty child. This was the era of Shirley Temple clones, and Sylvia seemed a natural. She was enrolled in dancing school, but as the family watched the row of little girls in abbreviated sailor suits tapping obediently to the tune of "Anchors Aweigh," it became obvious that whatever her other gifts, the one talent their daughter lacked was coordination.

Her stamina and determination were never in question. "Wait till you see me do 'Singing in the Rain,' Daddy," she promised. On the day of her first recital, as she rushed eagerly onstage, virtually attacking it, she caught her umbrella on a stage prop. It pulled inside out, but the plucky child pranced out undismayed, clutching the shattered umbrella valiantly as she struggled with the step. "Dark Eyes," her final number, was a true showstopper. While dancing about the gypsy circle, Sylvia created a sensation by stumbling into the canned fire. Glancing down in dismay, she realized what she'd done, but quickly forced a determined smile and danced back into the fire, hoping by her air of cheery abandon to convince the audience that it was all part of the act. Her memory of the occasion is of looking anxiously out over the crowd and spotting her father, head buried in his hands.

Sylvia's whole life became one of performance, of dedication. She was determined to please, to entertain, and to soothe. Her efforts and the self-discipline she had to learn served as a kind of conditioning. It was as though she were a young athlete training for the big meet.

Late one night, while lying sleepless, Sylvia was startled by the vision of two masks superimposed on the wall before her—the classical Greek comedy and tragedy masks. Their significance was explained by Francine, who told her, "Sylvia, this is your life."

The words were prophetic. Death and its many implications—reincarnation, mediumship, documentation of soul survival—play a daily part of her life. And so does comedy. Anyone who's ever watched Sylvia Browne on stage or television has witnessed a superb comedienne at work. Humor is the spoonful of sugar that enables us to laugh at the dark mysteries of life and death. Without it and its comedic corollary, the psychic lacks humanity.

As time passed, Francine made herself increasingly visible. She's an imposing figure, an Indian woman standing 5'6", slender with long black hair and brown, almond-shaped eyes. She speaks simply and precisely, conveying much in just a few words. Her message has always been one of tolerance, compassion, and forgiveness, her direct approach both modest and practical.

In the beginning, she talked with Sylvia about things a child would respond to. At first the little girl was primarily interested in games. It was amusing to Sylvia to repeat to the family conversations that she couldn't possibly have overheard. The surprised reaction was instant validation, and it further reinforced the confidence of the young medium.

As their friendship grew, Sylvia asked Francine questions about herself. Iena/Francine had been born in northern Colombia in the year 1500. She identified herself as an Aztec/Inca, a term that would later confuse many. Francine explained that although Hunayna Capac, the Inca ruler, was dominant, the influence of Montezuma, far to the north, was also felt by her people. There was much communication between the two cultures—a blending that is only now being verified by archaeologists.

Sylvia was fascinated by Francine's childhood, her teacher's training, and her betrothal at the age of 16 to a young silversmith. When Francine was 18, she was married, and within a year a baby girl was born. Sylvia often pictured the large open-air market that adjoined the emperor's vast grounds, where Francine went often with her toddler daughter to sell her husband's wares. It was here that a runner from an outlying village came one day to warn of strangers who'd invaded their land. It wasn't long before the Spaniards arrived to plunder the city. Hundreds of Indians were murdered, and Francine was among them. She was impaled by a spear while trying to protect her child.

This was, Francine told Sylvia, her one and only life on Earth. Though she had but one goal—to help people—she had no wish to return to the world as a mortal. From 1520 until Sylvia's birth in 1936, Francine was training to become a "communicating guide," which would allow her to perfect quickly without incarnating on Earth. Sylvia and Francine first met shortly before Sylvia went down the tunnel into a fetus. They were two very different personalities sharing one very important mission.

Despite her powers, Sylvia had no memory of any of this. It was necessary for Francine to explain it in a manner that a child could understand. There's nothing mysterious about a spirit guide, Francine told her. A guide is very much like a human except that he or she resides on the Other Side. The guide's job is to help a given individual through the present incarnation. Most everyone on Earth has been or will be a spiritual guide for someone.

The spirit guide's purpose is to research, suggest, nudge, and encourage the person whom he or she may be guiding through life. In most cases, the guides operate in the individual's subconscious, appearing as the "voice of conscience." They will illustrate lessons and speak of what the individual is here to learn, but they never interfere with choices. They are extremely careful never to preclude the opportunity for a person to learn a life lesson. If the subject is headed toward an event that will teach a valuable but difficult lesson, a guide may point out an alternative route. The decision remains with the individual; if that choice involves pain and struggle, the guide won't prevent it.

According to Francine, spirit guides may use a variety of methods to communicate. They convey knowledge through dreams, or as a flash in the mind's eye, even occasionally as a voice. It's a frustrating task, Francine told Sylvia, because few people take the time to really listen.

As Sylvia was growing up, Francine was a constant advisor and companion, slowly and carefully imparting the wisdom that would become the medium's philosophy. "Someday you will be a great psychic," Francine informed Sylvia. "You will help many people and will be asked to speak before large groups of people."

Remembering her failed career as a dancer, Sylvia was anything but pleased by the prospect. Seeking comfort from her grandmother, she pleaded, "I don't have to do that if I don't want to, do I?"

Ada patted the little girl reassuringly. "Of course not, but when the time comes and you're ready, you'll be able to do it."

The shy little girl *would* grow into an audacious, spirited woman. The time would soon come when Sylvia would seek a life of her own.

The spirit would warn, but the woman would not hear the message.

CHAPTER THREE

A Psychic in Love

Joe studied Sylvia intently, admiring the woman, remembering the girl. In many ways they were much the same. She'd always been special. The warmth, the humor, the enthusiasm, and yes, the sex appeal.

It was obvious to this out-of-town visitor touring the impressive offices of the Nirvana Foundation that Sylvia Shoemaker was a long way from Kansas City. "What was it like growing up with Sylvia?" one of her staff asked him.

Joe paused, thinking back over a friendship that had begun when they were children more than 40 years before. "No big deal," he replied at last, "although we always seemed to be waiting for her to tell us what was going to happen next."

Sylvia smiled, recalling many such times. Joe turned back to her. "Do you still have that lady talking into your ear, telling you things?"

"Yes, Francine's around. I don't think she'll check out until I do."

He watched her, still searching for traces of the impetuous but vulnerable friend he remembered. "Are you happy in California? Do they treat you right here?"

"Yes—yes, I'm really very happy," she assured him.

"You know you can always come home. We take care of our own in Missouri," he reminded her.

"Protect me like the village idiot? That's comforting," she teased him, amused, but also warmed by memories of the past. It seemed in retrospect that the Kansas City of her childhood had been frozen in time. Families stayed in place, neighborhoods remained unchanged. Everyone knew everyone, everyone knew *everything* about everyone—and before long they took it all for granted. Without realizing it at the time, Sylvia had been provided with the perfect shelter, the shelter so sorely needed by a psychic.

She'd done her first psychic reading at age eight. It had happened spontaneously when a friend named Mary Margaret had complained. "What shall I do about my mother? She's getting so cranky."

"I don't know about that, but I *can* see your mother falling down and breaking her arm." Although Sylvia had always known things, this was the first time anyone had deliberately sought information from her. Her inadvertent response to Mary Margaret's question had somehow revealed her psychic insight. She could actually hear a question and have it answered. "Your mother's going to break her arm!" she repeated, amazed at herself. Then she added, "Your father—I see him, too. He's going to lose his job."

Mary Margaret accepted the news matter-of-factly, not nearly as surprised as Sylvia. Since she'd known since toddler days that her friend was a bit different, this new development didn't appear particularly remarkable. "What about me?" she asked. "Is anything bad going to happen to me?"

"No—well, a little bad. You're going to slip and fall on the ice. Don't be afraid. You won't break anything."

Mary Margaret nodded, then went on to chatter about other things. It was the same Mary Margaret—by then calling herself Maggie—whom Sylvia would overhear ten years later attempting to explain Sylvia's strangeness to two visitors from a nearby men's college. "Sylvia might seem a little different—sometimes she knows things before they happen—but she's really lots of fun. She's just like anyone except for that."

The "Sylvia's one of us" attitude of her friends, possibly fostered by her own down-to-earth exuberance and humor, has accompanied the psychic all her life. The conflicts and challenges that have beset Sylvia are numerous and varied, but in this one area, she has remained truly fortunate. She grew up with the same group of boys and girls, attended school with them for 12 years, and continued on with many of them to

St. Teresa's College. Although her psychic gifts and tensions might have set her apart, the affection, support, and casual acceptance of life-long friends formed a protective shield to her vulnerability.

"What about you, Joe?" Sylvia asked, her eyes returning to the man who still watched her thoughtfully. "I hear you married four times. Which wife was your favorite?"

"That's easy. The first."

Sylvia's eyes filled as she thought of that long-ago marriage, *their* marriage. She'd been 16 when her father announced that he'd at last met the woman he couldn't live without. Stormy threats of divorce and tearful attempts at reconciliation were all she'd ever known from her parents. Now Celeste and Bill really had something to quarrel over—their children. Being placed in the middle of a custody battle was agony to a girl whose entire young life had been devoted to pleasing everyone. How could she possibly choose to live with one parent at the expense of the other? Sylvia was literally ill from the rage and fear she absorbed psychically from both parents.

At this period in her life, Sharon was a shy, introverted child who clung to her mother for support. She would live with Celeste, of course. But what about Sylvia? Probing psychically, she saw herself being sent to live with her mother as well. The sense of Bill's pain, his loneliness and desolation, was overwhelming.

Then, while sitting in algebra class, the answer came to her. Joe Tschirhart. If she married him, the decision of which parent to live with would be moot. Of course, her other boyfriend, Warren Becker, would be disappointed, but hurting her father or mother would be far worse.

Joe was easy to convince. How could he resist when Sylvia explained that he was the only one who could help her with this terrible problem? Besides, he'd hoped to marry her anyway—someday. That night, Sylvia located her birth certificate and altered it so that her age read 18. The following day after school, the two teenagers took a streetcar across the state line to the other Kansas City.

The enormity of it all engulfed Sylvia as she stood before the justice of the peace. Had she really signed her whole life away to this boy beside her? She was a Catholic girl; marriage was forever. A giant wave of homesickness swept over her at the thought of what she'd done. Sylvia had just been pronounced a wife, and all she wanted was to be her parents' little girl.

"What about our honeymoon?" Joe had asked, surveying his bride, who'd selected a white pinafore with matching bobby sox and oxfords for the occasion. "It's Friday, and we've got two days before we have to go back to school."

"I don't think my parents would like it," Sylvia demurred. "Let's just keep it our secret for a while."

Joe wasn't entirely disappointed. He had his own parents to contend with. Agreeably, he'd taken Sylvia home, settling for a quick but ardent kiss before leaving her on the doorstep.

Celeste was waiting in the living room, her eyes on the clock. "Where have you been?" was her first question. "What's that bulge under your dress?" was the second.

Sylvia looked down at the telltale bulge. Why had she been so careless? Of course she had to tell her parents something; that was the whole point of the runaway marriage. But not now. She wasn't ready. Would she ever be ready? The runaway marriage that had seemed like such a grand and daring solution was obviously a disaster. Sylvia felt sick with remorse. Her hand strayed to the front of her pinafore, trying to push it down. "Oh, just a license," she murmured.

"License! License to what, for God's sake?" Celeste yelled as Sylvia fled sobbing up the stairs. Mrs. Shoemaker retired with unprecedented urgency to her bath as Bill pounded on their daughter's door, demanding to be admitted.

"You can't come in, Daddy, I'm a married woman. I'm in charge of my life now," Sylvia announced in a quavering voice.

Not yet, she wasn't. To Sylvia's immense, but secret, relief, Bill had the marriage annulled in record time. Unfortunately, there was nothing that he could do to prevent the appearance of the wedding announcement in the vital statistics column of the newspaper.

The punishment agreed upon by both sets of parents was that Joe and Sylvia would refrain from seeing one another socially. The romance was over before it began.

Grandma Ada came to the rescue as she had so many times before. "What are we going to do with Sylvia?" Celeste demanded of her.

"What are we going to do with *you*?" had been the answer. As a result of Ada's firm but tactful mediation, a compromise was reached once again, and life continued at the Shoemakers.

After a few months, Joe Behm came along and filled the void in Sylvia's affections. This Joe was a bit older. His formal education completed, he had a good job with a trucking firm and felt ready for marriage. Sylvia, too, was maturing; her elopement and its embarrassing aftermath had been a crash course in reality. Joe talked of a farm and six children. To Sylvia, with her growing need for security, it sounded wonderful. But there was one major drawback. Joe was ready to settle down and make a life together right away.

Sylvia was torn. She loved Joe—or thought she did—and fantasized about the life they might have together. Her dreams of becoming a teacher, maybe even a teaching nun, dated from early childhood. But she'd recently begun to reconsider. Would having children of her own be even more satisfying? She pondered the question endlessly.

Many of Sylvia's friends planned to marry soon after high school. There was a seductive sense of independence about the idea of having one's own home, one's own family. Sylvia viewed marriage as romantic and simple, easily ignoring the tumultuous relationship of her parents. The idea of a tranquil, uncomplicated life with a very solid young man who adored her was highly appealing.

For once, neither Grandma Ada nor Francine were of help. Francine, despite her life on Earth as an Indian woman, was amazingly liberated. For all her supernatural powers, she refused to take seriously the pressures of an era that introduced the family room and delighted in *I Love Lucy*. By Francine's otherworldly standards, the child-centered, family-oriented decade that marked Sylvia's transition from girl to woman was merely a temporary aberration.

Grandma Ada hoped so, too, but lacked a discarnate spirit's concept of time. Years were years to her—not instants, as they are to Francine. Somehow, Ada realized, Sylvia must come to terms with *this* world, yet the destiny she perceived for her granddaughter was a far cry from the craze for domesticity that was sweeping the country.

Ada had seen women function brilliantly during two world wars; she remembered the independent New Woman of the 1920s and the strong dominant females called forth by the Great Depression. Now, surveying the young women of the 1950s with their cinched waists, voluminous skirts, and multiple petticoats, she realized that most of them regarded careers as mere time-passers to be readily abandoned when the right man came along. Although Joe *had* come along a little early, who was to say that this serious-minded young man wasn't just the thing for Sylvia? "Wait," was all that Ada could or would say. "When the time comes, you'll know the right thing to do."

As her high school years drew to a close, Sylvia realized that her adored grandmother was having serious problems of her own. She had a critical heart condition. An attack, the doctors said, would certainly be fatal. Ada had listened calmly to the diagnosis, accepting the death sentence implicit in the warning with equanimity. To her, death as we know it was merely "going Home." Why should anyone fear that? Her only concern was Brother. "I can't leave this world without him," she told Sylvia. "No one can ever understand and care for him the way I have."

"But you're not going anywhere, Grandma," Sylvia insisted, hoping desperately that the very intensity of her desire could somehow make the words come true.

She was almost 18 and in college when the call came that Ada had been hospitalized. "Your grandmother wants you to have this," a nurse said, handing Sylvia a black crucifix. Ada was enclosed in an oxygen tent, her eyes shut.

"Grandma, you have to get well. I love you," Sylvia said as she knelt beside the fragile body.

Ada said nothing, but her china blue eyes opened briefly. "Go on, Sylvia." The words were never spoken, but the sobbing girl heard them as clearly as if they'd been shouted.

Sylvia sat for hours beside her sleeping grandmother. It was late evening before she returned home. There was a light on in Brother's room. Pulling a chair up beside his bed, Sylvia sank down wearily. Taking the crucifix from her purse, she offered it to him. "This should really be yours."

Brother didn't want to keep it, but Sylvia insisted. The two, each seeking solace and finding some measure of comfort in their shared grief, then said the rosary together as they had so many times during Sylvia's growing-up years.

The next day Sylvia returned to the hospital and began a vigil that would last several days. She was seated alone at Ada's side when her grandmother died. Celeste was home in her bathtub. Two days later, returning from her grandmother's memorial service, Sylvia paused in the doorway of Brother's room. "Grandmother looked beautiful," she started to say, then stopped. Her uncle was having convulsions.

Brother was rushed to the hospital. He died the next day. The autopsy report read "cause unknown." Equally baffling were the stacks of neatly folded clothing discovered that night in Brother's room—he'd never folded an article of clothing in his life. His affairs in order—papers carefully stacked beside the garments, Brother had died before Ada was even in the ground.

In the days that followed, Joe Behm was constantly at Sylvia's side, offering love and support. "Why not quit college now? What's the point? We'll just be getting married when you graduate anyway," he urged. Bill, admiring the young man's progress in the trucking line, had come to agree. "You don't need college to be a wife and mother," he told his daughter. Celeste was vague. "Do what you want most, hon," was her only advice.

Francine remained adamant. "You'll need this training," she insisted. "You will need your college education for the work that you will do. Teaching will be a part of it."

Joe continued his efforts to persuade Sylvia to drop out of college, but as the months passed, an exciting new world opened up, exerting a powerful claim of its own. Despite her grief over her grandmother's death, Sylvia was enjoying college more and more, and soon would not hear of abandoning it. She was majoring in both education and literature with a minor in theology. Her old desire to teach had returned full force, yet a part of her still craved the security she believed came only from marriage. Now it appeared that, although she'd tried with some success to exorcise the paranormal side of her life, she still lived in two worlds. One was college life—late nights spent in philosophical and metaphysical discussions on Huxley, Kafka, Camus, Sartre, Bertrand Russell, and Alan Watts. The other world was the "real" one inhabited by Joe and the solid, home-centered life she envisioned with him.

Joe was an easy man to be around. He adored Sylvia and accepted her uncritically. Remembering his quiet strength during the bleak months following Ada's death, Sylvia felt certain that Joe would be a fine husband and father. As graduation approached, the pressure to make a decision increased. "That young man won't wait around forever," Bill warned. "He's too good a guy to let slip away," her girlfriends cautioned. Added to this was the longing that Sylvia read in Joe's eyes. She could feel the pain her reluctance was causing him. For a young woman whose whole life had been centered around pleasing others, this was the worst part.

Finally, in her senior year, Sylvia agreed to the marriage. Having at last made a decision, she felt immense relief. Whether it was the right one or not scarcely mattered; a weight had been lifted from her. Now she allowed herself to be swept into a flurry of preparations for a June wedding. Joe made a down payment on a house, and the couple were in the process of selecting furniture when again fate intervened.

Business, not philosophy, was Joe's forte. Though only a few years older than Sylvia's college friends, he sometimes felt out of place with them and rarely attended the parties she gave nearly every week. Sylvia has always wondered how her life might have differed had he been present that cold, winter evening when someone new walked in.

"Meet my rescuer," Maggie announced dramatically. "I was stuck in the snow and—"

Sylvia didn't hear the rest. She was staring into the greenest, most compelling eyes she'd ever seen. His smile, the force of his almost animal magnetism literally took her breath away. *"Tragedy, Sylvia!"* The words were sharp and clear, a kind of psychic telegram from Francine, who'd remained in the background for the past two years. It was the first time in months that she had communicated. *"This is the beginning of the most difficult time of your life."*

Alarming the message was, but Sylvia was 19 and looking into the eyes of her first true love—a tall, dark stranger.

"I'm the hostess with the mostest," she introduced herself with the glibness that came so easily to her, but that disguised her vulnerability.

"I can see that."

He moved his rangy body with a graceful ease that reminded Sylvia of a panther. She found it immensely attractive. Everything about him was attractive—even the broken nose that Sylvia thought very masculine. All evening Sylvia could feel his eyes on her until finally she could stand the mounting tension no longer. "Why do you keep staring?" she asked him.

"Because I have big eyes for you."

To a romantic teenager, it was movie dialogue; here, obviously attracted to her, was a man as handsome as any screen star. She felt dizzy with excitement. It was a moment out of every romantic novel she'd ever read, and now it was actually happening to her. As the party drew to a close and guests gathered to take their leave, the stranger swept Sylvia into his arms for a long, lingering kiss. Bantering farewells halted abruptly. Who was this older man who'd barged into a private party and was making time with one of the most popular girls on campus?

He was yet another Joe—Joseph Stemkowski, but Sylvia quickly named him "Ski." That evening, almost at the moment of their meeting, her engagement to Joe Behm ended. Sylvia would tell him in the morning. For her, suddenly, passionately aware of the reality of love, it was as though their long relationship had never been.

Ski was slightly mysterious, new in town; he'd come from New Jersey to study flight engineering. Dazzled by his good looks and charm, swept away by the force of their mutual attraction, Sylvia spent every possible moment with him. She was happier than she'd ever been before, but bewildered, too. Hidden behind the excitement was a nagging feeling that something wasn't quite right. It was as if, in Ski, Sylvia had found the other half of herself. It was ecstatic, yet just beyond the radiance there were shadows. Try as she might, Sylvia could neither dispel nor penetrate them.

Released from the time constraints her engagement to Joe had imposed, she resumed her readings. She received all sorts of information for others, but none for herself. "What did you mean by 'tragedy'?" she asked Francine again and again. "If there's something I should know, tell me," she pleaded. But after her initial warning, Francine remained curiously silent on the subject of Ski.

Then one afternoon, Sylvia encountered another engineering student, a friend of Ski's. They chatted amiably about trivialities, while Sylvia debated quizzing him. If anything was wrong, did she really want to know? At last she forced herself to probe for the answers that had eluded her psychically. "Ski's wonderful, but why do I feel that something's terribly wrong?"

He looked away, uncertain, avoiding her eyes. "Aren't you the one who's supposed to know everything? Don't you have that lady in your head who tells you stuff?"

"Not about me. I've never gotten any help from her with my own personal life—nothing about the future," Sylvia explained. "It never mattered much until now. Francine always said when the time came, I'd know what I needed to know. Now she doesn't say anything, and I sense there's something I need to find out."

"Well, there is," he admitted after a long pause. "Ski's married. He's got a wife back in New Jersey. A wife and two kids."

In that instant, the world grew dark and dirty. Sylvia was suddenly conscious of grime everywhere. Tattered papers blowing in the street, littered gutters. The sun had vanished for her. *I'm going to have to live my whole life in twilight,* she thought. A Catholic girl, a married man; it was impossible. She drove to the flight school, determined to confront Ski. Perhaps there was a mistake, Sylvia reasoned, but she knew there wasn't. Ski knew the moment he saw her. "It was only a matter of time before you found out," he said dully.

"Why didn't you tell me yourself?"

"I didn't want to lose you."

Sylvia nodded. Unbidden, a picture of a dark-haired woman with a small boy and girl appeared before her.

He attempted to explain. "I was very young, a sailor away from home for the first time. She got pregnant. I had to marry her, but I really tried to make it work. It never did. That's why I came to Kansas City to study. I thought distance would give me some perspective. I never dreamed I'd meet someone like you. God knows I never meant for it to happen."

Sylvia felt a wave of pain and guilt as she thought of Joe Behm. This terrible emptiness must be what he'd experienced. What a callous child she'd been. Life in that perpetual twilight, deprived forever of the warmth that was Ski, seemed a just punishment for her thoughtlessness, her cruelty. But how could she survive it?

"Will you see me tonight—one last night?" Ski pleaded.

Sylvia nodded, unable to speak. Two weeks passed, each night, "the last one." The two were more in love than ever, a frantic, devouring kind of love. Then one afternoon a messenger came to Sylvia's French class. Father Nadeux wanted to see her immediately in his office.

Sylvia had taken theology and Christian marriage classes from the Dominican priest. Once, in an impish mood, she'd scrawled, "Don't let this lead you into false conceptions," in a textbook written by the teacher—knowing all the while that he was watching. Father Nadeux had been more amused than annoyed. Since then, Sylvia had often been singled out for special praise or encouragement by the portly, good-natured man.

Entering his high-beamed study, she mentally reviewed her school conduct. Since Ski had come into her life, the pranks that had marked her college career had ceased. What could she have done this time?

Father Nadeux didn't keep her long in suspense. She'd scarcely seated herself before he began. "I have a letter from a Mrs. Joseph Stemkowski. Someone has informed her of her husband's involvement with one of our girls. Do you have any idea who that might be?"

"It is I, Father."

He turned away, looking absently out at the spring landscape— tender green shoots of life everywhere. "Do you love him?"

"Oh, yes, more than anything in the world."

Sighing, he turned back to face her. "That makes it more difficult. You know, of course, what you must do."

"Father, I can't give him up. I've tried, but I can't."

"You must, Sylvia. You know that." The priest knew her well. "You'll find the strength to do what has to be done."

His words echoed eerily. Sylvia could hear Grandma Ada not long before her death saying, "Within your weakness, there lies your strength sleeping." What did *that* mean? *Grandma,* she screamed inwardly, *where are you? Explain it to me! Help me!*

Sylvia left the room without another word. Somewhere, nuns were chanting, "Lord have mercy, Lord have mercy." *What could they know?* she thought bitterly. None of them could ever have had anyone like Ski in their lives, anyone so handsome and humorous, tender and poetic. Loving him was an addiction. He'd made her feel like a woman, the most beautiful, desirable woman in the world. How could she give that up? Could anyone hurt as much as she did and not die from it?

"For every hurt there is a reason—a reason to grow and to understand." The words were there suddenly, a response from Francine, but what good could they do? Francine's life on Earth was over, her own just beginning. The years ahead stretched before Sylvia, an empty wasteland.

She waved her hand over her right shoulder in a gesture used since childhood to dismiss Francine. "I'm tired of your spirit-world platitudes. Go talk to someone else."

"They won't hear me."

"Because they're not crazy."

"Don't start that 'crazy' notion again."

"Do you know any sane people who have spirits talking to them?"

"You always ask that when you're overwrought."

"Overwrought! I want to die!"

"You won't," Francine said and then was silent. The internal dialogue had ended.

At home later that afternoon, Sylvia did call Ski. She told him about the letter and described her conversation with Father Nadeux.

"I've got to see you," he pleaded.

"No, no more. Never again," she forced herself to say, and then hung up before he could reply.

Sylvia refused to take Ski's calls, fearing the effect of his voice on her shaky resolve. On the third day, a nun summoned her from class. "You know it's against the rules," she reminded Sylvia, "but since your cousin is on his way to Korea and will only be in town a few hours, I decided to bend the rules." Ski was standing behind her in the hall, pale-faced, hollow-eyed.

"No one will believe this," Sylvia said as the nun departed. "She's the one we call Old Ironsides. You must have really charmed her."

"Maybe she sensed how desperate I am. I had to see you. School's over. I have to decide what to do—stay here or go back."

"You know the answer to that," she said, pushing him from her with all her force and running back into the classroom.

There was one last call from Ski. Celeste had answered the phone. After listening to his message, she handed the receiver to Sylvia. "I think you'll want to take this call," she said. The following evening Sylvia drove Ski to the bus station. "When this life's over, I'll meet you on the second star to the right," he said, getting out of the car.

"It's a date," Sylvia replied, trying to smile.

"Maybe if this reconciliation doesn't work out, I can—"

She shook her head. Failed promises were scattered about them like punctured balloons. It was no use. They'd had five months together. Sylvia knew it was all they'd ever have. Perhaps Ski knew it, too, and perhaps on some level he knew even more.

Just before he boarded the bus, he turned to Sylvia and said, "Write to the Browns."

"What?" she exclaimed in surprise. "Which Browns? Who do you mean?"

"I don't know," he answered, looking at her in bewilderment. "It just came into my head. It must be from a song or something." Then he was on the bus, the last passenger to board.

The engine started, and slowly the bus began to pull out. Sylvia moved forward. Ski was trying to get the window open, but it was stuck. Sylvia was running now, trying to keep up. Ski finally got the window open, and she reached up, touching his face with her fingers. Ski kissed her palm; she could feel his tears.

It was June. Sylvia was 19. Within a week she would graduate from college, but her world had ended.

Create a void and something invariably fills it. As if Ski's departure were not enough, Sylvia seemed almost to be seeking an acceleration of her pain. Perhaps it was a secret wish for punishment, a need to flagellate herself still further for real or imagined sins. Or possibly it was a perverse desire to enkindle deadened senses. Whatever the latent cause, Sylvia's excoriation took the form of fear. College classes in abnormal psychology had opened a Pandora's box of doubts. According to the textbooks, there were seven levels of abnormal behavior. Sylvia fit at least four. Her agile mind leaped to the worst possible conclusion.

She was schizophrenic. After all, those struck with the disorder heard voices and saw visions. She was haunted by memories of the crazed neighbor who'd tried to kill her as a child. Again and again, she pictured Brother's battered, bloody body. How could a potential maniac even consider working with children?

Earlier, diverted by Joe and his constant talk of marriage and later by her passionate romance with Ski, Sylvia had been able to push those ugly thoughts from her mind. Now, with her whole being focused on teaching, her doubts virtually paralyzed her.

Teaching had always been natural for Sylvia. From earliest childhood, her favorite toy had been a small blackboard and chalk. Playing school was a cherished memory. She'd delighted in "teaching" anyone she could corral. When she'd entered college, there'd never been a question of what she would study. And, as in her paranormal life, Grandma Ada had encouraged her. "You will be a fine teacher, Sylvia, an inspiration," she said many times. Unfortunately, by the time Sylvia had reached her abnormal psychology class, Ada was gone.

"How can I teach children when I might be crazy?" she asked almost frantically of anyone who would listen. No one took her seriously. "Of course you're not crazy," Sylvia's young women friends would invariably respond, surprised that she'd even consider the possibility. Then they'd change the subject to their love lives. "What does Francine say about Dave?" they would ask, or "There's this new guy…" Celeste and Bill, occupied as usual with their ongoing drama, would nod absently, assuring Sylvia that she was perfectly sane and suggesting that she forget teaching for a year and just have fun. Then they would go back to their bickering.

Finally, Sylvia took the problem to her family doctor and then to her priest. What about the children, her pupils—could she hurt them in any way? Both men were certain that she couldn't; but at her insistence, they referred her to a psychiatrist. This physician interviewed Sylvia extensively and subjected her to a series of tests. At last he responded, "I see a young woman who has a great devotion to her family and who wants very much to please. Is that bad? Hardly, as long as she remembers to please herself as well."

Sylvia breathed a sigh of both exasperation and relief when he concluded, "You're quite normal, but something *para*normal is going on." She knew *that*.

Again, Francine was of no help, refusing to even discuss the question of Sylvia's sanity. "Of course, you must teach. It will be an important part of your training," was all that she could or would say. Often, when Sylvia brought up the question of her sanity, Francine would disappear, as if annoyed.

Finally, with considerable trepidation, Sylvia arranged for an interview with Sister Regina Mary, the principal of a small parochial school. Within an hour, she emerged with the promise of a contract. Sylvia would be the only lay teacher in a faculty otherwise comprised of nuns.

In September 1956, one month short of her 20th birthday, Sylvia began her teaching career. It was the first job, teaching or otherwise, that she had ever held, and she was terrified. "Will they like me?" she asked Francine again while driving to school the first day.

"Of course they will," the spirit replied in her no-nonsense fashion. "Haven't you spent years preparing for this?"

The reminder was of little help. Sylvia had begun to fear that all her past efforts had been misdirected. She'd dressed carefully that morning, discarding several choices before selecting a tweed suit with a tight skirt and a loose-fitting Chanel jacket. Sylvia had grown to her full height of 5'7", and was slim enough to be a model if she'd desired. Following Ski's departure, she'd cut the long red hair he'd so admired as a ritual gesture of independence. Getting out of the car with her lecture easel and her empty briefcase, she nervously patted her ducktail hairdo into place. Inside the school, 55 students waited for her. The impact of their eyes was palpable as she entered the assigned classroom and carefully set up her easel, glad to have something to hide behind.

"I'm your teacher for the year," she announced, and then she turned and wrote her name on the board in big, bold letters. "Sylvia Shoemaker." A boy in the front row snickered. Sylvia turned. "Now then, what are you laughing at?"

"Nothing."

"I'd really like to know," she persisted.

He laughed again, looking around at his friends for support. "I just wondered if your father made shoes."

Sylvia took a breath, then asked, "What's your name?"

"Ronald Necessary."

She suppressed a sigh of relief, thinking that God must certainly be with her on this one. "No, Ronald, my father doesn't make shoes," she answered, "but we'll see before the year's out just how necessary you are to this class." The other children roared. Score one for Shoemaker and zero for the class bully.

In addition to her traditional teaching efforts, Sylvia sometimes held the wastebasket for the children when they threw up, and occasionally she pulled their teeth. She showed them how to close their eyes and visualize what they wanted to be. And every day she told them how much she loved them.

None of the children ever seemed to think it strange that their teacher knew that they were angry or upset because they hadn't had any breakfast or had witnessed a violent argument at home or overheard an older sister tearfully announce that she was pregnant. No one ever said, "How do you know?" when the teacher took them aside for a reassuring little chat. It was simply taken for granted that Miss Shoemaker knew everything.

Late on a Friday afternoon in November, Sylvia sat at her desk grading papers. With a happy sigh, she set the last one aside and sat back surveying the room. The basement classroom might be the least desirable one in the school, but it was *her* room and she loved it.

Besides, she'd made it all so bright and cheerful with pumpkins and autumn leaves that you hardly noticed that there weren't any windows. Sylvia's confidence was growing. Some of the spit-and-polish shine was off the patent-leather teacher, but the enthusiasm had endured. "What do you think, Grandma?" she asked aloud. There was no answer, but Sylvia felt a warm glow envelop her. Happily, she gathered up her belongings and carefully locked the door behind her. That evening she and her friend, Maggie, treated themselves to dinner and a movie.

The next afternoon the phone rang. It was Sister Regina Mary. Sylvia caught her breath fearfully. The school principal never called on weekends. She must have done something awful, but what?

"Is everything all right?" she forced herself to ask.

"Well, yes and no," the nun answered.

It's my teaching, Sylvia thought, her old fears returning. A few weeks of student teaching simply hadn't prepared her for the responsibility of a whole class of her own. How could she have imagined that everything was going smoothly?

"Tell me what it is," she was almost whispering.

"I don't know how to begin—"

"Please, Sister," Sylvia urged.

"I hope you won't think I'm crazy," said Sister Regina Mary apologetically, "but the strangest thing happened just now."

"Won't you tell me, Sister?"

Haltingly, the woman began to explain. "I came to the school this afternoon to finish some reports. Naturally, the school was deserted. I was in my office working when I heard a noise downstairs. I knew I was the only one there, and I couldn't imagine who could have gotten in without setting off the alarm."

Relieved, Sylvia couldn't help smiling as she thought of the school, a veritable fortress. The nun continued, "The more I listened, the more it sounded like someone walking, so I picked up my crucifix and ventured down to the lower level."

Sylvia smiled again. "Lower level" was a euphemism if there ever was one for a basement complete with furnace and ducts. "The door was open, which in itself was strange because all the teachers are expected to lock their rooms before leaving."

"Oh, I did, I did, I remember locking it," Sylvia interrupted.

"Yes, I know you did," Sister Regina Mary agreed. "I always check everything myself before I leave. Your room was properly locked last night, but just a few minutes ago I looked in and the door was wide open and there in the middle of the room was an elderly lady."

"What was she doing?" Sylvia asked, mystified.

"Nothing, just looking around. I asked if I could help her and she said, 'No, just tell Sylvia I wanted her to know I think she's doing fine. I just stopped by to have a look at her room.'"

"Did you ask her name?" Sylvia spoke very softly.

"Yes, but all she said was, 'Never mind, she'll know.' I went back upstairs to answer the phone. When I returned, she was gone. There's just no way that she could have gotten in or out without my seeing her or without triggering the alarm. I don't mind telling you, Sylvia, I just don't know what to make of it."

"What did she look like?" Sylvia inquired, beginning to tremble.

"She was a tall woman, with pure white hair done in a kind of Gibson-girl style. She wore a navy blue dress and smelled of lavender. The scent lingered in the room after she left. Do you know her?"

"Yes."

"What's the meaning of it, Sylvia? Who was it?" The principal's voice was suddenly stern.

"My grandmother."

"But how did she get in and out?"

"It was easy for her."

"What do you mean?"

"She's dead."

"I see." The nun abruptly changed the subject to a trivial school matter and soon terminated the conversation. The incident was never discussed again.

Grandma Ada's visit was a turning point in Sylvia's professional life. It was affirmation that she was, indeed, at the right place at the right time doing the right thing. She would never doubt her sanity again.

CHAPTER FOUR
Growing Pains

Sylvia laughed so hard, she cried. She cried so hard, she laughed. Determined to forget Ski, she threw her energies into teaching, into parties, into readings. It didn't help. It wasn't enough. Nothing was enough.

Then one day a nun, one of her teaching colleagues, asked Sylvia for a reading. That was nothing new. Sylvia had inadvertently revealed her gift in high school when, psychically aware that a teacher was grieving over her family's financial loss, she'd come forward to offer reassurance. Word had spread among the sisters until eventually they all had come to her.

But this request was different. The nun who tentatively approached was in her mid-50s. "Could you tell me what my life might have been like if I hadn't become a nun?" she asked. "There was a man. I loved him very much, but..."

In her mind's eye, Sylvia got a clear picture of a vital, handsome man in his early 20s. "He loved you, too, but there was so much pressure from your family. You just weren't able to stand up to them."

The nun nodded. "Yes, that's right. At the time, I felt there was nothing else that I could do, but now, sometimes I think of him and wonder..."

Sylvia hugged her spontaneously. "Of course you do, but I'm afraid I can't tell you anything about what your life might have been. What I read are blueprints. Yours was to be a nun, and you're following that blueprint. There's nothing else to read. The life you're leading is the one you were always meant to lead."

After the sister had left, Sylvia sat for a long time speculating on her own blueprint. For a short time, Ski had been her entire life. She loved him now as much as ever but had accepted the fact that he could never be hers. Sylvia mourned her lover as though he were dead, for indeed, he was dead for her. She adored teaching and now took pride in knowing that she was good at it, but that wasn't enough. No matter how much of herself Sylvia poured into her career, it was never enough. An enormous void remained. Her life lacked purpose.

That evening Sylvia called her priest, Father O'Cannon, and made an appointment. The two talked for hours. "Perhaps the reason that you knew Ski's love and yet were strong enough to deny it is that you were meant to be a nun," he suggested.

Sylvia, remembering her childhood fascination with convent life, listened thoughtfully. Throughout her growing-up years, the church had been a refuge, providing solace and retreat from the ongoing chaos at home. A few weeks later, without discussing her plans with anyone, Sylvia sat down with Father O'Cannon and petitioned to enter the Franciscan order.

The formalities would take six months, she was told. Sylvia continued her life without change. "It's the only way you can be truly certain that convent life is for you," Father O'Cannon assured her. Since Ski's departure, Sylvia had dated a number of young men, and finally one special one, John Elwood.

John was a big, gentle teddy-bear type whose self-appointed mission was to heal Sylvia's broken heart. One evening, as they sat drinking tea, he broached the subject of Ski. "I know about it," he said. "I've made a point of finding out about you."

"Why?" she asked, her great brown eyes searching his face.

"Because I care," he replied, meeting her gaze. It was she who looked away.

"It doesn't matter, honey. I'm here to help you get over it," John assured her. In the background, a record played. Billie Holiday was singing, "And maybe someday a baby will climb upon your knee..." His hands reached for her, pulled her toward him.

They sat for what seemed like hours. She felt soothed and comforted, very much like a baby. It was wonderful. Finally, John broke the silence. "The only thing is, I don't know if I'm ready for this trance thing you do."

"Oh, hell," she said, and she started to pull away. Sylvia liked doing readings and wasn't about to give them up.

"I don't mind the psychic stuff. It's that Francine. I just don't think I like the idea of you leaving your body and some other gal taking over and talking through you. How will I know who's who?"

Relieved, Sylvia giggled. "You'd know, all right. Francine's very different from me, very independent. Men aren't all that important to her."

"Ah, one of those lesbians. A lesbian spirit, that's intriguing."

"No, it's more like she's beyond all of it. There's a male entity in her life, but she's very much her own person—if you can say that about a spirit."

"But I still don't like the idea of her just coming in and taking over."

"That's only happened once," Sylvia explained. "The psychology department of the University of Kansas City was offering a special hypnosis class. I signed up out of curiosity. During a demonstration, I slipped into a trance and Francine took over. It was her way of showing me what trancing was all about. It's never happened again. The last thing she wants is to dominate me, and she would never, never play tricks on anyone."

John's fears were allayed, and the two settled into a pleasant, easy relationship. Some of the pain connected with Ski had subsided to a dull ache that could sometimes be forgotten. Sylvia loved teaching and in a few months would become a nun. In the meantime, John was a pleasant companion. Despite his easy manner, Sylvia's new friend was sophisticated and intellectual. She found him quite different from Ski or the neighborhood boys she'd been dating for years, and that added to his charm. A Princeton graduate, John was finishing out his Army time shuffling papers. He came from a wealthy family and envisioned a dazzling future that didn't include Kansas City.

Their romance had a bittersweet "ships passing in the night" quality to it that appealed to Sylvia. They laughed a lot and flirted, Sylvia refusing to take any of it seriously. She was surprised, then, by John's obvious sadness when his military service ended and he prepared to return to his home in Peru, Indiana. "You will write to me, won't you?" he urged her. "You won't do anything foolish like commit yourself to anyone else? You will let me come and visit you at Thanksgiving?"

"Yes. No. Yes," she answered, still laughing, but a little puzzled by his unexpected ardor.

John left and Sylvia found herself missing him, much more than she'd anticipated. She looked forward to his letters and answered them by return mail. Sometimes she found herself speculating about the kind of life they might have together. A man who loved her, children of her own—they were surely valid considerations that deserved to be weighed against the advantages of convent life. More than anything, Sylvia wanted to be settled and secure. Marriage or a convent? The painful uncertainty again emerged; the need to decide once and for all loomed large as her 22nd birthday approached.

Weeks before, Sylvia had picked up psychically that her parents were planning a surprise party for her. She purposefully avoided making plans for that Friday night, but when the evening arrived and she came home from school, the house was quiet. Finally, unable to bear the suspense, she asked Celeste, "What happened to my party?"

Her mother gasped, half annoyed, half marveling, as she had so many times over the years. "Can't we keep anything from you? We had to postpone it until tomorrow night."

At loose ends, she called her friend, Maggie. "What shall we do tonight?"

"I have a date," Maggie told her. "Jerry finally asked me out."

"Jerry, the policeman? The one you've been after for months?"

"The very one. Suppose I call him and see if he's got a friend."

"A blind date? I don't think so. I'm sort of going with John and besides, I'm almost a nun."

They both laughed, realizing how outrageous it sounded. "I'd really like you to come," Maggie persisted. "I'm awfully nervous. Having you there would really help. We'll stay together, and even if you don't like him, we can have fun just going out. You don't want to stay home on your birthday, do you?"

Sylvia didn't, and Maggie called back a few minutes later and announced that Jerry did indeed have a friend. The two officers were to get off duty at nine; Sylvia, still feeling apprehensive, went with Maggie to meet them at the police station.

Gary Dufresne had sharp features redeemed in Sylvia's opinion by intense blue eyes. Not bad really, for a blind date, she decided. "I'm Sylvia Shoemaker," she introduced herself, adding, when he remained silent, "I'm a schoolteacher."

Maggie had forgotten all about introductions; she'd also forgotten her promise that they'd remain together. "Jerry and I will go in his car, and you can meet us somewhere," she announced.

Gary smiled at last, a rather nice smile, Sylvia thought. He took her arm as they walked to his own car. She sat far over to the right, suddenly recalling her father's repeated admonitions that cops were "no good." They could rape you and no one could do a thing about it. As if able to read her thoughts, Gary turned into a dark alley and parked.

Sylvia tensed, her hand grasping the door handle, but Gary merely got out of the car and came around to open the door for her. Together they walked down the alley and into the back of what turned out to be a bar, Sylvia's first.

What a relief to find Maggie and Jerry already seated in a booth. There was a flurry of small talk and then a lull, broken by Gary. "Now, Miss Sylvia Shoemaker, schoolteacher, if we were alone, I'd ask you to tell me about yourself."

Sylvia hesitated, but not Maggie, who explained, "She's part Jewish and Catholic, and she can tell people about their future."

"A fortune-teller, huh?" Gary remarked. He eyed Sylvia speculatively, then added, "I've never cared much for Catholics, or Jews either."

Sylvia instantly dismissed theirs as an amazingly brief, uncomplicated association and looked about the room. It was cheap and shabby. She felt a wave of misery and loneliness. Sylvia was picking up vibes again, and they were awful. The next incident did nothing to relieve her depression.

There was a commotion in the back of the room. Gary leaped to his feet and ran toward the noise. Someone had fallen out of a phone booth. As Gary approached, the man grabbed at his legs. Instantly Gary drew his gun and pointed it menacingly. "Get up and get out of here," he ordered. Without hesitation, the man rose and fled from the bar.

"Do you always carry a gun—even when you're off duty?" Sylvia asked.

"Always."

"Why did you pull it just now?"

"To scare him." Gary's impatient tone indicated he wanted no more discussion. Sylvia was glad a few moments later when he suggested they leave. The two couples separated, Sylvia and Gary returning to the car in silence. "Where to?" he asked.

"Take me back to the station; my car's parked close by."

"You haven't been around much, have you?"

"No, I don't suppose I have."

Neither of them said anything more until he unlocked her car for her. "How about going out some night?"

"Sure," Sylvia replied, though she had no intention of seeing him again. She was surprised by his suggestion; it seemed so obvious that she wasn't his type. She wanted nothing more than to end the evening as quickly as possible. Explanations or arguments would only have prolonged it.

"Maybe that's the way cops are—unpredictable," Maggie suggested the next day, adding, "What do you think of Jerry?"

"It doesn't matter," Sylvia replied. "He's not the one for you."

"Now you're beginning to sound like my mother."

Sylvia shrugged. "Sorry about that," she said. "I have to tell you what I see. Jerry's fine, but he'll only be a short-term thing in your life.

There's someone else—you haven't met him yet." She went on to describe the heavy-set red-haired man her friend would eventually marry. "He's in the Army. You'll meet him in a year; six months later you'll be married."

"And what about you?" Maggie challenged.

"If only I knew. The longer I teach, the more I'm around children, the more I'd like to have my own. But then I think about the Church, the peace, the wonderful tranquility that it offers. Who can tell about marriage? Suppose I ended up like my mother."

"I should think Francine could give you some help with this."

"She's no help at all. The best I can get from her is that my blueprint already exists and I have only to follow it. What good is a message like that?"

While Sylvia puzzled over her future, John's letters arrived regularly. There were frequent phone calls, too. Sylvia found his deep voice very reassuring. As comforting, she reflected, as Gregorian chants.

October drew to a close. It was Halloween night and Sylvia was ready for some excitement. When the phone rang, it was Gary, inviting her out for a late dinner.

"Why not?" she surprised herself by responding, but she had barely hung up when her misgivings began. A few minutes later she called him back. "I'm awfully sorry, but my aunt's visiting us and she just broke her leg. I have to drive her to the hospital."

"That's a shame," he said. "I was really looking forward to seeing you."

"I *am* sorry," Sylvia said, "maybe another time." But she vowed there'd never be one. That evening, she and Maggie went to a horror movie. "Gary called a few minutes after you left," Maggie's mother informed them when they returned. "I had no idea you'd lied to him, Sylvia. Naturally, when he asked where you girls were, I told him. Really, I should think you'd know better than to tell such a ridiculous story to a policeman."

"I never lie to anybody. I hate lies. It was stupid of me and I'll never do it again," Sylvia said and meant it.

The incident wasn't the end of Gary. To her surprise, he called again and again. The fourth time she gave in, but insisted that Maggie accompany them on a date. Gary's mild disgust was thinly veiled, and this time Sylvia was certain she'd seen the last of him.

The night before Thanksgiving, John arrived. He talked with Sylvia about her future in the Catholic Church—she saw no reason to mention Gary. John was having enough trouble thinking of her as a nun.

Sylvia listened with interest as John told her about his return to civilian life. "Mother persuaded me to spend the winter with her. I've been away so long and with Father gone, she gets lonely," John explained. In the late spring, he'd be moving to Chicago to begin his career as an executive in the family insurance company.

"Chicago's a very exciting place; they've even written a song about it," he reminded her before leaving the following Sunday. Sylvia promised she'd spend Christmas with him and his family in Indiana.

When the young police officer took to dropping by unexpectedly after work, Sylvia realized that Gary Dufresne wasn't the type to be easily discouraged. Though exasperated at first, she began to look forward to his visits when she discovered that beneath the laconic exterior was not only a dry sense of humor but an agile mind. Gary and his friends were older, more worldly than the men she'd known. Their cops-and-robbers world was new and exciting to her. When two whole weeks passed with only fleeting thoughts of Ski, Sylvia began to hope she was getting over him.

As the days flew by, Christmas was approaching, and with it her promised trip to Indiana. Sylvia, traveling alone for the first time, felt a glow of anticipation as she boarded the train. It was still the era of polished wood club cars and porters in white starched uniforms. Despite some trepidation about John's family, she felt very sophisticated in her new suit. In one of the few significant intuitive insights that Sylvia had ever had about herself, she received a clear picture of a protective mother and two doting sisters.

The train pulled into Peru, Indiana, at twilight. The town, blanketed in newly fallen snow, looked like a fairy-tale village. John was waiting—ruddy, smiling, big, and warm. "Come on, Mom has dinner waiting," he said after a giant bear hug. It sounded cheery enough.

They drove out into the suburbs. "That's Cole Porter's house," John said, pointing to a mansion, "and this is my house." He drove through the iron gateway that flanked the drive of the equally impressive estate next door. As they approached, Sylvia stared in amazement at the magnificent facade before her. "Why, it looks like Dragonwyck!" she exclaimed, remembering a Gothic movie she'd seen as a child.

The house, with its turrets, its towers, and its broad, sloping grounds, was a monument to old money. Sylvia tried not to feel intimidated, but she was. The greeting extended by John's mother merely added to her growing discomfort. "Miss Shoemaker, how pleasant of you to grace us with your presence," Mrs. Elwood said, standing back to inspect her.

Sylvia struggled to think of an appropriately effusive reply, but couldn't. "Thank you," she murmured, extending her hand as if across an icy chasm to Mrs. Elwood. John's mother was a short, stout woman with rigidly styled hair and a thin, pursed mouth. There was an air of disdain about her features, as though she'd either tasted or smelled something unpleasant.

John's sisters turned out to be clones of their mother. The holiday stretched out before Sylvia like a life sentence. "Are you having fun?" John asked the next day. "Aren't they wonderful?" He was shocked when Sylvia suggested that his family didn't like her. "They love you as much as I do," he insisted, and he appeared to honestly believe it.

After four days of confinement, Sylvia insisted that John take her out alone. He reluctantly agreed, but his resolve weakened as he stared at his mother's stricken face.

"That's all right," Mrs. Elwood said, her hand straying to her heart. "Just go along. I'll be fine."

"Is anything wrong?" John asked, bending anxiously over the great wing chair where she sat.

"Nothing really, just my heart. Now and then it acts up a bit—nothing for you two young people to worry about. I'll be happy here all alone, knowing that you're having a good time."

"We'd better not go," John said.

Sylvia could stand it no longer. "Whatever you decide to do, I'm going for a walk." She was already out the great, massive door when John caught up with her. The light of the full moon was bright on the snow. It was a night out of a Russian fairy tale, but the couple scarcely noticed. The snow crunched noisily under their feet—the only sound, for neither of them could find words to express their disappointment. Finally, John began a halting discourse on his career plans. Sylvia had heard it all before but now doubted that he would ever leave home. She responded absently, knowing John's mind was really on his mother's heart, an organ that Sylvia suspected would outlast her own.

Sylvia wasn't able to bring their conversation around to the situation; perhaps she didn't really try. Finally they trudged back through the snow to the house. Pausing just inside the door, John kissed her good night. He was staying with his married sister because Mrs. Elwood didn't think it proper that he sleep under the same roof with an unmarried woman.

Sylvia hurried up to her room, hoping to avoid Mrs. Elwood. As she was preparing for bed, she received a precognitive vision. John's mother was planning a surprise party, during which Sylvia's engagement to John would be announced. Sylvia had never felt less centered, more insecure. Without any further thought, she made her way to the upstairs phone. Her hands were trembling as she dialed. It was her father who answered.

"How do you feel about it?" he asked after she'd told him the story.

"If I ever had any idea of marrying John, it's gone now. I'd be marrying his mother right along with him, and probably his snooty sisters, too."

"Then there's nothing keeping you there. The sooner you leave, the better. You've got your return ticket." Typically protective, he offered, "I'll call the depot in the morning and get a train schedule for you."

"Thank you, Daddy."

"For what?"

"Just for being there." She was trying not to cry.

A little choked up himself, he changed the subject. "Speaking of people being there, Gary has been over here every night since you left."

"How come?"

"Come on, Sylvia, you can figure that one out. The guy's crazy about you."

"Don't tell me that! I've enough to worry about right here. I want out!"

"I'll get on it," he promised.

Just as Sylvia was hanging up the phone, she heard a clicking sound. She was certain Mrs. Elwood had been listening. Sylvia hurried back to her room with the very unpleasant sense that she was being spied upon. Finally, after lying awake for hours, she fell into a fitful sleep. It was late morning when she awakened. Dressing quickly, Sylvia hurried downstairs to find John and his mother waiting for her in the breakfast room. One look at their faces verified her suspicions; they were clearly aware of her feelings. "I want to leave today," she informed them.

John banged his cup down in frustration, but before he could say a word, Mrs. Elwood spoke. "I hope you're not getting angry at your mother, Johnnie. It isn't I who disappointed you."

That was enough for Sylvia; she turned away, intending to go back to her room, and John rose to his feet and crossed the room in an instant, pulling her to him. "I love you," he said in a hoarse, pleading voice. His mother's hand went to her heart.

"Not enough—or *not as much*, I'm afraid," Sylvia said, thinking of Mrs. Elwood. Pulling free, she went to the hall phone, and without a word, dialed her home number. Once again, her father answered. "How soon can I get a train out of here?" she asked.

"There's one at 6:45 this evening. It'll get you in around midnight. We'll be there to meet you."

"I'll be on it."

"Oh, no you won't! You're not going anywhere," Mrs Elwood, now standing beside her, said with quiet authority.

Sylvia gasped, "What do you mean?"

"Exactly what I said. You're not going to embarrass John or myself. A gathering has been planned. All our friends have been invited. I expect you to be there."

"I heard that!" Sylvia's father was yelling into the phone. "Tell her if you're not on that train, I'll rent a helicopter and land on her damned house."

Sylvia didn't have to repeat the message, for Mrs. Elwood could hear every word. Her face turned white. "Johnnie is well rid of you," she said, and walked stiffly away.

"Be there, Daddy, I'm coming home." Sylvia hung up the phone and hurried up the broad staircase to her room. She'd barely finished packing her few things when John knocked on the door. It had been his air of gentleness that had first appealed to her; now she reflected that the gentleness was possibly weakness.

"Why don't we go out somewhere for lunch?" he suggested.

Sylvia agreed, but insisted on taking her bag with her. She had no intention of ever returning to the Elwoods' house. They drove through the snowy countryside for hours before John finally took her to the station. Lunch had been a desultory affair. John wanted nothing more than to change her mind, but there was nothing left to say. Sylvia didn't need psychic ability to predict what life would be like with Mrs. Elwood for a mother-in-law. Beyond that, the image of John as he catered to his mother was an even more potent warning. Sylvia was relieved to see the train waiting, and was eager to board.

John got on with her, and together they walked through car after car filled with holiday passengers. At last, they found a vacant seat by a window. John placed her bag on the shelf above her and then sat down, holding Sylvia's hands in his. "Was it the party? Maybe you just felt that you were being rushed," he suggested.

She shook her head sadly, but he ignored the gesture. "We talked so often about the kind of life we could have. You know I love you. I really thought you loved me, too."

Sylvia's eyes filled with tears. "I do—in a way. But it just wasn't meant to be." The train jolted, then very slowly began to move. "I'll never forget you, John," she promised. "You were there for me when I really needed it. I'll always remember what a good friend you were."

Reluctantly, John rose and she with him. They hugged briefly, and then he hurried from the moving car. Watching from the window, she saw him leap onto the platform. The train was moving faster now. John was gone.

Sylvia stopped waving and leaned back against the leather cushions. She listened to the click of the rails, a very comforting sound. Ski had said good-bye to her; she had said good-bye to John. Another chapter was ended. Outside, the snow fell heavily against the darkening sky, but the interior of the car felt warm and safe. The pressures of the previous months faded away. A sense of peace and confidence enveloped Sylvia. She was going home. This was a moment frozen in time, complete, and to be remembered always.

CHAPTER FIVE
Following the Blueprint

Sylvia's train had been delayed by near-blizzard conditions. At half-past three in the morning, when it finally pulled into Kansas City, the station was filled. Revelers celebrating the new year were everywhere. Scanning the many faces, Sylvia saw her father almost immediately, then Celeste, and behind her, Gary.

"When your dad said you were coming home, I thought I'd better meet your train," he explained. "I've got this party—I'd like you to go with me. If I waited till tomorrow to ask you, you'd probably have something else to do—like taking your aunt to the hospital or something."

Sylvia winced. Her father answered before she could open her mouth. "Of course she'll go."

"Will you, Sylvia?" Gary persisted.

"Why not?" She was too tired to respond to the embarrassing jab.

By the time they reached the house, Sylvia had nodded off. It was Gary who awakened her. "You really will come? You won't forget or change your mind again?" he gently prodded while helping her out of the car.

Sylvia agreed dazedly, her thoughts only of sleep. It had been a very long day. "I promise," she said. At the front door, Gary kissed her quickly and was off into the icy dawn.

That evening, after sleeping most of the day, Sylvia felt refreshed and almost happy. She dressed with special care, accenting a sleekly simple black silk dress with a pearl necklace and earrings—her father's Christmas gift. Her hair, allowed to grow again, was swept into a French twist. At 22, she'd loved and lost. Hardly a woman of the world, Sylvia still sought to pass for one. She winked at herself in the mirror, suddenly pleased with the image reflected there.

The young man who greeted her downstairs shared more of her newfound confidence. It was a Gary she'd never seen before. He actually appeared nervous. Their arrival at the party was greeted with eager enthusiasm. The police officers and their wives who crowded about them seemed oddly conspiratorial. Sylvia began to feel like the key character in a mystery plot.

A pretty, dark-haired young woman approached and introduced herself. "I'm Barbara Crowther. Don works with Gary." Sylvia liked her instantly, and before long, the two were chatting like old friends.

"I'm so glad Gary met you," Barbara confided. "He used to keep Don out half the night. Now I finally get to see a little of my husband. Besides, I can tell you're good for Gary."

"We're not really going together," Sylvia hastened to explain. "We're simply good friends."

Just then, Gary appeared, "May I borrow Sylvia for a minute? I've got a big deal to discuss."

"Of course," Barbara agreed, smiling. "I've a notion that she and I are going to be seeing a lot of one another from now on."

Puzzling over Barbara's knowing manner, Sylvia followed Gary into the strangely deserted family room.

"Did your folks say anything?" he asked as they seated themselves on the large couch.

"About what?"

"Never mind."

"What is this?"

"Don't you know—psychically, I mean?"

"Really, Gary, if I've told you once, I've told you a thousand times, I don't 'know' everything! Maybe once in a while a message comes through for me, but not often, and never when I try."

"It may seem a little strange to you at first—since we haven't exactly been dating—but I've known since the first time I saw you."

"Known what?" Sylvia asked, feeling herself drawing away.

"I'll get to that in a minute. Maybe I should tell you a little about myself. I never like to talk about personal stuff, but now I guess I'd better. I was an Army brat. I lived in nearly every state in the union, then went to high school in Japan and spent four years in the Marines. I've been with the police department for nearly three years. I like it here. I'm ready to settle down. I *want* to settle down." In Gary's mind, everything was about to be settled.

"That's all very interesting," Sylvia prompted him, "but I've been through a lot lately. I want to know where this conversation's going."

"I'm getting to that." He turned to face her squarely. "I've loved you since the first time I saw you two years ago."

"Two years ago!" Sylvia exclaimed, giggling nervously. "We just met two months ago."

Gary smiled. "Some psychic you are! You don't even know what's going on in *this* world. Do you remember two years ago when your friend Maggie had a stalled car on the college campus? A police officer came to take the report. Do you recall him?"

Sylvia remembered the incident very well. The principal's voice announcing through the loudspeaker that Mary Margaret Ryan was to report to her car. Maggie had been doubled over with menstrual cramps at the time. "You go, Sylvia," she'd pleaded. "They probably want to tow my car somewhere. You take care of it."

Sylvia arrived in time to see a policeman writing a ticket. He explained to her that he'd been called in to investigate the possibility that the car was stolen. "Either the young lady has to have the car fixed, or she can expect to have it towed at her own expense," he explained.

Sylvia had been furious. "Don't you cops have anything better to do than harass college girls? Why aren't you out catching criminals?" she'd demanded to know.

"Some temper you got, cutie," he'd commented, not in the least annoyed.

"Don't you cutie me!" she'd snapped.

"What's your name?"

"Sylvia Shoemaker. Are you going to give me a ticket, too?"

"Not this time," he'd said, handing her Maggie's ticket, which actually turned out to be merely a warning. "I can still remember you flouncing out of that office. 'I certainly hope you fill your quota of tickets,'" he mimicked.

"That was you?" Sylvia asked incredulously.

Gary nodded. "I was determined to find you, but there must be a hundred Shoemakers in Kansas City—and they all spell the name differently. Finally I gave up calling, but never hoping. You can't imagine how I felt when I saw you that night in the station. It was like a dream had come true for me."

"But why didn't you say something?"

"I kept thinking that you'd remember me at some point, but instead you kept doing everything you could think of to get rid of me."

The story seemed terribly romantic to Sylvia, suddenly very much aware of how badly she'd treated Gary. She studied him. He reminded her of a big cat—not an unattractive image.

"I found out right away about that guy in Indiana—I gather that's over now," Gary continued, taking her hands in one of his. "I also know you've petitioned to become a nun. I hope you won't go through with it, because you'd be ruining all my plans."

"What plans?" Sylvia asked, her voice almost a whisper.

"I found you again in 1958. I want to marry you in 1959."

Before Sylvia could say a word, he'd reached into his pocket and brought out a blue velvet box. When she didn't take it, Gary removed the top to reveal the largest diamond she'd ever seen.

The events of the last 24 hours were just too much. Sylvia began to cry. Gary put his arms around her reassuringly. "You'll get used to the idea, honey. Your parents are already delighted. They like me. You know they weren't very happy about either of your plans. Moving to Chicago was bad enough—but the convent! They're praying you won't enter. Either way, they'd be losing you. You're everything to them, you know that."

She did indeed know. The choice between John and the convent had been only part of her dilemma. From the beginning, there'd been a missing piece of the puzzle, a piece that she'd attempted to ignore. Sylvia had always been the glue that held the Shoemaker family together. What would happen to them without her?

Sylvia imagined her mother's loneliness if she were to finally lose Bill after all these years. And her father—*I am the light in his eyes,* she acknowledged matter-of-factly. He had always seen her as the best, the prettiest, the cleverest person in the world. Knowing it, she'd excelled. At first it had been school; Sylvia learned so fast she'd skipped a grade. Later she'd become her father's little sweetheart. As a girl, she'd been barely into her teens before they'd begun entering dance contests together and winning. Sylvia remembered the black lace dress he'd bought her when she was 16. It had cost a hundred dollars, a fortune in those days. How proud he'd been of her when she stepped forward to receive the first-prize trophy they'd won together.

But now—didn't she deserve her own life, a life apart from the needs and desires of others? Sylvia shook her head as though to clear it, and returned to Gary. "I don't know what's best for them, me, anybody," she admitted.

He closed her hand over the ring. "Keep it awhile and think about it. Please, Sylvia, it won't hurt to just think about it."

At that moment, the other guests burst excitedly into the room. It was obvious that they could contain their impatience no longer.

"Congratulations!"

"How thrilling!"

"We're so happy for you both!"

"When's the wedding?"

Once again, Sylvia felt she was the central character in a drama, one that was becoming more romantic and exciting all the time. It was hard not to get caught up in it all. "We'll see," she murmured. "We'll see."

Returning home in the early hours of 1959, she found her parents waiting up anxiously. It was obvious that they were solidly behind

Gary. Their reasoning was persuasive. After all his years of traveling, Gary was eager to set down roots—happily in Kansas City. Sylvia's life with him could be really good, giving her the children she wanted and the security she needed. And her parents supported a match that would bring them the grandchildren they longed for and keep their little girl from straying far away. Why, there was even a nice apartment for rent just down the street. Celeste was certain that it was just the thing for her daughter. She and Bill would be more than happy to help with the furnishings.

Sylvia listened absently. Perhaps they were right. She admired Gary's self-assurance. No doubt about it—here was a man who knew what he wanted and went right for it. She could learn a lot from his single-mindedness.

When John Elwood called later that day, Sylvia told him about the proposal. "But what about *us*, Sylvia?" was his response, an even weaker one than she'd anticipated.

It was a bitter young woman who still longed for a lost sweetheart who answered. "Gary wants to marry me in April," she said. "If you can detach yourself from your mother and marry me before then, okay. Otherwise, I'm going ahead with it." Once said, the words even shocked Sylvia. She'd spoken spontaneously, without thinking, aware only that she'd lost Ski, and that John had rejected her in favor of his mother. Now it was she who was calling the shots. Without realizing it, Sylvia had made a major life decision as easily, as heedlessly, as one might change TV channels.

John made it even easier for her when he announced, "Mother needs me for some family business—she really does—and I can't possibly be free until August."

"Fine. That settles it," she told him. "I'm getting married on April 2."

"What do you know about this guy?" asked John, attempting to reason with her.

"I know that he loves me, and I know he's a man who lets nothing stand in his way. That's enough for me."

The next day Sylvia went to see Father O'Cannon. Telling him of her plans was more difficult, but there was some compensation in the marvelous sense of relief that accompanies the final resolution of a difficult issue. The assurance it brought carried her through the interview. At last it was settled once and for all. Sylvia would have children of her own; she was marrying a strong, dynamic man who excited her. She would soon have her own home. And in pursuing this course, she was pleasing her parents and possibly even preserving their marriage. Happier and more relaxed than she'd been in months, Sylvia felt almost giddy.

Soon her life centered entirely around Gary. For the next few weeks, she taught, came home, and rested. At midnight, Gary got off duty, and they spent three hours together. Then Sylvia went to bed and slept—if she was lucky—until it was time to get up and teach again.

Friends called, leaving messages, but there wasn't much time to return their calls. Finally, one Sunday afternoon a group dropped by. When they pressed Sylvia about her absence, she flashed her diamond mischievously and replied, "I've been busy."

There were excited shrieks. "You and John finally did it! When's the wedding?"

"April 2, but not John," she announced, enjoying their surprise and suspense. She'd been part of this close-knit group for so long that the sudden transformation to mystery woman was delicious. She was heady with the knowledge of what she'd done on her own, without discussing it with anyone.

"Who is it?" they asked at once.

"Gary."

"Gary who?"

"You haven't met him yet. He's a policeman." Her elation began to dissipate in their silence—a silence, she realized, that implied doubt and concern. "He loves me," she added defensively.

"You can't know him very well."

"Two months—that's long enough," she insisted.

"And Francine, what does she say?" a friend who'd known Sylvia since grammar school asked.

"She says that I'm destined to follow my blueprint."

"What the hell does that mean?"

"Whatever it means, it's happening," Sylvia declared briskly, putting an end to their questions.

Going all the way before marriage was a mortal sin, but that didn't mean that it didn't happen. Sylvia wondered occasionally why Gary didn't even try. It must be because he respects me so much, she reasoned. Such reticence from a man who'd seen so much of life was touching. It also made life less complicated for her in the hectic weeks before the wedding.

Sylvia and Gary were married April 2, 1959, at St. James Church. The magnitude of what she was doing hit her finally the night before the ceremony. It was as though she'd awakened from a dream. "What am I doing?" she asked Maggie. "I don't love Gary. I don't even know him."

"It was a rebound romance; we all knew that," Maggie said. "We all tried to tell you."

Sylvia buried her face in her hands and began to cry softly.

"You don't have to go through with it," Maggie reminded her. "It's not too late to stop."

But for Sylvia it was. All the plans had been made—the invitations, the gowns, the flowers, the caterers, the music. For days, she'd been receiving wedding gifts. The priests, the attendants, her friends, her parents, and, of course, Gary, all were expecting her to fulfill her promise. How could she disappoint them?

The night was long and sleepless. Sylvia's mind raced, but she knew there was no acceptable alternative. The wedding would go on as planned. The next morning, Celeste greeted her with an elaborate breakfast, but all Sylvia could do was look at it. Such "jitters" were to be expected, her parents sagely agreed. The dishes were quickly cleared.

Celeste, Maggie, and Sharon helped Sylvia dress and then donned their own finery. Bill beamed at them proudly, certain that he would be escorting the best-looking women in Kansas City. Just as Sylvia was about to step into the car, a young man driving by slowed down and called out the window, "I just want to say that you're pretty as a picture." Sylvia's spirits lifted, but not for long.

In the crowded church, Sylvia was suffocating. She wanted to scream, but no sound came from her smiling lips. Once again she performed on cue, walking down the aisle on her father's arm. As she knelt before the priest, she noticed that his shoes needed shining. Sylvia stole a look at Gary. Who was that stranger?

Then the final words—awful and irreversible—were spoken, and the service was over. The newlyweds were walking back down the aisle and out the door amid a shower of rice. At the lavish reception, where champagne flowed freely, Sylvia discovered Gary in the adjoining bar drinking something stronger. *Did he too have regrets?* Sylvia wondered.

The time came for them to leave. Tears, hugs, good-byes over, they were finally alone in Gary's car. For more than an hour they drove, half-hearted attempts at conversation going nowhere.

It was late Thursday afternoon. Both had to be back at work on Monday morning. "Where are we going?" Sylvia asked at last.

They were approaching a sign that read, Sedalia, Missouri. "This looks like as good a place as any," Gary said, turning into a Motor Inn with an adjoining restaurant. Gary ordered liver and onions for dinner; Sylvia had the same. Wasn't it the companionable thing to do? Both seemingly at a loss for words, the dinner stretched on interminably.

At last the check came. Gary paid it, and they rose and walked silently to their room. It was drab, cheerless, ordinary. Sylvia turned on the radio. The tune playing was a current hit, "Love Is a Many-Splendored Thing." She scarcely knew whether to laugh or cry.

The debacle of her honeymoon was a stunning blow to Sylvia's self-esteem; typically, she blamed herself. It was ten days before the marriage was consummated. Lacking experience, Sylvia speculated endlessly—*If only I were worldlier, sexier, prettier.* Reared in a tradition that deferred to men in every way, it never occurred to her to challenge Gary or even to question him. It was years before Sylvia learned the whole story of her husband's tragic childhood. Later, much later, he confided that his mother had run off with a snake medicine salesman when he was two, and that seven years later he'd discovered the body of his grandmother hanging from a self-tied noose.

At the time of her marriage, Sylvia knew only that the man who'd been so desperate to make her his wife, to bask in the warmth of her enthusiasm and humor, now seemed intent upon changing her, determined to mold her into another person entirely.

She had entered the marriage seeking comfort and approval, and in their place found only criticism. Very soon Sylvia realized that nothing she could ever do would satisfy Gary. But that didn't stop her from trying.

On the surface, theirs was a successful marriage. They were both gregarious and enjoyed a lively social life. Their private disappointments remained private. Sometimes Sylvia found a grim humor in her situation, remembering that she'd once wanted to be a nun. Then on December 9, 1959, at half-past nine in the evening, she became pregnant. Sylvia thought the event something of a miracle, considering the infrequency of their sexual intimacy. She was certain that she knew the very instant that conception had taken place. "Yes, you are, indeed, pregnant," Francine confirmed, telling Sylvia that her child would be a boy and would one day stand 6'5" tall.

Gary was furious when he heard the news and refused to speak to Sylvia for a week. He resented the financial responsibility and the intrusion into his life. For once, Gary's opinions didn't matter. Sylvia was wildly happy, for this was the child she'd longed for, the treasured entity who, for a short time at least, would be hers alone.

When, on a day early the following August, Gary asked Sylvia what she was planning to give him for his birthday, she laughed and said, "A son." Paul Jon Dufresne was born nearly a month early, arriving at 2:32 on the afternoon of August 19, 1960—his father's birthday.

By the first week of September, Sylvia was back in school, teaching. Her joyous expectations proved short-lived. A postpartum depression was the last thing that she would have expected, yet week after week she walked through her tasks enveloped by a soul-crushing malaise. To make matters more difficult, Paul was a colicky baby. Gary, already resentful, was enraged by the baby's crying. Sylvia was up half of every night walking the floor with the baby, trying to soothe him. Finally, exhausted and totally dispirited, she begged Gary to allow her to stay home with their child for one year. He would have none of it. "We need your salary," he insisted. "Don't even think of quitting." Obediently, Sylvia handed Gary her paycheck of $276 a month. She had no idea how much her husband made.

"Why do I have to go through all this?" she asked Francine. "Unless you experience many things now, you'll be unable to help others later," was the answer. Sylvia laughed aloud. With her own life a perpetual twilight of depression, how could she possibly help anyone else? But Francine promised, "One day you will be a star." Sylvia would gladly have settled for a good night's sleep.

As bad as things were, they could—and did—get worse. When Paul was five months old, he caught the staph infection that was raging throughout the city. Sylvia watched, panic-stricken, as her baby's temperature shot up to 105 degrees and remained there. She was on the phone hourly to the doctor. The hospitals were full. All Sylvia could do was try to keep Paul comfortable with cold-water baths and lots of water. She held him all night long.

The next morning, Paul's temperature was even higher. Frantically, Sylvia called the doctor. Then called him again and again. "I promise I'll let you know the minute there's a place for him," he attempted to soothe her. "In the meantime, just keep giving him baths." She hung up and carried Paul into the small bedroom of their apartment. The child was delirious; his head rolled from side to side as though to escape pain.

Helplessly, Sylvia sank into a rocking chair. "Please, God, don't let him die," she pleaded aloud, and then added, "Grandma, help me. I know you lost your Paul; please don't let me lose mine."

Sylvia had no sooner said the words than she felt a wave of cool air. Paul opened his eyes, then cooed and blinked. He seemed to be looking at something beyond her right shoulder. "Grandma, it's you!" Sylvia cried out, and just as she said the words, a Mass card that had been wedged for years in the mirror of her dressing table actually flew into the air and landed on the floor at her feet. It read, "Ada Coil; died July 13, 1954."

Sylvia was weeping uncontrollably when the phone rang. It was the doctor. There was a bed for Paul, and she was to bring him in immediately. Sylvia was there in 15 minutes and then waited alone for hours, unwilling to bother anyone. "If the baby dies, it's your fault," Gary had warned. Unaccountably, he blamed her for Paul's illness.

But Paul didn't die. After 26 hours in isolation, he began to recover. After a week, he was allowed to come home, and a marked change quickly followed. It wasn't long before he was sleeping through the night, and so was Sylvia. Slowly, her intense depression began to lift.

When Gary suggested, none too delicately, that she make more of a financial contribution, Sylvia knew that life had returned to normal. Obedient as ever, she got a Christmas job selling candy, and during the following summer she sold trailers. Their bank account grew rapidly, and when it reached a few hundred dollars, Gary decided that a house of their own was a testament to their upwardly mobile state. A cluster of tract homes was under construction nearby. The couple walked through the models and selected the one that Gary preferred. The down payment was made, and Gary importantly directed Sylvia in the paperwork. A month later, their house completed, the Dufresnes went down to inspect it for the first time.

"There's something wrong here," Sylvia said as they stepped inside.

"What do you mean?" Gary asked, thumping the wall. "It looks okay to me."

"No, it's not okay, not at all. Something's wrong here. We don't belong here," Sylvia said, almost frantic.

"We'll belong as long as we manage the $104 a month."

"I'm serious," she insisted. "We don't belong here."

"Don't give me that spook stuff. We paid for this place, and we're moving in."

"The time has not yet come for you to be believed," Francine explained.

They moved in, but from the beginning, things were wrong. Sylvia had selected a room on the top floor of the tri-level for Paul. It was the lightest and brightest in the house and had a sunny morning exposure. She'd taken great pleasure in planning the decor. Broad shelves held his teddy bears and other toys, and the furniture had been painted a bright blue to harmonize with the yellow and white wallpaper. She thought it a very pleasant room for a baby and imagined his pleasure at awakening in such a setting.

Unfortunately, Paul never had the opportunity; he refused to even sleep in it. Sylvia had scarcely placed him in his newly painted crib when he began to scream, pleading to be picked up. Gary was working at night, leaving Sylvia alone with Paul and Thor, their German Shepherd, so the baby slept in the room with her. Had Thor had his way, he would have, too. As it was, the dog lay across the entrance to Sylvia's bedroom.

Sylvia lacked the energy to really focus on her apprehension about the house. Every day it seemed she felt a little worse. One afternoon when she'd finished her school day and brought Paul home from his babysitter's, she felt totally exhausted. Wearily, she placed the child in his playpen and entered the kitchen intending to fix dinner. Without warning, a wave of dizziness overcame her. It was the last thing that Sylvia remembered.

Just how long she lay unconscious she never knew. An angry, unsympathetic Gary aroused her when he came home for a dinner break. The next day Sylvia was too ill to go to work. "A little rest is all I need," she told Gary. "I'll go tomorrow." But when tomorrow came, she was even weaker. For ten days she lay on the couch, so ill that even the effort of moving her head brought on a violent wave of nausea.

Realizing at last that rest alone wasn't going to cure her, Sylvia asked a neighbor to drive her to the doctor. The physician, an old friend, rose to his feet, greeting her warmly as she entered his private office.

Sinking into the chair opposite him, she forced herself to smile back. It was reassuring to see a face she'd known since childhood.

But the doctor was anything but reassured by the sight of her. "What's the matter?" he asked.

She tried to joke. "I don't know, Jim. I seem to be developing a color scheme all my own."

"What do you mean?"

"Well," Sylvia replied, hesitating, "my urine is black and my you know what is white. Oh, yes, my eyes. Did you notice, they're turning yellow."

She was still speaking as he reached for the phone and dialed. "Emergency coming in," he informed someone on the other end. There were a few words that she didn't catch, then he hung up.

"What about me?" she asked, hurt and annoyed that his mind was on another patient.

"I'm afraid you're the emergency."

Sylvia was admitted to the hospital within an hour. By the time the day had ended, she'd been examined by five different physicians. Their diagnosis was acute hepatitis. At first she was too euphoric to worry. They'd given her a shot to control the nausea, and, for the first time in what seemed like weeks, her stomach was calm. But in the days that followed, her body heat became unbearable, and most of her skin surface was raw from scratching herself. "Bile salts coming to the surface," a nurse explained. Sylvia had never heard of bile salts; she knew only that she was in agony.

Learning that an operation was scheduled, she asked Francine, "Am I going to die?"

"Not now, too many things are planned for you," was the answer.

Sylvia wanted to cry at the prospect of more work, more unhappiness, more pain. Death had seemed a merciful release.

The surgery lasted for nearly five hours. A portion of Sylvia's liver, intestinal tract, and gallbladder were removed. She awoke suddenly in agonizing pain. No medication seemed to work. She began to pray, her eyes focused on the light above the bed. Then, sensing a presence, Sylvia turned her head warily, wondering what they were going to do to her next.

There beside her was Grandma Ada. "Is it really you?" she whispered, her voice hoarse from the tubes that had been inserted during the operation.

"Of course it is, sugar heart. Did you think I'd let you go through this alone?"

"Grandma, I can't stand the pain."

"It will be all right now. They've found the right medication for you. It's on the way."

"I've made so many mistakes, nothing really turned out the way I intended. I have so much to tell you."

"You will one day, you will," Ada assured. Just then, the nurse entered the room and approached the bed.

"My grandmother's here," Sylvia informed her.

"No one's allowed in here," the nurse said, leaning forward to take Sylvia's pulse.

"You don't understand, my grandmother's dead."

"Of course she is," the nurse agreed, giving Sylvia's arm a little pat.

"She doesn't believe me, Grandma."

"Of course I believe you," the nurse placated her.

"Just close your eyes," Ada soothed. "Everything's going to be fine."

Sylvia woke up back in her hospital room. Bill was crying, Celeste was wringing her hands, Gary was staring out the window. Sylvia turned to Sharon, who was sitting beside the bed. "I just saw Grandma." The four of them looked away, looked at each other, looked everywhere but at Sylvia. "Really, I saw her. I even talked with her," Sylvia insisted, frustrated that they didn't believe her. In reality, they had taken the incident as a sign that she was dying. They were certain that Ada had come for her.

Seven days passed and Sylvia was still hooked up to the machines. Not even her stomach functioned without a tube while another apparatus drained the bile from her body. Gary refused to come to the hospital; the smell disturbed him. It was Bill who came every day. Invariably, he arrived just as Sylvia was vomiting. Joking, he accused her of saving it up for him, but it was obvious that he was very frightened. His little girl was growing weaker every day.

Alone in her hospital room, Sylvia thought about her situation. How wonderful it would be to just slip away to wherever Grandma was. The thought of death had never frightened her, and now the prospect seemed like utter bliss—until she thought of Paul. If she died, he would be left with Gary, who'd never wanted him. She thought, too, of Francine and her continuing insistence that they had a job to do. Whatever it was, Sylvia realized that she would have to get on with it, and that meant getting well.

Gingerly, Sylvia reached for a spoonful of Jell-O. She took a bite, then realized what an exercise in futility that was. What nourishment was there with everything going out the stomach tube? Later, when the doctor came by on his rounds, she demanded that he remove the tubes immediately.

"Now Sylvia, you have to have patience," he said, attempting to soothe her.

"If I'm any more patient, I'll be dead. I'm never going to get well if everything that goes in goes right out of me," she argued. Then she threatened, "If you don't pull these tubes out, I will." The tubes were removed, all but the one that extracted bile. Almost immediately, Sylvia felt herself growing stronger.

One afternoon, as she continued to improve dramatically, Sylvia heard the nurses talking about a patient who had no visitors. Sylvia decided to pay a "call." She wheeled herself down the long hallway, carrying her bile tube and bottle with her.

Pausing in the doorway to catch her breath, she was struck by a flame of bright red hair flowing across a pillow. "Hello, I'm Sylvia," she introduced herself, pushing the wheelchair forward.

The woman turned feebly. Her face, nearly as pale as the bed linen, was quite beautiful. "I'm Maureen," she replied. Her smile was touchingly eager.

Soon Sylvia learned that Maureen was only a year older than she. Maureen had a husband, but he'd left her. She also had four children and a mother who resented having to care for them while her daughter was hospitalized.

"The nurse told me you're here for a lung operation," Sylvia ventured.

"Yes, one of them's gone. They're going to fix the other today."

Sylvia knew almost instantly how the operation would turn out; it was very clear that she'd come to this room for a purpose. Wheeling herself up to the bed, she took Maureen's hand. They talked for hours, Sylvia sharing the wisdom that she'd received over the years from Francine.

"It's so scary to think of dying," Maureen confided. "Are *you* ever afraid?"

"No, no, not at all. I'm really not, because I know what the Other Side holds for me," Sylvia explained. She paused and said, "It's something to look forward to, not to fear."

"You mean it really is heaven?"

"Heaven, paradise, nirvana—whatever you want to call it. All those words describe the same place, our eternal Home where our experience of God and each other isn't restricted to the limitations of time and space. Beauty and wisdom are there waiting for us. All the pain and trauma of life fades to a pale memory. The degree of our soul's perfection is the badge of having lived." Sylvia found herself parroting Francine's words to her new friend.

"I'm not sure my soul's all that perfect," Maureen confided.

"Well, neither's mine; but we're both doing our best—aren't we?"

Maureen nodded. "I've tried very hard."

"That's what it's all about, trying hard and learning lessons. We'll have lessons to learn on the Other Side as well, but there won't be pain attached to it. You can believe me, dying is like going Home—only better, much more wonderful than any home in this world could ever be."

"Oh, that sounds so nice," Maureen sighed, leaning back. She seemed to have attained almost total peace.

"Yes, it *is* nice, it's really heavenly—so heavenly that if we could envision it clearly, we'd all want to go there now rather than wait. The problem wouldn't be feeling frightened at leaving this world, but rather sad at the pain of having to stay here knowing there's something so much better beyond."

Sylvia stayed with Maureen throughout the preoperative procedure, holding her hand until the attendants came to take her to surgery. As they were wheeling her out, Maureen gave Sylvia's hand a final squeeze. "I'll never forget you," she promised. "When you get to the Other Side, I'll be there to welcome you."

Eventually, Sylvia went home, but, despite Gary's impatience, she wasn't allowed to work for a month. At night, she and Paul were alone in the house. Paul still refused to sleep in his room. Even Thor refused to go upstairs, raising his hackles and digging in his paws whenever anyone tried to force him.

It was lonely now; Gary came home only for meals and to sleep. One evening Sharon came to spend the night. The two young women had just finished dinner when Sylvia entered the bedroom she shared with Gary to get the television log. Confronting her on the wall above the dresser were three mysterious markings: a blue glowing star, a half moon, and an insignia that looked like a swastika. Despite her familiarity with metaphysical phenomena, there was a sense of menace about the apparitions that caused Sylvia to panic. Her frightened scream brought Sharon running.

Summoning their courage, the two women approached the markings. "Maybe they're reflections from something," Sharon suggested. She seemed somehow less shaken than Sylvia.

"From what?" Sylvia wondered, glancing about. To accommodate Gary's need to sleep days, they'd installed black nightshades that kept out all light.

Thoroughly mystified, Sylvia and Sharon hung blankets over the nightshades and stuffed the door jambs. The markings remained. In the daylight, they would vanish, only to return the following night.

"Why don't you ask Francine about it?" Sharon suggested.

Sylvia laughed nervously. Why hadn't *she* thought of that?

"Your house is built on an Indian burial ground," Francine told her. "They resent your intrusion. You will not be happy in this house."

Sylvia doubted that she would be happy anywhere, but nevertheless told Gary what her guide had said.

"That's crazy," he insisted. "The marks—if they exist—have to be lights from somewhere, and the burial-ground stuff sounds silly. I don't believe it."

Sylvia knew that the swastika was an Indian symbol. The next day at the library she was able to find an old land grant and map. As near as she could determine, their house actually was built squarely on an old Indian burial ground.

"Well, so what?" Gary responded when she told him. "Don't you suppose somebody's buried everywhere?"

"Maybe," she conceded, "but the point is, we're not meant to be here." Gary returned to his television program, effectively tuning her out.

Then the events leading to their exodus came in rapid succession. A few days later, a tornado hit their house—and only theirs. It was the only structure touched. Fortunately, the damage was slight. "Don't you think someone or something might be trying to tell us—" Sylvia suggested, then stopped. Gary had elaborately turned his back and returned to his newspaper.

Then, a few days later, Gary was suspended from the police force. Before long he found a position as an insurance adjuster, but he showed little aptitude for the job. A month later, on the very day that he was discharged, the house caught fire without any apparent cause. There was some damage, but as with the tornado, no one was injured. The next day, Thor was literally thrown through the screen door. There was no discernible cause. That night, Gary placed a long-distance call to Sunnyvale, California.

His old friend Don had left the force the same time he had and was currently working for the Sunnyvale Police Department. "Come on out," he suggested. "I know I can get you on here. Put Sylvia on," he said in conclusion. "Barbara wants to talk to her."

"It's wonderful in California—no more snow to shovel," Barbara enthused.

"What do you think?" Gary surprised Sylvia by asking after she'd hung up.

"I think I'd go anywhere to get out of this house."

"Okay!" he yelled.

Six weeks later they'd sold the house and most of their furniture, had shipped the dog, and were heading west. Only once, thinking of the family and friends she was leaving behind, did Sylvia turn and look over her shoulder. But on the far horizon she saw the swirling cone of a tornado. That was enough. There was no more turning back.

CHAPTER SIX

Nirvana

"Your marriage—it won't last much longer. There's another woman coming into your life, a somewhat older woman. She'll be much better for you."

It was Francine speaking. Sylvia, oblivious to the handsome, dark-haired man sitting opposite her, was literally entranced.

Later, returning to consciousness, the medium was aware of the man's thoughtful manner. "Was it bad news?" she asked anxiously.

"Don't you know? Don't you remember anything?" he asked as he studied her curiously.

"Never. Once I've asked Francine to come in—once she takes over—I'm out of it. It may be my lips moving, but I have no idea what they're saying. Whatever is I or me or Sylvia is out in space somewhere. Then Francine leaves and I come 'home' again."

"Aren't you afraid of not coming back?"

"No, I'm really not. Francine's my best friend; she'd never do anything to hurt or frighten me. Besides, the last thing she'd ever want would be to be stuck in *this* world."

"I don't understand how you do it."

"Nor do I, really. It's something that just happened one day, and then over the years I've developed shortcuts. But I'm more interested in you. You're sad about something that Francine told you."

"Yes," he admitted. "It's my marriage. You—Francine—said it was going to end."

"Francine reads blueprints, but of course there's such a thing as free will. It's possible that what she sees is simply a strain on your marriage, a problem area that you can work on."

"I'm not sure I want to."

Sylvia smiled sympathetically. "It's that bad?"

He nodded and then sat silently for a few moments. Sylvia felt his depression and empathized. She thought of numerous platitudes, but none seemed appropriate. The baby within her kicked. In less than six weeks, he'd be making his presence felt in the world. Sylvia pulled herself heavily to her feet.

Her subject rose, too. Dal Brown, at 22, was the youngest captain in the history of the Stanford University Fire Department. Sylvia thought him the handsomest man she'd ever met. What a pity he was so unhappy. Was this the natural condition of life?

"Francine doesn't give information that you're not meant to hear," she reminded him."But what you decide to do about it—that's your choice."

"But you're psychic, too, aren't you? It isn't just Francine?" he persisted.

"That's right."

"Well, can't *you* tell me something? Francine mentioned another woman."

Sylvia strained inwardly, but surprisingly, her mind's screen was blank. Then, very slowly, a woman appeared next to Dal. "Yes, there is someone. She's tall, red-haired...that's funny!"

"What's funny?" Her subject was intense, eager.

"Not amusing, but strange. I can't seem to see her face. I always see faces—why can't I see hers?"

"Francine said she'd be good for me," he ventured.

"Yes, she will be, I can tell that. She'll be very good, and her boys, you'll like them, too."

"Her boys?"

"Yes, I see two of them." Sylvia paused, searching for more. "I just can't see her face...but there's a business, some kind of business, you'll go into it together. It will make you both very happy."

"Anything else?"

Confused, Sylvia shook her head. "I'm sorry, but that's all I'm getting."

The door opened and Gary looked in. "You two about done? It's getting late."

"We're finished," Sylvia replied. She reached for her coat. Outside in the living room the other firemen were waiting to say goodnight. She'd read for each of them that evening. On the way home, Gary quizzed her. "How did it go?"

"You know better than that," she answered wearily. "How should I know? It was a trance, not a reading. You'd have a better idea than I. You saw each of them as they came out."

"They really seemed impressed, every one of them. You were the hit of the evening. The guys really go for all that spook stuff."

She smiled wryly at the note of surprise in his voice. It was always like that. Sylvia repressed a sigh. Lack of recognition in her own home was the least of her problems. Gary's pleasure at the indirect admiration her abilities brought him was one of the few pluses in their troubled relationship.

Her mind moved, as it often did, over the two years since their arrival in California. The move had changed nothing. Gary's bad luck had continued. Don Crowther had been unable to find him a place on the Sunnyvale Police Force. For a while it was Sylvia who had supported the family, this time by teaching at St. Albert the Great Elementary School in Palo Alto.

Then, one morning six weeks after their arrival, Sylvia opened the door to confront the smiling faces of Bill, Celeste, and Sharon. Bill had resigned the vice presidency of his company, and the Shoemakers had sold their home and moved to California, arriving without warning to surprise their daughter. Sylvia's feelings were mixed. Although she'd often felt guilt and concern about leaving them behind in Kansas City, there'd been a sense of relief at being removed from their problems. Now the respite the separation had brought was over. For more than a year, both families lived together, Sylvia frantically juggling the demands of husband, child, parents, students—striving as always to please them all. The Shoemakers moved out of Sylvia and Gary's home only when the two families purchased a duplex and settled down to live side by side.

But there had been one reprieve for Sylvia. On one evening every week she escaped into another world. Sylvia had enrolled in the English literature master's program at San Francisco University. As challenging as undergraduate college life had been to the young girl, the woman was even more stimulated by graduate work. As time passed, Sylvia's originality and enthusiasm were noted by her creative-writing professor, Bob Williams. Soon the two were enjoying vigorous literary debates at a campus coffee shop. "*Ulysses* has been my favorite assignment thus far," she surprised him by announcing one night.

"Most students find it difficult, hard to relate to."

"Oh, no!" she exclaimed. "I know exactly what Joyce is talking about. That part about the tower in the tarot deck—it's as though he were talking to me."

"Really?" Williams leaned forward, intrigued. "Do you mean you actually understand the tarot cards?"

"Yes, of course. Each card represents some aspect of our journey on Earth. The whole wonderful deck is a kind of compendium of knowledge, a symbolic record of human experience."

"And the tower?"

"Well, the traditional meaning is a sudden conflict or catastrophe, but, as an upset of the existing order of things—the old notions—it could bring enlightenment as well."

"You sound like a fortune-teller! Do you read the cards?"

"I love the tarot; those symbols have so much beauty and truth in them, but I don't need cards to know what's going to happen."

Williams nearly dropped his coffee cup. "You mean to tell me that you're really psychic?"

"It's more like I'd rather *not* tell you that I'm psychic. Back home in Kansas City, everyone knew me, and no one cared that I was different. People just took it for granted that 'Sylvia knew things.' I'm afraid it wouldn't be like that here. When we moved to California—when I began a new life—I made up my mind not to tell anyone." Sylvia felt a growing sense of apprehension as she studied the professor's expression closely. "Now don't *you* tell."

The professor promised to keep her confidence, but pressed for details, and soon Sylvia found herself telling him all about Francine. "Could you come to class an hour early and do a reading for me?" he urged.

Reluctantly, Sylvia agreed. A few days later, she arrived at the promised time and found not only Williams waiting eagerly, but two of his friends.

The following week, when the creative-writing class concluded its survey of *Ulysses*, Williams announced that Mrs. Dufresne would discuss tarot symbolism and give a demonstration of divination. Sylvia was furious with him, but there were 50 pairs of eyes trained on her. The perennial people-pleaser found it impossible to say no.

Later, it became obvious that those 50 people had told at least 50 more. Sylvia very soon found herself speaking to other classes, to women's clubs, even to business organizations. Inevitably, the demand for individual readings grew to be tremendous, but somehow Sylvia managed to accommodate everyone. Nothing terrible happened. Friends and acquaintances continued to accept her, and, as many appeared to benefit from the information she was able to give them, Sylvia concluded that perhaps Bob Williams had been somehow meant to blow her cover.

But Bob's role was much more than just a teacher. He and Sylvia loved one another deeply, and during the next four years, all of Sylvia's spare time was with Bob. They were a perfect match, shared the same loves, moved effortlessly together, and were simply dreamy-eyed with each other. But the match had a single flaw, a twist of fate that prevented a full union—one that Sylvia would have gladly overlooked—but one that eventually led to Bob's death.

During their time together, Bob toured Sylvia through the vastly interesting world of Haight-Ashbury in San Francisco. This was in the time before drugs ruined the scene, when San Francisco was the mecca for "love children" and their social reforms. Among those drawn to SF were swamis, mystics, and gurus, most of whom Bob knew. He took Sylvia to every little place that hosted such people in order to show her what they did and to remind her that her talent was far and away above them all. Under Bob's wing, Sylvia began to see a more public direction for her gift. With his compelling, loving insistence, she agreed that they could actually create a place where psychic talent is legitimate, done professionally, and made into a respectable business. This, then, would be their child, the only way they could have a child of their own creation. But the world turned another click, and Bob was drawn to a faraway place.

Bob's teaching career was fixed in place, with no real opportunity for advancement. He wanted something more, like to be head of a department. As it happens, a university in Australia had a need for just such a person to head up the English literature department. Bob applied and was accepted.

The joyous news was appalling to Sylvia. "Bob, don't go," she pleaded. "It's not right for you to leave. Because if you do, you'll come home in a pine box." Bob replied, "This is my big chance, I'll only be gone one year, and the money is just fabulous. When I get back, we'll open a psychic foundation. I could fund it, just like we've discussed."

"Why, Bob," said Sylvia, "why are you ignoring my warning? I've been so right so many times, you've seen me. What's wrong with your brain today?"

"Yes, but I also know that Sylvia the woman cannot see for herself."

Bob did go to Australia two weeks later. He returned in ten months, one of the first victims of AIDS.

During the next months, adjustments were made, and a new life pattern emerged. Gary eventually found a job with the fire department at Stanford University. The Dufresnes and the Shoemakers had bought their duplex together. Sylvia was teaching at Presentation High School in San Jose and looking forward to the birth of her second child. She hoped that the baby's arrival might herald a reconciliation with Gary.

Christopher Michael Dufresne was born on February 19, 1966. He was a healthy infant from the beginning, and Sylvia was spared the crushing depression that had followed the birth of her first child. She adjusted easily to the necessary changes in her routine—mothering, teaching, attending classes, and giving readings. She loved every minute of her busy days.

But there was no improvement in the relationship with Gary. Their continued inability to achieve sexual intimacy left her lonely and frustrated. She tried to compensate for her own imagined shortcomings by working harder, doing and earning more. Months passed and finally years. Then one day it became suddenly clear. She could *never* do enough to please her husband. It was a "no win" situation.

Sylvia then and there took stock of her life. At 35, she could make it on her own. She *was* making it on her own—both economically and emotionally. What was the point of continuing in a marriage that served only to undermine her self-esteem?

That was the day Sylvia walked out.

In the weeks that followed, the ringing phone usually meant that the Shoemakers were calling to urge their little girl to come home to them. "How can I?" she asked. "There's only a thin wall between you and Gary." Actually, Sylvia was grateful for the excuse. Bill and Celeste had been devastated by her sudden decision. Having their daughter and grandsons practically in the same house with them had been a dream come true. They refused to believe that anything could be seriously wrong between Sylvia and Gary and took every opportunity to importune her to return to him and to them.

Sylvia, Paul, and Chris had taken "temporary" refuge with the newly married Sharon, but as their stay stretched on and on, nerves grew frayed. Sylvia spent every possible moment searching for an affordable home that would allow children, have a fenced area for her boys to play in, and was near a babysitter. "Is it possible?" she asked Francine in desperation.

"The perfect home is waiting for you," Francine reassured her, but would say no more. Sylvia was beginning to suspect that her guide was referring to the Other Side.

One morning, as she returned from a frantic round of house hunting, she was met by a curious Sharon. "A very interesting-sounding man called."

"Well, if it wasn't Daddy, it has to be someone wanting a reading. I just can't take time to do any more until I'm settled. You were supposed to explain that to people," she reminded her sister.

"Well, it's sort of like that, but all this fellow wanted was to tell you that you were right on. He *did* break up with his wife."

"Who was it?" Sylvia asked, sinking wearily into a chair. *Why are people always so surprised when I am right?* she wondered absently.

Sharon consulted a pad of notepaper by the phone. "He said his name was Dal—Dal Brown."

"Dal Brown!" Sylvia perked up immediately. "Dal Brown's separated? Did he leave a number? Oh, he's quite a guy." Sylvia studied the number a moment, then quickly picked up the phone and dialed. Soon they were talking.

"I always thought you were the perfect happily married couple," Dal said. "Gary used to give me advice on how to treat Margaret."

"No wonder your marriage failed!" Sylvia exclaimed, finding herself laughing for the first time in weeks. "Why don't we get together, maybe have dinner?"

"I don't think that would be right. I only left yesterday," Dal explained.

"Then how about an affair?"

Sylvia was joking, of course. Or was she? Sylvia and Dal went out that evening and never separated. It was the kind of union she'd always dreamed of, a true merging of souls as well as bodies. The following day, Sylvia and her two small boys moved into Dal's new apartment.

Gary was furious, and so were Celeste and Bill. While married to Gary, Sylvia still belonged to her parents. Dal was an unknown, someone who might somehow estrange her from them. They fought the match in every way possible, even going so far as to back Gary in an attempt to have the children taken from her. For one of the few times in her life, Sylvia defied her parents, standing firm in her resolve to remain with Dal.

On January 4, 1972—the very first day they were both legally free—Sylvia and Dal Brown were married in Reno, Nevada. (Sylvia later added the *e* on the end of her last name.) It was a joyous occasion, different in every respect from her first marriage. Sylvia could scarcely believe her ears when Dal announced, "You've been working too hard for too long. It's time that someone took care of *you* for a change."

At his insistence, Sylvia remained at home for a few months. For the first time in her adult life, she had time and space for herself, precious hours in which to think and to read, to both cultivate friends and enjoy solitude. Best of all, there was the opportunity to really get to know her children. She began her teaching again as a substitute when classes resumed in the fall.

A few months later, Dal and Sylvia attended a lecture by a well-known San Francisco–area psychic. As the evening progressed, Dal, always sensitive to Sylvia's moods, was aware of her growing tension. When the psychic asked for questions from the floor, Sylvia repeatedly raised her hand, but to her frustration, she was never recognized.

Finally, the demonstration ended, and as the Browns joined the others filing out of the auditorium, Dal asked, "What did you think?"

"I thought it was awful, really awful!"

"But she seemed to be on target."

"Yes," Sylvia agreed. "Most of the time I think she was, but you cannot just leave people dangling like that."

"What do you mean?" he asked, puzzled.

"Oh, there were so many times. That woman, for instance, the one who asked if she and her husband had a chance of making their marriage work."

"You mean the plump blonde woman whose husband had been her son in a previous life?"

"That's the one. The medium made it seem absolutely hopeless. You can't just take someone out of an audience and dump on them like that."

"I seem to remember Francine giving me a little bad news," he reminded her.

Sylvia grinned. "As I understand it, she also gave you a little ray of hope."

"She did indeed," Dal agreed as he slid his arm around his wife.

"I'm serious, Dal."

"I'm serious, too. Here's a coffee shop. Shall we go in and have some coffee—or maybe tonight you'd like something a little stronger?"

"Don't you think I've spirits enough?"

"Coffee, then," he agreed, opening the door for her. Later, after they'd ordered, Dal pressed her further. "Don't you believe a medium should give a negative message if she gets it?"

"Of course I do. I believe I wouldn't get the information in the first place if I wasn't supposed to pass it on, but I also believe that a medium has a responsibility. Sometimes counseling is required. Besides, just because the woman's husband was her son in one life doesn't mean that they can't work it out as man and wife in this one. It simply means that there's a problem area that needs to be allowed for and worked around. The medium might have given her a little advice on that. Instead, she left her feeling that her marriage was hopeless."

"Have you ever considered being a medium?"

"Really, Dal!" Sylvia stared at him in shocked exasperation. "What do you think I've been doing all my life?"

"I mean full-time."

Sylvia turned inward, silently reflecting on her four glorious years with Bob. Their endless hours of planning to open a psychic foundation, to put a professional image on psychic work, to be with Bob every day—all dashed by fate. She cried softly, but deep inside she could still hear Bob telling her to go for it. Her longing for Bob became unbearable. Sylvia *had* to have a part of him again, so in her need for Bob's love, she created their child, which was named the Nirvana Foundation for Psychic Research.

CHAPTER SEVEN
The Other Side

The Nirvana Foundation began with a small ad in the classified section. It read:

Husband and Wife Offering Classes in Psychic Development

Twenty-two people showed up for the first class in the Browns' tiny apartment. Those 22 told another 22, and soon there wasn't room for them all. Somehow, Sylvia and Dal managed to scrape together enough money to rent a small storefront office. Her mind still very much on soul-survival research, Sylvia named their enterprise, "Nirvana," which means something like "heaven" or the "Other Side." Determined to have a nonprofit foundation, the couple took out a $2,400 loan to cover legal expenses.

Sylvia was concerned with credibility. "I don't want anyone thinking this is some fly-by-night outfit," she explained. "Madame Lazonga, I'm not."

"There really is no way to certify a psychic," their attorney reminded them. "The only 'proof' will be your reputation." Sylvia nodded, certain at last that she was doing the right thing.

Almost immediately, that confidence was vindicated. People began to clamor for private readings. The office couldn't accommodate them all. In the early days, Sylvia charged five dollars and used tarot cards. People didn't always realize that the cards were merely a means of altering consciousness and achieving focus. At one session, Sylvia told a client that she had a throat problem. "Yes, you're right," the woman responded, "but where's the sore-throat card?" Before long, Sylvia realized that she no longer needed the cards; she could confront her clients' problems head-on.

Although most of her time was spent giving readings, Sylvia's true focus remained on research. On a spring evening soon after the foundation was formed, a small group gathered to attend Sylvia's first open trance. Every person had at least one question to ask Francine.

The evening began as Sylvia made herself comfortable on the couch. Dal sat beside her, acting as a kind of protective buffer against sudden shocks, noises, or other disturbances, for Sylvia was quite literally "out" when Francine was "in." A loud noise occurring just as Francine was entering or vacating Sylvia could be dangerous to Sylvia. Dal began to count, "One thousand and ten, one thousand and nine, one thousand and eight, one thousand and seven..." Slowly, almost imperceptibly, Sylvia's face began to change. Her features somehow seemed to broaden, and the "doe" eyes that are almost a Sylvia Browne trademark became hooded and more penetrating.

Slowly, cautiously, a young woman barely out of her teens edged forward. "Can you describe yourself?" she asked the spirit guide.

"Yes."

There was a low chuckle at the literal reply. "*Will* you describe yourself?"

So Francine, the entity who'd first appeared to a frightened child so many years before, described herself to the eager group and then went on to tell them that her information came from three major sources—Akashic records, individual spirit guides, and messages from the Godhead.

"The Akashic records are actually God's memory," she told them. "They are stored in a kind of library. There, all of the events of each individual's life are continually being recorded. It's like an epic motion picture in which everything that happens—past, present, and future—is depicted.

"Secondly, everyone has a spirit guide who is fully aware of the blueprint his or her person reflects. I am able to consult with that guide for detailed personal information." Francine reminded the audience, "The spirit guide is one's most intimate friend and companion on the Earth plane. The guide's knowledge of a subject's motivations, perceptions, and life is total. Churches sometimes call these beings 'guardian angels.'

"Information from the third source—the Godhead—comes in different forms," Francine continued matter-of-factly. "Every entity on the Other Side has complete communion with God. His presence is felt in a very tangible way by each soul. When I need information to guide Sylvia, I go to special groups of entities who speak for God with great knowledge and spirituality. But at other times I may simply pray directly to God for guidance—and He always answers. This type of information is known as 'infused knowledge.' It is available to all who ask."

The group digested this for a moment, and then another woman spoke. "But how does infused knowledge work, and what exactly is a spirit guide? What are *you*, Francine?"

"Infused knowledge is information that comes directly from the Holy Spirit. It's placed directly into the mind without the aid of any of the senses. It's an immediate acquisition of knowledge that you simply know without knowing how you know it. This information is to be shared with others—otherwise God would not have given it to you.

"A spirit guide is simply an entity—just like you. I am an entity just like you. My job and the job of all other spirit guides is to help those on Earth perfect themselves, as others have in turn helped us. No doubt many of you in this room will one day choose to be spirit guides when you make your transition to the Other Side."

A white-haired man in his late 70s asked, "Just what is the Other Side?"

Francine paused, as though searching for words. "It's simply another dimension," she replied at last, in a soft voice so different from Sylvia's deep, husky tone. "It's paradise, it's heaven, it's the ultimate reality of existence. It is the living world; yours is moribund by comparison. You reside in a temporary state of unreality. The puny lifespan of 100 years is a tiny drop in the great sea of eternity."

Once she had warmed to her subject, Francine's persona became more apparent. Although totally different from Sylvia's ebullient candor, her voice rang with quiet conviction. "Most of us reside on your plane of existence at one time or other in one or more lives in order to experience negativity. There is no negativity on the Other Side nor, for that matter, in the true reality of any existence. But since negativity is part of knowledge, and since the whole purpose of creation is to garner knowledge and experience, almost all of God's creations choose at some time to come to Earth as part of our continuing education.

"In other words," Francine said becoming noticeably more intense, "the true reality of existence is in another higher-frequency dimension that is called 'the Other Side.' That dimension—which is beyond the realm of the five senses—is where we reside for eternity, except for our brief sojourns to planes of unreality. We live in these planes temporarily to experience negativity for the evolvement of our souls. The Other Side is our—and your—*real* Home."

The older man, obviously pleased by the answer, persisted. "Just *where* is the Other Side?" he inquired.

Many now leaned forward intently, for it was a question puzzling everyone.

"It's right here," Francine surprised them by saying. "The Other Side is superimposed on your plane, but it is approximately three feet higher. This is the reason why those of you who have seen 'ghosts' or 'spirits' often see them floating slightly above ground level. Your plane and that of the Other Side share the same space. It is only because of the higher vibrational frequency of our matter that you are unable to see or perceive our existence. You are like 'ghosts' to us as well, but by concentrating, we're able to activate our senses to a keener pitch in order to bring you into clear focus.

"Because the laws of physics are different on the Other Side, we have more space in which to live. Without losing volume or size, hundreds of persons may be comfortable in a nine-by-twelve-foot room. Our physical laws allow us to do this without becoming microscopic because space on our plane is entirely different from yours. Consequently, we have more entities on our plane—approximately six billion—but we also have much more space and are not in the least crowded. This applies as well to land, bodies of water, and all material things."

As though anticipating the next question, Francine continued. "If you can imagine the most beautiful thing you have ever seen and multiply it a hundred times, then you might be close to the beauty of the Other Side. The colors are brighter, and the flowers are more gorgeous and far larger than on your plane. All the beauties of nature exist here—mountains, seashores, lakes, trees. All the animals that you have on Earth exist here as well, except that here they are friendly with each other. There is no aggression or hostility.

"It might be interesting for you to know that the pets that reside on your plane come to the Other Side when they die. If you have loved a dog or cat, it will be waiting for you when you come Home. My dear Sylvia has a large area in which all the pets she has gathered throughout her incarnations live. When she comes Home, there will be a big reunion.

"We have beautiful fountains and plazas, courtyards and parks, as well as gardens and meditation areas. Although our architecture is predominantly classic Greek or Roman, we have areas that cater especially to an entity's fondness for a special lifestyle—a castle, an Elizabethan cottage, a log cabin, or a hacienda."

A teenage boy who was sitting on the floor near Sylvia moved a little closer. "Are there other inhabited planets?" he asked.

"There are millions of planets like yours on which entities in a variety of sizes and shapes exist," she told him. "Like your planet, they also have an 'Other Side.' There are millions of 'Other Sides,' and each is a duplication of beauty like the one for the planet Earth. We all exist in the same dimension and can travel back and forth at will."

The boy sat quietly for a moment, imagining the possibilities of what Francine had said, and then asked another question. "Do we each have a body on the Other Side?"

"You most certainly do," Francine assured him, "and you and only you select it. You can choose from all the physical attributes that you'd like to have—your hair, weight, height, features, eye color—everything."

A smartly dressed woman in her late 30s spoke next. "What other abilities do we have on the other side that we don't have here?"

"There are three major areas," Francine explained. "Entities on the Other Side are able to communicate telepathically and generally do this when conversing in small groups. But with larger gatherings—in order to avoid confusion—we use verbal communication. Although all languages are used from time to time, our main language is Aramaic. We have selected Aramaic because it is ancient and simple, yet descriptive.

"We also have the ability to bilocate. Perhaps we want to visit someone or someplace and still continue our work. We then concentrate on being in that other place. The shift is accomplished easily, and many entities choose to appear in several places at once for purposes of assistance. Our Lord, Jesus Christ, can appear in millions of places when needed.

"All knowledge is open to us. We not only have memories of what we have learned on Earth as well as here, but we have access to the Akashic records, which contain all knowledge—past, present, and future—for the planet that you call Earth."

The questioner's fingers moved rapidly as she jotted all this down in a small notebook. Then the woman looked up, a puzzled expression on her face. "Do we keep our Earth identity on the Other Side? I'm rather attached to mine."

"Yes," Francine reassured her. "Your personality—your individuality—is a composite of all your experiences, whether they were gained on the Other Side or on Earth. Your experiences, whether good or bad, influence you as a person. If you have lived in various locales around the world in past lives, the experiences you garnered contribute toward the personality you have today in your present life.

"When you get to the Other Side, your personality remains the same but functions at an optimum. Imagine yourself at the happiest period of your life, with your personality at its peak, exuding charm and happiness. Then take this feeling and magnify it 100 times, and you will get an indication of how your personality works all the time on the Other Side."

"But what about the people we don't like on this planet?" someone asked. "Will we suddenly like everyone when we get to the Other Side?"

It was a question that struck a responsive chord among everyone in the room. Francine responded without hesitation. "Likes and dislikes are a part of an individual's personality and are directly attributable to one's own experiences. If one individual does not care for another, it is usually due to the fact that the individual's experience with her or him has been negative. Dislike is not created existentially in an entity. It must be formed from one's own experience with the object of that dislike.

"If, for example, an individual has a strong dislike—perhaps even a hate—for an uncle, this may have been created by the behavior of the uncle toward that person as a child. Perhaps the dislike is fully justified. On your plane, feelings may be altered by forgiveness or may remain unchanged. But on the Other Side, our awareness vastly opens up. We understand why the uncle treated us badly. Perhaps it was caused by too much pressure on the uncle, or possibly it was a learning experience needed by the soul. Whatever the reason, this knowledge gives us an entirely different outlook. We love all the souls of creation because each is a part of God, just as we are.

"Perhaps in some cases we don't desire intimacy with a person, but we still love that individual's soul. Each and every entity has a choice to associate with those it chooses. All of us have our close friends—that is part of the personality—but I know of no one who hates or even dislikes another entity on our plane. There is just too much love and harmony.

"The main reason for that love and harmony is the lack of ego involvement. There is no competition on the Other Side. Everyone works together for the common good. Pride and jealousy no longer have meaning for us because we have learned that the true purpose of our existence is to love and obtain knowledge about God. It is easy to help one another on our side because there is no negativity to confuse us."

There was a low murmur as people discussed this answer, and then a man spoke up. "But what about *this* world?" he asked. "We've got so much negativity to contend with. Is it okay to get angry at people or situations?"

"It is not only permissible, but *right*," Francine surprised them by saying. "You are not on the Other Side yet; you're still human. Anger is inverted depression. It is inverted because you cannot stand up and be who you are because you are afraid of peer group disapproval. And yet whom do you admire in life? Who but the eccentric, the person who does what he or she pleases.

"No one can drain you. You allow yourself to be drained. It is because you are angry but feel that you cannot say what you would like to say. Instead, you put up with someone's maudlin whining and wonder why you are exhausted. You lack the intestinal fortitude to stand up and say, 'I do not like this. This bothers me. I do not need it.' Would this be hurting the other person? No, it is hurting you *not* to say it.

"If you have spent a year or two with an individual and the relationship does not improve, you are wasting your time by allowing it to continue. You have every right to get away from a constant, painful situation. You do not have to wait till you get to the Other Side to be happy, but do know that the happiness you enjoy here is nothing compared to what you will experience on the Other Side."

Another teenager seated on the floor, this one a girl, moved in closer. "What about social activities, Francine? Do you have parties on the Other Side?"

"Indeed, yes," the girl was assured. "We have innumerable social activities, so many and so varied as to appeal to every taste. There is music and dancing in large ballrooms, there are lectures and debates on almost any subject held in large forums, there are art shows and galleries featuring every kind of art, there are sports events and science exhibits, fashion and design shows—everything that you can imagine. Whether one wants to view these things as a spectator or be a direct participant is up to the individual.

"But in addition to the large events, there are smaller gatherings, such as poetry readings and chamber concerts. There are also spas to visit and wilderness areas to explore—swimming, sailing, mountain climbing, tennis. Although eating isn't necessary, some people enjoy gourmet cooking, and nearly everyone likes to invite others in for a get-together.

"When you come Home to the Other Side, you will find yourself hard-pressed not to engage in some sort of social activity frequently. Although you certainly don't have to participate, most so choose. I myself am what you might call a party girl. I love parties and dancing and go regularly to those to which I am invited. Sylvia sometimes jokes about the fact that when I am not around her, I am off at some party. I do love them, as most entities do."

It took awhile for the group to digest that answer. It was so different from the traditional view of "heaven." Finally, it was the teenager's pretty blonde mother who broke the silence. "What can anyone do for all eternity?"

It actually seemed that Francine was surprised by the question. "You work, you socialize, you learn, and you enjoy your existence," she answered. "It is interesting to note here that we are all 30 years of age on the Other Side. This is the perfect age, as you have the ideal combination of youth and maturity. The Elders have the appearance of being older, but that is due to their projection of wisdom and learning. Our sense of time is so different from yours—your lifetime is only a few minutes to us—and our lives are so full that eternity exists for us as a state of bliss."

A man in his late 20s spoke next. He was seated toward the back of the room, his hand clasping that of a woman seated beside him. "Do you have marriage on the Other Side?" he asked.

"Since we live in some cases many lives on your Earth plane, we may have had, in various incarnations, several husbands or wives. It is not likely that we would want to be permanently united with so many. Indeed, we might choose to merge with one soul mate."

The sweet-faced young woman seated beside him leaned forward and asked, "What does the term *soul mate* really mean?"

"Its meaning is often misunderstood by those on your plane," Francine admitted. "Let me begin by explaining the difference between 'soul mate' and 'kindred soul.'

"When we were created by the Godhead, we were basically and intrinsically whole—for the most part. I say for the most part because a soul mate is actually the other half of oneself—unless you were created as a single, unattached being for the purpose of experiencing that single state. The soul mate comes together with you when you have both determined that the time is right for this duality relationship to occur. It is, in essence, a marriage for all eternity.

"Soul mates exist singularly until they have reached their own chosen level of experience and evolvement. Once they have more or less gone through their training, they come together. This can take eons, depending on the individuals involved. Some have already gone through this process of learning and are now together, while others are still evolving. When the time is right, they will come together.

"An entity may or may not have a soul mate, depending upon whether or not that entity is a singular creation or whether or not it has reached the time of coming together on this plane.

"Kindred souls are souls that have a very deep love for each other. Most of us have literally millions of kindred souls that we can relate to, but we will usually have only one soul mate. If, for example, you have a deep, loving friendship in this life with someone, chances are very good that you are kindred souls on the Other Side. All of your close friends on the Other Side are kindred souls. We have a kind of soul merging here that is nonsexual. It's an act in which one entity enters another and experiences a merging of mind and body that is very intense and pleasurable. The mental high is indescribable."

The woman hesitated a moment. Her pale face colored slightly as she asked, "Is there sex on the Other Side?" Everyone in the room reacted in varying degrees, some leaning forward eagerly, others stirring uncomfortably, a few laughing. Sylvia remained supine on the couch; only her lips moved as Francine's voice came through.

"Yes, we do have sex on the Other Side. We call it merging. It is difficult to explain because it is both spiritual and physical. There is nothing that compares with it on your plane. If you take the most intense and pleasurable orgasm that you have ever had and multiply it by a hundred, you might come close to what an orgasm is on our side. Our orgasms also last much longer. Imagine an orgasm on your plane that lasted for several hours.

"All of us on my side participate in merging with each other, whether we have met our soul mate, are single, or waiting for their return. You must understand that there is no moral judgment for this act between those who aren't soul mates because they always come together with the purest intent: love.

"Morality as you know it does not exist on the Other Side. There is no such thing as 'bad' because all entities are loving and without ego involvement. We have no need for laws.

"On our side, soul mates come together in a traditional way. The male entity proposes to the female entity. If she is inclined and if both are at the level of evolvement that they want to reach, she accepts and they go to the Council to receive a blessing. Once this is given, they begin to live together. However, this does not diminish any of their prior social customs, activities, or friends. Many soul mates live very happily doing things together, while others may prefer to pursue their own interests in a singular manner for a portion of their time. Either lifestyle is commonly practiced."

The group was quiet for a few moments, each person occupied with private thoughts. Finally, a portly, gray-haired man asked the next question. "Do you work on the Other Side?"

"All entities work on the Other Side, but the word *work* is probably misleading to you because it sounds like drudgery. We all enjoy working very much in our chosen fields of endeavor. It's not like on your plane, where you work to feed, clothe, and house yourselves. We do not work to survive. We work because we enjoy it and gain knowledge from it.

"It is interesting," Francine continued, "that all the knowledge garnered on your Earth plane, new inventions as well as rediscoveries of ancient knowledge, is gained from our research and then introduced into your plane by implantation into the brain of a researcher, scientist, philosopher, or whatever. All inventions, all medical cures, all new scientific discoveries are transmitted from our plane to yours for your benefit and use. Even such things as music, art, and new designs are implanted by us into individuals on your plane.

"Since time as you know it does not exist on our plane, we have plenty of leisure to pursue hobbies. Each of us enjoys at least one in addition to 'work.'

"Of course, we do keep track of time in your dimension so that we can understand world events on your side, as well as what is going on in a specific individual's life. We need an awareness of your time in order to monitor your progress.

"When your loved ones pass over into our plane, they often have a difficult time relating to your problems because of the time factor. They realize almost immediately that you will soon be with them and your problems seem very short-lived and insignificant. You may have years to live, but to your loved ones it seems only a few minutes before you will be Home again, safe and secure.

"It is like a child of yours who pricks a finger with a thorn. You may be sympathetic, but you cannot get too concerned because you know the pain will soon go away and the child will be laughing again. This is the reason that a 'communicating guide' like myself has to go through such extensive training. Without it we would not be able to relate to your human experience. We forget about negativity on the other side—*your* side—and must reintroduce ourselves to it in order to work with a medium—Sylvia, for example.

"So do not feel upset if some dear loved one passes over and you do not feel his or her presence or receive some form of communication from beyond the grave. This person may be very involved in his or her own work and just waiting for the short period to pass until you come Home."

A small woman in her early 40s seated in the back of the room spoke next, asking, "If life is forever, why do we have such a fear of death?"

"You come into life with a subconscious memory that life is forever, but that memory soon is blocked by the nature of the life experience on your plane, which forces you to only consciously remember what you have experienced there. It is somewhat like this: Have you ever lived in a house that you were afraid to give up because you might not find another? Or have you gone on a long trip and thought, *Will I ever get back to the old house?* Or perhaps, on returning from another trip, you said to yourself, *I had forgotten just how very good home is.*

"That is very much what life on your plane is like. Don't you often feel sorrow at the realization that your body separates you from others? Don't you long at times to pull another person into yourself? Don't you often feel a sense of isolation? Once you begin to recognize and understand this principle, the fear of death will dissipate; and, when you pass over, the memory will burst upon you at that very moment. Then your soul will breathe a sigh of relief: *That is all over and I am Home.*"

The woman sighed audibly. "That does sound so nice, but I wonder, then, what is the purpose of it all? What is the purpose of living?"

"You are all messengers from God sent here to carry His word. But that message is coded, and you must break the code yourself. It is true that God exists within you, but *all* of you are a part of Him as well. You will live forever, you have lived forever, and no one will ever be lost or diminished.

"Spirituality means, in essence, to find yourself, to find the God within and without, and to fight the battle against negativity. You see, even if just one of you will go out and light the way for another, some of the grayness will be banished. This is how negativity is fought, and it only takes a handful of you to accomplish a great deal.

"Each of you is here to evolve your soul. You have chosen to experience life in order to perfect more rapidly. You are an evolving part of God, perfecting one aspect to Him. God experiences through His creations.

"Start looking at life as something you must survive. It can be fun at times, but it can also be very tedious. Think of life as a school in which the dormitory serves poor food and there is no worthwhile transportation. Yes, it will help if you maintain a sense of humor about it all."

The older, gray-haired man laughed heartily with the others, but then questioned, "Why does God need me for learning? Can't He experience directly?"

"God, having all knowledge, needed to experience His knowledge. From this need arose all creation, a manifestation of God's power and intellect. Every facet of God can be found in His work. The perfect love of our Father became so great that it began to multiply itself and in so doing, created all of us. Since that time we have been the direct experiencing, emotional side of Him.

"You are, literally, a part of God. As such, anything you experience is also experienced by Him. If you are in some difficulty, then God, too, experiences it. If you discover a joyous facet of life, then God, too, is there.

"It is true that God needs us to experience. Yet it is more correct to say that God *is* us, and thereby He does experience directly. But He does have experience over and above what we have. This is true because He has all knowledge, whereas we have very little by comparison. For example, say someone in your life has all knowledge of biology—they have read everything in the world about it. Then say they have no practical experience of biology, they lack the sense and feel, the experience of that science. By knowledge alone, they can experience much, but not as much as by experiencing biology directly. People are the sensing, feeling aspect of God's awareness. Yet because of His boundless knowledge, His perception of our experience is far greater than our own."

The man nodded, considering what Francine had said, then asked, "What signposts mark our path? How can we know when we're on the right track?"

"Self-acceptance and self-knowledge indicate that you are doing well. You will feel good about yourself. You will begin to realize that, regardless of what adversity you may go through, you can handle it spiritually. Circumstances may temporarily derail you, but there is always an inner faith and glow that draw you back to inner peace. It is an intuitive awareness that you are okay, as well as a love for yourself that is totally necessary. This will, in turn, bring a heightened understanding and sensitivity that will enable you to hear guides and feel their presence."

The whole room was still while each person mentally evaluated his or her progress. At last, a woman in her late 20s spoke. "Do you have houses on the Other Side?" she wondered.

Francine paused a moment, as though considering how best to answer the question. "Many of us prefer communal apartments—I do—because of the opportunity for social life. But others, particularly many of the soul mates, may prefer houses. These houses may be of any kind of architecture. Some will be elaborately furnished, and others are very simple. Some entities choose to build their houses in the conventional way, enjoying the act of construction. There are carpenters and other artisans on our side who can do anything.

"Others create a building merely by thinking it into being. For example, suppose we want to construct a new forum. After the site is selected, several architects outline the contours of the building using their thoughts alone. If you were watching this being done, you would actually see lines forming in midair, almost as though the architect were drawing them on a draftsman's table. Sometimes the builder will outline the contour of the building, decide he doesn't care for it, and then erase the 'energy' lines and start anew.

"Once the style of the building is established, other entities gather and together they create the substance of the building—the walls, roof, windows, and interior furnishings. All of this is done through concentrated thought processes that condense the real matter.

"Sometimes we follow the same type of process in determining our appearances. If, say, after several eons, you wish to change your appearance, you merely concentrate on the changes you want to make and, as easily as that, change from dark hair and brown eyes to being a blue-eyed blonde."

The woman nodded, acknowledging the answer, then decided to venture another question. "Do you have some form of government on the Other Side?"

"No," Francine answered. "We do not have a government per se, but we do have a hierarchy. This is in the form of a Council of Elders. We also have, in a decreasing order of responsibility, communicating guides, sixth-level entities, fifth-level entities, fourth-level, and so forth.

"The Elders are old souls who have a very wise and beautiful Godlike love for everyone. Much information comes from the Elders. You might call them spokesmen for the Godhead, at least in a spoken form. They are humanoid and—unlike the rest of us—choose, with their white hair and beards, the appearance of age. The Elders are wise and loving, and their knowledge is vast. If any edict is to be pronounced, they perform that function.

"Archetypes are also humanoids in form but are very different from any of the other entities on our side. They all look alike, almost like android robots in human form. Another difference is that they all communicate telepathically with each other, but do not communicate with others. That doesn't mean that they do not respond to us—they do, but it is like dealing with a deaf-mute. They are all very bright and actually seem to glow with an energy that no one else has. Many times, if you look at one for an extended period, your eyes react as if you had a flashbulb go off in front of you. The Elders say that the purpose of the archetypes is protection for those on your plane as well as ours. They are very powerful creatures, and spirit guides use them frequently to help guide their earthly protégés. In your Bible, they have been called archangels, and

Sylvia's maternal grandmother, Ada, at age 30, a well-known practicing psychic in Springfield, Missouri.

Grandma Ada's family, from left to right: Marcus Jr. (had cerebral palsy, everyone called him "Brother"), Marcus Sr., Celeste (Sylvia's mother), Paul (also psychic, died at age 21, told Celeste she would have a girl child who must be named Sylvia), and Ada.

Grandma Ada's brother, Henry Kaufholz, who was a medium and Spiritualist in the old "camps" in Florida and Oklahoma.

Sylvia at age 2 1/2.

Sylvia at age 6 with her mother.

Sylvia at age 7 with her little sister, Sharon. Sylvia was the caretaker for the new baby right up to adulthood.

Sylvia, age 14; and her sister, Sharon, age 8.

Sylvia, age 20; and her dad, Bill Shoemaker, at the Fathers and Daughters dance at St. Teresa's College.

Sylvia's first house with husband Gary in Kansas City. Built on an Indian burial ground, strange images appeared on the walls, the dog was tossed out the door, a tornado hit it (and only it), and it caught fire.

Moving to California in 1964, Sylvia again ended up in a haunted house. But with Francine's instructions, she did her first "house blessing" and brought peace to the place.

Paul Dufresne, Sylvia's older son, at age 7, holding his little brother, Christopher, at age 1. Both boys grew up to be 6'6" tall.

Sylvia's younger son, Christopher Dufresne, inherited the psychic talent and began doing readings at age 16.

Family portrait done in 1994. On the left is the Paul Dufresne family: Nancy, Jeffrey (age 1), Paul, then Sylvia in the middle. On the right is the Chris Dufresne family: Chris, Angelia (age 1½), and Gina.

Angelia Sylvia Dufresne at age 5, Sylvia's granddaughter by Christopher and Gina. She renamed herself "Eya," is super psychic, and is Grandma Ada reborn to continue the spiritual work Sylvia began.

William Christopher Dufresne at age 5 months (already 25 pounds!), Sylvia's grandson by Christopher and Gina, named in honor of Sylvia's father.

Jeffrey Dufresne at age 4 1/2, Sylvia's grandson by Paul and Nancy.

Christopher Dufresne, age 32, an excellent psychic in the family tradition, works alongside Sylvia on a daily basis. Sylvia's older son, Paul, is a successful mortgage banker.

Montel Williams Show—Sylvia tapes nine shows each year with Montel. Here is one show where the "psychic dynasty" was all together: Chris, Angelia, and Sylvia.

UNSOLVED

mysteries

Unsolved Mysteries had Sylvia come in to de-mystify a ghostly threesome at a seaside tavern.

Home Improvement: Tim Allen.

In the Heat of the Night: Howard Rollins, Carroll O'Connor.

"Wild Card": Cindy Pickett.

WEDNESDAY GUIDELINES

☐ With Halloween just around the corner, **Unsolved Mysteries** scares up some ghost stories. Psychic Sylvia Browne comments on theories about the "ghost" of Moss Beach, Cal., while another segment investigates reports that the Drum Barracks Civil War Museum in Wilmington, Cal., is haunted by the ghosts of Union soldiers. —8 PM ④⑥

for six months. Burns co-wrote and co-produced his brother Ken's *The Civil War.* —9 PM ㉘

☐ **Movie:** A seasoned performance by Powers Boothe as Preacher, a former Episcopal priest turned gambler, distinguishes 1992's **"Wild Card,"** a ★★ cable drama. Cindy Pickett costars as his love interest. Boothe also preached

'Mysteries' enlists psychic's help with ghost

■ **NBC series: Unsolved Mysteries:** 8-9 p.m. today, WPTV-Channel 5, WTVJ-Channel 4.

By PAUL LOMARTIRE
Palm Beach Post Staff Writer

Psychic Sylvia C. Browne talks to a ghost on a segment of NBC's *Unsolved Mysteries* tonight and doesn't care a bit about convincing people of her mental gift.

"That's right," Browne said last week by phone from her Campbell, Calif., office. "People either believe or not. Although I'll tell you the truth, I love skeptics because skeptics sometimes can be the easiest to topple.

"And it's OK if there's skeptics. Who wants somebody pushing something down your throat all the time?"

Tonight, Browne talks to ghost Mary Ellen Morley, who died in 1919 as the result of a car accident.

The woman, seen and heard by various people around Moss Beach, Calif., is known as

Browne

the "Blue Lady." She's been known to warn children to stay away from the area's steep bluffs and has spoken to employees of a restaurant called the Moss Beach Distillery. Morley also appeared, dressed in blue and covered with blood, to two men whose car ran off the road after they attended an uneventful seance at the Distillery.

The restaurant's owner brought Browne in to validate or dispel the rumor. But, according to the *San Francisco Examiner,* it took owner John Barbour a year to get Browne to take the job.

"When John Barbour called, he was kind of concerned about it because he was a big skeptic," she said. "Needless to say, he's not a

skeptic anymore."

Browne found there are four, not one, Moss Beach ghosts. Morley also told Browne about a love triangle Morley was involved in.

As Browne relates all this, her voice is even, reassuring. The 56-year-old woman with a staff of about 50, including family, works from offices in Campbell as well as Los Angeles. She charges $200 for a one-hour reading. She works with police departments, lawyers and those seeking facts about missing or murdered family members.

She has worked in television for 22 years including, she says, 15 of those as consultant for a network about audience research. But she turns down most TV invitations. "I don't want to be treated as entertainment.

"I will not go on a show in which it's going to be a silly thing ... I don't want any goofy

Please see 'MYSTERIES'/A0

Wednesday
GUIDELINES

☐ **Haunted Lives: True Ghost Stories** is entertaining scare fare concerned not so much with spirits haunting people as with the haunts that spirits haunt. Reenactments take place at a Northern California toy store and a Southern California hotel room. —8 PM ②

Sylvia was the star of this national CBS special, which aired May 15, 1991. Her brilliant performance helped bring in a rating of 10.3 with a 19 share, nearly beating the long-standing champ *Unsolved Mysteries!* The show was so good that CNN, *Entertainment Tonight*, and NBC and CBS news all broadcast Sylvia's story.

Winchester Mystery House (San Jose, CA) is one of Sylvia's "haunts" when looking for ghosts. There are three earthbound ghosts in residence who simply will not leave.

Ghost image of Johnny Johnson—Sylvia was asked by the TV show *That's Incredible* to communicate with the spirit haunting a toy store in California. The photographer caught Johnny in this infrared photo, upper left image of a man standing, leaning to the left. Sylvia is the bright white blob in the lower right.

Society of Novus Spiritus—Sylvia founded a new church to celebrate the all-loving God. Here is the first group of ministers at their ordination ceremony.

Sylvia with Chris. This is the photo on the cover of his book *My Life with Sylvia Browne.*

Sylvia dancing with Chris at her 60th birthday party in 1996—the party was planned and hosted by Chris and Gina.

Sylvia lectures all over the country each year. Here is a surprise visit from Montel at one of her Manhattan lectures.

Sylvia and Montel Williams are clearly "kindred souls." Sylvia says that Montel is an angel from God who has been instrumental in helping her bring a new Spiritual Message to the world. Montel also does God's work by helping people on his TV show, as well as giving behind-the-scenes assistance to many in need.

This photo was taken in May of 1998. Sylvia shows no signs of slowing down as she enters her 60s.

because of their brightness and energy, they have sometimes been seen by those in your dimension and confused with an apparition of Christ. Not too much is known about them. They are still something of a mystery even to us, but the love and protection they have given to us is not.

"Communicating guides are advanced and evolved entities who act like spirit guides but perform additional duties, such as communicating with your plane through mediums in various ways. This communication can take the form of verbalization through a medium who is in a trance, channeling verbalization through a clairaudient medium, both of which I do. Or it can involve manifesting physical phenomena through a physical medium and channeling energy through a psychic healer. All of these functions of the communicating guide require extensive training because, if they are not done properly, the medium could be seriously injured. It takes many of your years of training to become a communicator, while most everyone performs the function of being a spirit guide at one time or another.

"For the purpose of categorizing and organizing groups of entities according to their experience and vocation, seven levels have evolved on the Other Side. These are not levels of spiritual evolvement, but only of experience.

"The first and second levels are levels of orientation—temporary states experienced by entities that have just passed over from your plane to mine.

"The third level embraces all entities who choose to work with animal husbandry, with agriculture, or with a craft such as carpentry.

"Fourth-level entities select more aesthetic pursuits, such as art, writing, sculpture, or music.

"Those entities who are counselors in such areas as business, science, and medicine are in the fifth level.

"The sixth level comprises entities who are organizers, teachers, and philosophers.

"Seventh-level entities are those who choose to go back into the Godhead and therefore do not really reside on the Other Side for an extended period. I might add that very few entities choose the seventh level; those who do lose their individuality, since the energy of their creation is taken back into the Godhead. Those who do elect this level are very spiritual and evolved, for their love of God is so great that they wish to be absorbed back into Him.

"Because of the experience needed by managers in various types of vocational endeavor, the fifth and sixth levels take more responsibility and become heads of research projects and orientation centers and majordomos of large areas of residence on the Other Side.

"If one were to say we had a form of government, it would most likely resemble the pure form of the ancient Greek democracy. There is complete interaction with all on my side, and everyone has the power to act or contribute if they choose. As there is no ego involvement on the Other Side, everything functions with complete love and harmony and a desire to do the best, both for each individual and for the whole.

"Regardless of what level we have chosen to live in, we are all a part of the same dimension. There are areas on my side in which all are predominantly on the same level, but that state is for convenience and lifestyle or vocational purpose. All levels are equal and are designated only by experience and vocation. Usually, the higher levels are chosen by entities who have more experience in life. They have usually been on the Earth plane in more incarnations and so have gained more experience with negativity."

The teenage boy who'd spoken earlier raised his hand. "You don't have to do that," Dal reminded him. "You're not in school."

"I don't know," the youth responded. "Maybe I am, but I sure like this kind of school better than my regular one. What is the purpose of negativity?" he asked Francine. "Why experience it at all?"

"While the Other Side is the Home and true reality for us all, most who reside there choose to incarnate briefly to the Earth plane in order to experience negativity and to learn how to deal with it. Since negativity is a part of knowledge, we would be incomplete without having experienced it.

"It is much easier to be positive in a perfect environment, so we come to test our mettle on your plane. It is something we undertake for our soul's evolvement."

"Can we see God or Christ on the Other Side?" It was the gray-haired woman speaking again.

"God is always present on our side, though not in a bodily form. His presence is so powerful that it is felt through every pore of one's being. He constantly communicates with all on the Other Side through mental infusion. That manifestation of the energy of His love is always there, but there is another way of communicating with Him. It is called going behind the seventh level and is in essence the energy of all the entities who have chosen to go to the seventh level.

"Since all of us are a small portion of God's energy and contain a portion of His knowledge, the many entities who have chosen to go to the seventh level have magnified this force into a power that potentially contains all of His knowledge. It cannot be defined or described.

"Christ exists on our plane in bodily form and lives with his soul mate, Mary Magdalene. His power and goodness are constant as he walks and talks with entities on the Other Side. Since he can divide himself and appear in many locations, there is ample opportunity for anyone to seek his counsel at any time. On some occasions he may be seated by a fountain in serious and loving conversation with one person while laughing happily with a group.

"Our Lord has a wonderful sense of humor and enjoys parties, yet remains the ultimate philosopher and counselor. His time is spent in simply being there for all who need him."

The teenage girl who'd spoken earlier in the evening moved forward slightly, a shy smile on her face. "Would you tell us about your life on the Other Side, Francine?"

"Most of my time is taken up in guiding Sylvia and watching her loved ones. In addition, I spend some time researching for my communications to those of you on the Earth plane to whom I speak through Sylvia's body in a trance session such as this. The rest of my time is spent like most entities in attendance at lectures, concerts, and parties.

"I have a soul mate, and his name is David. We love each other very much, but do not do everything together. We have our own individual interests as well as our shared ones. Sometimes, when David and I want to do something together, I ask Raheim—Sylvia's other guide— to watch over her, but I am never away from her for long.

"Being the communicating guide for a medium such as Sylvia can be somewhat confining in comparison to my former lifestyle. But in the overall scheme of things, this is very temporary. The span of Sylvia's life on the Earth plane seems much longer to you than to us on the Other Side.

"I discuss my work with friends as much as possible and will often consult with Raheim, the Elders, and Christ about Sylvia and her life's work. I keep in touch with the latest developments in the arts and sciences on your plane in order to understand better the various forces that affect Sylvia's life, as well as the lives of those who come to her for help.

"When I finish my job as Sylvia's guide, I will go back to my normal, more relaxed lifestyle. I will return to my work at the orientation center where I help those who are making their transitions from your side to mine.

"I have chosen to evolve and perfect my soul by doing work on this plane rather than going into a great number of incarnations. My life as Iena was my first and last incarnation on your side. This method is slower, but what is the hurry? I have eternity."

Dal brushed a strand of Sylvia's hair back from her forehead. "This has been a long session. We don't want to tire Sylvia," he reminded the people. "Francine may have eternity, but Sylvia's a very busy lady with readings to do first thing tomorrow."

Gently he gave her the command to return to consciousness. Within instants, Sylvia was Sylvia, sitting up, smiling, and joking. "Did Francine tell you who your prom date will be?" she asked the pretty girl seated on the floor before her.

"I forgot to ask. As a matter of fact, there are still a few other questions I'd like to ask some night."

"Only a few? What a lucky girl you are." The elderly man, her grandfather, had come forward to thank Sylvia. "I fear that most of us have many more questions. Isn't it lucky there's all eternity to work on them?"

CHAPTER EIGHT
The Reading Room

Sylvia's office was the best that she and Dal could afford, but it was awful. There were two tiny rooms—a minuscule waiting room and Sylvia's scarcely larger office.

She settled in early in the morning on June 11, 1974, placed a photograph of Grandma Ada on the desk before her, and sat back. Sylvia had anticipated a sense of pleasure at having her own office, but instead she had a feeling of mounting panic. The walls were closing in on her. *I can't stand this a moment longer,* she realized. *I'm getting claustrophobia.* She alleviated the problem with a quick trip to a nearby department store.

When Dal dropped by later that afternoon, he stopped short in amazement. "I didn't remember a window here," he said. Puzzled, he pulled the drapery cord. The drapes parted to reveal a blank wall.

"It makes me *feel* like there's a window," she explained.

Other problems weren't so easily resolved. The smell, for instance, at times seemed overwhelming. That week one of her first clients commented on the strong odor of Lysol.

"Well, yes, I suppose it is rather heavy," Sylvia admitted, "but I thought it was better than that other smell."

"Other smell?"

"Yes, can't you smell it? No matter how much Lysol I spray around this place, I can't get rid of that ammonia smell. I just can't figure out where it's coming from."

The client, a heavy-set grandmother type, laughed. "Maybe you'd better pay some attention to *this* world, honey. Didn't you notice the diaper service next door?"

Sylvia laughed with her client, but later reflected. She was reminded of the ancient saying, "As above, so below." The universe was not about to allow her to become too spiritual. Like it or not, she was well grounded in the everyday world. But it went further than that. Now it seemed that all the factors that had clouded her life—her father's infidelities; her affair with Ski; her depression, illnesses, and unhappy marriage—had all been for a purpose. She had needed those experiences to give her greater empathy for all aspects of the human condition. She was not, she realized, a priestess dispassionately channeling from aloft. It might be a cliché to say, "I know where you're coming from," but in Sylvia's case, it was true. Sylvia had been there, too.

Not only could she read for her clients, she could feel their pain. This personal understanding would enable her to avoid the worst pitfall she'd observed in open readings where the medium dumped information with no apparent concern for any subtleties of feeling within the individual receiving it. Now, with so many total strangers coming into her life, it was a relief for Sylvia to realize that her hard-won empathy would enable her to heal rather than hurt.

Looking now at the woman before her, Sylvia "saw" a husband suffering with multiple sclerosis. She questioned her gently. "You know that your husband is seriously ill, don't you?" she asked.

The woman nodded her head and replied, "Yes."

As Sylvia probed psychically, she knew her client was ready for the whole truth. "He'll be gone in two years."

"That's why I came to see you," the woman replied. "I wanted to know how long we have together. I want to arrange things so that we can make the most of it."

In those early days, it was the money issue that troubled Sylvia the most. It had been one thing to accept money for teaching, a skill she'd spent years training to acquire, but doing readings was something else entirely. Sylvia had *always* been psychic; now it seemed she was suddenly being paid for simply being herself.

When Sylvia officially opened the doors of her storefront office at 249 East Campbell Avenue, her fee was $7.50. The first week there were five clients, one of them an avowed skeptic. He sat in the slightly battered secondhand armchair across from Sylvia, his hands clenched into fists. As she talked, he shook his head violently.

"What's the matter?" Sylvia asked at last. "Does your neck hurt?"

"I'm shaking my head 'no.' You're totally off. That marriage stuff— forget it. I've parted company with one wife; there's no way that I'm going to go through that again."

"What do you mean 'no'?" she challenged him. "How can you shake your head 'no' when I'm talking about the future? If you could foretell the future, you'd be sitting here and me there. Now let's get down to business. Who's this Penny person, whom you call Puff?"

The identifying question stopped him cold—exactly what Sylvia had intended. Such statements about the present establish the medium's credibility to foresee the future, soothing and reassuring clients and allowing them to benefit from the reading. Some of Sylvia's early clients were so skeptical that she felt she was arm-wrestling them into submission, but this enabled her to get on with the real business of finding helpful material.

The second week, there were 30 clients. One of them was a small, rather thin woman in her late 40s. Her face was tense, her manner anxious. She had barely seated herself before Sylvia got a picture of a young woman lying dead in a dark alley, her chest covered with blood.

If I receive the message, she's meant to hear it, Sylvia reminded herself, but her heart sank at the ordeal of describing her vision. "I see a young woman. She's thin with blonde hair," Sylvia began.

"Yes, yes," the older woman said, leaning forward, her hands pressing against the edge of Sylvia's desk.

"Her skin is rough, almost pockmarked," Sylvia continued. "She's off at a distance. In the east—a very large city."

"That's my daughter. I came to you about her. The last I knew she was in New York. Is she all right?"

Sylvia took a deep breath. "No, she's not all right. I have to tell you, she's going to die. In fact, she may even be dead now."

"Thank you," the woman responded, her voice soft, controlled. Her quiet dignity put Sylvia at ease. "It may surprise you to hear this, but I've known for a long time that my girl was headed for disaster. She's been involved with drugs since she was a teenager. She's mixed up in a drug ring with no way out." The woman began to sob quietly. "There's nothing that I could do, nothing that anyone could do, but the waiting, the uncertainty, is so terrible. I imagine them hurting her, torturing her, and I feel such helplessness."

"No," Sylvia was relieved and happy to say. "It's not like that. It's very sudden, a gunshot wound. She may not even know what hit her."

"Thank you," the woman said again. She pulled herself wearily to her feet.

"Would you like—shall I try to see what else—" Sylvia began.

"No, perhaps I'll come back another time. This is enough for now. Don't feel sad. You think you've given me bad news, but actually you've done me a favor. I don't have to be afraid anymore, to dread anymore. You've told me the worst, and even that isn't as bad as it might have been."

Sylvia rose, crossing the small room in an instant and opening the door for the woman. The two hugged briefly. "You've a wonderful gift; please don't stop using it," the woman urged, and then turned and walked away. Sylvia closed the door softly behind her and leaned against it for a moment, certain at last that she had made the right decision. It was indeed time to come out of the closet, to really honor Bob's trust in her.

Within a month, it became clear that Sylvia not only needed more space, but help as well. Her father, Bill, quit his job and came to work at the Nirvana Foundation as office manager. Soon he was joined by Larry Beck, a student at San Jose University. Before long, Larry's friend Laurie Halseth was a staff member as well.

One day Laurie approached Sylvia tentatively. "Do you think Larry and I will ever marry?"

"Yes, I know you will," Sylvia told her. "You two will marry, but it will only last five years. There's someone else out there for you—someone for Larry, too." (Actually, the Becks' marriage lasted five years and eleven days.)

Meanwhile, the Nirvana Foundation moved to larger quarters. The Goodwill sofa supported by bricks was replaced by a newer model. Sylvia raised her rates to $15. Before long, another move was necessary, and then another. To cover the cost of her growing staff and activities, Sylvia's fees climbed to $30. Reflecting on the accounting, financial consulting, and law firms that shared the building with her, she thought sometimes of her former neighbors, the diaper service, and laughed.

Today the comfortably furnished Sylvia Browne Corporation (successor to the Nirvana Foundation) occupies an office with 3,000 square feet and is within walking distance of the first office. The full-time staff of 14 includes Larry, who serves as business manager; Sylvia's son Chris, who does readings; and Sylvia's sister, Sharon. A variety of classes and other services are regularly offered, as well as an array of cassettes and booklets. But the focal point remains the reading room.

It was obvious to Sylvia from the beginning that with each client who came there, she was essentially reading a blueprint. "Where does this come from?" she asked Francine.

"Each and every person creates his or her own blueprint from birth. Each person decides the kind of parents and childhood that he or she will have, the kind of marriage, career, health, death—"

"But why should anyone choose the awful things that so often happen?"

"Life's lessons are necessary. Only through adversity does one's soul progress. Think of it, Sylvia—what have you learned from the good things that have happened?"

Sylvia considered, then admitted the results weren't impressive. The hard times, however, had made her strong. She remembered vividly the dark days of her depression and the sense of accomplishment she'd felt when she thought, *I made it. I may have gone through a lot, but at least I got up and brushed my hair and moved around and took care of Paul, taught school, cooked for Gary, cleaned the house—all of it.* Now, surely, those memories increased her rapport with clients facing the same kinds of problems. Because of her experiences, she was better able to help others and that, apparently, was *her* blueprint.

But there were some people that Sylvia could not help. One was Curtis Bitney.

Curtis had come into her life as a friend of her son, Chris. When he was a teenager, the activities at Nirvana were like food and drink to Curtis. Attending his first open trance, Curtis had surprised everyone by greeting Francine as an old friend. While others remained in awe of the spirit, Curtis walked right up and sat down by the couch where Sylvia was lying entranced. "Hi, Francine," he greeted her cheerily. "How are you?"

"Very well, Curtis," she'd replied. "It's good to see you here."

Curtis was eager to learn everything about the supernatural. He participated in research projects, helping Sylvia in every way he could. He enrolled in her hypnosis class, hoping to learn past-life regression. One day as Sylvia looked at him seated in the front row, she had a terrifying vision of him lying dead on Highway 17, his smashed motorcycle beside him.

"This is important," she told him. "I don't want you riding your motorcycle on the freeway. Stay away from Highway 17. I mean it. Will you promise me?"

"Sure, sure," he agreed. Laughing, he looked away from her. Three days later he was dead. A car had sideswiped his motorcycle on Highway 17.

Sylvia was distraught. Why hadn't he heeded her warning? Bitterly, she thought of those who accused her of trying to control the lives of her clients through mediumship. It was impossible. Everyone fulfills the destiny they create themselves. For whatever reason, Curtis had programmed himself to die at that time in the exact manner that he had. Sometimes the blueprint was unalterable—she could not change it.

But on other occasions it seemed to Sylvia that she herself was part of the client's blueprint, that her message was meant to divert disaster. When Kent Herkenrath came to her for a reading early in 1979, she saw the wreckage of a plane and sensed it was in the Midwest sometime in May. "Don't go flying off somewhere in May," she warned him.

"But that's exactly when I'll be returning from a business trip to Chicago," he told her. "I can't let something like this ruin my life."

"It's up to you, of course, but I see it very clearly. You're in an airport running for a plane. I wouldn't get on that plane if I were you."

Two months later, Herkenrath was in O'Hare Airport. He was late, hurrying to catch a plane back to San Jose. As he turned from the ticket counter, he glanced absently at the airline calendar. It was May. Sylvia's words flashed through his mind. Almost running, he approached the gate. Passengers were already boarding.

Herkenrath started to give his boarding pass to the agent and then pulled back. The man looked at him, puzzled. "Sorry, I guess I've changed my mind. I'll take a later plane," he mumbled, embarrassed, and he turned away.

That plane, an American Airlines DC-10, crashed shortly after takeoff, killing 275 people. It was May 25, 1979.

Sylvia had thought often of the two men, the one who took her advice and lived, and the other who chose instead to die. Could it be, she wonders now, that for whatever reason, it was part of Kent Herkenrath's blueprint that he should come to her to receive a warning that would save his life?

Sylvia had been aware since girlhood of the existence of blueprints that guided the lives of most of her subjects. But now, as more and more people came to her, she realized that each particular script lacked one component.

"My life is a mess," each client would almost invariably insist. "Everything's wrong." But as Sylvia investigated psychically, she realized that it wasn't everything that was wrong, it was some *one* thing. And curiously, it was this one problem area that was usually the most difficult for her to read. As always, with one exception, the individual's life was psychically accessible to her, each aspect clearly delineated. Invariably, one area would be vague, the conclusion undecided. With some it would be finances, with others love, with still others a career.

Puzzled, she consulted Francine. "What does it mean?" she asked.

"Those areas—the vague, undecided ones—are option lines," the spirit guide explained. "Each individual, when deciding upon his or her blueprint, also selects an area to leave open. This is what makes life interesting."

Sylvia disagreed. "This" was what made life painful. All around her she saw sorrow and frustration. It became increasingly obvious to her that few people came to a psychic in a happy state. Most were battle-scarred, so very tired. Sylvia came to feel that the reading room was a kind of "MASH" unit where she had to patch people up quickly and send them on their way, because outside there were a hundred others waiting for help.

On the other hand, Sylvia's good friend, William Yabroff, an associate psychology professor at Santa Clara University, who'd begun working with her on psychic research, observed her remarkable process in action. Again and again, Sylvia was able to penetrate to the heart of the problem almost instantly and was thus able to effect healings that might take a conventional therapist several years.

Now, as in the early days, much of Sylvia's work focuses on option lines. There are seven of them—health, career, spirituality, love, finance, social life, and family. Despite her avoidance of subjectivity, Sylvia came to realize almost immediately that her own option line was family. No matter how hard she has always tried, it has been impossible to reconcile the members of her family to one another. Bill and Celeste continue to quarrel; and Sylvia's sons, Paul and Chris, are not always the best of friends. Sylvia's continuing struggle is to please them all. It is an often-futile effort.

The difference today is that Sylvia is now aware of what is going on, aware that at one point at least she did have some choice in the matter. Sylvia elected while on the Other Side prior to this incarnation to confront family problems as her option line during this life. It is this realization that enables her to maintain her hard-won equilibrium. It's the helplessness, the sense of being a victim, that makes life most difficult, she now concludes.

Early on, Sylvia noted that problems with option lines cause people to believe that their whole lives are in shambles. "Everything's terrible," a client once complained to her.

She looked at the distinguished man in his late 40s and shook her head. "No, it isn't," she surprised him by saying. "Your health is fine, so are your finances, your career," she ticked each area off on her fingers. "It's just your love life that's off—way off. You've chosen one nymphet after another. Sooner or later you grow bored, the whole thing becomes disillusioning, and you become depressed. Or else the women leave you for someone younger, making you even more depressed."

"Yes, you're right," he admitted. "That does seem to be my pattern. Whichever way it goes, I end up alone and feeling rotten. Maybe the rest of my life is pretty good, but what's the use of having the other things if there's no one to share them with? Why, I wonder, do I always meet the wrong women?"

"The room could be full of women, and you would still choose the wrong ones—at least they're wrong for you if you truly want a lasting relationship."

"I do want that, I really do," he insisted. "I feel awful and I'm sick of it."

"Then program yourself," Sylvia advised him. "Decide what you really want in a woman. Write it down, if that makes it easier. Whatever you do, get really clear. 'I want a woman four years younger. I want some-one with a good mind, a sense of humor, someone who is at ease with all types of people, someone warm and caring'—whatever it is that you real-ly want in a woman. Make certain that you know what you really want, then go after it and don't accept substitutes. You are in control. You—are—not—a—victim. You don't have to go off with the next bimbo you see. You can really have the woman you want, the relationship you want, the life you want—if you decide to program yourself for it."

Sylvia found that this same type of advice worked well on other option-line problems. A woman with terminal cancer turned her life around and three years later was living a healthy, normal life. A man on the verge of bankruptcy programmed his way to solvency.

An option line is literally an option. Often this fuzzy area seems to permeate one's whole life, but Sylvia feels that the healing process begins with identifying the central problem and deciding on remedi-al measures. One can either consciously decide to make positive changes with no waffling allowed, or one can elect to recognize the option line, realize that it was personally selected for a reason, and learn to live with it.

She herself has chosen the latter. By recognizing her family situa-tion for the growth opportunity that it is, Sylvia has learned to flow with it. The frustration, the frantic desire to flail about, is gone, enabling her to get on with the business of life.

CHAPTER NINE

Haunting Expressions: Ghost-Hunting Protocol

When Dr. Marshall Renbarger moved into a new office in San Jose early in 1975, he was delighted by the convenient Crown Avenue location. But then strange things started happening.

First he heard loud, clanging church bells. But there was no church. Next, he began to sense that he was not alone when he was alone. Finally, there was the presence of strange dark-robed men gliding silently about his office.

When he discovered that no one else heard or saw the things that he was experiencing, Dr. Renbarger got concerned. "Maybe I'm going crazy," he confided to a friend. "Wait till I tell you what's happening around here."

The friend stopped him. "I'll be right over to see for myself."

Fortunately for Renbarger's peace of mind, his friend was Sylvia Browne, who was able to tune in to the situation immediately.

Upon entering the office, she was suddenly assailed by the smell of incense. "What are you burning?" she asked. "It's so strong." Renbarger looked at her, puzzled. "Nothing," he replied. "Nothing at all."

As Sylvia looked about the office waiting room, she began to see a series of scenes seemingly imposed over one another. She saw a steeple, then a bell. As she looked about her, the walls seemed to give way. There was a small baptismal font and, off to the side, a row of small cells in which she saw monks kneeling in prayer. Then, right before her eyes, another monk walked through Renbarger's waiting room ringing a bell.

"What do you see?" the doctor gasped. "What are you looking at?"

"I know it sounds crazy, but there's a whole other world going on right here, right at the same time our world is going on. There's a kind of church here. It's very small, a chapel, really."

"What does it look like?"

"It's very simple, primitive, *old;* I've never seen anything like it."

"Like a mission?" Renbarger ventured.

"Yes! That's it exactly. It's a tiny mission, a Spanish mission."

"And people?" he asked, almost whispering. "Do you see any people?"

"Yes, I see several monks. They're wearing long brown robes. They're very busy. They're all over the place performing all kinds of tasks. They seem so happy here."

"I certainly don't feel very happy sharing my office with a lot of dead people."

"You've nothing to fear from them, really," she assured him. Renbarger was doubtful, but the arrival of his first patient prevented any further conversation.

Sylvia suggested that Renbarger do some research at the county recorder's office, where he found the verification he was seeking. During the early days of California, a Spanish chapel had stood on the site of Dr. Renbarger's office.

"Sylvia, you were right, the old land grants show a mission on this property."

"Not to worry," she reassured him. "It's all very peaceful. The priests seem to have settled happily into their earthly routine; they don't want to leave it. You don't exist in their dimension, but of course, even if you did, they would never harm you."

Renbarger's experience brought another to Sylvia's mind—her own. The mellow vibes of the doctor's office were a far cry from the sinister aura that seemed to envelop the Missouri tract house where she'd lived some years before with Gary. How frightened she had been then, how helpless she had felt. But hadn't some of that been a reflection of her own emotional condition at the time?

Now that Sylvia's life was coming together with a new marriage and a burgeoning career, she felt confident and eager, ready to take on a new area of paranormal research. Her foundation was already dedicated to documenting survival phenomena. Weren't ghosts and haunted houses merely another aspect of this?

Unlike most psychic researchers, Sylvia had access to an insider, a true expert. "Just what causes a haunting?" she asked Francine. "How does it come about?"

"Hauntings often are caused by earthbound spirits, entities who have a sense of unfinished business," her spirit guide replied. "The priests you saw are an example. They simply do not know that they are dead and so continue in their familiar rituals. In this case, the lives remembered are peaceful, happy ones, but that isn't true for all earthbound spirits. Often with others there is a sense of confusion or frustration. They seek a lost person or object; they attempt to right a wrong.

"But," she continued, "the phenomenon that you call haunting may have another cause as well. Energy implants[1] may also be responsible. Sometimes the energy is positive—happy times evoke a light, pleasurable ambience—but at other times the opposite is true."

Sylvia immediately thought of the house in Sunnyvale where she and Gary had lived until their separation. The duplex, still owned by her parents, had been the scene of so many angry battles when she and Gary lived there. In recent years, her parents had rented it to a series of couples with disastrous results for the tenants' marriages. Now Bill and Celeste were considering its sale.

Many of the tenants had been newlyweds, and all had initially seemed happy and affectionate. But no matter how blissful the couples appeared at first, the neighbors soon were complaining about the noise, shouting, and screaming coming from that half of the duplex. Violence occurred with almost every couple. The turnover was frequent and always for the same reason—divorce.

"I don't know what came over me," the man would almost always say, vainly trying to explain his brutal conduct. "It's so strange; he was never like that before," his wife would complain.

Surely, Sylvia reasoned now, there was something that could be done about it.

---

[1] Energy implants, also called "residual hauntings," result from a strong emotional impact leaving a psychic impression that is detectable by sensitive people. Think of it as a fist striking clay—the impression of the trauma remains, but not the actual event.

"It is time for you to do an exorcism," Francine surprised her by announcing.

Sylvia was shocked. She knew nothing about exorcisms, had no idea how to go about performing one.

"It is quite simple," Francine assured her. "Use a white candle, salt, and holy water. Encircle the house with the salt, and seal each door and window with the water. Do this at night, lighting your way with a white candle."

Sylvia was dubious. "Where would I get holy water?"

"Make it yourself. Holy water is created by leaving ordinary water in the sunlight for three hours. Make the sign of the cross over it three times during that period."

Now Sylvia was even more dubious. It all sounded so hokey.

"It is *not* hokey," Francine assured her. "Such rituals have power because they are so very ancient. Just do as I tell you, and you will see for yourself."

Reluctantly, Sylvia agreed. She realized that, if the exorcism was to be done at all, it should be attempted as soon as possible. Sylvia went alone very late at night, hoping that the tenants would be asleep. Happily, she noted that the house was dark. Getting out of the car as quietly as possible, she walked all around the building with her candle, stopping before each door and window to sprinkle salt and water.

At first Sylvia felt silly, but as she tuned in to the vibrations of the house, she could feel the hostility and pain. Softly she prayed for peace, a peace that would heal not only the young couple sleeping inside, but the house itself.

As she knelt before the French doors and began to pour a line of salt across the doorstep, a window opened next door.

"What the hell are you doing?" a man demanded to know.

"Just killing snails." It was the best excuse she could think of. There were a few moments of silence that seemed like hours while Sylvia envisioned herself burned for witchcraft, or at the very least, roasted in the morning paper. Then the window was lowered. Slowly, softly, deliberately, Sylvia continued her work. When every opening had been carefully sealed, Sylvia walked back to her car and drove home.

To her very great relief, the exorcism was a success—completely so. No more violence, no more problems of any kind have been reported. The tenants are happy, the neighbors are happy. The trouble has dissipated as mysteriously as it began.

Whether caused by energy implants or earthbound spirits, the phenomenon of haunting continued to absorb Sylvia. She was determined to seek out valid case histories and document them. Fortunately, it wasn't necessary to look far. One of the most famous haunted houses in the world was located only a few miles from her home.

At Sarah Winchester's famous mystery-shrouded mansion in San Jose, every night is a veritable Halloween. An aura of dark foreboding surrounds the massive, sprawling structure; the towering spires, minarets, and cupolas stand dark and still, silhouetted against what always seems to be a glowering sky. Inside are trapdoors, secret passageways, and doors that open into the air. The Gothic Victorian is a living monument to the dead. The spirit of Sarah Winchester, who tried to shut out the grim realities of life and death, is everywhere.

The story of Sarah Winchester—possibly the most enigmatic woman in the history of the West—is as fascinating as the legend of the house itself. To the pioneers of the 19th century, the Winchester repeating rifle was the "gun that won the West." But to Sarah Pardee Winchester, heiress of the fortune of the Winchester Repeating Arms Company, the weapon was an instrument of doom and a portent of her ultimate destruction.

According to the story, Sarah, the widow of the rifle manufacturer's only son, was informed by a Boston medium that the spirits of all those killed by Winchester rifles—and most particularly the Indians—had placed a solemn curse upon her. The medium advised Sarah that she might escape the curse if she were to move West and build a house. As long as the building continued, she was advised, the vengeful spirits would be thwarted and Sarah would live.

The unhappy heiress obediently took her "blood money," as she called it, and moved to San Jose, where she purchased an eight-room farmhouse. She proceeded to remodel and expand exactly as she had been instructed to. The construction project, begun in 1884, was to occupy the next 38 years of her life and would ultimately employ hundreds of artisans working around the clock, even on Sundays and holidays—all in accordance with the plans provided by Sarah Winchester's spirits.

Design conferences took place in the séance room, where Sarah retired alone each night. In the morning, the resulting plans, complete in every detail, were handed to the head carpenter. Hundreds of rooms were added, many of them only to be quickly ripped out to make way for new ideas from Mrs. Winchester's nocturnal architects. These spectral consultants were capricious and insatiable, demanding more and more rooms, balcony after balcony, chimney after chimney, tower after tower. The strange growth spread until it reached a distant barn, flowed around and adhered to it like a tumor, and finally engulfed it. Again and again, observation towers rose, only to be choked by later construction.

Today, 160 rooms of this baffling labyrinth still stand, the survivors of an estimated 750 chambers interconnected by trick doors, self-intersecting balconies, and dead-end stairways. Literally miles of winding, twisting, bewildering corridors snake their way through the house. Many of the numerous secret passageways are concealed within the walls. Some end in closets, others in blank walls. The door from one was the rear wall of a walk-in icebox. The halls vary in width from two feet to regulation size, and some ceilings are so low that an average-size person must stoop to avoid bumping his head.

The explanation for all this is that the house was designed by ghosts for ghosts. If stories from that dominion are to be believed, spirits dearly love to vanish up chimneys. Sarah, always obliging, provided them with not one, but 47 of these escape hatches. The séance room, where Sarah received her instructions, was off-limits to other humans. Those entering the forbidden sanctuary after her death were said to have found a small blue room furnished with only a cabinet, armchair, table, paper, and planchette board for automatic writing.

Despite her efforts to forestall it, death came to Sarah Winchester on September 5, 1922. Today, one can still see a row of half-driven nails where carpenters stopped when word came that the 85-year-old recluse had died quietly in her sleep.

Of her $21 million inheritance, the widow had spent at least $5.5 million preinflation dollars to please her discarnate friends. Unless ghosts are unspeakable ingrates, Mrs. Winchester should have been well received.

But the story didn't end there. The mansion, known as "the world's largest, oddest dwelling" became a museum soon after Sarah's death. Next it was declared a California Historical Landmark and registered by the National Parks Service as a historical place. Rooms, as well as the extensive gardens, were refurbished. The maintenance of so large a place is continual. Today, most of the sounds heard in daylight hours are anything but spectral. In fact, the carpenter's hammer echoes just as it did during the mansion's heyday.

But there have been other sounds as well—strange, puzzling sounds. Over the years, tourists and staff have reported a variety of phenomena—chains rattling, whispers, footsteps, cold spots, filmy apparitions. To Sylvia, this Gothic thriller brought to life was tailor-made for investigation, an ideal spot in which to cut her teeth as a psychic investigator.

The thought was the act, and she quickly arranged with the owners to spend a night in the house. There would be five in the party—Sylvia, Dal, a photographer, a foundation researcher, and this writer. Sylvia prepared for the evening by not preparing, making it a point not to check into the history of the house or its inhabitants. At the time, Sylvia knew nothing of Sarah Winchester, other than that she had been the one-time owner of the mystery mansion.

Upon entering the house, Sylvia established her base camp in Sarah Winchester's séance room, one of the few with electricity. Because of its susceptibility to fire damage, very little of the gingerbread Gothic has been wired. The séance room, bare now with only a naked lightbulb dangling from the ceiling, soon seemed a snug haven to the team. The meandering passageways beyond, daunting enough in the daylight, were even more formidable in the dark. The tape recorder was unpacked along with 12 packages of tape still sealed in cellophane, 6 cameras, packaged film, and a metal detector.

From the séance room, the small party made forays into other parts of the house. Each member of the group felt sudden gusts of icy wind and cold spots for which there was no discernible reason. Once they were startled by moving lights for which they could not account, a kind of psychedelic light show that exploded out of nowhere, only to disappear again. In Sarah Winchester's bedroom, while seated in total darkness, the party's resolve was tested by the sudden appearance of two great angry red globes that confronted them and then seemed to explode before their eyes, finally disintegrating into blackness.

Sylvia was the only one to hear organ music. The next day, however, when the tapes made that night were played back, the others heard the sounds as well. This seemed particularly important when it was uncovered in subsequent research that Sarah Winchester had loved to play the organ and reportedly had done so all night long when arthritic pains kept her sleepless.

As the rest of the group sat on the floor of the bedroom, clutching clipboards and cameras, Sylvia whispered a description of a couple watching from the doorway. During the 38 years that Sarah Winchester resided in the "mystery house," her servants and other employees remained fiercely loyal, protecting her privacy and defending her every eccentricity. They described her as strong-minded and firm, but always fair and kind. Each was well paid and often rewarded with lifetime pensions or gifts of real estate.

In death, it would appear that Sarah received the same attention. "The man and woman I see are dressed in turn-of-the-century clothing," Sylvia explained. "The woman—her name's Maria—is Spanish-looking. She keeps wiping her hands on her apron. The man beside her has red hair. He's wearing overalls with a red kerchief around his neck. There's a big black dog with them, a Labrador. They're caretakers. Their attitude isn't quite menacing, but they are watching us very carefully, suspiciously. They don't like strangers in their house. They don't like *us* here. They want us to leave."

As the night wore on, the frightening sense of being observed did not diminish. Sylvia and her companions sat for about an hour watching a ghostly shadow play across the dark walls. Each of them tried to explain the spectral light show in earthly terms. Moonlight? There was no moon. Passing cars?

At times, the tension was almost unbearable. It was a very long night.

It had been an eerie initiation into what would become a sideline as a kind of ghost chaser and exorcist. The following day, Sylvia and her research team learned that Sarah Winchester's reclusive nature had even barred Teddy Roosevelt when he came to call. It appeared now that the tormented woman had moved on, no doubt finding on the Other Side the peace that had eluded her here.

For whatever reasons, the caretakers had remained behind, guarding the house in death as they had in life. The present owners find some advantage in preserving the house's "haunted" reputation, but Sylvia feels concern over the spectral pair, locked as they are in a lonely vigil. She has returned to the Winchester Mystery House several times specifically to speak with Sarah's caretakers. She has hoped to communicate to them that they are dead and to encourage them to follow their earthly mistress into the light, where they can get on with the work of fulfilling their own destinies. But they remain steadfast in their determination to stay with the house. On one occasion, a TV cameraman who'd accompanied Sylvia was able to photograph an apparition walking back and forth before the second-story window.

Since that cold January night in the early days of 1976—Sylvia's first trip to Winchester Mystery House—her field trips have taken her to many bizarre locations. One investigation brought her to California's Mother Lode country to investigate a murder committed more than a hundred years ago. Robert Chalmers, the merchant prince of the Gold Rush capital, was not only a member of the state legislature, but also a prize-winning vintner. His beautiful wife, Louise, with her easy elegance and proud, imperious ways, was the undisputed social leader of the area.

At the apex of their success, this pair of high rollers constructed a four-story mansion that was to be a mecca for the Mother Lode elite. Among the attractions of their "Vineyard House" was a 90-foot ballroom and a music room.

But Robert Chalmers's pleasure was brief. Soon after completion of the showplace in 1878, his manner began to change. The former orator now spoke in whispers. Seeing a grave being dug in the cemetery across the street, he walked over and lay down to see if it would fit him. Soon, according to Louise, he was a raving maniac whom she was forced to chain in the cellar of their home. It was said that she came down often to taunt him, standing always just beyond his frenzied grasp. Chalmers's misery lasted for nearly three years. Then in 1881 he died under mysterious circumstances. Some said Louise had poisoned him, although no one could say for sure.

Visiting the scene of the tragedy a hundred years later, Sylvia was able to tune in to both spirits. The sad truth was that Robert Chalmers had literally starved himself to death because he feared that Louise might kill him. "I meant him no harm," the spectral Louise insisted. "I only did what I had to do to protect him. If he'd been free, he might have killed himself or someone else."

Another memorable investigation occurred at a nude beach resort in Northern California. Even on a sunny day, the place looked like a setting for a Gothic horror story. Coast Road winds its way through deserted stretches of hills and sea. On the November weekday the Nirvana research team visited, there was very little traffic.

A dirt road wound downward from the highway, twisting and turning around rolling moundlike hills. As Sylvia approached the isolated farmhouse that served as an office, she felt that she had stepped back in time a hundred years. If ever a house looked haunted, this one did. To Sylvia, the tall two-story structure seemed like some lonely sentinel, a mute survivor of penetrating fog and sea gales. *But of what else?* she wondered.

Ralph Edwards met the team at the gate. He was a tall, rangy man with a taciturn manner. "I hear you have a ghost," Sylvia greeted him.

"Better talk to my wife."

"You mean you never saw it?"

"I didn't say that." He turned back to his gardening.

Kathy Edwards proved the opposite of her laconic husband. She was full of stories—all of them frightening. "Things are relatively quiet now—those footsteps, they aren't much. They happen so often, Ralph wouldn't get any rest at night if he ran down to check every time we heard them. And the doors slamming by themselves, that's nothing. They do it most every day. My perfume bottles dance around a lot, and we hear the sound of crystal shattering but never find anything broken.

"But when the girls were living at home, that's when the house was really active. My daughters used to have a terrible time at night. Something seemed determined to shake them right out of their beds. Sometimes they'd make up beds on the floor, thinking they'd get away from it, but there was no escape. Every time they'd pull up the covers, something would yank them away. I remember Ronda was working as a medical secretary—a really demanding job that kept her very busy. Sometimes I'd hear her pleading with the bed to let her sleep.

"My son, Roger, didn't believe his sisters, so one night he slept in Ronda's bed. Nothing happened, and he soon was asleep. Then in the middle of the night, he awakened, thinking an earthquake had hit. The bed was shaking so violently that it seemed to leap right off the floor.

"Since the girls married and moved away, whatever it is seems to have shifted its attention to the first floor. People just won't stay overnight in this house. Our last guest was several years ago. A young relative sleeping on the couch was awakened by a rooster crowing. He could see its outline perched on the arm of the couch at his feet. But when he turned on the light, nothing was there."

The Edwardses have never kept chickens.

"One night," Kathy said, "Ralph's Navy picture flew off the living room wall and sailed five feet before crashing to the ground. The force of the crash was so great that some of the glass splinters are still embedded in the wood. The nail that had secured the picture remains in the wall.

"If you think any of this is funny, don't laugh too loud," Kathy advised. "I told a visitor about our ghost once, and he laughed at me. That skepticism didn't amuse whatever lives here one bit. Suddenly a drawer opened by itself, and a baby shoe flew out and hit him on the side of the head. That stopped his laughing in a hurry."

On Thanksgiving Day of 1975, Kathy Edwards was just opening the refrigerator door when a large plant left its stand and flew toward her—a distance of some 12 feet. Her daughter prevented a serious injury by grasping the heavy pot in midair. But the mess could not be avoided. The plant and dirt that had been in the pot crashed against Kathy and splattered the inside of the refrigerator. No fruit salad was served at that holiday dinner!

Ronda was the target of another attack that occurred one evening with nine people present. A glass of wine sitting on the piano flew through the air and deliberately poured itself down the front of the young woman's décolleté dress.

Sylvia had listened in silence as her senses tuned in to the vibrations of the house. "You feel a heaviness in your chest at night, don't you, Ralph?"

"Yes." He nodded.

She continued, "Things move around in this house. They seem to get lost, disappear for no apparent reason."

"They sure do," Kathy agreed. "The first year we lived here, we were ready for divorce court. I thought he'd taken things; he thought I had. Now I know that neither of us had. It was someone else, something else. Once I had a letter to deliver for one of the campers. It disappeared right out of my hand and appeared a day later in a laundry bag."

"I see an older man," Sylvia said. "He's wearing a raincoat and hat. I feel dampness, rain, mist. I think he was a sea captain. He walks about the grounds. In his life he killed an intruder. He doesn't like company even now."

Excitedly, Kathy explained that she'd found an old rain slicker and cap hanging on a hook on the back porch when they moved into the house. "At least a dozen people a year tell me they've seen an old man in a raincoat. I wonder sometimes if it couldn't be the sea captain who built this house in 1857."

"Yes," Sylvia agreed as she nodded, "I feel that it was." She was quiet a moment and then added, "The people who lived here before were an angry, unhappy family. There was a lot of hatred, a lot of unresolved problems. I see unhappy young people...a beautiful young girl...blood. There was a stabbing here. There were evil acts committed in the past."

Kathy gasped. "A young girl did disappear mysteriously while visiting her uncle, who owned the place. That was in the very early 1900s. No one ever heard from her again. But a few years ago, when Ralph and I decided to put in a barbecue pit, we dug up a skeleton. We thought it might be an old Indian burial ground and called in an expert from the University of California. He said the bones were those of a woman buried around the turn of the century."

One of the most grisly hauntings ever investigated by Sylvia occurred on Alcatraz Island. "Discovered" in 1775 by Juan Manuel de Ayala, the island of Alcatraz was known by the Miwok Indians as a haven for evil spirits. In 1934, a maximum-security prison was built there, the most hated and feared in the United States penal system. The notorious Machine Gun Kelly was among the hundreds of murderers, robbers, and rapists who ended their days there.

Because of the evil reputation surrounding the place, Alcatraz was finally closed in 1963. Today the stark island lies vacant, a sanctuary for seagulls, but as the prison crumbles, its legend grows.

On September 5, 1984, Rex Norman, a ranger spending a lonely night on the island, was awakened by the sound of a heavy door swinging back and forth in cell block C. Upon investigation, Norman could find nothing to account for the disturbance. When the sounds continued on subsequent nights, it was decided to bring Sylvia in on the case.

On September 10, Sylvia, accompanied by a CBS news team, began her investigation. One of the first areas toured was the prison hospital. As Sylvia was about to enter one of the rooms, she paused in the doorway. "I don't understand this, but I see all kinds of cards and notes all over the walls. They seem to be everywhere."

Norman stepped to her side. "Do you see anything else?"

"The letter S. I see an S. I don't know what it means."

"Perhaps it stands for Stroud," Norman ventured. "Robert Stroud, the famous 'Birdman,' spent ten and a half years in this room. People think he had birds in his cell, but that isn't true. He just studied birds. He had hundreds of notes and cards tacked up all over his cell—things he was learning about birds."

Moving down the hallway, Sylvia entered another room. "Oh, this is awful!" she exclaimed. "I feel such panic, such anguish. It's almost unbearable. There's something else...it's cold, it's so terribly cold here."

"This used to be the therapy room," Norman explained. "The most violent psychotic prisoners were brought here to be bathed in ice water and wrapped in icy sheets. It seemed to have a calming effect. Afterwards they would often go to sleep."

As Sylvia progressed to the prison laundry room, she had another strong reaction. "There was violence here. I see a man. He's tall, bald-headed, and he has tiny little eyes. I'm getting the initial M, but they call him Butcher."

Norman shook his head. "Could be," he said. "I just don't know." Leon Thompson, an ex-convict who'd done time on Alcatraz and who'd been invited to join the party, moved forward and stood beside Sylvia. "I remember a man we used to call Butcher. His name was Malkowitz, Abie Malkowitz, but we called him the Butcher. He'd been a hit man with Murder Incorporated before they caught him. Another prisoner killed him here in the laundry room."

Feeling pity for the spirit of this prisoner who, for some unaccountable reason, chose to remain in the island fortress, Sylvia held a séance in the prison dining room. With Dal's help, she was quickly able to go into a trance. Soon Francine was present.

"What's happening?" Thompson asked. "Do you see him? What's he doing?"

"He's walking toward us. He's standing now on the other side of our table watching us," she explained. Francine spoke now to the spirit. "You don't have to be afraid of us. No one wants to hurt you," she reassured him.

"What does he say?" Dal asked.

"He says, 'I've heard that before.'" Now she addressed the Butcher once again. "When I leave this mortal vehicle, I will return to the Other Side. Come with me, follow me into the light. You will be much happier there. You will find people who will care for you, people who want to help you."

"What does he say?" Dal asked again.

Francine sighed. "He doesn't believe me. He's going to stay here."

And apparently he has, for the rangers who look after the island fortress, now a state park, continue to report eerie disturbances late at night. The prospect of the Butcher's seemingly eternal sentence to the abandoned penal institution continues to prey on Sylvia's mind. She hopes to be allowed to return again to perform yet another séance.

In searching out potential haunts, Sylvia herself might have initially been drawn to Charles Addams–style Victorians with their long, dark corridors, widow's walks, and dramatic staircases. But the ghosts themselves show a profound indifference to such things.

The ghost, it seems, is concerned with *what* happened to him, not where it happened. In most accounts of hauntings, some spirits come back to erase, reenact, avenge, or simply brood about an awful event or unfulfilled longing. Others, meanwhile, seem inclined to continue in more comfortable earthly patterns.

Judging from the number of individuals reporting spectral contact, one doesn't have to be a professional medium to see a ghost. They attract believers and nonbelievers indiscriminately. What seems to be required is the ability to tune in to the electromagnetic field or "vibes." Many may have the ability to do this without even being aware of it.

To be a ghost hunter, one needs only a rational outlook, a good memory, a sense of humor, and an inquisitive, flexible mind. Basic equipment begins with a notebook and pencil. Tape recorders, thermometers, cameras, and Gauss meters can be acquired as interest increases.

Of all the locations investigated by Sylvia, her favorite remains the haunted toy shop.

Toys "R" Us in Sunnyvale hasn't yet erected a warning, "Beware of Swooping Teddy Bears," but it may well come to that, for popular local wisdom has it that the place is haunted. It all began in the early summer of 1978 with a talking doll that couldn't. A customer returned the toy to cashier Margie Honey, complaining that it was defective. Margie tilted the doll this way and that, but no sound would come out. Satisfied that nothing could be done, she placed the toy in a carton, intending to return it to the manufacturer. No sooner had she closed the lid than the doll began to cry, "Mama! Mama!"

Margie removed the doll but could elicit no sound. She and the customer both shook it repeatedly, but the cry was still absent. Back into the box it went. The lid was closed, and sure enough the crying began again.

"It ceased to be funny," Margie complained to Sylvia. "I called a clerk to take the toy away. It cried all the way to the stockroom."

A few nights later, Margie was sitting alone in the employee lounge. Suddenly a large bulletin board secured to the wall began to swing back and forth.

Then, on another evening, Charlie Brown, another employee, and no relation to Sylvia or Dal, was closing up. He had just locked the door when he heard a banging sound from inside. Brown opened the door, but there was no one there. When he closed and locked the door, the banging began again. The pattern repeated itself several times until Charlie finally gave up and walked away.

Judy Jackson, the store manager, was later confronted by a customer who complained, "There's something strange going on in the women's restroom."

Judy listened in amazement as the woman explained. "I turned off the water faucet," she said, "but by the time I reached the door, it had turned itself on again. I went back and turned it off, only to have it turn on again. This happened three times, and now it's on again."

One evening, yet another employee carefully stacked a group of skates on a shelf just before closing time. The next morning he returned to find them rearranged in an intricate pattern—on the floor.

None of these phenomena has ever been explained. These and similar cases, some involving merchandise or equipment being moved during the night, are particularly curious. The business is a no-nonsense one and is extremely well organized. The incidents described are entirely out of character.

Employees came to believe that well-secured shelves unaccountably falling, footsteps heard in empty lofts, and lights turning themselves on and off can mean only one thing—a ghost. But of whom—or what?

Ultimately, Margie Honey and another employee, Regina Gibson, decided to mount their own investigation. The search took them to the Sunnyvale Public Library. Among the archives, they found a cryptic note that read, "It is said that the ghost of Martin Murphy is seen on nights of the full moon."

Reputed to be descended from the kings of Ireland, Murphy was the founding father not only of Sunnyvale, but of the surrounding towns of Mountain View and Los Altos as well. An early pioneer who arrived on the first wagon train to reach California by way of the Sierra Nevada Mountains, Murphy purchased a 5,000-acre ranch and settled in what would eventually be Sunnyvale.

On July 18, 1881, Martin and Mary Murphy celebrated their golden wedding anniversary with a huge party at their mansion, a great frame building that had been brought from Boston in sections by boat around Cape Horn and reassembled like a great jigsaw puzzle. An estimated 10,000 guests partied there for three days and nights.

Many believed that the Murphy saga didn't end with Martin's death in 1884. Many past and present employees of Toys "R" Us said that his was a restless spirit still bound to earthly pleasures. They called their resident ghost "Martin." Considering him to be highly mischievous, they speculated about his intentions. Some were frightened.

Martin Murphy named the city streets for his numerous offspring, but his interest in young people extended further; the city father helped to found the University of Santa Clara and the College of Notre Dame in nearby Belmont. So, some speculated, what better vantage point could the ghost of this man—once so fond of children—have found to watch the world go by than a toy store on a corner in the city he had founded?

Sylvia decided to find out for herself. Arranging with the store manager to spend the night at Toys "R" Us, she and a small research team entered as the last shoppers were ushered out. As always, the staff straightened up the merchandise, putting each toy in place, then swept the floors. Each employee was checked out and the alarm was set. No one could leave or enter before nine the next morning without triggering it.

Despite these precautions, during the night a large beanbag set well back on a shelf tumbled to the floor. Several beach balls belonging on the shelves of Aisle 107 appeared on the floor of Aisle 206. Later that night, a weighted ball was found in the center of a corridor and put back on its shelf and barricaded in place by a box. Within an hour, the ball was back on the floor again—the box pushed to one side.

At midnight, the hour suggested by the television reporters present, Sylvia began her séance, an attempt to psychically "tune in" to the store. To everyone's surprise, she began to describe not Martin Murphy, as most had anticipated, but a circuit preacher whom she "saw" brooding over an unrequited love.

The clergyman's name was John Johnston, though it seemed to her that most called him Yon or Yonny. Sylvia clearly saw him pumping water from a spring that appeared to her bubbling out of a corner of the store. Yonny had stayed with a family who resided on the property, she explained. He fell in love with a pretty girl named Beth, one of the daughters of a prominent family. But she was scarcely aware of his presence and married someone else. Yon or John remained a bachelor. Sylvia saw him limping painfully about the store, blood pouring from an injured leg.

The names Murdoch, Josiah Abrams, and Kenneth Harvey also appeared in Sylvia's consciousness. She spoke of tremendous activity within the area now occupied by Toys "R" Us during the years 1881 and 1923.

The next day, a research team from the Nirvana Foundation attempted to validate Sylvia's psychic findings and discovered that a spring, now capped, flowed where the building occupied by Toys "R" Us now stands. Water was undoubtedly pumped there. But, more important, could Beth possibly have been Martin Murphy's daughter, Elizabeth, who eventually married William Taafee, a prominent citizen of the area? One thing, however, appeared certain. The Murphys— devout Catholics—would scarcely have considered an itinerant Protestant preacher as an appropriate husband for their daughter.

The Murphy wedding anniversary party—an event of such magnitude that court was adjourned for the entire three days to enable judge, jury, prosecutor, and defendant to attend—was held in 1881. The events of 1923 were less easy to pinpoint. Newspaper accounts of the time failed to turn up anything of note—but the team hardly knew what it was searching for. The significant events that Sylvia sensed were probably of a highly personal nature.

Although no connection with Josiah Abrams or Kenneth Harvey was discovered, an attorney named Francis Murdoch was found to have been the owner of the *San Jose Weekly Telegraph*. In 1860, Murdoch sold the newspaper to the Murphy family.

The most dramatic find was John Johnston, whose life was recorded in *History of Santa Clara County*. Johnston was a 49er who settled in the Santa Clara Valley. There he became a minister who was instrumental in the founding of the First Presbyterian Church of San Jose. He never married, and bled to death in 1884 as the result of an accident sustained while chopping wood.

Prior to the séance, Bill Tidwell, a professional photographer, had placed a camera next to Sylvia. "If you see anything, just pull this string," he'd instructed her. As she saw "Yonny" approach, Sylvia had followed his instructions. When the film was developed, it revealed strange, unexplainable white blobs illuminating the darkened room.

Of course, all the ordinary explanations were considered—faulty equipment, double exposure, light leaks or reflections, faulty development, refractions and, naturally, the imagination of the viewer. Any or all of these could have accounted for the phenomenon, but were ultimately rejected in favor of the spirit itself.

Sylvia was delighted that her information was verified, but she couldn't get the thought of John Johnston out of her mind. He seemed such a tragic figure, stuck forever in what must have been a very unhappy situation. Surely there was something that she could do to release him from so sad and unproductive an afterlife.

Another séance was scheduled. Sylvia returned once again to the Toys "R" Us store where John Johnston maintained his vigil. "It's time for you to move on, John. You've been dead a long time," Sylvia urged.

"No, no," the spirit responded as he shook his head. "I'm waiting for Beth to notice me."

"Beth has been dead a long time, too. If you go to the Other Side you'll find her. You'll be able to talk to her much more easily there. Everything will be better, I promise."

John shook his head again and began to walk away. He was becoming agitated. "I have to stay here, I have to look after things," he explained, then paused, looking about the large store. "It's different now; there are so many people around. They have so much company now."

"Yes, it must be very different," Sylvia agreed. "Lots of children running around."

"Yes, the children are so noisy...twin boys running, yelling..."

"Twin boys? Did you see them clearly?"

"Oh, yes, I was afraid they would break something. I have to watch things. Beth isn't here. I have to be responsible."

"John, you were a minister—you *are* a minister—you should know there's a heaven. It's waiting for you. Please don't fade out on me. Listen to what I'm saying," Sylvia urged. "Do you see the light? Walk toward it, John."

But John was shaking his head again, already fading away. It was obvious that it disturbed him to hear her speak of death or suggest that he leave his familiar surroundings. Sylvia called out to John, urging him to return, but he did not.

When the lights were turned on again, the store manager rushed forward. "Of course I could only hear your part of the conversation, but didn't you say something about twin boys?"

"Yes, John was complaining about them. He said that they were very noisy."

"Were they ever! Those kids came in here again today, hell on wheels. Their mother doesn't even attempt to control them, maybe she can't; they're too much for her. They really tear up the place."

Subsequent attempts on Sylvia's part to persuade Johnny to leave Toys "R" Us and move on to the Other Side were failures. He has no intention of abandoning his familiar habitat. In John Johnston's confused perspective, his assumed responsibility for looking after the place remains all-important.

"But you must remember that his time and ours are very different," Sylvia gently reminded the toy-shop staff. "Someday—maybe next week or perhaps a hundred years from now—the realization will finally come to him that his purpose in this world has been served. Then he'll move easily toward the light and take his place in the spirit world."

The toy-shop personnel are now in no hurry to see Johnny go. Convinced at last that their ghost means them no harm, they've adopted him as a kind of pet.

This acceptance of spirit phenomena and willingness to coexist with ghosts is not at all uncommon, Sylvia has found. Perhaps the most persuasive explanation of the continued popularity of the ghostly phenomenon is its implied optimism. A spirit has conquered death and come back to prove it. It is both a clue and an invitation to a world beyond our own limited reality, an offer to broaden our awareness to encompass everything and anything that just might be possible.

And who can resist that kind of challenge?

As a result of Sylvia's many explorations of allegedly haunted dwellings, a protocol has evolved that she now offers to aspiring ghost-busters.

Ghost-Hunting Protocol

NO ALCOHOL OR DRUGS BEFORE OR DURING TRANCE

1. The first visit to the location should be the research visit. All people involved should be in attendance; there should be no "test run" by any member of the research party prior to this time.

2. No research on the location should be conducted prior to the research visit.

3. All members of the team should jot down everything they know about the location prior to their arrival.

4. The team should determine before the research visit what it is that they wish to learn about the location while there— what they wish to check for psychically, what they antici- pate photographing, and what information they require from the trance medium. The purpose of the visit should be determined. Is it to discover if the house is haunted? If so, what material would back up this hypothesis? What ques- tions must be asked of the medium? What psychic impres- sions are important? Is the purpose of the visit to determine the history of the house via energy implants? If so, what par- ticular historical eras are important? If there are none, those in attendance should be prepared to ask a variety of ques- tions regarding different historical periods.

5. Researchers should enter the house together, and silence should be maintained until the initial walk-through ends. Those participating in the walk-through should record their impressions individually and without communicating with one another. Since such research often involves the owners or residents of the location under investigation, one team member should be designated as the nonsilent partner who enters the house before the others and makes certain that the group will have immediate access. He or she can also inform the group of any areas that might be designated "off- limits." The owner/occupants should be present, but should not give information during the walk-through.

6. After the silent walk-through, the group should meet to dis- cuss their impressions. If necessary, each may return to

specific areas for additional sensing. Before the general dis-cussion of impressions, all researchers should turn in their notes or tapes to a neutral party (possibly the nonsilent coordinator). Although this may seem an untrusting maneu-ver, its purpose is to protect team members from being accused of changing their notes to match those of other members.

7. Prior to the trance, the research group should discuss what they wish to know about the location, based on the impres-sions gathered on the walk-through. Two areas should be foremost: a) information from the communicating guide that either validates or invalidates the impressions gathered, and b) information that can be verified historically by library/museum/archives research.

8. The trance session should be taped.

9. If only to boost the morale of the research group, the back-ground information on the location should be investigated as soon as possible.

CHAPTER TEN

Why Am I Here?: Life Themes

The two-year-old looked intently and trustingly into Sylvia's eyes. "You died of blood poisoning in your last life," she explained to him. *"You—don't—have—to—die—now. Don't leave us."*

Little David, a leukemia patient, recovered, defying all medical prognostications.

Later, his parents returned to Sylvia, wildly happy but nonetheless puzzled. "How could David understand what you were saying—or did he?" his father asked.

"Kids know much more than most of us realize," Sylvia told him. "They understand what's going on from the very beginning. The next time you look into a new baby's eyes, tell me you don't see, 'Oh, hell, here I am again.' That's what he's *really* thinking. But what we usually say is, 'The baby looks so old and wise.' That's not it at all! He's actually saying, 'Oh, *shit*.'"

"It's that bad, huh?" David's father asked, shaking his head. "I don't understand. What's the point of it all? Why do we do it?"

"Francine says that the purpose of reincarnation is to perfect the soul by gaining different kinds of experience and knowledge in a negative plane of existence—our Earth. Perhaps, for whatever reason, it was necessary for you and your child to experience leukemia. That's been accomplished now, and you're experiencing something else—a healing. Your boy has literally healed himself just by deciding to do it. Can any of us really be the same after an experience like that?"

"But why do we need to incarnate?" the mother asked. "If it's so bad here in comparison, why can't we just stay on the Other Side?"

"Well, you can if you want to," Sylvia told her. "At least that's what Francine says, but the thing is, what all of us *really* want is to get better, to *be* better than we are. Some entities choose to work on their perfection on the Other Side, but the trouble is in their environment, where everything is so perfect, it takes so long. Most entities decide to come back to Earth every hundred years or so to have another whack at perfection. There are even a few who elect to spend all their time down here incarnating into one life right after another. I'd call that being gluttons for punishment."

"Then who judges us? Who decides when we're reaching perfection?" David's mother persisted.

"We do," Sylvia told her. "We judge ourselves. Doesn't that make sense? We're the ones who know what we need to learn. Francine says that when we're on the Other Side, we're much more understanding of everything. We're fully aware of our good points, too—as well as the bad. We're not confused there. We remember not only everything we learned here in our last past life, but everything we learned in all those other lives. Then, added to that, is all the knowledge we've accumulated while working on the Other Side."

When David's mother continued to look doubtful, Sylvia reassured her. "No one is going to be standing over your shoulder telling you to work harder, to get better. You're the only one responsible for your learning process. How fast or slow you progress is entirely up to you. There's no good or bad connected with it. It's really more of an evaluation of how you're coming along in your own progression. There's no St. Peter or anyone else to condemn you. If you decide that your accomplishment in a given life isn't at the level you want it to be, you may decide to live another life that's very similar, to see if you can do it better a second time. That's part of the reason reincarnation exists—to give each of us as many chances as we need to learn something, something at which we'd failed. Think of it this way: God's an equal-opportunity employer. Everyone gets all the opportunities that he or she wants to work toward any desired goal."

The man nodded in agreement. "I never believed in reincarnation—I thought it was all nonsense. But listening to you talk to our little boy, and then seeing him actually get well when no one thought it was possible...how can we *not* believe that there's something like that going on? But what I don't understand is why he forgot about those other lives, forgot about his blood poisoning, for instance. Why aren't we born with a continuing awareness of our past experiences?"

"Francine says it's so we can learn our lessons the hard way. She believes they have a deeper meaning that way and are more of an influence on our soul's development."

"But apparently David's past life affected him in *this* life. Is there a way of explaining that?"

"He was very confused, but fortunately I was able to get through to him. A reminder was all he needed. It's unusual to carry a physical ailment over from a past life, but it still happens sometimes. Then, such a reminder may help to dispel the new problem. It's a kind of unfinished business, something like the spirits that hang around a so-called haunted house."

Sylvia thought for a moment and then went on. "There's another kind of carryover as well. We bring our likes and dislikes with us. Our personalities have been deeply affected by previous incarnations. Past lives can have a tremendous influence on physical health, appearance, race, creed, religion, value system, wealth, habits, talents, sex—I could go on and on. There's almost nothing about us that isn't rooted in a past life. Some of what we bring is positive, but some is not—bigotry, for instance. We've all—at some time in some life—been both the perpetrator and the victim of that."

"This whole thing is so new to us, it's kind of overwhelming," David's mother admitted.

"Perhaps you might want to look at your lives and analyze them from the perspective of reincarnation," Sylvia suggested. "See how many of your interests, habits, likes, and dislikes could be the direct result of a past life. Is your house furnished in a particular decor? Do you prefer a specific kind of ethnic food? Do you vacation in the same place year after year because you feel drawn to it? You may be surprised where answers to these questions take you."

The couple left the reading room with lots to talk about. As Sylvia watched them go, she smiled absently, thinking of the many similar conversations she'd had with Francine over the years. The concept of reincarnation had always seemed natural to her, but the mechanics were something else. Once, during a particularly low period in her life, she and Francine had discussed suicide. "Couldn't I just leave now and come back another time?" Sylvia had ventured.

"Do you think for an instant that you can simply 'cop out,' as you humans say?" Francine replied. "It is quite impossible. There are no breaks, only your preordained exit points. There is no escaping life. You would only have to face the same problems all over again."

"But I'd be rested, it would be easier," Sylvia reasoned.

"No, it would *not*—it would not be easier," Francine said emphatically. "You would be pushed right back to Earth immediately. There would be no rest period allowed. You would be right back in the same geographical location, with the same type of parents, in the same kind of marriage or relationship, with the same work problems, the same financial situation. *Everything* would be the same, and you would just have to confront it all over again. Nothing would be gained by trying to escape. Think of it this way. What happens when children run away from school? Don't you put them right back in and keep them there until they graduate? Of course you do, and it isn't until they've learned their lessons and graduate that other opportunities are open to them."

Sylvia remembered, could almost feel her weariness at the time of that conversation, her exhausted frustration. "What will happen to me when I do get to the Other Side?" she had asked, as a child might beg a bedtime story.

"The same thing that happens to everyone. You will move through a dark tunnel toward a shining light where a loved one will be waiting to guide you. At the end of that tunnel, you will find an orientation center, our Hall of Wisdom. There you will sit before a screen and watch your whole life pass before your eyes. It is then that you will decide whether or not you have completed the self-assigned tasks of that life. Perhaps you may choose to reincarnate immediately, but more than likely you will choose to pursue your studies on the Other Side for a time."

"Why would I ever choose to return?" Sylvia had sighed wearily.

"Whatever your decision, you will have help," Francine had assured her. "A counselor will go over your life with you—your blueprint, your life theme—everything. You will decide together what is the best course to follow in order to achieve your own perfection."

"But why did I take on so much this time?" Sylvia had asked. "Why did I make it so hard for myself?"

"That is a tendency of everyone," Francine had admitted. "Life on the Other Side is so idyllic and one feels so strong that one tends to forget how difficult it is on Earth. You are counseled against taking on too much, but once again, the final decision is yours."

"I must have an awfully big mouth."

"Yes, Sylvia," Francine had agreed. "As I told you before, we retain much of our earthly personality on the Other Side."

"That's a comfort—I guess."

"But it is all your choice," Francine had insisted. "From the beginning of your creation, you, like every other entity, knew what you wanted to perfect, what your life theme would be, and how many lifetimes it would take to achieve perfection. It's that innate knowledge that drives each of us forward. The first one to know when it's time to incarnate is you. It's like a bell going off, an internal clock that says: '*Now.*'"

"Then what happened? How—where—did I go wrong? How did I get into all this?" Sylvia had asked, feeling and sounding petulant.

"You did *not* go wrong," Francine had reassured her. "You are moving according to plan—your very own plan. The first thing you did before incarnating—into this life as well as the previous ones—was review your past history. In the very beginning, in the early days of creation, all entities probed the future of all the planets that were enacting the reincarnation schematic. They studied all periods or ages of the planets—past and future—seeking the one that contained the right scenario for their particular perfection. The evolvement of the planet Earth contained a series of plateaus—the Atlantean era, the Neanderthal period, the Cro-Magnon period, the Stone Age, the Iron Age, the Bronze Age, the Golden Age, the Dark Ages, the Renaissance Age, the Atomic Age. In each of these ages, all entities could find the particular scenario that best fit them."

"Did—do we ever get whatever we ask for?" There was a trace of eagerness in Sylvia's voice.

"In a sense. In the very early days, we all sat in a vast forum scanning all those periods on a great board—a little like a stock-market board or a union hiring hall—which apprised us of all available opportunities."

Sylvia had been puzzled. "You mean life opportunities?"

"Yes. The boards listed information like geographical locations, parentage, ethnic and racial backgrounds, politics, economics—everything about a lifetime opportunity down to the most finite detail. Then some of us—you among them—took this information and, knowing our individual needs, bid on various opportunities."

It all seemed very strange to Sylvia. "Bid," she had repeated. "I don't understand."

"In the beginning, bidding was necessary because so many entities wanted to incarnate early. They were curious and eager to see what it was like on Earth and there were not enough opportunities for everyone at once. Now, of course, with the population so much larger, there is no longer a problem."

"I'm sure I'd be *glad* to give my place to someone else." Sylvia, thinking of the state of her life, had again been disconsolate.

"No, you were always very eager, very courageous about the tasks you set for yourself. You are still very courageous, Sylvia. You have no idea how much you give of yourself to others or what an inspiration you are."

Sylvia had shaken her head self-deprecatingly. Life had seemed very difficult at that point, getting through each day an effort. Only her responsibility to her children—and in some strange way she couldn't yet define, to Francine—kept her going.

But despite Sylvia's depression, she had been fascinated by her spirit guide's account. "What happened next?" she had asked.

"You—like everyone else—went to the Council, the governing body for the Other Side, and submitted a plan for your proposed incarnation. An entity does not *have* to do this, and a few have incarnated without the approval of the Council. But most prefer it, and all benefit from the counseling involved. It is like your earthly saying, 'Two heads are better than one.' The expertise and knowledge of the Council Elders combines with your own knowledge to select the best possible incarnation scenario. The Council went over your plan in great detail. They warned you of pitfalls that you had not considered, and they pointed out events that might change the whole complexion of what you wanted to accomplish."

"I wish I could remember," Sylvia had sighed wistfully. "Was the Council nice?"

"Oh, yes, very nice. Very loving and caring. They exist for our welfare and well-being. Frequently, a session with the Council causes entities to revise their plans until a final course is reached that takes in all contingency factors. Often an entity is warned about a particular incarnation and is counseled against going into a life that is too difficult or ambitious. Sometimes the Council may advise an entity to take two or three lives to accomplish what has been planned for just one. Of course there are always some entities who will not listen. They argue with the Council, insisting that they are right."

"What does the Council do about that?" Sylvia had wondered.

"Nothing, nothing at all. If the entity refuses to heed their advice, the Council assumes a passive stance. All entities possess free will and can incarnate as they choose. But I can truly say that I have never seen the Council make a mistake in reviewing plans for an incarnation, although I have seen many disastrous mistakes made by an overeager entity."

"Was—is—that the final step?"

"Oh, no. After that, you return to the orientation center, where you discuss the plan that you and the Council have decided upon with at least one Master Teacher. This is a time-consuming process for everyone because the Master Teacher must be totally familiar with every detail of what the entity wants to accomplish. Some entities spend many years of your time—years as you measure time on Earth—in the orientation center preparing for life. When you've completed this final preparation, you begin to search with the aid of a computerlike apparatus for the right parents, the right body, the right geographical location. Using this device, you decide upon the defects you might have, the jobs you might hold, what kind of childhood is best for fulfilling your destiny, what kind of midlife, what mate or children, what kind of death."

According to Francine, all these factors are weighed. "You yourself decide whether it would be better for you to be rich or poor," she explained. "Do you want a parent that will be a matriarch or patriarch? Do you want parents who will be divorced or killed? Do you want siblings? Will you marry? What entity or entities will best enable you to attain perfection? Will you have children? How many? What sex? What kind of dispositions should they have? What kind of associations? What kind of traumas? How many negative challenges should you have? Will you embrace one religion, many religions, or no religion? The list of possibilities and necessary decisions goes on and on."

Sylvia had sighed again. "With so much planning, how can it all go wrong?"

"It does *not* go wrong. There is no 'wrong,'" Francine insisted. "Things only seem wrong to you at this time. Actually, I have not told you all the decision making involved in an incarnation. There is more. After finalizing the basic plan, you and your Master Teacher view the major events of this planned incarnation on an apparatus much like a closed-circuit television. In this manner, you actually see the major events and choices in the life that you have planned in order to gauge your reaction and analyze your emotional response. You may look at your prospective life in a hundred different ways—variations made possible by unanticipated changes."

"Then I can make changes in the plan?" Sylvia had asked.

"There are many paths that an entity may follow, but only one 'blue track,' the path that must be followed to accomplish the desired perfection. If the entity gets off this track, some form of derangement may arise."

Sylvia had considered that possibility. "Derangement? What exactly do you mean?"

"Alcoholism could be one type of response, or perhaps some other form of mental or physical illness. In the most extreme cases, it could take the form of suicide. Of course, the entity planning the incarnation is carefully programmed to avoid the stress that produces such problems."

"It doesn't work very well, does it—that programming?" Sylvia had asked.

"Most of the time it *does* work," Francine had argued. "In most cases, the entity survives incarnation, although not always on the chosen track. The difficulty comes, as I have told you before, from the difference between your plane and the Other Side. Overcoming the problem is the reason for the extensive planning and, particularly, the intensive review. The plan must be programmed into the subconscious mind of the entity so that he or she can not only survive the incarnation but move forward toward perfection."

Sylvia had sat back, thinking about all that Francine had said. "And that's it?" she asked at last.

"Yes, that finally is 'it.' When all the planning, counseling, and programming have been completed and the 'blue track' has been embedded in the entity's subconscious mind, he or she incarnates."

"And then we're out here floundering around on our own," Sylvia had responded.

"Well, not *really* alone," Francine amended. "We spirit guides are always with you—if only more of you would listen to us."

Although until this time the mechanics of reincarnation had been a mystery to Sylvia, she had been aware of its principles operating in her life since early childhood. When she was scarcely more than a baby, she recalled being poisoned in a prior life and so insisted that her father taste all her food before she would eat it. As Sylvia grew older, pleasant memories of convent life contributed to her longing to become a nun in this current incarnation.

Then later still, Dal, shortly after their marriage, hypnotized Sylvia and returned her to an earlier life in Japan. "Are you psychic?" he asked.

"Yes," she replied. Then, while still under the hypnotic trance, Sylvia startled her husband by asking, "Are you one of my voices?" It was an insightful moment that seemingly transcended time and space. For an instant, two lifetimes separated by hundreds of years had merged into one.

This was a tragic life, one that Sylvia chose not to focus on for long. Her ability to hear voices that others did not hear, to see things psychically that others did not see, was highly threatening to those around her. At first, her words were dismissed as the ravings of a madwoman, but eventually a woman frightened by a prediction about herself stabbed the entity who was Sylvia in that incarnation. She died of those wounds.

Sylvia believes today that it was necessary for her to experience that negative potential of a psychic's life to fully comprehend the power inherent in this gift.

Later, an indication of a chain of lives influenced by psychic ability in Sylvia's past surfaced when another regression revealed a life as an oracle in Delphi. As usual, Dal had relaxed her, leading Sylvia deeper and deeper into a hypnotic trance. "Now open your eyes," he instructed her at last. "Look about you…what do you see?"

"Mountains, jagged mountains…they're all around me."

"What are you doing?"

"I'm climbing a trail. It's very steep and rocky."

"Are you a man or a woman?"

"I'm a woman."

"What are you wearing? First look at your feet. What kind of shoes are you wearing?"

"Sandals. I'm wearing sandals. Sandals and a long white gown, a kind of tunic."

"Are you alone?"

"No, there's a little girl with me. She's dressed as I am. I'm holding her hand. She's my daughter."

"Are you happy?"

"No, it's early morning, but I feel so tired, so very tired. At the top of the trail there are a group of cell-like rooms. I will go into one of them. I do this every day. Soon long lines of people will be climbing this trail to see me, to ask me questions."

"Do you foretell the future for them?"

"Yes, I do that every day from early morning until late at night. My little daughter is training to do it, too."

"Don't you like your life?"

"I have no life—no life of my own. All my time is spent reading for others. I see very little of my child."

"What about her father?"

"He's gone...long ago...I can't seem to remember. I'm very much alone in this life. It's all work, all readings. I have very little contact with anyone. The people who come to me stand at a little window in my cell. I'm busy all the time, but it's really very lonely."

"How do you die?"

"Tuberculosis. I'm not sorry. It feels so heavy, not just my chest, but everything. I am ready to move on."

After returning to consciousness, Sylvia had total recall of this past incarnation. After meditating on it, she came to the conclusion that the memory was meant to instill in her awareness of the necessity of balance in a medium's life.

In 1983, while vacationing in Greece, Sylvia became ill and was unable to accompany Dal on an eagerly anticipated excursion to Delphi. At her urging, he made the trip alone. On Dal's return to

Athens that evening, he started to describe the mountain sanctuary to her. "Wait a minute," Sylvia said, stopping him, "you forget—I've been there, too." And then she went on to describe for him the steep trails, the towering peaks, the massive columns and statuary.

Even for all of her experiences—not only from her own past-life memories, but from helping others to recapture theirs—Sylvia was unprepared for the wave of nostalgia that assailed her in 1981 as she stepped off the plane in Nairobi, Kenya. The trip had been largely unplanned. Client friends who had moved to Africa had invited Sylvia and Dal to visit them there. The Browns had accepted, but frantic schedules had kept them too busy to read or even to think much about the country in advance of the trip. Sylvia knew almost nothing about Africa, at least not consciously. Yet as soon as her feet touched African soil, she felt an immediate sense of coming home. As time passed, pictures and incidents appeared in her mind's eye. Sylvia is certain that she has lived three very happy lives in Kenya.

In the first of these, she saw herself dressed in the red wraparound robes of the Masai tribe. Sylvia's husband in that incarnation was killed on a hunting expedition, but her son—who is Chris in *this* lifetime—cared for her in a loving and tender way throughout her long life. In another incarnation, this one as a member of the Kikukyu tribe, it was Sylvia who was killed by a wild animal. She recalls this incarnation today as a short, almost idyllic life. In each of her African existences, Sylvia was both a woman and a shaman. She remembers this as a very natural thing that was well integrated into her simple life and taken for granted by those around her. Only in the final incarnation, that of a Samburu, did she achieve any kind of prominence. This occurred when she was able to effect a dramatic healing of a village child, but even this was a low-key experience that had little effect upon the simple rhythms of her life.

Sylvia believes that the purpose of these lives was to learn the value of simplicity and of a natural, uncomplicated existence. These lives also helped her to reach an understanding of a loving cooperation with others. Each of her African incarnations was dedicated to these principles, and a return to the areas served as a reminder of truths she'd always known but tended at times to forget.

It appears that there still remains a part for Sylvia to play in Africa. During the course of her holiday, she was interviewed by a local journalist, Kathy Eldon. Eldon had approached the assignment with some trepidation. She'd never met a psychic before and wasn't at all certain that she wanted to. Later she was to write, "I went cautiously, determined to wipe from my brain any transparent thoughts that could be 'picked up' and used to reveal me. But Sylvia in person held no terror. She's a big, comfortable lady with tinted blonde hair, huge eyes outlined in blue eye shadow, and a voice which is deep and husky."

In the interview, Sylvia talked intimately about her experiences, beginning with precognition in early childhood. She described the entrance of Francine into her life and outlined the scope of the Nirvana Foundation. "Suddenly," Eldon recalls, "in the middle of our conversation, Sylvia began talking about me. She told me how many children I have, their sexes, and gave accurate descriptions of their personalities.

"She discussed a trip I would be making, which I had planned only the day before. She talked about a book I would be writing and discussed medical complaints I had experienced in the past. She used words to describe me that only my best friend would have chosen, and pinpointed an incident two years back which led to my present job. I was astounded. Sylvia had no way of doing research on my life, and indeed, much of the information she imparted was known only to me."

Her earlier concerns completely banished, Eldon took Sylvia to meet Mark Horton, an Oxford don who had excavated ancient ruins off the coast of Mombasa. Sylvia was able to successfully date coins that he showed her and to identify where they had been found on a map of Kenya. Then she went on to point out a place where other significant artifacts could be found.

The journalist then introduced Sylvia to a most skeptical gentleman, Dr. Richard Wilding, the National Museum's Director of Coastal

Sites and Monuments. After commiserating with Wilding about a hip ailment that he'd had from birth, but which was not visible to anyone else, Sylvia set off with Wilding and Eldon for Gedi, a deserted city mysteriously vacated in the 15th century. After walking about the site for a few minutes, Sylvia began to sense the vibrations of the people who'd lived there. "This area drew a lot of children," Sylvia told Wilding, pointing to a mound of old stones. "Children of all ages came here with their parents."

Wilding looked at her in amazement. "We believe these to be the ruins of a family mosque," he told her. "Do you have any feelings as to why the city was deserted? Why did they all leave?"

"People died here...a lot of them all at once. It was the water. Something polluted the water system, and most of them died. The rest moved away and never came back."

"Yes! Yes!" he exclaimed, nodding, his earlier skepticism gone. "That could account for the exodus very well indeed."

The article that Eldon wrote about Sylvia for her newspaper, *The Nation*, touched a sensitive spot in many readers. Within a week, the journalist had received more than 50 letters and calls from people anxious to make contact with Sylvia, who by then had, unfortunately, returned home. Undaunted, two of these readers went on to telephone Sylvia in California for readings.

One woman, distraught by the disappearance of a teenage son, asked for information on his whereabouts. "Is he alive?" she wanted to know. "Is he being held under duress? How can we get him back?"

Sylvia's response was instant. Describing the events that had led to the boy's disappearance, she gave details about the people he was with, described where he was staying, and added, "Don't bother to look for him. You won't find him. He'll come home when he is ready." The family relayed the information to the police, who continued their search. Despite their efforts to follow up clues furnished by the boy's friends, the youngster wasn't found.

Then on Easter Sunday, the runaway boy came home—just as Sylvia had said he would. He later confirmed most of the information in Sylvia's prediction.

The second call to the United States was made by a Tanzanian reader of *The Nation* who was so distressed by his wife's mysterious illness that he felt that it was essential that he discuss her case with Sylvia.

But once again there was no need for details. "Your wife has severe headaches that constrict her circulation," Sylvia told him. After relating more information on the woman's condition, which the husband corroborated, she recommended a specific medicine.

The patient, who had for months consulted many doctors in her country, decided to try the new medicine. After one week, instead of being bedridden with incapacitating headaches every day, she reported only two mild headaches in six days. She appeared, on the basis of her conversation with Kathy Eldon, to be well on the road to recovery.

The article that Eldon had written for *The Nation* appeared in February 1982. At that time, Sylvia warned that there would be serious difficulties in Kenya during the end of July or the beginning of August. On the first of August, a coup attempt resulted in several deaths and a shakeup of the government.

The following year, when Sylvia returned, she was contacted by Cabinet member Philip Leakey, son of the world-famous anthropologists. During the course of the reading, Sylvia expressed concern about the safety of Kenya's president, Daniel Moi. "He should be very careful in Mombasa...I see him there surrounded by flags. He shouldn't be there. It's in September. He's in a kind of—well, at home we'd call it a fairground. Someone there wants to hurt him...he shouldn't go," she warned.

As it turned out, President Moi's executive duties did take him to Mombasa, where he attended an annual festival, very much like a large state fair. The atmosphere was very tense. Aware of Sylvia's warning, Moi ordered extra security and—most important—cut his visit short, possibly averting violence and death.

Today Sylvia is known in Kenya by the Kikukyu title, "Mumbi-1," which means "First Woman of the World." She has made many trips since 1981 and considers Kenya a second home.

❧

Sylvia has been told by Francine that she's had 54 lives. She recalls fragments of 12, but has no particular interest in further pursuing her own past history. These memories have come to her, she believes, for a specific purpose that has some bearing on *this* life. They are long-ago memories from long-distant times. More recent experiences have eluded her. Unless some occasion should arise in which past lives have immediate effects upon this present one, Sylvia remains content to leave them buried.

Once satisfied as to the continuity of the human spirit, mere curiosity isn't enough to justify to her the time spent on hypnotic regression. She prefers to spend the time and energy helping others heal themselves through knowledge of past-life experiences.

A dramatic demonstration of this was documented on television on October 9, 1982. The subject was Edwinna Moore, hostess of the San Francisco TV show *Pacific Currents*. Moore's problem was a fear of heights that was severely restricting her life.

Sylvia began by calming her subject, instructing Moore to feel the relaxation creeping slowly over her entire body, beginning with her feet and moving upward. "With each breath, you're going to go deeper and deeper," Sylvia intoned. "Now close your eyes and look at the bridge of your nose." Within a few minutes, Moore was in a deep hypnotic trance.

"Now go to the time when your fear of heights began," Sylvia directed. "Tell me what's happening."

"I'm climbing a mountain," Moore said, her voice almost a whisper. "I'm afraid, I'm so afraid."

"Go back before that time...tell me about yourself. What do you look like?"

"I'm young, about 15. I have brown skin."

"Where are you?"

"On an island, a very lush island...it's Hawaii."

"What's happening?"

"I'm running...I'm running away from someone, but it's hard, the mountains are so steep...something terrible is going to happen!"

"Be calm," Sylvia commanded, "take a deep breath, remove yourself from the entity you see, and get out of the picture to an observer's position. You are now calm, safe, protected; you are simply watching the following events, which will cause you no distress."

Sylvia continued, "Now just as an observer of events, tell me, who you are running from? Why are you afraid?"

"A woman is chasing me. She's very angry...she wants to kill me."

"Why is this happening?"

"Her husband—he fell in love with me. She hates me. I'm to blame."

"What's happening now?"

"I've reached a rope bridge...I'm running across a deep chasm. If I can get across, I'll be safe...the rope is swinging—it's hard to hold on. There are rocks below....Oh, she's on the bridge, too...she's reaching out. I can't get away from her...I'm holding on to the rope railing, but she's making the bridge swing. It's terrible. I can't hold on any longer. I'm falling! Oh, I'm falling—"

"It's all right," Sylvia soothed her. "That's all over now. You don't have to experience it. This is a new life that has nothing to do with the other one. You don't have to be afraid of heights any longer. You know now what caused that fear, and it's all over. This is a whole new life, and you're completely free. I'm going to count to three now, and then you'll awaken feeling well and rested. The fear of heights will be gone. One...two...three...wake up!"

Edwinna Moore did indeed awaken feeling well and rested. Four months later, on February 10, 1983, she wrote to Sylvia:

> I wanted to let you know that since our session, my fear of heights has virtually disappeared. I'm now able to drive Highway 1 without that shaky feeling in my legs. I can even stand on the edge of a cliff and not feel dizzy. Thank you for releasing me from that debilitating problem.

Not every client has been immediately accepting of the principle of reincarnation. One woman complained to Sylvia about sudden behavior problems that had developed with her four-year-old daughter. They had recently moved into a new apartment with no bathtub. When the child was confronted with a shower, she began to scream.

"Poor thing," Sylvia sympathized, "but can you blame her? She was killed in a Nazi gas chamber. The last thing she recalls is being led to the 'showers.' You'll have to explain it to her. She doesn't understand that this is a new life."

The client was shocked. "You can't know something like that!" she argued.

"Why not?" Sylvia countered. "It's no different from telling you what your new place looks like when I haven't been there."

The woman was unconvinced. "It's different to me! I don't believe in reincarnation." She dismissed the idea as absurd, but the following day she called back. The previous night she'd been about to step into the shower, when the little girl began to shriek, "No, Mommy, no! Gas!"

The tragic reaction was too much for the mother to deny. "You must be right," she admitted to Sylvia, "but what does it mean? Why would my little girl choose such a terrible life? And what about Hitler and the other Nazis? Why do these awful things happen?"

"I used to wonder about it, too," Sylvia told her. "I'm partly Jewish and so, of course, I've thought a lot about Hitler and the Nazis. Francine says there are actually group incarnations. In the case of the Holocaust, both the persecutors and their victims agreed prior to their lives on Earth to enact those horrors."

"But why? What purpose could it serve?"

"It was intended as a global lesson for all of humankind. The same kind of thing happened nearly 2,000 years ago in Rome. Both Christians and Romans incarnated together to enact that grim—but inspiring—scenario."

"Then you actually believe that Hitler chose to be Hitler?"

"Yes, I certainly do," Sylvia assured her. "What he did—his acts—was undeniably terrible, but we can never judge the soul of any person. Francine is always reminding me that we all choose lives to express many things. But the ultimate reason is the evolvement of our souls and, finally, of humankind. Some of us select lives in which we are pawns, thereby enabling others to attain perfection in some way. Perhaps the entity who is now your little girl was one of these pawns in her last life."

"I just don't understand that at all," the mother protested.

"We sometimes incarnate to create a certain situation or environment for someone else," Sylvia explained. "On our plane every victim must have a victimizer, every follower a leader. We're all here to help each other. All of us want to end the reincarnation chain so that none of us must live any longer than necessary with negativity."

"But the Holocaust was so terrible, so uniquely terrible—"

"Terrible, surely, but not as unique as you might imagine. Many more were killed by the Inquisition, which lasted for a much longer period—more than 500 years—and encompassed all of Europe as well as Mexico and Central and South America. We tend to think that everything that touches us is unique. We're always saying, 'I wonder if anyone thinks as I do?' You can be certain that somebody does, has, or will. No thought comes into your head that's new. Someone, someplace has already had that same thought. In the very early days, new situations on Earth were in great demand by incarnating entities, but now there's really nothing new. You may imagine that you're going through a unique situation, but be assured that someone has already experienced it. We are all brothers and sisters in experience."

"But when will it end?"

"It will end when all people have acquired the amount of knowledge necessary for their perfection, when all of us have been sufficiently exposed to negativity and learned all that we can from it."

"Then in other words, you're saying that Hitler was simply a volunteer or possibly an actor playing a part?"

"That's right," Sylvia said as she nodded. "As evil as the acts are that he committed, the entity was a kind of actor playing a villain in a cosmic drama."

"But what about all that karma stuff that people are always talking about? It seems like Hitler would have terrible karma."

Sylvia sighed in exasperation. "I'm so sick of that word. It seems as though just when we finally moved away from the fear of hell, some jackass had to substitute karma."

Deeply puzzled, the woman asked, "Well, just what is karma?"

"The true definition of karma is simply experience," Sylvia told her. "It's nothing more than the experience we seek while incarnating on Earth. Unfortunately, many people interpret it in a very negative sense. They think if I slap you in this life, you have to slap me next time, and then I slap you back, and we just go on slapping each other back and forth through eternity. Isn't that dumb? As though we didn't have enough to do."

"But if that isn't true, where does the negative connotation come from?"

Sylvia explained, "It began in Eastern philosophy, in which it is believed that 'bad' actions incur bad karma. Some are so extreme that if you were having an accident of some kind, a believer might refuse to help for fear of interfering with your karma. In our own society, the belief in a vengeful, wrathful God sometimes carries over into reincarnation, bringing a false interpretation of negativity to karma. What both of these factions fail to realize is that the whole purpose of life is for people to help one another. It's only in that way that we all progress toward perfection."

"It's hard for me to even think of things like Hitler and the Holocaust, much less imagine volunteering for them," the woman admitted. "But I do wonder about my daughter and myself. We're so close. Do you think perhaps we made some kind of contract before our incarnations to be together?"

"Very probably," Sylvia told her. "Francine says that each single incarnation is part of a highly sophisticated network of other incarnations—your own as well as those of others. Most are planned years in advance so that all the entities involved are subconsciously aware of all the major influences involved. Probably you and your daughter chose each other before you even incarnated. Perhaps you got together on the Other Side and went over your plans together. Very likely you may have done this with your husband as well, and possibly with your parents.

"Of course," she continued, "there are other cases where less time is devoted to planning, but the entities participating still know basically what to expect, even though they might not have conferred with one another. For example, an entity may incarnate without really knowing what soul will incarnate as her child. All she knows is how that 'child' will fit into her overall plan. This method is used less frequently, but is not unusual."

"Then making contracts is all part of the reincarnation process?"

"Oh, very definitely," Sylvia told her, "but the most significant contract is made with your spirit guide."

"How does that work?"

"Francine says that while we're on the Other Side, we usually choose a friend or someone we respect and have confidence in to become our spirit guide when we incarnate. This is a very serious and significant choice, for the spirit guide must know all our plans for incarnation in order to enable us to accomplish as much as possible. If for some reason we get off the track, our guides try to put us back. They also observe all our actions in life and help us to evaluate them after passing over to the Other Side. The devotion and effort of spirit guides are happily given, for they too have used the services of a guide at some point—everyone does—and they wish to help others as they have been helped. After all, this is how we all progress."

"Then how do we get it together? How do we get here?"

Sylvia was pleased with the insight the woman's questions demonstrated. "Remember, I don't recall any of this either," she reminded her. "I used to be as confused as you are. I'm only telling you what I've learned from Francine, but it appears that we enter a kind of tunnel—it's the same one that we leave by when our physical life is over. The tunnel connects the Earth plane and the Other Side. It's here somewhere that our conscious memory starts to fade. Many of us try to hold on to it, but it's never any use. Since thoughts are still things in the tunnel—as they are on the Other Side—we can think our way to the vehicle that we've chosen. We enter this vehicle by way of the pituitary gland. The whole process takes a little over two minutes. Sometimes the mother is aware when this happens, but most often not."

"Does this happen at conception?"

"No, somewhere between four and eight months into pregnancy. Sometimes at this point an entity, for any number of reasons, will change his or her mind. That's why there are so many miscarriages. It also explains many crib deaths and the high infant-mortality rate in developing nations as well. An entity can return to the Other Side at will until age four and does so if the soul finds it can't acclimatize to the negativity of Earth. If we thought it was tough on us having kids, it was even tougher on them getting here. The exit from the womb is very traumatic—those bright lights and rough hands; the cold, heavy atmosphere; and that tiny little body. Francine says it's terribly hard for arriving souls to adapt, but unfortunately, the birth process is the only way to incarnate. The birth experience really drives home in a hurry the fact that life on Earth is full of truly negative experiences."

As a striking demonstration of soul survival, reincarnation has a particular fascination for Sylvia. She's been actively involved in reincarnation research almost from the inception of the Nirvana Foundation, and today has some 1,700 histories on file. Never has a subject failed to remember some detail, however minor, of a past life—and most often this has been related to some problem in this incarnation.

All regressions at Nirvana are tape-recorded so that the individual will have a permanent record of all that transpired, as well as a copy for research purposes. Imagination, patience, and just plain luck are essential to anyone seeking to investigate his or her prior existence. Not everyone has led a recent past life, or even a life within the last several hundred years. Some of Sylvia's clients have recalled lives spent on other planets. One woman described a life as a computer operator on Uranus.

In the beginning, Sylvia made an effort to document the memories uncovered through her numerous regressions with startling success. One example was a woman who not only recalled her name in a past life—Selena Franklin—but her city of residence—Peoria, Illinois. Selena recalled her husband's name, Edward, and said that they'd both been born in 1804 and had lived all their lives in Peoria. A member of the foundation traveling to Peoria was able to actually locate both graves in a local cemetery and to verify several other details provided by Sylvia's regression.

For a time, Sylvia was very excited by such validations and worked extensively with the Federal Archives and Records Center in San Bruno, California, but now feels that the healing potential of regression offers much more real satisfaction. Not only are many of the lives recalled too ancient to document, but the time involved in this type of research appears wasted when compared to the benefits of the healings themselves. Is it really worth the effort to attempt to locate the grave of the teenage temptress who was Edwinna Moore in a previous incarnation, when simply determining the cause of her death in that life will cure the fear that had virtually paralyzed the entity in *this* incarnation?

One unique conclusion that Sylvia has drawn from her numerous hypnotic regressions is that all entities not only choose to perfect themselves, but they also select a major life theme with which to achieve that perfection. Sometimes there are two or three subthemes as well. Lately, Sylvia has begun to compare this concept to the choice of a major and a minor in college.

Each entity, Sylvia believes, carries that main theme through all its incarnations into a variety of environments and lifestyles. As each entity has a choice of theme, each also decides upon the degree of knowledge it wishes to acquire on that theme. Again, comparisons can be drawn to education. While some people might be quite satisfied to graduate from high school, others would be comfortable with nothing less than a Ph.D.

As Sylvia's research continued, she was astonished by the number and variation of themes. "Just how many are there, anyway?" she at last asked Francine. She was even more astonished when Francine responded that there are 45.

Soon it became obvious to Sylvia that when individuals lost sight of their themes—their inner missions—they became anxious or even ill. Slowly she began to categorize the themes and to study how each manifested itself in its particular entity. Wasn't this the very key to the question plaguing nearly everyone: *Why am I here?*

Sylvia suggests meditation after a careful reading of the list. Everyone will certainly be able to identify their personal theme, and its recognition may contribute significantly to maintenance and restoration of order in their lives.

Life Themes

Activator—The focus here is to perform tasks that others have failed to accomplish. These may be truly gargantuan or quite menial, but the focus is always on getting the job done right. Activators are the turnaround artists or the troubleshooters of the world, the ones who successfully reverse failure. Naturally, these entities are in great demand and so have a tendency to spread themselves too thin. Activators should make every effort to confine their energies to tasks where a genuine opportunity to achieve beneficial change exists.

Aesthetic Pursuits—Music, drama, crafts, painting, and writing are included in this category. An aesthetic theme is not to be confused with a little "flair" for one of those enterprises. When an aesthetic theme is present, the entity is driven by his or her innate talent. A need to create manifests itself at a young age and dominates the individual's entire life. If the secondary theme is a complementary one, the entity has a long and productive career. If not, the acclaim and privilege the entity receives only leads to dissipation and often tragedy. The life of Richard Burton is a recent example of this. The agonized existence of Vincent van Gogh reflects a very different but equally tragic application of a conflicting secondary theme.

Analyzer —Not only does this entity want to know everything, but how it works and why. Analyzers are afraid they will miss something or that some detail will be overlooked. The rest of us learn from their continuing scrutiny of the most minute detail. These entities thrive in scientific or highly technical settings, where their skills are essential. In everyday life situations, the challenge is to let go and trust the senses. Analyzers should, after a discreet analysis of the behavior of others, ask the Holy Spirit for enlightenment to transcend the physical evidence.

Banner Carrier—The first lieutenant of the cause fighter may be found picketing, demonstrating, or possibly lobbying; these entities also fight the battle against injustice. The key to success in achieving this theme is moderation, tact, and discrimination. It is far better for these entities to select one cause and see it through than to scatter their impact among many.

Builder—These entities are the cornerstones of society, the unsung heroes and heroines of wars and organizations. Good parents are often builders, enabling their children to go on to a much larger canvas. Mikhail Gorbachev is an uncharacteristically visible example of this life theme in action. Without these cogs, the wheels would never turn, yet builders rarely receive credit for the accomplishments made possible by their efforts. They need to keep in mind that not all prizes are won on this plane of existence. Often those who get the credit on Earth are not perfecting as rapidly as the builders who help to make their accomplishments possible.

Catalyst—Here are the thinkers and innovators, those agents of action who make things happen. Catalysts are the classroom stars whom everyone aspires to be, the ones invited to parties to ensure excitement. Catalysts—Ralph Nader is a prime example here—are essential to society for their innovations. Catalysts generally have boundless energy and actually appear to thrive on stress. They must have an arena in which to perform, or they become morose and counterproductive.

Cause Fighter—The number of causes is infinite—peace, whales, hunger, and so on—and the cause fighter will either be drawn to them or will create more. These entities fulfill an important function by speaking for others who are perhaps too absorbed with their own themes to address social issues. Cause fighters have a tendency toward impulsiveness that can place themselves *and others* in jeopardy. It is also essential that cause fighters consider the possibility that the cause itself is minimal compared to their ego involvement.

Controller—The challenge for this entity is obvious. Napoleon and Hitler were typical examples of this theme manifested in its most negative sense. The controller feels compelled to not only run the broad overall show, but to dictate to others how they must perform the smallest detail of their lives. In order to perfect, these entities must learn self-control.

Emotionality—Not only the highs and lows, but every subtle nuance of emotion will be felt by these entities. Frequently, emotionality is a secondary theme of poets and artists. As such, it will indeed enhance creativity while imposing a severe challenge. The recognition of a need for balance is all-essential here, as is the establishment of self-control.

Experiencer—It's not unusual for this entity to go from flower child to bank president to vagabond touring the world in a self-made boat. Experiencers dabble in nearly everything and master many of their pursuits. Howard Hughes is a well-known example. Wealth is merely a by-product of a multifaceted experience. Good health is essential to an experiencer; it is important not to jeopardize this by excesses.

Fallibility—These entities appear to be always at the wrong place at the wrong time, for they have entered life with a physical, mental, or emotional handicap. Helen Keller, who as an infant contracted a fever that left her deaf and blind, is an excellent example. Her triumph over these handicaps is an inspiration to everyone. It is important for entities with a fallibility theme to remember that they chose this path in order to set an example for the rest of us.

Follower—Initially, these entities might have preferred to be leaders, but on some level they decided not to make the necessary commitment. The challenge of the follower is to realize that leadership is impossible without them and so recognize their own importance. Perfection comes from accepting the self-chosen theme and providing the leader with the best support possible. Discrimination is essential here in deciding exactly who and what to follow.

Harmony—Balance remains all-important to these entities, and they will go to any length to maintain it. Their personal sacrifices are admirable up to a point, but the real challenge lies in the acceptance of life's wrinkles. What can't be changed must be adapted and accepted.

Healer—Entities with this theme are naturally drawn to some aspect of the healing professions, physical or mental. The good they do is obvious. The only danger is that they can easily become too empathetic. It is essential that those with a healer theme pace themselves so that they avoid burnout.

Humanitarian—While cause fighters and banner carriers cry out against the wrongs committed by and against humankind, the humanitarian theme takes these entities into the action itself. Humanitarians are too busy bandaging, teaching, holding, building, and so on, to have time for protests. Those in this category aren't much concerned with the concept of evil and they are inclined to excuse humankind for its faults. Since humanitarians rarely stop with family and friends, reaching far beyond to anyone and everyone who touches them, they are in danger of overextending themselves. The challenge for the humanitarian—Sylvia Browne's challenge—is to avoid physical burnout through self-love and nourishment.

Infallibility—These entities are born rich, handsome, attractive, witty, and so forth. When we consider that perfection is the universal goal, this theme becomes one of the most challenging. There is often a tendency toward excesses of all kinds. It is almost as though the entity wants to tempt fate. Curiously, there may often be a lack of self-esteem that causes the entity to fear that he or she is not lovable as an individual. The goal here is to truly accept the theme and learn to live with it.

Intellectuality—Here is the theme of the professional student. Charles Darwin, who used the knowledge that he acquired through intensive study to experiment, hypothesize, and eventually publish, is an excellent example of one who has perfected this theme. But since knowledge for its own sake is frequently the goal among intellectuals, there is often a danger that the knowledge that has been so ardently sought and painfully acquired will go nowhere.

Irritant—Deliberate faultfinders, entities with the theme of irritant are essential to the perfection of others for, in their company, we are forced to learn patience and tolerance. Though it's important not to play into the irritant's innate pessimism, we must also be nonjudgmental. We must remember that irritants are perfecting their themes so that we can perfect ours through them.

Justice—Many of our Founding Fathers, concerned as they were with fairness and equality, are examples of the justice theme in operation. Those with justice as a theme will eagerly give their names when they've witnessed an accident or crime. As admirable as all this sounds, it is essential that these entities use discretion in their choices. Mob violence is another misguided attempt to right a wrong. It is imperative that those with justice as a theme remain God-centered.

Lawfulness—Practicing or teaching law are obvious choices for these entities, who are almost obsessed by issues of legality. Some of those entities may also be found serving on governing boards. When elevated, these souls keep the world safe and balanced, but they must always be on guard against the possibility of using their power in a self-serving manner.

Leader—Those who pursue this theme are controlled and premeditated—rarely innovative. They become leaders in areas that are already established. Their drive is toward success rather than creation. Their challenge is to avoid power trips.

Loner—Though often in the vanguard of society, those with the theme of loner invariably pick occupations or situations in which they are in some way isolated. Sylvia, as an example, has recognized this as a secondary theme of her own. Being a psychic has set her apart from others. Loners are generally happy with themselves but should watch their irritation levels when people come into their space. If each theme recognizes the presence and significance of other themes, the result will be far greater tolerance and understanding in the world and—eventually—peace.

Loser—Entities with a loser theme are extremely negative, though unlike those with fallibility as a theme, they are born without handicaps. Often they have many good points, but choose to ignore them. Although their theme may resemble that of the irritant in the proclivity for constant criticism, they are different in that they invariably place the blame back on "poor me." These entities are prime martyrs, moving from one elaborate soap opera to another. By observing this theme in action, we determine to be more positive. It is important that we not judge the people who have this theme, remembering that their patterns were chosen to enable us to perfect ourselves.

Manipulator—This is one of the most powerful themes, for manipulators are easily able to control situations as well as people. By viewing people and situations as a chessboard, those with a manipulator theme can move people and circumstance to their advantage, as though they were pawns. President Franklin Roosevelt was a prime example of a manipulator in action. When such a person works for the good of others, this theme is elevated to its highest purpose. When the theme is misused, the ultimate goal of perfection takes a long time to achieve.

Passivity—Surprisingly, entities with a passivity theme are actually active—but about nothing. Although they will at times take stands on issues, it is always in a nonviolent manner. Although any extreme is hurtful to the individual, *some* tension may be needed in order to bring about the perfection of the soul.

Patience—The patience theme is clearly one of the most difficult paths to perfection. Those with this theme seem to desire a more rapid attainment of perfection than entities with less challenging themes. Often, they carry great amounts of guilt when they feel that they have strayed from their goal and become impatient. This attitude can lead to self-abasement and, sometimes, to suppressed anger. These entities must be lenient with themselves, for living through the circumstances they have chosen to express this theme is difficult enough.

Pawn—The biblical Judas was the classic example of this theme. Whether the means is negative or positive, pawns trigger something of great magnitude into being. We cannot evolve toward universal perfection without the pawn, but those entities who select this theme should preserve their dignity by only picking worthy causes.

Peacemaker—Entities who select the theme of peacemaker are not as pacific as the name implies. Peacemakers are actually pushy in their desire for and pursuit of peace. They work endlessly to stop violence and war, addressing a larger audience than those who've opted for harmony as a theme. Their goal of peace far exceeds an allegiance to one particular group or country.

Performance—Those with a performance theme find it highly rewarding but frequently exhausting. These entities are the true "party animals." Some will go into actual entertainment careers, but others will simply be content to entertain in their homes or offices. The challenge here is for those with performance as a theme to combat burnout by looking within, thus acquiring the ability to nourish and "entertain" themselves.

Persecution—This arduous theme is chosen to allow others to grow spiritually. Entities with a persecution theme live their lives in anticipation of the worst, certain that they are being singled out for persecution. Experiencing pleasure can throw them into a panic because they are convinced that somehow they must pay for it.

Persecutor—Those with a persecutor theme may range from wife beaters and child abusers to mass murderers. It's difficult to see the purpose of this theme within a single lifespan, but these seeming "bad seeds" have a self-chosen role to play that enables humankind to evolve toward perfection. Once again, it is imperative that we not attempt to judge the individual.

Poverty—The theme of poverty appears most frequently in developing nations, yet it can be even more of a challenge in affluent societies. Some entities with poverty as a theme may even have all they need to be comfortable and yet *feel* poor. With progress, the frenzy fades and is slowly replaced by a sense of bliss as the realization comes that the trappings of this world are transitory things whose importance will quickly pass.

Psychic—The theme of psychic is more a challenge than a gift, at least in the early stages. An entity with this theme is able to hear, see, or sense things in a manner beyond that of natural sense perception. Often it comes to those in strict backgrounds where authority figures strive to deny or suppress the gift. Eventually, the entity will learn to accept and live with the ability, using it for good in a spiritual, if not professional, manner. Sylvia, incidentally, does not carry this theme; psychic ability has never been a challenge point in her life.

Rejection—This challenging theme manifests itself early, with rejection or alienation experienced in childhood. The syndrome accelerates with entry into school and subsequent involvement in relationships. Often these entities are deserted by those they love—even their own children will adopt surrogate mother or father figures. The pattern can be broken once the entity recognizes what is happening and surrenders the action and the ego involvement to God.

Rescuer—One often finds the rescuer working alongside the cause fighter, but when the cause fighter moves on to another cause, the rescuer remains to care for the victim. Even when the victims have obviously created their own problems, the rescuer is determined to "save" them. Often, in so doing, it is the rescuer who is victimized. An entity with a rescuer theme has a high degree of empathy and can manifest strength for those in need. This theme presents a tough road to travel, but the spiritual rewards are great indeed.

Responsibility—Individuals who have chosen the responsibility theme embrace it with fervor rather than obligation and feel guilty if they don't "chicken soup" everyone who comes into their orbit. The challenge is to decide what is immediate and necessary and then to stand back and allow others to share in the assumption of responsibilities.

Spirituality—The quest to find a spiritual center may be all-encompassing for entities pursuing a spirituality theme. When the full potential of this theme has been reached, these entities are farsighted, compassionate, and magnanimous; but while still involved in the search, these entities must guard against being narrow and judgmental in their views.

Survival—For any number of reasons, real or imagined, life is a constant struggle for those who've selected a survival theme. At their best in a crisis situation, these souls take a grim view of day-to-day existence. The obvious challenge here is to lighten up.

Temperance—Very probably the entity with a temperance theme is dealing with an addiction of one kind or another. The challenge here is to avoid extremes. Perhaps the entity has conquered the actual addiction but is still dealing with a residue of feelings about it. The key to combating the fanaticism that often characterizes those with temperance as a theme is moderation—the true meaning of temperance.

Tolerance—Entities choosing the tolerance theme must be tolerant about everything—world affairs, relatives, children, politics, and so forth. The burden is so great that they often will only choose one area to tolerate, remaining very narrow-minded to all the rest. By recognizing their theme, these entities can meet the challenge and so grow more and more magnanimous.

Victim—These entities have chosen to be sacrificial lambs. By their example—dramatically displayed by the media—we are made aware of injustice. President John Kennedy is an example of one pursuing a victim theme—not merely his means of exit, but his back pain, his family name, and the pressures placed upon him by his parents. Many victims, after having played their parts, may choose to rewrite future scripts by altering their masochistic tendencies.

Victimizer—People's Temple leader Jim Jones was a prime example of the victimizer theme in action. Within the framework of one's own viewpoint within life, it is almost impossible to see the full purpose of Jones's manifestation of this theme, yet it is obvious that many lives, as well as many life themes, interacted with his. In the tapestry of life, Jones's unique role may have been to focus public attention on cult abuses.

Warrior—Entities with a warrior theme are fearless risk takers who assume a variety of physical challenges. Many go into some form of military service or law enforcement. With humanitarian as a secondary theme, they may be particularly effective. Although it is important to temper aggression, it still remains that without warriors, we would be prey to tyrants.

Wealth—This theme sounds like a great choice, but invariably it is more like a burden and leads to destructive behaviors if unchecked. As always, the goal of a theme is to overcome the negative aspects, and wealth is a seductive tempter that acts like an addiction—it is very difficult to gain control of this theme, and it usually becomes one's master. People will be obsessed with acquiring wealth, growing it, and hoarding it. They will not be concerned with the methods of acquisition nor the consequences of their actions in their quest for more. Moral values are of no importance to this theme. Usually it takes many lives to overcome this theme due to its powerful effect on a person. When people do finally master wealth, then you find them giving away their wealth freely, with no regard for anything in return.

Winner—Unlike those entities with infallibility as a theme, to whom everything comes easy, winners feel compelled to achieve. They strive to win with great tenacity, often gambling or entering contests. Perennial optimists, they are always certain that the next deal, the next job, even the next marriage will be the best. No sooner has one deal fallen through than they pick themselves up and go on to what they know will be a winning situation. President Dwight Eisenhower was a positive example of this theme. As a general, his unfailing optimism was inspiring; as a president, his confidence had a calming effect. The challenge for these entities—which Eisenhower appears to have met— is to take a realistic approach to winning.

Unlike some Eastern reincarnationists, Sylvia does not believe that reincarnation endlessly evolves through all eternity. She is certain that it stops for an entity when he or she has learned everything necessary on this planet. Her own current life is her last one here, Sylvia believes, but she stresses that this does not in any way imply perfection on her part. After many lifetimes here, she has learned her Earth lessons and will pursue her perfection on the Other Side, where she will assist some other entity as a spirit guide.

CHAPTER ELEVEN

Medicine and the Medium: The Laboratory Technique

The doctor is stymied. His patient does not respond to treatment. What to do?

For the internist, the response may be, "Let's run another series of tests."

For the psychiatrist, "Back to the couch."

With either course, the patient must spend more time and money before a cure is effected.

Now, at last, there is an alternative—the psychic.

Sylvia's link with the medical community was forged in an unexpected way. Just prior to undergoing minor surgery at El Camino Hospital in Mountain View, California, she looked up at her anesthesiologist and informed him, "Your wife's going to have an automobile accident. I see her crashing into something. I think it's a phone booth. She'll be okay, but the side of your car will be bashed in."

The doctor was obviously not impressed. "Fine, thank you very much," he replied, "now just relax...." The last thing that Sylvia remembered before fading out was his condescending smile.

As it turned out, the joke was on the doctor.

When Sylvia regained consciousness a few hours later, he was sitting beside her bed. "How did you know?" the astonished man asked. It seemed that as he had left the operating room, a call had come from his distraught wife. She'd just crashed into a telephone booth.

Since then, Sylvia has read for nearly half the staff of El Camino Hospital.

Before long, doctors were sending patients to *her*. Jerrod Normanly, a Sunnyvale neurologist, referred patients to Sylvia. "I had a phone call from a patient I sent to you sometime back," he wrote Sylvia. "She expressed gratitude over the help you gave her. She had problems with chronic tension that just wasn't responding to various medications and other approaches.

"I must say that I consider your presence in the community a definite resource because there are certain patients who will respond to the way you deal with them far better than to orthodox medical approaches to their problems.

"I have appreciated the patients you referred to me; they have been complex to the extreme, and I hope that you have been able to do something with the results of my consultations."

Sylvia now participates in a two-way referral service with some 75 doctors. If, while reading for a client, she senses a specific health problem, she's able to recommend an appropriate specialist. And doctors also consult Sylvia about their diagnoses and sometimes prescribe readings with her for their patients.

Again and again, Sylvia's intuitive gift has enabled her to give inspiration to those who have lost hope, enabling them to challenge the medical establishment in seeking new paths and possibilities.

Almost any working day brings a health problem of some kind into Sylvia's reading room. Early in 1988, a middle-aged woman entered. Before she could open her mouth, Sylvia stopped her. "Don't sit down. You've got to go to a urologist right away. Do you know one?"

When the woman shook her head in bewilderment, Sylvia suggested a doctor she'd worked with before and offered to call him.

Alvin Rutner of Mountain View agreed to see Sylvia's client immediately. Two hours later, the doctor called back. "That woman is seriously ill. If she hadn't come in when she did, she'd be in deep trouble. How did you know? What did you see about her that told you something was wrong?"

"I can't tell you, Al," Sylvia replied. "It wasn't anything about how she *looked*." She struggled for an explanation, but gave it up. "I just knew—how do I know *anything?*"

Sylvia's files are jammed with testimonials. Karen Guy of San Rafael, California, is an example. She wrote, "My skin has improved since you stressed no dairy products and L-Phenylalanine. Blood tests showed that I did have too much iron in my blood as you stated. And it wasn't until I got home that I realized that you were right in what you said—I *do* have 'flukey' periods."

A mother wrote, "My daughter wanted a baby more than anything else in the world but couldn't seem to get pregnant. She went to doctor after doctor, but no one was able to determine the cause. Finally, she came to you for a reading. You said that her problem was an ovarian cyst and suggested she go to a Dr. Nola. Sure enough, this doctor discovered ovarian cysts and has begun to treat them."

Pat Silva of Sunnyvale has written yet another testimonial. "Sylvia was very accurate regarding my need for niacin and ferrous sulfate," she wrote. "My headaches are almost gone. Also, my memory level is way up since I started taking the iron you suggested."

And Jean Turner of Fremont, California, wrote, "You were right about my allergy to dairy products. Since I stopped using them, I look and feel much better."

A more dramatic case was that of Sue Lange, who had attended a seminar given by Sylvia in Santa Rosa, California. During a question-and-answer session, Lange asked about her health. Sylvia surprised her by advising that she have her thyroid checked. Lange's swollen body and inability to concentrate had heretofore been attributed to Sjogren's Syndrome, a rare blood disease. As a result of Sylvia's suggestion, Lange learned that her thyroid was indeed very low, but could easily be treated, alleviating a number of problems previously thought to be "incurable."

On another occasion, when Sylvia was lecturing on therapeutic hypnosis in Marin County, California, a former subject, Sue D., rose from the audience and described how a lump under her arm had disappeared as Sylvia worked with her hypnotically on a drinking problem.

Rarely is Sylvia able to help members of her own family, but a dramatic exception occurred on November 29, 1980. Her nephew, Crisjon, was taken to Kaiser Hospital in Santa Clara, where his condition was diagnosed as osteomyelitis. The treatment was to be three weeks of continual intravenous injections in the hospital followed by three weeks of bed rest at home.

But Sylvia began to have very strong feelings that something was amiss. "It's all wrong," she told Sharon. "Crisjon doesn't have osteomyelitis. He has aseptic necrosis—the treatment shouldn't be nearly so extreme. Get him out of there. You'll feel better about it if you take him to a doctor named Marvin Small, but I promise you the disease will run its course in ten days. He'll only be out of school for two weeks."

Sharon and her husband, Richard, succeeded in getting their son discharged from Kaiser Hospital over many strenuous objections from the doctors there. Crisjon was taken to Small, whose x-rays confirmed Sylvia's psychic "diagnosis." The boy did have aseptic necrosis. Within ten days, he was completely recovered, and four days later was back in school.

The healing may take many unanticipated turns. One morning, Sylvia studied the woman who'd just sat down before her and "saw" that her client was mortally ill. "You know, don't you, that you have cancer?" she said, a statement rather than a question.

"Yes"—the woman nodded—"but what I don't know is how much time I've got. The doctor has some radical treatment that he wants me to try. The side effects are very unpleasant. If there's no hope, I'd rather be left in peace to enjoy my last days."

"If you take the treatment, you'll have six months to live," Sylvia said without hesitation. "If you don't, you'll have three."

The client sighed. A difficult choice was suddenly easy. She would decline the treatment.

Her death was an easy one, her last months uncomplicated by difficult, expensive treatment that would have brought nothing but pain. She and Sylvia talked often about her transition. When it came, the woman was ready to walk into the light.

Winifred Woods received comfort of a very different nature.

In 1978, Woods, who had muscular dystrophy, had been told that she could die at any time. She'd had a series of colds and had recently suffered from the flu, which had developed into a severe case of pneumonia. Having barely recovered, she was told that the next malady would in all likelihood be fatal.

One morning, Woods lay in her bed watching a favorite television program, *People Are Talking*. The face she saw smiling out at her from the screen was that of Sylvia Browne. For a time, her numerous problems were forgotten as she watched Sylvia "reading" members of the audience.

A man had risen and was challenging Sylvia. "You told my wife some things—they were sort of true, but I still don't believe this stuff. My father and I haven't spoken in years—"

"And that isn't going to change," Sylvia interrupted him. "He's one of those people who always has to be right so you're automatically wrong. Besides, there's another person involved, a male family member. It's a three-way ego conflict."

The man had looked surprised. "Yeah, that's true," he admitted.

"Sure it's true, so now I'm true about your wife and I'm true about you, so shut up and sit down," Sylvia said, grinning at him impishly, and he laughed back at her.

A little of Winifred's depression lifted as she found herself chuckling along with them. Before she realized it, she was watching eagerly, and when the program ended, she jotted down the address of the Nirvana Foundation as it flashed before her on the television screen. The doctor had said that she could die at any time, but wouldn't it be nice to know how much time she really had? Winifred thought of the fence-mending she wanted to do, the affairs that could be put in order. Impulsively, she reached for a pen and paper lying beside her bed.

A few days later, the answer came. To her surprise, the letter was anything but the death sentence she'd envisioned.

"Your death is far, far in the future," Sylvia had written. "Don't even think about it. You have more to do in this life."

Woods looked up from the letter and caught her reflection in the mirror. The woman she saw was glassy-eyed from medication, her body badly bloated. She felt like a helpless blimp, but how could she not feel that way? From the very beginning, her doctor had said that her disease would grow progressively worse until she was completely helpless. Now she'd reached the point where her right hand was having difficulty managing a fork, and her left was too weak to hold half a sandwich. And her recent siege of respiratory ailments had left her physically and emotionally exhausted.

Winifred Woods studied her reflection, searching for the woman she'd once been. *If I'm not going to die, that means I've got to live— really live,* she reasoned. *I've got to begin taking control of my own life.*

Her eyes wandered down to the throw that lay across her knees. The binding had come loose, and she'd been waiting for someone to mend it for her. Next thing Woods knew, she'd wheeled herself over to the cupboard where her old sewing basket was kept, found a needle and thread, and secured the binding herself. The small incident proved to be a turning point.

Woods blamed the medication she was taking for her sluggishness. *It's my life,* she decided, *to heck with the doctor!* She cut the dosage, and within days was feeling clearheaded and optimistic. A few weeks later, she'd gone from a size 22 to a size 14 and was looking and feeling better than she had in years. The fingers that had had difficulty with utensils were busily crocheting an afghan. She didn't feel "sick" at all!

Wonderful as all that was, it wasn't quite enough. Sylvia had said that Winifred Woods had something to accomplish. The woman wondered what it could be. Though still confined much of the time to a wheelchair, she was getting about, doing some of her own housework, and taking charge of her life in a way that no one had thought possible. Woods began to meditate. It wasn't long before an old longing resurfaced. Years before she'd written a newspaper column and planned one day to write mystery novels, but instead, marriage and a family had claimed her attention. Now there was plenty of time, but could she write?

The meditations continued until an idea came to her and she set to work. The mystery novel was half completed when Sylvia came to the area to speak. Woods, with the help of her daughter, was able to attend. During a question-and-answer period following the lecture, the aspiring author was one of those called upon. Woods was so excited that she forgot to tell about the health prediction that had come through. Instead, she asked, "Will my project be a success?"

"Yes, your *book* will be a success," Sylvia replied.

As of this writing, Winifred's book has been completed and is being readied for publication.

Sylvia has been able to bring insight into mental and emotional problems as well as physical ones. Thomas Peters, a Campbell, California, psychiatrist, has worked with Sylvia since 1975. "We have consulted with each other freely about families, adolescents, and children in need psychologically and emotionally," he says today. "Her liaison with the medical profession has been outstanding. In the psychiatric and psychological area, Sylvia's intuition has been particularly useful to me in terms of diagnosis and insight into family dynamics."

A few years back, Sylvia became aware that her eyes were rapidly deteriorating. "What's the matter with me?" she asked Francine.

The reply was simple. "There are too many things you don't want to see," Francine told her. After many years of psychic diagnosis, Sylvia is in enthusiastic agreement with the theory that many illnesses are caused by emotional factors. Once these are recognized, steps may be taken to correct the condition and heal or at least alleviate the medical problem. *What is it that I don't want to see?* she asked herself when the eye problems appeared to accelerate.

The answer seemed quite clear—problems confronting Sylvia daily in the reading room.

Perhaps on some level she was tired of leading others around and wanted someone or something to lead *her* for a change. But since this is Sylvia's chosen work, all she can do is recognize the strain and make a conscious effort to distance her inner self from it. The condition now has stabilized.

Sylvia is certain, too, that the weight problems she has suffered from for many years are the result of "carrying" others in her effort to protect them. Smoking, an addiction she has conquered, represents to her a subconscious desire to hold evil at bay—a modern-day replacement for the bonfires of old.

This provocative theory extends to many areas of possibility. Sylvia perceives upper-respiratory ailments as an immediate response to trauma. You "cry" and sniff with a cold, but if you don't succeed in getting the problem "off your chest," something more serious may develop—such as pneumonia or possibly even breast cancer.

Not enough "sugar" or love may result in low blood sugar or hypoglycemia. Too much sugar—an unrealistic Pollyanna approach to life—could result in the opposite, diabetes.

Back problems? Who or what are you carrying around?

Arthritis? Could it be that your energy is bulging at the joints?

Is your heart "broken"? Look out, a heart attack could result.

Mouth problems? Too much mouthing off. Does your blood "boil" at times? Better calm down; high blood pressure may result. And so it goes.

Once when Sylvia was attending the National Congress of Regression Therapists, she and James Fadiman, president of the Association of Transpersonal Psychologists, were discussing their health problems. "I've had a bladder infection on and off for four years," Sylvia had complained. "What do you think causes it?"

"You're smart enough to figure that one out," the psychologist reminded her. "What do *you* think?"

"I don't know. I've tried everything, one specialist after another, but I just keep getting one case of cystitis after another."

"Okay, if you can't get the answer now, drop it. But tell me, how's your family?"

"Terrible!" Sylvia fairly exploded. "That mother of mine, she really pisses me off!"

"Well, there you are!"

The two friends looked at one another and laughed, but the moment that Sylvia said the words, she knew that her bladder problems were over. Once her mind had made the connection, the healing took place.

Sylvia has since been able to use that insight again and again to help her clients. "Who's the pain in your neck? Your husband? Your children? Your parents?" she asks, often with startling results.

The list goes on and on. Dizzy spells? What's keeping you off balance?

Back problems? Who's on your back?

Bleeding ulcer? Who can't you stomach? The possibilities for healing are endless.

Sylvia is certain that the anxiety that causes these reactions results from the soul's need to expand. The instinctive reaction of the conscious mind to the spirit's challenge is, *No, you don't*. It responds, she believes, out of fear of the unknown.

The solution comes, Sylvia believes, when we consciously allow the soul to give birth to a new self. When the devil is named—when the ailment is acknowledged and the connection recognized—the healing can begin. It all comes down, she is certain, to assuming personal power. Just how readily we give that away is illustrated by the story of a client who, when given a penicillin shot by her doctor, immediately felt better until informed that the shot wouldn't take effect for at least 24 hours.

According to Francine, chronic pain "grooves in," continuing to send its signal long after the inflammation has run its course. Her suggested method of dealing with a traumatized nervous system is to respond to it by saying, "I have received the signal; I now produce my own anesthetic." It's like talking to God and saying, "That's enough. The groove is too deep, and I don't want to put up with it anymore."

Sylvia's spirit guide also urges that we prevent pain before it starts by being more self-centered, more caring for ourselves. "In doing this," Francine says, "try for one week to do everything that *you* wish to do—just for you. For one week, try it. I guarantee that by the end of the week you will not only be doing for yourself, but you will be doing more for other people than you ever have before. The reward of self takes very little effort, but it brings a wealth of love that begins to emanate in all directions."

In response to Sylvia's suggestion that this might be "selfish," Francine responded that there is no such thing as selfishness—there is only fear that causes a person to become introverted and closed off to others.

In order to enable all of us to not only make the connection necessary to reach the cause of our illnesses, but to effect their healing, Francine has transmitted the Laboratory Technique.

"The Lab," she says, "is a special place where you can go to receive healing, counseling, or help with any type of problem. As you know, on my side, thoughts are things. When you mentally construct your own Lab, we on our side can see it and then go there with you in order to help with problem solving. *But you must create that reality for us.*"

The Laboratory Technique

In your mind's eye, build a rectangular room in a size that feels comfortable and right to you. Leave the far wall open. From the windows you will see a beautiful view of water—the sea or perhaps a lake—which will add power to the healing. Also visualize three walls of a soothing green color. In the center of the room, place a table, large enough for you to lie on. Give the table some "character," with carvings or other types of ornamentation.

The more detail you give to your room, the stronger its existence will be for you. So decorate it with furniture, paintings, and other objects of art that you like. Now place a stained-glass window in the open wall. This can be of any design, but the colors must be bright—blue, purple, gold, and green in big blocks or bands.

After you've finished mentally constructing the Lab, walk through it. The best time to do this is at night as you are going to sleep. But please complete the Lab *before* falling asleep; otherwise there won't be any Lab to use. When you enter the Lab, stand in front of the glass window and allow each of the colors to penetrate your mind and body.

The blue brings tranquility to the soul and spirit, increasing awareness. The gold is for heightened dignity and intellect, the green for healing, and the purple for increased spirituality.

Allow the shining colors to enfold you in warmth and happiness. Try to actually see each as it enters you and cleanses your soul. Now ask for the white light of the Holy Spirit to surround you and make you well. Feel yourself starting to become whole now, with a new feeling of stability, power, and control in your life.

Go to the table and lie down, still wrapped in the glow of God's love. Ask the master teachers and doctors on the Other Side to work on a specific area of your body. Although you can always ask to be relieved of mental and emotional pressures, work only on one physical problem each session. Surrender yourself totally to these spiritual helpers, for they come to you directly from God. Once you've created the room, placed yourself on the table, and identified your problem, it's all right to fall asleep. Actually, you may have a hard time staying awake because the Lab itself has an anesthetic quality.

Use the Laboratory for any problem in your life. You may also bring a loved one into your room for a healing. First, you create the room mentally. Then, place your person in the white light of the Holy Spirit, and put your "patient" on the table. Ask the master teachers to help with the problem.

There is no limit to what you can do using this phenomenon. The only block you may encounter could arise because the individual you desire to help doesn't want that help. If you find that this is the case, then release yourself from the trauma by recognizing the free choice of another.

CHAPTER TWELVE

The Psychic Detective:
The Temple of Quiet

San Mateo County coroner's investigator Bob Jesson was angry. The last thing he wanted to do was consult a psychic. "The boss said to call you," he admitted, the irritation apparent in his voice. "We've got two bodies and no I.D. on either."

"Yes, yes, I see them," Sylvia soothed him. "One woman's short and dumpy, the other's tall, a brunette with a heart tattooed above her left breast."

"Where are you?" Jesson demanded, looking into the phone, down at the floor, then up at the ceiling. "Is this some kind of joke? Where are you hiding?"

"Just calm down. Listen to me a minute. I'm trying to help you," Sylvia reassured him.

"But I didn't even tell you they were women," Jesson retorted angrily.

His confusion faded as he heard Sylvia say, "Just listen while I sort them out for you. The brunette is young. Her name is Vivian— yeah, Vivian. I can't seem to get the last name—check the missing-persons' files in Petaluma. The short woman—her name's Clover—is from Monterey."

Within 24 hours, Jesson had verification from both Marin and Monterey Counties. Two missing-person cases had been solved.

Gary Boozer, a sergeant with the Santa Clara County Sheriff's Department, was another skeptic. He'd reluctantly sought Sylvia's help with a homicide case. "Forget about that for a minute," Sylvia had advised. "I've got something much closer to home, officer—closer to *you*. It's drugs."

"I'm in homicide, not narcotics," he'd reminded her.

Sylvia shrugged. "What can I tell you—you're going to make a big drug arrest. There's a brown two-story building with a kind of run-down trellislike railing. It's an awful-looking place with writing sprayed on the walls. The street has some kind of bird name. It's off Evelyn Street. There's no grass or anything in front—just dirt—it's a mess." Sylvia paused, warning, "Watch out, you could get killed there."

Two weeks later, Boozer was unexpectedly transferred over to the narcotics division. Only a few days later, while driving down a side street, he slowed to read an address. It was Lark Street, he noted. Ahead was the Evelyn corner, to the right a brown two-story building with a railing. Remembering what Sylvia had said, Boozer decided it was the wrong place for him to be alone. He drove off, intending to survey the house later with his partner.

Within an hour, Boozer got a call. There had been a shooting in the house; one man had been killed. He returned immediately to investigate with reinforcements and discovered a cache of drugs on the premises. The arrests that he made that day put a narcotics ring out of business.

As a result of many such successes, Sylvia had been asked to speak to a number of law-enforcement groups resulting in many working relationships with police officers. Gary Robinson of the Los Altos Police Department is one. Robinson was so impressed with Sylvia's presentation at a meeting of the homicide investigators in Sunnyvale that he called her regarding the notorious "ski-mask rapist," a man who'd been terrorizing the entire San Francisco Bay Area for three years.

Twenty-six women, ranging in age from 16 to 83, had been brutalized, although the police believed that there were many more victims who'd been too terrified to file a complaint. Police teams throughout the area were frustrated in their many attempts at apprehension because the criminal never left fingerprints or used a car that could be traced. He said little to his victims, and only two of them had seen his face, for he invariably wore a characteristic blue ski mask. Adding to the mounting terror was the rapist's uncanny knack for knowing when his victims would be alone. The assaults most frequently occurred in schoolyards, but women had also been violated in their homes, in vacant office buildings, and, in the case of the oldest victim, in the confessional booth of a church. Invariably, the rapist threatened his victims at gunpoint, bound them, and, after sexually assaulting them in a variety of ways, demanded cash, jewelry, or automatic teller cards.

"What can you tell me about him?" Robinson asked Sylvia.

"I can see him!" she exclaimed, overcome, as always, with excitement at her vision. "He's husky, dark-haired, white, but looks somewhat African American. I can't quite get the name, but I know the last name begins with an *S*." She paused momentarily, then continued more slowly, "I realize that it sounds kind of funny to say a rapist is gentlemanly, but in a way he is."

Robinson looked up from his notebook, eyeing her intently. "What do you mean?"

"I don't know, really. It's like I said—crazy as it sounds, it's like he's almost polite about it."

"It does sound crazy," Robinson agreed, "but several of the victims have told us that even though the guy threatened to kill them and showed every evidence of meaning it, he was apologetic. 'I've killed before and I can kill again, but I'm sorry' sort of thing. There's never been anything in the newspapers about this trait, but it's a theme that keeps coming up again and again in each of the victims' descriptions." Robinson was eager now, leaning forward. "Anything else? Think about it...some little detail. Never mind if it sounds crazy."

Sylvia nodded. "Yes, there is something else. He works for the city."

"That's pretty broad. I do myself. What do you mean?"

"I don't know exactly what he does. It's like he draws lines on the street—or else he works *under* the street. Yeah, under the street, but there are lines connected with it someplace. He does something with lines. I don't get it."

"Neither do I," Robinson said as he shook his head. "Anything else?"

"It's going to happen next in Redwood City," she told him. "You better start doubling up in Redwood City, because that's where you're going to catch him. He's thinking about Redwood City. He wants to rape someone there, but instead you'll get him."

On November 30, 1987, a cold Monday night, police caught George Anthony Sanchez—the man with the initial *S* that Sylvia had "seen." The 26-year-old San Jose city sewer repairman was breaking into a Redwood City home where a woman was living alone. A search of Sanchez's home and vehicle revealed possessions belonging to victims of the ski-mask rapist, as well as a second ski mask similar to the one he was wearing.

One hundred and one felony charges were filed against the man, who is currently serving a lifetime sentence.

Although Sylvia feels an obligation to use her psychic gifts to assist the police whenever possible and has frequently volunteered her services to them without charge, she is well aware of the risks involved. For this reason, she tries whenever possible to maintain a low profile.

Francine, who frequently assumes a protective mantle, has suggested that Sylvia begin each day with a prayer:

> *Father/Mother God, I ask that the white light of the Holy Spirit surround and protect me this day and every day. I ask that it cleanse and purify my soul. I release to the light now any negativity as so much dark smoke to be absorbed by the white light, causing no one harm. Let nothing but love and positive energy pass into or out of this protective bubble.*

Sylvia had difficulty truly feeling this prayer until she remembered Glinda the Good Witch from *The Wizard of Oz*, who always appeared within a clear bubble. With that image in mind, it was easy for her to envision a similar shield around herself and so evoke the white light. Now Sylvia includes her family within the protective bubble as well.

Although much of Sylvia's time is spent assisting law-enforcement officers in the apprehension of criminals—she calls it being a psychic detective—she much prefers locating missing persons. A frequent function here is "simply" a matter of providing much-needed solace to distraught loved ones.

One day, Mary Ellen Stewart of San Jose contacted the medium. Frantically, she described the details of her daughter Marion's disappearance. "Is she all right? Where is she? Will she ever come back?"

"Yes," Sylvia reassured her. "I see her—I see her clearly. She left of her own volition, and she'll come back when she's ready. She'll come back in March."

On March 29, 1983, Mary Ellen Stewart called again, her voice choked with emotion. "You were right," she informed Sylvia. "Marion came home this morning."

Sometimes Sylvia is able to provide tangible information that facilitates the search. In 1987, Maria Elena Ulery called about her missing daughter. "She's 15, she has reddish-blonde hair, braces on her teeth—"

"Sure, sure, I see her," Sylvia interrupted. "She's with two friends—a blonde girl, I think her name's Kathy, and Kathy's boyfriend. The boy has dark hair and blue eyes. Kathy's parents don't want her to see him. Do you know who I'm talking about—that small blonde girl, Kathy?"

"Yes! Yes, I do," Ulery gasped.

"Talk to her parents; they know something that will help you," Sylvia advised.

A short time later, the medium received a note from the much-relieved mother: "Thanks very much for your help at the very moment I needed it so much. What you told me was right. You helped me through the most terrifying moments of my life. My daughter is back, and I hope I can find a way to guide and help her."

Sometimes the police use information received by Sylvia to recover a missing child. One such episode involved Sarah Jane Dalitz, who'd been missing for two years despite repeated efforts of law-enforcement officers to locate her. The grieving mother despaired of ever seeing her child again until Sylvia told her: "Sarah Jane was kidnapped by a man who seems very fond of her."

"Can you see him?" the detective asked. He'd been reluctant to accompany Dalitz to Sylvia's office, but now was suddenly eager. "Describe him—what does he look like?"

"Yes…he's short and stocky with a lot of sandy hair," Sylvia replied.

"Why, that's my ex-husband!" Dalitz responded, fairly shrieking.

"You never thought he might be the one?" the detective asked.

"No, I really didn't think he cared that much…it's a relief to know that Sarah Jane's safe, but I want her back. Imagine him putting me through all this!"

"Do you know where he is?"

"No," Dalitz said, shaking her head, "I've no idea. It's been so long since I heard anything from him."

A map began to appear before Sylvia's mind's eye. "She's in the Northwest." A state began to stand out, and finally, a city. "It's Seattle," she announced. "Seattle, Washington."

Dalitz looked blank. "So far as I know, there's absolutely no connection to my husband. He's never worked there, he's got no family there, no friends."

"Why not give it a try?" The detective shrugged. "We've tried everything else. Let's give it a shot."

Two days later, the two flew to Seattle. Within a week, Sylvia received a call. "You were absolutely right," the happy mother reported.

"She was in Seattle living with her father, but now she's home with me."

Not all of Sylvia's psychic searches have such happy endings. It is always difficult for a medium to report tragedy to a hopeful loved one, but at least there is the awareness that the waiting, the uncertainty, is at last at an end. One such case received nationwide coverage.

In the late spring of 1982, Milton Tromanhauser went off into the wilderness to meditate. The 53-year-old Martinez, California, building contractor was a deeply religious man. He had traveled extensively in India and the Middle East and could quote the Bible in depth. Tromanhauser had fasted in isolated areas many times, believing that this enhanced his meditations and furnished him with insights into the problems plaguing mankind. Each year the mystic made a pilgrimage. That summer, Tromanhauser's goal was to fast for 40 days and 40 nights. No one knew his destination.

The pilgrimage had begun May 10, 1982. When 40 days had passed, Terri Ball, a close friend of Tromanhauser's, became alarmed. She first called the East Bay Regional Parks ranger who referred her to the Contra Costa County Sheriff's Department, who sent her to the East Bay Regional Parks security division, who added to her growing frustration by suggesting that she again talk to the Sheriff's Department. This time the Sheriff's Department sent her to the Martinez Police Department. By now she was desperate.

"Perhaps someone would pay attention to me if I could tell them exactly where to look," she appealed to Sylvia. "Part of the problem is that he never told me where he was going. Last year he climbed Mount Tamalpais in Marin County. Do you suppose—"

"No," Sylvia stopped her. "Not Marin, he went to the east—Contra Costa County. The place where he is—it's called devil something—devil—Devil Mountain?"

"You mean Mount Diablo?"

"Yes, that's it," Sylvia exclaimed, then hesitated. "I'm sorry to have to tell you this, but he's dead. He's been gone for some time. You'll find his body in the water."

When the Contra Costa Sheriff's Department scoffed at the idea of a psychic sighting and refused to follow up on this lead, Terri Ball enlisted the aid of two ranchers, who went into the wilderness area on horseback. Within three hours, they'd found Tromanhauser's body floating in a small spring on the slopes of Mount Diablo.

Terri Ball's agonizing vigil had come to an end.

Although Sylvia does charge for psychic readings and hypnotic regressions, she refuses to take any payment for her police work or for her efforts to locate missing persons, believing that it is her obligation as a psychic to help those in need. "How can I possibly make money from the grief of others?" she asks.

In another volunteer project, Francine provided the information for one of the medium's most unique assignments. William Yabroff, a psychologist and associate professor at University of Santa Clara, approached Sylvia with this challenge. One of his graduate students was working on a project involving suicide victims.

All the student knew about the ten people involved was what she had read in the papers, and the details were very sketchy. A man might have shot himself, but where? In the head, in the chest? A woman might have died of an overdose, but what was the drug used? The purpose of the study was to find out more. What were the motives behind the act, and exactly how did the death occur?

So Yabroff brought his student to Sylvia's office at the Nirvana Foundation. Sylvia's husband, Dal, placed her in a deep trance. Very slowly, gradually, they began to feel another presence and, of course, it was Francine.

When the spirit guide indicated her readiness, only the ten names were submitted to her one by one. Sylvia, Yabroff, and the student knew only that the names belonged to suicide victims, but they had no other information. This lack of knowledge on their part was intentional and important. It eliminated the possibility of mind reading.

As each name was provided, Francine unhesitatingly described in detail the circumstances of the case. Not only was she able to say exactly when and where the deaths occurred, but she also pinpointed the motivation and its evolution and the exact method used, including, in one instance, a complex drug compound.

Then shortly before the trance ended, Francine spoke directly to the young graduate student. "George is here with me on the Other Side," the spirit guide informed her. "He's very anxious that you know that his death was an accident. His gun discharged by mistake. There was absolutely nothing that you could have done to help him."

The young student gasped in astonishment. There were tears in her eyes when she and Yabroff left. Yabroff later described their departure to Sylvia. "What was that all about?" he'd asked as they drove back to the university.

"I suppose it's the whole reason that I became involved in the suicide study," the student told him. "I'd been a volunteer at a crisis center. One night a man named George called and told me he was going to commit suicide. He said he had a gun in his hand. I talked to him for a long time, and I thought I had him talked out of it. Then suddenly there was this noise—it was horrible. I knew that he'd shot himself. I've thought so many times that it was my fault, if I'd been better—if someone else had talked to him—perhaps it wouldn't have happened, he wouldn't have done it. I've felt so guilty—"

It was a very happy young woman who was able to verify Francine's descriptions with the San Jose District Attorney's office. Francine had been entirely correct about the time, place, and motivation for each of the deaths. Nine of the ten described were correct down to every detail. In the case of the tenth, Francine had said that the man had shot himself in the head, when in reality it had been the chest.

In stress situations, those involving unusual demands, Sylvia often retreats to her own "temple of quiet," a special meditation technique, an ultimate refuge. She regards it as being of particular value where missing persons are concerned.

The Temple of Quiet

Begin by calling on your spirit guide and entreating him or her to take you to the temple. As you approach, you will see a short flight of stairs before you. Climb those stairs, then enter the eminence of the temple.

The floor at first looks like marble blocks, but as you advance toward the center of the room, you will see that each block emits a beam of light that centers on you. Each is quite lovely. Some are pink, others mauve, blue, and green.

When you reach the center of the room, ask that your dilemma be resolved. As you phrase your request, an octagonal crystal set in the wall before you will emit a beam of light into your third eye. As this occurs, the circumstances of the problem will be reenacted before your eyes, and all available options will be revealed to you.

You can enter the temple with any kind of problem—a lost or endangered loved one, job conflicts, tests, finances, personal relationships. You can program the resolution of the problem any way you please, but first view all the options.

For example, suppose you lose a job. What is the next option? What about a better job, or possibly an opportunity to change careers? Ask that a variety of options be played out before your third eye like a movie scenario. Then select the resolution that feels best to you.

When dealing with a stressful situation, you may want to say, "What is the worst thing that can happen?" You may be surprised that the "worst" is really not so terrible, and even that possibility can be reprogrammed to something better.

Remember, you can always reconstruct characters and situations in a manner that will contribute to your evolvement. Make certain, though, that you consider the evolvement factor in your planning. Remember that we are all interconnected, and each of us has a right to determine in accordance with our free will. Each person is his or her own chairman!

CHAPTER THIRTEEN

Novus Spiritus:
The Tenets of Novus Spiritus

On April 12, 1986, Sylvia looked out over the capacity crowd at the Flint Center in Cupertino, California. It was question-and-answer time.

A small gray-haired woman called out, "Will my marriage stay together?"

"Bite the bullet. Hang in there," Sylvia advised her. "September will be the turning point. Be patient just a little longer. It will be worth it in the long run."

A younger blonde woman rose from the audience. "My husband's going into business—" she began. But Sylvia stopped her. "Are there two other people involved—a man and wife?" When the woman nodded excitedly, Sylvia was emphatic. "No, no—don't do it! Don't let him do it!"

A small dark-haired woman in her late 20s waved her arm eagerly. When Sylvia nodded at her, she was suddenly reluctant. "Yes, yes—go ahead," Sylvia urged, "you can ask me anything."

A faint blush tinged the woman's cheeks as she faltered. "My—my boyfriend—he and I have a son. Do you think—will we ever—"

"Get married?"

The woman nodded vigorously, then broke into a broad smile as Sylvia continued. "Yes, you will, and I think you'd better hurry up about it because there's a daughter on the way."

"You mean I'm pregnant now?"

"If not now, then in the next ten minutes," Sylvia said over the laughter of the audience. "*Really*, I'm only half-kidding. You better get on with the marriage soon. It's a little nicer that way, better for the kids, easier for them later on."

"What about you, Sylvia?" a man seated far in the back of the auditorium called out. "What's coming up for you?"

The medium's reply was characteristically matter-of-fact. Looking out over a sea of more than 2,000 faces, she announced, "On the way over here, I decided to start a new religion."

And she did.

At that moment, Sylvia embarked upon the most important chapter of her life to date. The symbiotic result of her devotion to God and her prophetic gift is Novus Spiritus, or "new spirit." The religious organization was founded to serve individuals who find no reasonable explanation for life, who seek another dimension to their faith, or who are confused or put off by traditional religion.

Dal was furious. "What are you doing to me? We can't start a church. Things are going great now. Why are you doing this? I don't have the time to run a church and Nirvana both."

"How dare you!" replied Sylvia. "All you do each day is play video games in your office. You even hired people to do the work you should be doing. And since I pay all the bills, it really is none of your concern."

"Fine. I'm sorry that I'm not psychic so I can make some money."

"Get off your pity-party-for-one. You chose to quit your job to help me, but when will I get any help out of you? My 75-year-old father works harder than you.

"Besides, Dal," Sylvia continued, "I was very remiss in waiting so long to start the church. Some 15 years ago I laid out its basic structure, then Larry did the incorporation, and it was all ready to go. But you said no, and I am very mad at myself for letting you win. Not this time—you are not going to block me again!"

Novus Spiritus differs from Western theology in three major areas. First of all, it represents the return to the belief in reincarnation, which was an integral part of Christianity prior to its drastic restructuring under Emperor Constantine at the Council of Nicaea in the fourth century.

Second, Sylvia's church is unique in that it is the first religion in more than 2,500 years to embrace the female, as well as the male, aspect of the deity. The Mother Goddess is alive and well in Novus Spiritus. She is co-equal with the male—that is, she is the emotional dimension as opposed to the pure intellect of the male principal. Combined, the two comprise the Godhead.

Finally, and perhaps most important, the new religion provides a forum for the expression of the love and joy that is God without fear, guilt, or punishment. Through her church, Sylvia hopes to give the world a means of understanding the always-benign God of life and human existence.

"For the record, God is blameless," she reminds her congregation. "She/He is not prone to the human traits of vengeance, hate, or just plain crankiness. He/She is constant, pure, a loving intellect. God does not sit around all day, then suddenly invoke damnation on a helpless person. *Never*.

"There is no room in Her/His perfect being for such nonsense. Inherent in the perfection of the deity is a steady love for His/Her creations, a never-wavering compassion, and a constant companion along the way. Whatever you experience, God, too, has felt it, right by your side. For within you lies a spark of the Divine. God is simple; people are complex."

It is within this complexity that evil arises. "Evil is *not*," Sylvia stresses, "a creation of God. From simple adversity, evil has developed into the concept of the devil, complete with horns and a tail—a mythological being in direct competition with God. In reality, evil is merely a logical opposite to the concept of good.

"Since every person has an innate knowledge of good, it's inevitable that each must also possess an awareness of its direct opposite. All through our lives we are constantly choosing between the two modes of expression. The parable of Satan tempting Eve—*Eve* means 'life' in Hebrew—to partake of knowledge closely parallels the Novus Spiritus interpretation. Only by living and facing adversity can one perfect one's soul—that is, know the difference between good and evil."

"Why a church, Sylvia? Aren't you busy enough already?" many asked in the early days of Novus Spiritus. The answer was yes, of course, she was and is. Sylvia does between 15 and 20 readings a day and may receive more than a thousand letters and calls within a week. Additionally, she participates in numerous research projects, missing-persons searches, and volunteer work with the police department. She also teaches ongoing classes in hypnosis, counseling, and psychic development.

The Nirvana Foundation now has more than 25,000 members, and a staff of 14 assists Sylvia. A very significant member of the team is Sylvia's younger son, Chris, who has inherited her psychic gift and has been doing readings on a full-time basis at the foundation since 1983.

Novus Spiritus grew out of a need. "I can't find what I'm looking for in any church," clients complained to Sylvia again and again. "I was raised on the Sylvia Browne philosophy. It's what I believe," a young woman said one evening at a foundation meeting. Then she asked the question that set everyone to thinking: "Shouldn't it be accessible to more people?"

"It's not *my* philosophy—at least not originally," Sylvia was quick to remind her. "I'm only the channel. What I've shared with you over the years is Francine's wisdom, the knowledge of the Other Side." That night, Sylvia was awake a long time. Since 1974, she had received thousands of pages of information culled from hundreds of deep hypnotic trances. These transcripts, catalogued and cross-referenced by members of the Nirvana Foundation, had formed a tremendous knowledge base not available from any other source. Wasn't it her obligation to share these unique spiritual insights with anyone who might desire them?

The responsibility seemed enormous. Just being a medium was often a burden. People imagined that she was perfect. As the founder of a new religion, her followers would expect a saint.

"You are always yourself, Sylvia," Francine reminded her. "No one grows by leaning on someone else, yet everybody seems to be seeking a guru to direct them. You are very honest about your frailties to everyone who cares to listen—on the radio, on television, and from the lecture platform. How can anyone ever do an exposé of you? You've already exposed yourself!"

It was all quite true, Sylvia realized. She was forever pounding away at the fact that she, like everyone else, had needs and emotions of her own to deal with. She was *very* human. All her life she had been required to follow her blueprint from day to day, just like everyone else. The insights she received from Francine were always for the enlightenment of others, not herself.

It had finally become quite clear to Sylvia that the new religion was the realization of her long-term humanitarian dream, the enactment of her karmic theme. There was no question about it. After having absorbed so much of Francine's otherworldly perspective, it was obvious to her that traditional religions no longer addressed the needs of today's world. The insight was so startlingly clear that she wondered why she hadn't realized it earlier. Hers was a clear call to refine and promulgate the wisdom that she'd received from Francine. Perhaps a degree of her own perfection and refinement might come from dealing with the criticism she would undoubtedly encounter for following this controversial path.

The basic tenets of the new faith were revealed by Francine. First, of course, was the practical task of forming the credo itself. Soon Sylvia realized that she could do this coincidentally with the beginning of her ministry. "Our culture cannot live by rules set down 2,000 years ago," she pointed out at her first service, or "celebration." Sylvia's message reflected her confidence.

"The fact is that human intellect grows, and the capacity for learning grows with it. We need an intellectual basis for God. Novus provides that basis. Does it really matter whether you wear jewelry? Does it really matter if you practice birth control? Does it really make any difference whether you go to church every Sunday? Is dancing really an instrument of the devil? Come on, *think!* Do such restrictions matter one iota in the grand scheme of life or, for that matter, in the evolvement of your soul? Novus Spiritus thinks they don't. Two thousand years ago, Our Lord said: 'Love your neighbor as yourself.' We all got the neighbor part. We don't always do it, but everyone agrees we *ought* to. The self part we ignore because we equate *self* with *selfishness.* It doesn't mean that at all. Loving ourselves means nothing more than the essential awareness of the God Center within ourselves and of our interconnectedness with God and with each other."

What makes Sylvia's church truly unique is the total absence of fear or guilt, for Sylvia—and Francine—believe guilt to be counter to both life and to a living, breathing religion. Novus Spiritus is a practical, portable philosophy, a viable belief system applicable to all the trials and the triumphs of everyday life, a religion that can accompany one anywhere in the world. Although it's reassuring to enjoy the camaraderie of church services and to respond to the inspiration of the sermons, one does not, according to the tenets of Novus Spiritus, have to go to church to find salvation. Salvation exists when that fruition is reached entirely within one's own heart.

The way of all peace is to scale the mountain of self. Loving others makes the climb down easier. We see all things darkly until love lights the lamps of our soul.

Those words form the first tenet of Novus Spiritus. Within them lies the basic philosophy of the church. Life is discovery—a long, long journey of discovery, wherein everyone must meet and love themselves, overcome individual fears, and learn the great truth about loving. It is a process of perfecting the innate, God-given beauty of the soul.

The journey for most takes numerous lifetimes to achieve. Novus Spiritus embraces reincarnation. "How could it be otherwise?" Sylvia asks. "Perfecting one's soul is the most important task that each of us ever performs. It is more than a task; it is the continuing life process. Consider how most of us learn. Isn't it almost always by trial and error? We do a new task repeatedly until we do it correctly—even the most trivial tasks require repetition. Has anyone ever tied their shoes on the first try?

"But then are we to assume that God has no patience with us? Will She/He be upset if we are not perfect after merely one life? Would His/Her anger condemn us to roast in hell because tying our shoes took a whole month to learn? We think not. Reincarnation is the most reasonable concept to explain the inequities of life in the light of an all-loving God. The alternative—a God of hate—is simply not tenable."

Every person, indeed every sentient being, can be likened to a newspaper reporter working for God, the editor. The whole reason for life is to witness for God all of Her/His knowledge—this, indeed, *is* life. Along life's journey we must learn the meaning of being good and, in so doing, perfect our souls.

The concept of perfection is very much a part of the Novus Spiritus creed, as is the knowledge that each of us is obligated to perfect our souls. No one is expected to reach the ultimate perfection of God. The idea is for all people to reach the level of perfection that they have chosen, with which they will be content through all eternity.

Francine has used the analogy of the thimble and the bucket to illustrate this point:

> A thimble and a bucket both stand empty. Each must realize its full potential. The bucket begins its journey through life. As the waters of experience are added, the bucket slowly fills. The little thimble then starts its journey. In a short time, the thimble has filled itself and is content. Yet the bucket has much more work to do until it, too, stands full. Now which one is fullest?

The answer, Francine reminds us, is neither. Both are full to the brim, and that is sufficient. The fact that the bucket contains more is not important. The goal is to seek and find a level of perfection that exactly fits *you*. Upon reaching that level, you are full—as perfect as you can become.

Naturally, we must give full credit to the bucket. Obviously, it has learned a great deal—which is very important to the bucket. In the course of its labors, the bucket enjoyed a richer understanding of many things. More insight, more beauty, and more knowledge are available to the bucket. Yet this does not mean the thimble is unfulfilled or unhappy. Indeed, the thimble cannot even conceive of those things that the bucket most treasures. The thimble is completely happy with its own level of perfection and cannot be happier. It's really a matter of capacity.

Much of the church's sentiment can be found in this communion prayer:

> *Dear Mother and Father God:*
>
> *We ask you to witness this communion, which is a symbol of finding our own God-centeredness and Christ-consciousness.*
>
> *In doing this action of taking bread and wine, we are impressing on our higher consciousness that we are dedicating our lives to God's will.*
>
> *The symbol of this communion for us through Novus Spiritus means we wish to be born into the new spirit of true spirituality and let go of all guilt and karmas of our past lives and start fresh and new. From this time forward, we will be on track fulfilling our themes and walking with the blessed aura of God's Light.*
>
> *We do this as an activation of our will to symbolize to ourselves and the world that we walk in grace, free of all negativity.*
>
> *We ask this in Your name.*
>
> *Amen.*

Services are warm and intimate. There are simple prayers and hymns. Sermons are practical and to the point, invariably dealing with issues of personal and national concern, such as battered wives, AIDS, or teenage pregnancy. An integral part of the service is the meditation, during which the congregation sits quietly with palms upturned while Sylvia or one of her ministers points the way toward self-healing, goal achievement, or other desired paths.

Another important part of the service is the healing that is given to all who seek it. Those desiring healings may also ask to have their names added to the prayer list. A group meets each Wednesday evening at the church to pray and send healing energy to those on the list.

Sylvia's files are jammed with letters from men, women, and children who have been helped in this way. An example is Eleanor Moore of San Jose. Moore had been diagnosed by her gynecologist as having an ulcer in her urethra. She was referred to a urologist, who informed her that an operation was necessary, and a date for the surgery was set. In the meantime, Moore, although in great pain, attended a Novus Spiritus service and requested a healing. Almost immediately she felt better. Later in the week, she called the church and asked for a remote healing from the prayer group.

A few days later, she returned to her doctor for her scheduled examination. "I *knew* I was healed," she said later, "but I still went through the motions. My doctor confirmed my feelings but insisted that I be examined again by the urologist. I agreed, and once again the two doctors agreed, but this time their joint decision was 'No operation.' I didn't need one; I was completely recovered."

In addition to holding weekly services and prayer meetings, Novus Spiritus ministers maintain a 24-hour crisis line; offer spiritual counseling, hypnotherapy, and meditation classes; and provide convalescent-home visits and carpooling services for the elderly and the handicapped. Plans are now under way for an AIDS hospice to be funded by Novus Spiritus.

Sylvia's very special partnership with Francine continues to unfold from day to day. Novus Spiritus is in every sense a living religion where the word of God is often revealed on a daily basis. As the ability to comprehend grows; new and deeper truths are manifested. For years, Francine has been saying, "If you think of a question, the answer will be found."

Sylvia's challenge is to provide those answers.

The 21 tenets of Novus Spiritus—along with a complete description of each one—are included in *If You Could See What I See*, which immediately follows this book.

If You Could
See What I See

I

*The way of all peace is to scale the mountain of self.
Loving others makes the climb down easier. We see all
things darkly until love lights the lamp of our soul.*

II

Whatever thou lovest, lovest thou.

III

*Do not give unto God any human pettiness such as
vengeance, wrath, or hate. Negativity is man's alone.*

IV

*Create your own heaven, not a hell.
You are a creator made from God.*

V

*Turn thy power outward, not inward,
for therein shines the light and the way.*

VI

*In faith be like the wind chimes: Hold steady
until faith, like the wind, moves you to joy.*

VII

*Know that each life is a path winding toward perfection.
It is the step after step that is hard, not the whole of the journey.*

VIII

*Be simple. Allow no man to judge you,
not even yourself, for you cannot judge God.*

IX

You are a light in a lonely, dark desert who enlightens many.

X

*Let no one convince you that you are less than a God.
Do not let fear imprison your spiritual growth.*

XI

*Do not allow the unfounded belief in demons
to block your communion with God.*

XII
*The body is a living temple unto God,
wherein we worship the spark of the Divine.*

XIII
*God does not create the adversities in life.
By your own choice they exist to aid in your perfection.*

XIV
*Karma is nothing more than honing the wheel of evolvement.
It is not retribution, but merely a balancing of experiences.*

XV
*God allows each person the opportunity for perfection, whether you
need one life or a hundred lives to reach your level of perfection.*

XVI
*Devote your life, your soul, your very existence, to the
service of God. For only there will you find meaning in life.*

XVII
War is profane; defense is compulsory.

XVIII
*Death is the act of returning Home; it should be done with grace
and dignity. You may preserve that dignity by refusing prolonged
use of artificial life-support systems. Let God's will be done.*

XIX
*We believe in a Mother God, Who is
co-Creator with our all-loving Father God.*

XX
*We believe that our Lord was crucified, but did not die
on the cross. Instead, he went on to live his life in France
with his mother and Mary Magdalene, his wife.*

XXI
*We Gnostics kept the knowledge hidden that Christ's lineage
exists even today, and the truth long buried is open to research.*

Dear God,

As the years pass like the dead leaves in autumn, let me never lose sight of You. Let me always walk with my hand in Yours, and when human beings may fail me and all hope seems to die, let me feel You walking beside me.

I have a great journey ahead of me, of which I am master. If it lasts for only a day or stretches throughout many years, keep me pure of heart and true to the principles I hold so high. Let me always be patient with those around me. Let me see life at its fullest and yet smile bravely at death. Let me see and appreciate the beauty of Your creations and the extent of Your power. Only when I have done these things will I be able to look to heaven and know "I have lived."

Through the years when my dreams fall around me, I will know that dreams should not only be made up of hope that stretches like a translucent web over reality, but built out of the hope that burns into the future and is left in our lighthouse of memories.

Sylvia Shoemaker (Browne)
Notation in my Bible . . . May 1954

INTRODUCTION

It's been almost 20 years since I wrote my first book, *Adventures of a Psychic*. As I look back, it seems like yesterday . . . and yet a lifetime away (like so many things). To recap just a bit, as most of you know I was born psychic, as my grandmother Ada Coil was, and her mother and her mother before her—and on it goes for approximately 300 years. My son Christopher Dufresne also has the gift and has taken up the family mantle; today he is an established psychic in his own right.

Throughout my life, especially since *Adventures of a Psychic* came out, my soul has been tried to the limit. Everyone thinks that because you're on television or are in the public eye, you're living a glamorous, wealthy life. Not true—I walk the same path you do. While my psychic ability isn't affected by "normalcy" (which I give God credit for), Sylvia Browne the woman still goes through hurt, joy, pain, worry over family and friends, divorce, bills, cars breaking down, a garage flooding, and on and on it goes. . . .

I've spent many a sleepless night worrying about people I can't get to fast enough. I pray that I'm doing God's work every day. I get nervous before I go onstage to do a lecture or workshop . . . again praying that I'm able to help others and do God's work. I try to put up with the mean-spirited detractors (not skeptics—those are normal), but just to be a target for someone's hateful, unfounded untruths hurts. I find as I get older, however, that I pay less attention to it. I never really got involved in negative publicity, but I worry about the younger psychics coming up who aren't as thick-skinned as I am. I keep telling them that if we're doing the best we can for God, no one can take anything away from us.

What keeps me going are the 21 tenets you'll find in this book.

When I've gone back to the words contained herein, I've gained such strength. At times they've seemed like a map for life, while other times they're almost a prayer or a meditation. In this work, not only will I explore each one in depth, but I'll also incorporate stories from my own life that illustrate them. When we look at the tenets from different angles, we can see that they take in *all* of life, including what bedevils us or makes us happy on our spiritual quest.

Discovering the Tenets

These 21 principles came directly from my spirit guide Francine. For those of you who don't know, Francine has been with me my entire life. I first "heard" her at the age of seven, for I'm not only a trance medium and clairvoyant, but I'm also *clairaudient,* which means that I hear my spirit guide talk to me. Although I hear her, I can't take listening to her for very long because her voice comes into my right ear and sounds like a bad Alvin and the Chipmunks record. I therefore prefer to go into trance and have Francine speak through me and give me information. The tenets came from her while I was in such a state, and they were brought back from the ancient Gnostic texts. Even before the Dead Sea Scrolls and the Nag Hammadi codices were made public, Francine had already related what mirrors many of the passages of Thomas and James, which are part of the Nag Hammadi library.

These tenets have been a part of the Sylvia Browne Corporation for about 30 years—even before the Society of Novus Spiritus was ever established as an accredited church and religious organization by the state of California. They were our rules to live by. Now, while these 21 principles might seem very simplistic, when you go deeper into them you'll discover that they're far more spiritual, and in many ways carry a deeper meaning, than they may seem to be on the surface. Maybe if you could see what I see or hear what I hear doing 15 to 20 readings a day, you'd know that their depth goes far beyond what the words seem to hold. It's almost like the Mona Lisa's enigmatic smile: What does it mean? What secret is she keeping from us? What does she know that we don't?

Here I'm going to do something I've never done before: I'll go through the tenets one by one and show you how they relate to me and my journey. Some of you may respond to what I discuss, while others may feel that it's too far out there for you. Just think of what I'm about to share with you as a chronicle of a life—that is, don't simply look at it as a *psychic* life. Of course that's part of it, but so much of these principles refer to all of our lives in one form or another.

In the tenets of our Society, and the stories that accompany them, you'll see your existence (and that of your loved ones) reflected; you'll also note how we struggle to get happiness out of life and not succumb to that dark place of futility or depression. This book is not a course, but rather a very direct commentary on things we don't understand. Maybe I can shine a light on it so that it's not so confusing.

Gnostics and Novus Spiritus

You'll see that this book is an autobiography in a sense, but it almost has to be to show you how I came upon these tenets, which are the cornerstone of our church's beliefs. I started (or, should I say, "attempted to start") a Society in 1973, but it became a nonprofit foundation for research of the paranormal. As life so often turns in wondrous ways, we did investigate everything from astral projection to past lives, psychic phenomena, hauntings, poltergeist activities—

you name it—and all the while, a strong survival of the soul and spirituality was coming out . . . not just in droplets, but floods of knowledge of the afterlife, including our purpose and our learning for God. My staff and I kept copious notes and statistics—in fact, our archives are filled with affidavits too numerous to mention and too similar to disregard.

Take, for instance, the afterlife. How could so many people, when finding themselves on the Other Side through various means (including near-death experiences, astral trips, dreams, and past-life regressions), find the same topography, buildings, research, services, and even populace searching for the God we know and love? These were everyday people from different countries, creeds, religions, and backgrounds who had been immersed in widely varying schools of thought.

One of the things I'm grateful for is that today, the Society of Novus Spiritus is thriving, with hundreds of study groups around the world. For years the Gnostic movement has tried to form a religious organization, whether it was the Cathars, the Knights Templar, or the Essenes, and all were either wiped out by the Catholic Church and reigning powers, or they went underground. A Gnostic is one who searches for truth constantly with the grace of an all-loving and all-knowing God, and uses spirituality and love as weapons against negativity. A Gnostic also holds truth in the highest esteem, for only with truth can you find true spirituality and be as one with God.

The remnants of the movement today basically consist of the Freemasons and Rosicrucians, which are more fraternal and philanthropic organizations than religious ones. I'm positive that there are some Gnostic organizations out there, but they're basically either kept private and secret or they've gone totally underground. You'll find a few of them on the Internet, but they don't have any religious services to speak of and are mostly information sites.

The Gnostic movement is very ancient and wasn't just confined to Christianity, as most people think. In actual fact, it existed before the time of Christ, but was mostly obliterated by the 5th century after the Roman emperor Theodosius I officially recognized only one branch of Catholicism. Now I'm not trying to single out the Catholics as the only persecutors of the Gnostics, but their history isn't exactly bloodless or lily white. The Romans and the Sanhedrin also did their share of persecution in trying to put down what they called "rabble-rousing groups" that ran around like Jesus did and taught and followed the philosophy of an all-loving God. Gnostics have been burned, tortured, and driven out, whether it was in France or Jerusalem or other parts of the world. They were either killed and their possessions taken, or they went underground and met secretly for fear of reprisal from the religious politics of the Church or the establishment at that time.

The Gnostics have risen up at least four times and were put to death, branded as heretics, and just got tired of the embattlement of the fear-based churches, so they disbanded publicly . . . only to quietly keep their beliefs buried in their hearts and secret societies. They had their various schools of thought and theology (as most religions do) brought forth by different scholars, prophets, or leaders. Perhaps the most famous was Valentinus, who founded a Gnostic movement in the 2nd century A.D. that spread throughout the Middle East, North Africa, and Europe. The Valentinian school existed for more than 600 years and still has influence today despite constant persecution from the Church.

As the Gnostic movement was waning due to persecution, another movement arose that was founded by the inspirational writings of the prophet Mani. The Manichaean movement spread not only to Europe, but to Central Asia and China as well, and it still exists in small pockets today. Both of these movements incorporated reincarnation in their philosophy and advocated it strongly, and both had numerous writings attributed to them of an apocryphal nature. Several of these Gnostic movements can be studied at **www.gnosis.org**, with many related links to other

Websites that also provide much insight into Gnosticism.

Gnostics are not a threat to anyone except those who want occult control. We accept everyone; and profess religious tolerance and an all-loving God Who gets rid of the fear, guilt, and karma that has been laid on the shoulders of humankind (which both kept people in line *and* gained more members for various religions).

* * *

I do want to pause here to clear up some information about Gnosticism and our church. Not only has Gnosticism been around for thousands of years, with philosophers such as Plato espousing it, but there are many schools or teachers out there in the world today. Not all of Gnosticism is Christian based, and even Christian Gnosticism has different sects and beliefs. There are many aspects of Gnosticism that Novus Spiritus doesn't practice or believe in, but we *have* tried to form a religion that has its basis in Gnosticism and one that especially follows the teachings of Christ and the dualism of our Creators (that is, Mother and Father God).

At the Society of Novus Spiritus, we don't purport to know every truth. Since the whole concept of Gnosis essentially means to "seek truth," we're constantly in flux as we do so. That's why we basically have no church-made dogma or rules other than the "golden rule"—that is, we try to help others by doing good works with love—and the belief in our Lord (Jesus) and the duality of God. Our 21 tenets reflect what we believe, and they're added to as truth becomes apparent.

We accept all, regardless of their beliefs, race, ethnic background, gender, and so forth. No one is turned away, especially those who are seeking truth, enlightenment, or a loving God. We have services, but we just talk about God's love and light and the Christ Consciousness; we also do meditations and pray for the sick. After a service, we do healings wherein we have people stand up and tell the congregation what they need, and we pray for them. We have a prayer line that goes 24/7. We have literally hundreds of study groups where we meet in someone's home and discuss the tenets, as people did many years ago—we've tried to reproduce how it was in the time of Christ. We also do research, give solace to each other, and help the sick and the elderly. It's a moving, hands-on, living spirituality that's promoted by all.

So the Society of Novus Spiritus, which is going into its 19th year, has spread across the United States and other countries in hundreds of study groups. We used to meet in our offices in Campbell, California, but our congregation grew to be too big. Now we have four so-called churches (or I should say "meeting places"), and we're still growing.

Who Am I to Start a Church?

I won't ever lie to you, but to form Novus Spiritus was very frightening to me. This is where I had to put my silly ego aside. For perhaps a week I walked around muttering to Francine, "It's bad enough to put yourself out there as a psychic, but now we want to start a church!"

She replied, "Do you know how many religions were started from a vision or a revelation? Quakers, Mormons, even Moses and his burning bush."

This made me feel better, especially when I looked at Buddha and his enlightenment or Mohammed and his message. Now please understand that I'm not implying I'm comparable to these messengers, but there is truth in revelation and spiritual communication. This truth isn't mine alone, but it has logically sprung from what I've researched for more than 50 years, compounded with the considerable amount of research from so many thousands that I've read for, as well as the work of our church's ministers and others from around the world.

Anyway, the Society of Novus Spiritus was founded and accredited, and the tenets that had sat there gathering dust began to take hold and form the basis for our beliefs. They seem to echo the Beatitudes from the Sermon on the Mount, the Eightfold Path of Buddhism, and the gentle portions of text from the Koran—and they serve to bring into focus the simplicity of what every one of them tried to say. The tenets aren't new (they're as old as time), but they have been condensed. The ministers and I often say, "After we've gone to the Other Side, we hope that humankind doesn't corrupt the simplicity that's so real and tangible, which carries such a gut-level truth."

It's interesting to note that since my books have come out, the e-mails and letters have poured in, and each in their own way has said, "This says what I've felt forever," "I always believed, but was afraid to say it for fear that people would think I was different or crazy," or "I know this is right, not only in what my heart tells me, but my intellect confirms it."

So each of the tenets was formed out of our Gnostic philosophy, and the only problem we encountered was that when people thought about God, they tended to think in the singular sense of God the Father. Thus, we added a tenet to recognize the duality of God and to acknowledge the existence of God the *Mother*. Several of our tenets are also highly controversial to standard Christian belief, but by no means do they take away from the Divinity or teachings of Christ. Yes, they impugn the beliefs of the early Christian church in some areas that are still believed in today, but new information and research in the last few years is starting to show that these beliefs are false anyway.

I'm highly controversial as it stands, so why not just put all the truth out there for everyone to read and see . . . besides, where would the fun be if I didn't? So, having said that, I hope that you enjoy accompanying me on the very personal journey I'll be taking you on in these pages.

✳ ✳ ✳ ✳ ✳ ✳

TENET I

The way of all peace is to scale the mountain of self. Loving others makes the climb down easier. We see all things darkly until love lights the lamp of our soul.

My life started out being psychic, and maybe thanks to sheer ignorance, I went with it. God knows that it hasn't been an easy road, but I'd never change it. It's been rewarding, of course, but I've also experienced rejection and skepticism of the highest order. Yet when we write our chart (the life plan we plot out before we're even born) and have a goal for God and our own soul's perfection, we follow it the best way we can.

When I wrote *Adventures of a Psychic,* many individuals I mentioned in it were still alive, so I had to couch what my life had been like in somewhat vague terms. People are very smart, so when I wrote about my childhood, they read between the lines. . . . Now, however, so many of them are gone that I can go into greater depth about what my life was really like.

Shortly after my first book was written, I had to declare bankruptcy and was hit with an astronomical IRS bill. This was because my then-husband Dal, out of ignorance, not malice, opened up a gold mine recommended by an attorney. He forgot to fill out a securities form, so they came down on us like a ton of bricks. I'll never forget the judge saying, "It's unfortunate, Mrs. Browne, but you're the one making the money, so you'll have to pay. I'm very sorry."

Now in my experience (as probably in yours), when you fall in love there doesn't seem to be any mountain too high to climb. We can almost float up rather than climb because we're so euphoric and our endorphins are racing, not to mention our hormones. But when that goes south, the journey down is miserably hard—we feel foolish, battered, rejected, and bruised in our soul. We then look valiantly for someone to love, or who loves us, after the long journey of paranoia, suspicion, and hurt begins to dim. For some it (sadly) never does, and they spend their lives in the nightmare of what could have been. They don't understand that not everyone needs to be paired—and what if it doesn't work out if they *do* find someone else?

When I was a young girl, I truly dreamed of a house and children and a husband who loved and supported me. Well, when my chances came, I kept telling myself, *It's not right.* For example, I was engaged to Joe Behm, a wonderful guy who loved and wanted to make a home with me. He later did get married, have children, and support his wife. This dear man died just a few months ago, and one of the last conversations we had (yes, we kept track of each other over all those years) points out the differences of our charts and the "what could have been" scenarios.

I started out by asking him, "What if it had been the other way and I had agreed to marry you?"

Joe wisely replied, "No, Sylvia, it wouldn't have worked. The world was calling you so loudly that even I could hear it." But still, in the human part of our brain we wonder (chart or no chart), *What if?*

And that's how I felt when my marriage to Dal broke up. We divorced partly because of my anger resulting from trying to be so loyal and aboveboard, even as I let someone else foolishly jeopardize the church and foundation I'd built. I went from having not one smudge on my record to people running amuck with money I didn't have. But it was my fault, too, because I was so busy with lectures, ministers, and readings that I left the business end to someone who'd made a catastrophic and foolish mistake.

I felt that my life was over. My home and car were gone, and all my possessions had to be sold. I had no credit, so I had to try to pay for everything in cash. On top of that, I was taking care of my aging parents and my friends Linda and Larry. (Linda is a kindred spirit who's been with me almost 30 years, while Larry was a friend who was trying to help me out of the mess I was in.) My father had some money and helped me some, but since he'd worked all his life for what he had, I couldn't take his nest egg. Consequently, I had to raise enough money to get us all a place to live. The two apartments we wanted would cost $1,100 each, for a total of $2,200. I remember the day we had a huge garage sale . . . during which we made $2,300. I got my mom and dad an apartment; and Linda, Larry, and I got one adjacent to it.

Talk about your uphill climbs! The economy at that time in the late '80s was pretty bad, but I managed. I started to do 25 readings a day to keep my church, family, and staff going. I never missed a payroll. My son Chris, who was barely starting his psychic career, helped some, but it was just enough to keep him afloat because he'd recently gotten married. They say these things are cathartic, but the memories are still painful and debilitating. But wait . . . it gets better and then worse—which is the story of all our lives.

My parents were in their late 80s at the time, and they were failing. My mother's behavior, which was always a real nightmare, was becoming more erratic. My father (who was working with me) was also taking a turn for the worse. On top of that, my book *My Guide, Myself* (later to be known as *Adventures of a Psychic* and published by Hay House) had flopped because the publisher, New American Library, had been sold to Dutton, leaving my book to fall through the cracks. And *People Are Talking*, a local show in the San Francisco area—on which I often appeared and had been my main public-relations (PR) outlet—was suddenly canceled.

Larry, my friend since he was 19, tried to keep my spirits up, but it was hard. I have a tendency when things go wrong to pull in and away and regroup inside myself and go forward. Not because I resent help, but as you know, there are times when no one can help you but you. Every area I looked at seemed pretty hopeless, but as I've taught and do believe, you stay in the light and keep on going.

I started traveling to other states to set up "in person" readings, as my PR outlets were at a standstill. Then Steve Ober, an old producer friend of mine from *People Are Talking* who was now producing in Los Angeles, called and asked me to be on *AM Los Angeles* with host Steve Edwards. So I went . . . and watched as my numerous appearances caused my PR to pick up. Yet I was still grieving over the end of my marriage and the fact that my life was in financial ruin—plus, I was really feeling the strain of trying to keep my staff and Novus Spiritus afloat.

It was during this time (which I called "the dark period") that I happened to pick up the tenets, and at that moment, I began to see their surface *and* deeper meanings. "Dear God," I whispered, "this is truly the treasure map to keep us on track." It reminds me of a painting that used to hang in my grandmother's home, which depicted a woman standing against a rock on the ocean. Her hair was back, and she looked as if she was being battered by the weather. Her arms were thrown wide open, but again, like the Mona Lisa, there was that smile. This time, it seemed to convey, "Bring on the waves and the storms—I can stand it! I will embrace it and be strong!"

My grandmother used to say two things that I carry with me: "Within your weakness lies your strength sleeping" and

"Save your tears for when you really need them." Well, I was recently in the room of my 12-year-old granddaughter, Angelia, while she was doing her homework. I sat down on the bed and happened to glance over at a piece of paper that looked as if it had been torn from a diary. It said, "I must remember as Bagdah [that's her name for me] says, to save my tears for when I need them, but it was hard to lose my pet mouse." I didn't say a word, but my heart ached as all of us do when someone we love feels pain, yet I was also very proud that something I'd said hit home.

A friend of mine whom I'd first met and read for more than 20 years ago in Kenya (where she was a journalist) just called me. She's writing a book that starts out with a reading I'd given her many years ago, which she hadn't believed at the time. I'd told her that she was going to get divorced, move to California, and receive an award for her son. I truly didn't see his death—looking back, I should have been able to warn her, but then I also know that I wasn't supposed to. You see, the young man had to fulfill his destiny, and if I'd seen his death, it might have taken him off course. I always pick up things for a reason, and I don't always know that reason or why I don't get something—other than the fact that it might derail someone from their chart.

Anyway, my friend is now divorced and living in California. She also received a posthumous award for her son from the State Department—for he was a photographer killed in Bosnia. She managed to climb her own mountain, and now she's writing and helping other mothers who have lost children. And she's truly happy.

Everything passes and everything changes—what's bad today can turn on a dime tomorrow, and what's good can also turn bad—none of it lasts. If we're depressed (and some people do need pharmaceutical help due to chemical imbalances in the brain), we can alleviate it by loving outside of, and getting above, ourselves. All the lights will come on, especially the light of the soul.

I'm reminded of a family I just saw in Florida who wanted

a private session because of the death of a loved one. The mother asked me, "What do I do with the rest of my life?"

I said, "Well, you have your grandson, your daughter, your husband, and your friends; and maybe you can go out eventually and help other mothers who have lost children."

She visibly brightened and then hesitantly asked, "Is my son really happy?"

"He's happier than we are," I replied.

I know that type of advice isn't much consolation at times, but it sure is an absolute truth that those on the Other Side are better off than we are. After all, they've finished the journey of climbing this mountain—not only of self, but of adversity and negativity. Their lamp is lit, and they've gone to the Home we'll all go to one day.

How Can This Tenet Help You?

From a spiritual standpoint, the whole meaning of this first tenet points to climbing the mountain of your own ego, or the false self that can fool you and lure you into believing that you're more than you are. The mountain of ego isn't that difficult to climb if you begin to realize it only means the *essence* of you, or the sum total of who you are, including all the good and bad. Climbing this mountain is difficult until you come to the understanding that you're a spiritual being who came here to experience for God and yourself. When you get that, then it's just like being in physical love: You'll float down the mountain and realize that loving others really does light the lamp of our soul.

Now how did *I* climb the mountain of self? I don't have much false ego—not because I'm necessarily such a good person, but because I've always been so external. However, I did have a tough time with my ability. When it came to seeing and hearing things, I just wanted to turn it off at times. It isn't that I don't love my psychicness, but I certainly didn't want to be viewed as "crazy." (Strangely enough, when I was a schoolteacher, the priests, nuns, and even the kids just took it in stride that I was different, or it was just "Sylvia's thing.")

My psychic grandmother had told me many times that I came from a long line of psychics, but then I went to college and took abnormal psychology. I started to wonder if we were really a long line of genetically flawed people with an aberration of the mind. I very stubbornly stuck to this viewpoint until the day Francine asked me, "Have you ever had any motive to hurt anyone?"

"Of course not!" I answered angrily.

"Are you more right than wrong?" she countered.

"Well, yes," I replied. "I guess so."

"Have you made people feel better with the truth?"

"I suppose . . . ," I said.

Then she asked, "Sylvia, why don't you live with it and do it for God, and quit trying to scientifically put it in a box?" So not really having much choice, I did climb the mountain of myself and gave it all up to God. I also had encouragement from some people who just seemed to find me.

Even today before each lecture, TV appearance, book signing, or reading, I take a deep breath and ask God to keep me a pure channel. I also surround everyone with the white light of the Holy Spirit and ask that my insight be clear and clean and that no part of Sylvia gets in the way.

I can't say this enough: *If you get out of yourself and give to God, you get out of your own way.* Is it hard? Sure it is, but your love and passion for something outside of you makes your spiritual engines run. Sure, the corny expression "If life gives you lemons, make lemonade" is great, but it better be sweet or else you're just left with sour lemon water. The sugar is what you add to life.

When you stop to help a person, and truly love them unconditionally for who they are, you're fulfilling your chart. In turn, you'll like or even love yourself for the good that you've done. I think it's very important to do this many times, without fanfare and recognition. It's like that movie *Pay It Forward,* or what my ministers and I call "a magnificent obsession"—that is, to prove what people have wandered the world to be assured of: that God is good and loves us unconditionally.

My staff often jokes in a kind way that I can have a temperature of 103° (which I've had) and be as sick as a dog, yet I still go on reading. I've gone on after deaths in my family, a hurtful divorce, and so on, and my ability seems to work aside (or *be*side or *in*side) of me without anything interfering with it. I was doing readings six days after a hysterectomy that I had when I was 40. Is it constitution? Maybe, but the ability is far beyond my physical self.

So on whatever level you choose to look at the first tenet, it begins to take on new meaning—as it has for me every time I read it. Francine has also said to "be above the body" because we're only "renting" this vehicle for a time. Our soul is larger than our body, and if we get too earthbound, we're going to get too caught up in the woes of this world.

Shakespeare said that a coward dies many times before his death. No one on this planet can ever be a coward, since just to come down here is an act of bravery. The only cowardice that comes into play is when you sink into darkness and forget how to love. It doesn't matter if it's for your animals, your friends, your garden, or your family, the key here is *"to love."* So light your lamp of love, and the world that may seem dark becomes the light of your own Christ consciousness (or whatever your beliefs may be).

✳ ✳ ✳ ✳ ✳ ✳

TENET II

Whatever thou lovest, lovest thou.

I'm sure that your reaction when you first read this tenet was like my own: "Hey, that isn't always true." When we love others, we have the high expectation that they're going to love us back, but I've certainly cared deeply for another person and not had that feeling returned. Well, I'm not just talking about the affection between a man and woman here, although that takes up a big part of the "loving game." Poetry and literature certainly have that passion as their dominating feature, but we also love parents, children, friends, relatives, pets, and so on.

So many times we do pick the wrong person to care about because, as I'm convinced, love is not only blind, but deaf and dumb as well. Yet we can't just blame everyone else. We have to be honest with ourselves: Are we lovable, or are we too demanding? Are our expectations beyond the norm of reality? Are we in the state of loving someone unconditionally? The majority of us mothers (good ones, that is) love our children in this way. We might not always like what our kids do, but we love them without reservation. Even "tough love" has an unconditional component in that the mother really does hope that her child will straighten up for his or her own good.

In the many readings that I do, I hear variations on the same theme from my clients: "My husband of 25 [or 30 or 35] years left me." And a doctor friend recently told me that almost half of his patients are women being treated for depression over their husbands leaving. But let's not leave men out—sorry ladies, but in my experience, it's not just the men who cheat . . . women do, too, and frequently. The only defining line here is that women don't tend to tell, and they usually don't break up their families over an indiscretion.

In no circumstance do I believe that a person should stay with an abusive spouse. I did in my first marriage, because I was ashamed and thought it was my fault. But keep in mind that abuse can be mental as well as physical, and women (who from the beginning of time have been the keepers of hearth and home) often put up with it longer than we should. Society has always had a tendency to blame the woman, from Eve to the modern-day divorce that happens because the wife didn't make the husband happy. Just as so many therapists blame the mother when a child goes wrong—no one stops to think that maybe this just is a rotten kid!

Sometimes, though, even when what we love isn't good for us, it can lead us to a better place. My first marriage, as abusive as it was, led me to California, where my career took off. There I formed a foundation where many people could work and help others (it was first the Nirvana Foundation, and then it became the Sylvia Browne Corporation).

No one on either side of my family had ever divorced, except for me. And then, with my dreams in hand, I tried it again. Dal and I did have a happy marriage for many years, but eventually it didn't work. My third (and last) husband seemed to be a kindred soul, but he left me for another woman, claiming that I was so popular now that I didn't need him! Of course I sat back and wondered, "What in God's name is *this* about?" Once again, looking on the bright side, this was not a fun time in my life, but since then my career has taken a giant step forward, and my eldest son, Paul, has stepped in to help me.

The thing I'd hoped secretly in my heart was that my sons would be part of my spiritual mission, and it happened. Chris, my precious psychic son, has worked beside me for 19 years as an excellent medium (and that isn't just a mother's pride talking . . . well, maybe some), but now my dear Paul also really helps me in my work. This would have never been possible if my last husband had stayed, because he'd tried to alienate everyone from me.

So I've had to learn just like anyone else. Every story has two sides, so perhaps I *was* too busy and caught up with my church, people, and career, causing my last marriage to go by the wayside. I have a real problem with people who take adultery lightly, but that's probably my upbringing. I have a problem with it even in my readings, and I know that it doesn't come from me—it really is linked to our Gnostic motto (which is in our logo and even in our jewelry): "Loyalty, Gratitude, and Commitment." I guess you can say that for me, adultery is more about loyalty than anything else—when I link myself up to someone, I tend to be there through hell and high water. I used to call it my "defect," but now I can thank God for that defect!

Now three years out, life is full of love again. My time is filled with friends, companionship, pets, clients, and all of you—and it's all good. A friend of mine says that having a bad relationship is like having an elephant in the front room: You can't hide it, you can't dust it off enough, and you have to clean up after it. No matter how much you pretend, it's still there.

We can also do this with the ghosts of long-lost loves,

whom we begin to make better than they were. The mind is very strange in that it has a habit of somehow forgetting the bad and remembering the good. In other words, if there were only five good times in a relationship of 20 years, that's where your mind goes, blanketing out the fights, the hurts, and the infidelities. When you think about these long-lost loves and the "what ifs," you don't have to force your mind to go to the negatives. It's time to look at things realistically: For whatever reason (yours or theirs), they didn't work out—and they never would have, no matter how much you tried to move that elephant out of your front room.

So, to go back to the second tenet, I know that it may sound like an oxymoron considering what we've been discussing, but here comes the spiritual insight. You gave your love to the wrong person . . . so where does that love go? Well, as Francine says, it's like electricity: It can never be destroyed—no, it may not have hit the target of your focus or attention, but it did go somewhere. Love is one of the emotions, believe it or not, that's stronger than hate or vengeance. It has conquered countries, built the Taj Mahal, and so on. It's the one emotion that's more pliable than all the others put together, and it can be directed more easily and is more convertible than any other.

When my beloved father died, and Chris and I walked out of the hospital into that bright April day, for just a moment I wondered how people could be driving, eating lunch on the lawn, and laughing when my dad was dead. Chris looked down at me, with his beautiful blue eyes filled with tears, and asked, "What do we do now, Mom?"

I said the only thing I knew to say—or perhaps the only thing that gave reason to what I was charted for: "We go back to work and love and have compassion for all the people we talk to today in our readings."

You see, love doesn't go away . . . it stays in our hearts for our lost ones, but it also spreads out to others who love us back. I hear my clients sometimes saying, "I don't care, I just want Sam [or Suzie or whomever] to love me—I don't care about anything else!" Well, I've been there myself enough times, until spiritually I began to realize that love takes many forms.

I've been onstage many times when a voice will ring out through the darkness of the audience: "I love you, Sylvia!" I always reply, "I love you, too!" and I truly do. That phrase is so often held back, and it's a shame. That voice in the dark is someone I know either here or on the Other Side, because as I say in my lectures, we're all strung like golden beads worn around the neck of God, our all-loving Father.

My dear friend Danny Levin and I were once talking about the fact that I was so glad I'd canceled a trip to Egypt, especially when I found out that it had been hit by a bomb at one of the Hilton hotels. I laughingly said, "That's all I'd need—to be taken hostage."

Very seriously, without even a second's hesitation, he replied, "Well, I'd go in on a moment's notice with a SWAT team to get you out." Is that love? Of course it is, and it's tucked away in my memory box that reads I'VE LOVED AND BEEN LOVED.

Yet when it comes to one of the greatest love stories I've ever witnessed, I'd like to take you back with me to when I was about 12 years old. At the time, I was attending St. James Church, which was being renovated. (Those of you who are—or were—Catholics will remember how much time we spent in church: whether it was confession, choir practice, holiday and feast days, Mass every day, or what have you.) Well, I remember this young construction worker who seemed to be a loner. Everyone made fun of him because he didn't seem to be attached to anyone, and every day during his lunch break, he'd dart into the church alone.

One day I heard someone half-mockingly ask, "Jack, what do you do in there?"

Jack put his head down and said, "I just run in and say, 'Jesus, this is Jack—I love you, and remember me.'"

Months went by, and we were filing in for choir practice when a scaffolding came loose and fell on Jack, killing him instantly. Besides me, maybe 15 or 20 kids plus workers heard the following right above Jack's body in midair: "Jack, this is Jesus. I love you, too, and remember you always." Now you can say or think what you want, but we all heard it.

Would Christ or God love us no matter what? Of course, but it was the miracle of a lonely young man apparently loved by no one who truly captured the greatest love of all. Even today I get chills, and I remember it as if it were yesterday.

* * *

We can't get into the second tenet—and it certainly wouldn't be complete—if we didn't address the Christian dogma of forgiveness. Yes, we must have unconditional love, but I don't believe that we have to forgive evil. It sounds like a contradiction, I know, but think about it: If we love evil, it can't love us back, nor does it hit its mark. It's true that if love doesn't hit its mark it goes somewhere else, but why give our love to someone who's dark and unworthy? We're not at fault and we can learn from it, but we don't have to keep loving and giving and casting those proverbial pearls before such swine.

Of course we can be duped, as the Germans were by Hitler, and the people who followed Jim Jones were waylaid by occultism (which was actually evil) taking the form of love. It's not wrong to hate evil: Who's going to love the men who put millions to death for being supposed witches; and who would love Hitler, Stalin, or Manson? How sick would we have to be to love and forgive such evil creatures? The best thing to do is to give such feelings to God, but don't have guilt about experiencing these human emotions.

And keep in mind that there are some things that are just too big for us to forgive, such as a mother who has had her child needlessly killed, or a trusted family member who deceives his loved ones and takes the inheritance. I talked to a man the other day who said, "Sylvia, I raised my brother when we were growing up. Just before our dad died, my brother doctored the will and had my very ill father sign it so that he'd get everything." It wasn't just the money, which was a lot, but this man's father had promised him a ring and some keepsake photos that his brother denied him. My client went on to say, "I feel so bad—I can't forgive him!"

"Then don't," I said. "Yet don't let it take over your life."

Forgiveness is Divine, and even though we're genetically a part of God, we're not totally in the state of Divinity until we get to the Other Side. We're still in human form, just like Jesus was. Even though he was a direct reporter and messenger from God, the human side of him knew anger (in the Temple with the money changers) and despair ("Why hast thou forsaken me?"). This was his human side, just as we have the foibles of the humanness of being in a body that the soul doesn't really fit that well into.

How Can This Tenet Help You?

Instead of living with the rejection of those few people who can't or won't love you back, find someone who will. My grandmother, who was full of proverbial folksy sayings, used to say, "Sylvia, if you take your wares to a poor market, no one will buy." So true . . . if you happen to be a victim like I've been, then you can understand that gut-wrenching feeling of rejection. You feel as if your heart is broken and it will never be mended, but sorry is the person who has lost love and cannot love again.

If you fall into the trap of "Why me?" or "I did everything right and I don't deserve this" for too long, then you might as well crawl into that dark hole and stay there. All of us have a tendency to do this somewhat, but you've got to get out of it as quickly as possible, or you're going to wither away. You must excuse my use of clichés here, but sometimes they can really make a point. For example, our Lord said, "Don't cast your pearls before swine," but like me, you may have found someone and—sure enough!—you looked in your bag of love and found just a few more pearls. Well, "you can't make a silk purse out of a sow's ear" (my personal favorite). I don't care if you put diamonds *and* pearls on it— it still stays a sow's ear.

When my last husband left, I was devastated, but then I slowly began to see what others had been aware of all along. I won't go into a barrage of attacks on him, but after our breakup, my old boyfriend's words kept coming back to me: "The world called you." So I just told myself that the planet and the people in it are my love affairs—as it should be for you, too. Get rid of your elephant in the front room, throw out the sow's ear, and go out on a crusade to find someone you can love . . . because it will come—maybe not in the person you want, but in so many truly loyal and meaning-ful ways. Passion is great but fleeting, while true love is ever-lasting and constant.

Love your friends, the grocer who helps you with an extra good cut of meat, and the old lady whose eyes light up when she sees that you've come to visit her at the nurs-ing home. Love your children, your friends, and your pets. . . . Love spills out everywhere, and if you put it in the right places, it will come back to you a thousandfold. The world is full of things of every size and shape to be loved, includ-ing people of all creeds and colors, sunsets, animals, nature, or even the first cup of coffee in the morning. When you've been hurt, start with the small, and then grow spiritually into bigger things.

Children love unconditionally (at least most of them do) until the world gets a hold on them. But from birth to death, pets give out a pure form of unconditional love— they love you no matter who you are or how you look or feel. Humankind could certainly learn from animals! And while it may seem that children and animals are the only sources of unconditional love, I *have* also seen rare instances of it in human relationships.

So you can love and not be loved back or lose your love, but I promise you that, just like it did with me, someone or something will fill its place if you're not too blind to see. The life you live goes in circles that widen, and if you let it, it will take in more people to love. (Don't forget that you can have a wonderful love affair with the teachings of Christ, Mother or Father God, or your guides and angels, too.)

✸ ✸ ✸ ✸ ✸

TENET III

Do not give unto God any human pettiness such as vengeance, wrath, or hate. Negativity is man's alone.

This third tenet is especially dear to my heart. I have researched it, logically gone over it, and seen it in action as miracles, but it really just comes down to plain ol' street smarts.

Where does one begin, I asked myself almost 40 years ago, *to try to explain our Creator, Who has been defamed for centuries?* Christianity is not the only religion responsible for this, although it does seem to be the front-runner. When you look at what its alleged messengers have had to say—and what humankind has made of it—it's just a travesty of lies.

All throughout theological history, humans have viewed God as not only the Creator, but also a Being who played favorites. He was supposedly capricious, jealous, wrathful, and punishing, and He played for favor. He even told Abraham to kill his son (of course, He did later change that desire, but the very fact that God would even ask anyone to kill their son is anathema). When we discover that the God of the Old Testament wanted the Ammonites killed, we have to ask ourselves, "Who made the Ammonites? Why would a loving God even take sides in a war?" God wouldn't, for we all belong to the same genetic family.

Theologians have argued for centuries about this Being called God, and there are as many varied opinions as there are words in the dictionary. Yet one logical truth keeps resounding in the hearts and souls of humankind: Is God vengeful or loving? Let's say for the sake of argument that we've never studied this subject, but we just know that we were created by God. Even with that simplistic premise, the logical question is: *Why would a Creator Who made us condemn us to a life of suffering and hell?* (Granted, life *is* hell, but coming here helps us learn and perfect.) Whatever religious text we read, we still find that God can be good *and* bad—so which is it?

Let's not go into the theological areas here; instead, we'll just go with plain, honest logic. For example, whenever I've sat down with any religious leader, no matter what Supreme Being they follow, I always start out with these questions: "Isn't God good? Isn't God all-loving? Isn't God omnipotent? Isn't God all-forgiving? Isn't God perfect love?" And the answer to all of these questions is, of course, yes. "Okay, then," I tend to respond, "how can He/She be mean, hateful, and capricious?" The silence from these ministers, priests, clerics, rabbis, and theologians has always been deafening. (Although one had the nerve to say to me around 1989 that God must have an evil side in order to create evil. I hit the proverbial roof! God can *know about* evil, but didn't *create* it. Total perfection is what God is about.)

Most of this concept of fearing God and "my god is better than your god" is from the Old Testament of the Bible, which is basically a history of the Judaic people. The Bible was formed to show ancient humans that our deity was stronger than any of the pagan gods of Babylon, Egypt,

Greece, and especially Rome. All of these ancient gods had human qualities (for example, Zeus could rape women and Isis played favorites), and you made sacrifices to all of them to gain favor. Yet sacrifices were also made quite often to God in the Old Testament.

Now I've always had a hard time understanding why Christianity insists on embracing the Old Testament (other than perhaps because it presented a history of Christ's lineage), since it certainly portrays a Creator of human emotions Who is in direct contradiction to the type of God that Christ taught about. Well, the reason this text is embraced is because the early Christian church included it in its holy books. Apparently, it doesn't matter that the Old Testament really doesn't belong in the Bible—especially since a lot of it is part of the Judaic holy scriptures and books. To get it right, the New Testament should be the Christian Bible, but then most Christians don't know the history of how their Bible came into being—or, for that matter, the history of the early Christian church that compiled it.

Anyway, no matter how you portray Him, God has always been constant, loving, and perfect. Once we were all created from good by God, Who gave us free will, and we all made our own choices. So if we have a loving God, then we logically have to stay with that—we can't waffle. Once we grasp this logical, well-founded concept, then we're in league with the God Whom Christ loved and followed, and we can see as he did the hypocrisy and pettiness of humankind. Then we, as Christ said, become the temple in which God resides without vengeance, hate, jealousy, or pettiness.

Many religions seem to try to make their personal god more powerful, intelligent, and even more vengeful. They don't do this out of meanness or spite—fear is actually the common component of the ancient religious teacher's philosophy. You see, Carmelite nuns sequestered themselves in convents to pray for the world, while holy men have sat on mountains to atone for the world for centuries. Please believe me when I say that none of this is wrong—it's each person's individual preference as to how to worship God. I just find it interesting that when you read so many of these antiquated scripts, no messenger ever comes forth and says that this is the law. In other words, it doesn't make sense to have people believe that the only way to achieve redemption is to wear hair shirts, beat themselves bloody, or what have you. How can a loving God want you to mar the temple He/She created in His/Her image and likeness?

I always encourage everyone to read *all* the great religious works—not just our Christian Bible, but the Baha'i *Thief in the Night,* the Talmud, the Koran (Qur'an), and Buddha's Eightfold Path as well. In these varied texts, to make your god more powerful and make your religion prosper, it seems that love was left out, and fear, rules, and dogma reigned supreme. Well, do people today take into account the fact that these early writings were basically for an ignorant mass of people who were continually at war and changing religions to that which was most expedient—namely, the one practiced by the conquering nation?

The uneducated can always be controlled by fear, for they have no knowledge or grasp of the basic concepts related to God. This ruling of the masses by fear led to a tradition that's been carried out to this day: ruling *educated* masses by fear. It's so inbred now in major religions that even a highly educated person, who logically knows that much of what he or she is being taught by their practiced religion makes no sense, still falls into the trap and follows blindly because so many others do.

The role of fear in religion plays on the insecurity of humankind. We're afraid because we categorically don't know who's right or wrong. We seek solace and comfort in the fact that there's a full cathedral, church, mosque, or synagogue—after all, if so many people believe in this practiced religion and attend, then they must be right. Religious leaders know this; consequently, they try to convert as many as possible to their own belief. Truth is thrown out the window, for what has worked for centuries is still working, although there are more and more people who are starting to think for themselves and leaving organized religion in droves. Most of them still believe in God, but they can't abide the stupid rules and dogma that's been handed down for centuries and makes no connection in the modern world . . . especially in light of recent research and just good ol' common sense.

I don't want to pick on any religion, but at one point, if a Catholic ate meat on Friday and died on Saturday, he or she went to hell. Then the law was changed—but what happened to those who'd already gone to hell? Were they told to come back up? Why would God even care what we ate? The Old Testament has David and Solomon partaking in grand feasts, and the New Testament has Jesus being entertained and fed grandly at the house of Martha and Mary . . . nowhere does it say that if it was Friday, no one could have meat. I know I'm oversimplifying what was originally considered a "sacrifice of abstinence" for God, but it was a stupid part of human-made dogma. This was only eliminated a few decades ago—what in the hell took them so long to change it? Tradition and the refusal to change are the bane of all religions. (I don't even want to go into the fact that this particular church only allows men to be priests, for they're not alone in that overt discrimination.)

I'm not particularly in favor of tattoos for myself, but I do feel that it's an individual's right or preference to have them. The Torah prohibits Jews from getting tattoos, which is why Hitler tattooed numbers on concentration-camp victims. Yet we hear of monks or even nuns sleeping on beds of nails or flaying or gouging themselves until their skin is scarred and mutilated, punishing themselves for unworthiness or some sin that they felt they'd committed. Why would God want you to harm yourself—or be accountable for what an evil madman would do to people who had no choice? When your intellect and logic start to work, it can really make you so confused (and even half crazy) trying to sort it out.

We come here to acquire knowledge by making up our charts and learning for God. Think of it like this: God is all-knowing, because He/She knows that to experience is part of knowledge. We (His/Her creations) are the experiencing side of God—not only do we learn for ourselves, but we feed data back to our Creators.

* * *

More times than I can number, people have asked me, "Why is God doing this to me?" First of all, be reasonable—God doesn't play Russian roulette with our lives. And even in an inverted-ego scenario, why would you or I be so important that God just picks on us; or, for that matter, so good that we find favor in becoming a martyr? We need the true presence of a good God, not a critical one.

Every day when I do readings, I seem to hear: "God took my son [daughter, husband, or what have you]" or "I'm mad at God." Don't get me wrong—being human, you can get angry at our Creator. Even though it's useless, sometimes it's as the saying goes: "We always strike out at those we love." Well, the Almighty is no exception. I've had some real screaming matches with God. When a dog bit my granddaughter's lip, I have to say that I gave God a piece of my mind. Angelia's lip is all right, but at the time I had so much fear for her, and I was completely frustrated because I was hundreds of miles away. When my intellect kicked in, I realized it was her chart at work—then my spiritual knowledge chimed in, and I realized that I can't control the destiny of others.

God doesn't take offense, because He/She doesn't have the human pettiness to get mad or hold grudges. Time is the great teacher, and when you look back, nine times out of ten, tragedy turns into greatness, even if it means that you grow spiritually . . . which is what it's all about anyway.

Not long ago, for instance, I was counseling a woman about her three-year-old who had died (the most horrible thing anyone can go through is the loss of a child), and she wailed, "Why did God take my son? What did I ever do so wrong in this life or a past one to incur this?" The answer is simply . . . nothing! In situations like this, we tend to automatically feel that we've failed somehow, and we wonder why bad things happen to good people. This pill is unbearably bitter, and we're often unable to swallow it—until we realize that our loved one didn't die in vain. But how do we figure this out?

As I told my client, "Aside from the unbearable pain, has the death of your child led you anywhere?"

"I don't know what you mean," she said.

I replied, "Isn't that why you're starting to read and search or even call me?"

She was quiet for a moment. Then, as if a light suddenly went on, she said, "Sylvia, I have. I've started searching for answers."

I said, "Well, that's the big first step toward learning about spirituality."

My grandmother's son Paul died when he was a young man, yet she still talked to him every day of her life. She'd tell me (God love her), "If it wasn't for you, Sylvia, I'd love to be with him." She knew she would someday, but she said, "I have to see you on your way." Not until I was almost 18 did she let go and "graduate." I wasn't ready to let her go (are we ever?), but I can see that she saw me through the developing years of my strange family life, and she helped me face my psychic ability.

You see, if a loved one dies and you just give up, their death hasn't been in vain because they completed and learned from their chart, but it will be in vain for *your* learning process. This "why me" has a definite answer: You simply chart to learn, and the toughest things tend to be left until the last life or incarnation. I used to wonder why, but logically it makes sense that we pick the hardest tasks to learn from, and then graduate so that we don't have to come back into life. At the same time, we also carry a greater amount of

accumulated knowledge in the soul to deal with these tragedies.

"Will I see my beloved again?" is also a question I receive
quite a bit. Yes, all of us meet each other again because (you
guessed it) we have a loving God who allows us to learn and
gain a higher understanding, and to even ascend to a higher
level of spirituality on the Other Side.

So, if we have an all-loving God, He/She then truly loves
us, forgives us, and is always with us. Yes, He/She can interfere with our learning, but does not because we contracted
to do it. Does that mean prayer to this loving, perfect God is
useless since everything is in its order and place? Of course
not! It helps elevate us to God, bringing about grace and
a deeper spiritual understanding that at best life is short
(sometimes I feel that it's actually very long), but it gives us
time to fine-tune our souls.

You and I are partners with God in this journey of life.
You might ask, "Why doesn't God always answer prayers?"
He/She does, but often has to turn down your pleas—not
out of malice or pettiness, but because it would be against
your learning curve. It's much like telling your school counselor that you don't want to take speech and calculus, and
then being told, "That's fine, but you won't graduate."

So when you feel yourself abandoned, just know that
you're not. God holds you forever in the palm of His/Her
hand. God loves all people of all creeds, colors, sexes, and
religions. How could He/She not—didn't He/She make all of
us? If God plays favorites, then here we go with a humanized God. . . .

How Can This Tenet Help You?

Remember that if you're obsessed with the idea of retribution, then it's like the ancient proverb says: "When you
go for vengeance, you had better dig two graves: one for you,
and one for the person you go after." It may seem that evil

prevails sometimes, but it doesn't. You just might not see the justice you're seeking in this life, for it will be done in God's time, not yours. Evildoers have to keep coming back until they're finally absorbed into God, while we keep our own identity as a shining example of His/Her goodness.

We've got to get back to the basics of loving God and accepting His/Her never-ending love for us. God is love, and that love doesn't hurt, is never cruel, and accepts us for the sum total of who we are and who we were made to be—rather than what religion's human-made rules have placed upon us. If we just followed what Jesus taught and did, then we'd be on our spiritual, simplistic track and love the God Who is gentle, kind, and omnipotent.

Everyone has searched for the right God, and He/She has always been there for us . . . always constant, always forgiving, and always loving. If we just stick with how Jesus addressed his Creator—and know and love God as our Father/Mother Who is not only in heaven, but always with us—then we're guaranteed to be on the spiritual path.

✳ ✳ ✳ ✳ ✳ ✳

TENET IV

*Create your own heaven, not a hell.
You are a creator made from God.*

I know that at times this book may seem more like a self-indulgent autobiography rather than a text on spirituality. This is partly because I'm sharing what these 21 tenets have helped me learn from my own life, but I'm also including what I've learned from *your* lives. To prove that point, I have to tell you about Sister Francis.

At the time (40 years ago), I was working at St. Albert the Great, teaching second grade. Sister Francis was a fellow instructor, and we'd try to spend our free time between classes or at lunch together. That always meant going outdoors, because Sister Francis dearly loved to be out in nature. She and I would go out rain or shine, and she never failed to say, "What a beautiful day this is! Look at the splendor God has laid out before us!"

At first I thought she was exaggerating, but gradually I began to see what she saw: the variances in temperature, the cloud formations, the soft beat of the rain, and even the cold that made your face pink and flushed when you came back inside. Sister Francis truly had heaven in her own mind.

Then there was my grandfather, Marcus Coil, who'd become a millionaire in Springfield, Missouri, by starting up some of the town's first laundries and mercantile stores. By the time the family had moved to Kansas City, however, he'd lost every penny in the stock market. Although it was during the time of the Great Depression, every day my grandfather would press his now-shiny-with-wear suit and shirt (which Grandma Ada had to keep repairing the frayed cuffs on) and sit in the waiting room of Pacific Gas and Electric looking for work. And every day, the head of the company would come out and say, "Sorry, Marcus, we have nothing for you today."

For one year my grandfather followed this routine. Finally, the CEO told my grandpa that he was sick of seeing him every day and that anyone who had that type of perseverance deserved a job. My grandfather was given a menial position, but in six months he became the head of the whole district office. He kept telling Grandma Ada, "I made it once; I know how to do it again." Was this all about money? God, no—it was about providing for his family and taking a positive and undaunted attitude. My grandfather was able to create a heaven out of his hell.

On the other side of this coin you have my mother. It's hard to understand how she could have come from the same family as my wonderful grandparents, her brother Marcus (who had cerebral palsy but was an angel on Earth whom everyone called "Brother"), and her brother Paul, who was also psychic and used to talk to God daily before he died of cancer at the age of 21. Out of this family of beloved people came my mother. I used to obsess about not liking her until Francine told me many years later, "You can only honor your parents if they are honorable."

My mother was not only abusive physically, but her

greatest forte was to try to damage her family members with mental abuse. I was too tall, not pretty, and too strong willed. I also thought I was smart, even when she told me I wasn't—this seemed to set a fire in my gut to make her wrong. I was also my father's favorite, which endeared me to her even less.

Now I could have wilted under her abuse and become like her, but instead I went under my beloved grandma's wing and basked in the light of my dad's approval. My poor sister, Sharon, wasn't so fortunate, however: My mother got her claws into her and for a time controlled her and almost made her an invalid. To this day, my mother's influence has affected my sister's life—and not in a positive way. (You can say that I was stronger, and that may be so, but I also chose my chart.)

Being psychic didn't help me in my mother's eyes, even though she'd grown up with a psychic mother, brother, grandmother, and uncle. With all due respect, she may have had enough of it, but instead of encouraging me as Grandma Ada did, when I was ten years old, she told me, "Keep this spooky thing up and I'll have you locked up." I can remember being so frightened that night that I could see my heart beat through the blankets on my bed, and I truly prayed that my gifts would go away.

When I hesitantly told my grandmother about the incident, I remember her listening carefully and getting a grim look on her face. She silently put on her coat and grabbed my hand, and we both marched off to see my mother. Now this was one of only two times I saw my grandmother get angry in the 18 years that I was with her. Seething with anger, she went up to my mother, put her face close to hers, and said, "Celeste, if you ever say that to Sylvia again, I'll personally see to it that *you* are locked up!" So that ended that . . . except for the constant snorts and sighs of disapproval my mother directed toward me over the years whenever I'd do mini-readings for friends or come out with a zinger of psychic insight.

My psychic ability was even accepted by my childhood friends (who will attest to it). In fact, I recently attended my 50th high-school reunion, and my classmates all told me they were proud of me. Even the nuns and priests, believe it or not, were good to me back then—while they didn't always understand how I knew what I knew, they never condemned me. In fact, all throughout Catholic high school and college, and even during the 18 years that I taught in Catholic schools, I was never made to feel that I was evil or an oddity. At Presentation High School in San Jose, California, they even let me teach world religions, which I have to confess had Gnosticism on the agenda more than the Bible, Bhagavad Gita, Koran, or Talmud. Of course I gave time to all of these, but I kept coming back to a loving God and the fact that life is what we make of it inside our soul . . . because, after all, that's where our heaven and hell reside.

Getting back to my childhood, as I grew into my late teens, my father was making $3,000 a month. That was a fortune in those days, so I didn't have an underprivileged upbringing in those years, but I truly would have foregone that for a semblance of a happy home. Yet I can honestly say that I was happy overall because I had the rest of my family and my friends. I chose to respect my mother, while at the same time putting her on a shelf in the back of my mind.

During this time, my grandmother fell on hard times. My grandfather had died, and Grandma Ada was taking care of Brother. It's very difficult for me to relive this portion of my memories, for my mother stuck them both in a literal flophouse. You may wonder why my father didn't intervene, but it's more unbelievable and complex than that. My father left everything to my mother to handle because he traveled all the time and really didn't know what was going on with my mother's family. I was right there when she lied and told him that no one would take Brother because of his cerebral palsy. Well, she never even looked—nor was she about to spend any of her considerable allowance to have them taken care of.

I remember the day Grandma Ada and Brother moved into this three-flight walk-up that my mother had put them in. Brother was afraid of stairs because his disease threw his balance off, and then a drunk came out brandishing a knife. I think I was so full of grief that I turned on the man and screamed, "Get back in your room before I use that knife on you!" He looked befuddled and stunned. I guess so . . . seeing a 13-year-old girl going into what looked like a manic fit.

I saw that my beloved family members were going to be reduced to living in a dirty one-room flat with a communal bathroom down the hall. I kept thinking, *Please, God, let me grow up fast so that I can take care of them.* The room contained a bed, one straight-back chair, two hot plates, a few large windows with no curtains, a small sink, and a dresser—and that was it. (Oh, except for the two dishes, glasses, and sets of eating utensils; along with a pair of sheets and a flimsy blanket, plus two pillows and towels that my extravagant mother had so thoughtfully provided.) This is what my grandmother—who was of German nobility, escaped the war, gave to charity, healed the sick, and helped as many people as she could—had been given by her own daughter.

Grandma Ada sat down on the chair, and for a moment I saw what looked like a cloud cross her china blue eyes. But then she threw her hat on the bed and sat down. Then, like my granddaughter, Angelia, still does, I flung myself on my grandmother's lap—all 13 years of me. She must have seen my pain because she said, "Look at those windows! Brother can look out every day and see the sights, and we'll have light all day long." She patted me and said, "It'll be just fine, darling. I'll make it great in no time."

I'd like to take a moment here to talk a little bit more about Brother, who lived with my grandmother until her death at age 88. He was one of the most brilliant people I've ever known. He read everything—history, religion, politics, you name it—and could talk about it. He was very frail, with reddish hair and blue eyes, and stood only about 5'8". His head was tilted to one side because of his cerebral palsy, and his neck would bob violently when he was agitated or nervous. When I walked down the street with him and people stared (as they're wont to do), I glared at them, silently daring them to say one word.

When she was asked about how hard it was to take care of him, my grandmother, without hesitation, would say, "Are you kidding? Look what joy and company I have in my older years—we have fun, read, talk, and laugh; and without him, I'd be alone. How can this blessing be a burden?" Once again, as you can see, out of a hell (or what's perceived to be one) lies a heaven in disguise.

My grandmother never really read for me because we couldn't for each other, but she did say that I'd have two boys, would go to California, and that people would know my name. "Me, a girl from Missouri? I think not! And how will they know my name?" I pressed her.

She replied, "You'll carry the torch that was built upon itself for 300 years." *How poetic,* I'd think, but then I rationalized that she loved me so much she was blinded by it. In fact, in a half-kidding way I once asked her while we were cooking, "Grandma, how much do you love me?"

She stopped what she was doing, looked at me, and said, "My heart would hear you and beat if it lay for a century dead." Now try to top that one!

My grandmother was a writer, too, and someday I'm going to publish her letters. Every one is filled with quotes, all of which were gloriously optimistic. She *always* made a heaven out of a living hell. For example, in that room that she and Brother shared, she got ahold of some donated fabric and made a skirt for the dresser and one for the sink to hide the utensils and dishes, and she made another sheet for the bed . . . but it was still a rattrap.

When my father came home two weeks later, I immediately went to him and tried to explain how awful it was. He had some business issue on his mind, so I could tell he wasn't with me. My mother came in and said, "Bill, don't listen to her—she's always so dramatic anyway. You can go see for yourself what a cozy place this is," knowing full well that he wouldn't. He either wanted to believe her or was afraid not to, I'll never know. I do know that after that, he'd slip me money to take to Grandma.

I can remember on more than one occasion skipping school with money in my pocket, taking the streetcar in the blinding snow to 18th and Baltimore, and walking up to that damn run-down building. I'd look up and see a form in the window, standing there with that Gibson-girl hairstyle she had, smiling and waving because she psychically knew that I was coming (after all, she had no phone). I'd climb the steps and give her the money, prompting her to clap her hands together, tell me what a good man my father was, and remark that we were going to have a feast. That meant a soda, cheese, milk, and her famous hamburger hash.

As painful as it was, Grandma could even light up a dingy cell-like room with love and joy. She'd always say, "Isn't this cozy?" or "Aren't we lucky?" or "Aren't we happy to have each other?" I decided to believe her. And it didn't take long for people to again find out where she was. Long lines began to form to see her—priests, laypeople, old people, and sick people . . . she'd see everyone. I used to say, "God, please let me just be one-tenth as strong, brave, and positive as she is throughout *my* life."

Well, I won't lie or be humble, but I can't honestly say that I've arrived at the point that my grandparents or Sister Francis reached, but I try valiantly. I *can* say that when I got divorced from my abusive first husband, Gary, and was relegated to tenement living (where there was algae all over the pool in back), I told my boys that it was just water lilies. However, after two ear infections, I decided that enough was enough.

Not only did I have Paul and Chris, I also had my adopted daughter, Mary, whose mother had simply given her to me when the child was only 6. (Mary left us when she was 22 and is now married with two girls and living near Boston.) And I was so strung out at the time with my ex-husband's threats to kill us that I didn't know if I was coming or going. The police actually told me that Gary could stand on the sidewalk in a threatening manner and there was nothing I could do about it. One officer said that the only way I could stop Gary would be to pull him into our apartment and shoot him. Since I could never ever hurt anyone or anything in that way, that wasn't a viable option either.

Yet, even through this horrendous period, the kids and I managed to scrape by. People were so caring. For example, when Chris had a terrible earache (the attack of the "water lilies"), the woman next door came over with what I deem were no less than magical drops for his ear—and he was fine from then on. Mary was a love, and together, even at her age, we'd laugh about all the pork and beans we ate.

At this same time, my mother went to a lawyer to try to get my children. My lawyer was flabbergasted: Here I was, a Catholic schoolteacher and a good mother, and she was going after custody with my ex-husband. The reason, she explained later, was that she didn't want to lose us. *Huh?*

At one point in my late 20s and early 30s, as I was raising the kids by myself, teaching school, doing readings, *and* attending classes, I began to see that my life wasn't going the way I wanted it to. It felt like an endless circle of readings, teaching, raising children, school, and nothing else. Then I began to ask myself, "What do *you* want, Sylvia?"

I really wanted to teach and help people, but I also needed to give the children a good home. So I quit my job as a schoolteacher and opened my foundation. We had two rooms and taught classes in the evenings, and I brought my kids with me. They'd sit in the back and do their homework—then we'd go to Denny's, eat dinner, and talk about everything. Sure, finances were really tough, but the trade-off was great. It was the process of selection: I had my family with me because when they were in school I did readings in my home, and three nights a week, they went with me to lectures or teaching.

Life went on and on . . . it can take on a Shakespearean quality (or even a comedy of errors), but you roll with it. Life also gives you grief and sorrow in large measures: It can deceive and disappoint you, but it also gives you happiness; ecstasy; satisfaction; and loving friends, pets, and family—all part of the montage that makes your life how you perceive it: a joy.

When my third husband, Larry, exited three years ago, things became quite difficult. I like having partnership at this point in my life, but I also feel that people my age or even younger should find fulfillment by doing what they feel is right, not what society dictates. Anyway, right in the middle of the divorce, Dal Brown (my second husband whose name I still carry, although I added an *e* to it) showed up at my office and told me that he was getting an amicable divorce from his wife of two years. He was working as a store manager in Auburn, California, and had come to the Bay Area on business when he decided out of the blue to stop by and see me. His children had moved away, and we talked about old times. We'd kept in touch sporadically since our divorce, and one thing led to another. . . .

Although Dal has had many serious health problems (including heart trouble and several operations that left him on disability for a while), shortly after both our divorces were final we decided to become companions for one another. After all, I'd known him for almost 40 years, and we had 18 years of marriage together. All the old hurts were forgotten—what he'd done with our finances had been out of stupidity, not malicious intent. So we're friends . . . and even though he doesn't share any part of my business, it's nice to have someone around who knows me. He has his life, and I have mine, but we try to spend as much time as we can with each other.

As you can see, with the closing of one door, another opens. Even though I was hurt by my last divorce, I found solace in the fact that there was so much good in my life. These days, my perfect setting is coming home from being on the road and sitting next to the fireplace with Angelia, needlepointing and talking, while my grandson Willy plays with his toy trucks, with a stew on the stove that we can eat whenever we want.

And then I feel all the loved ones who have passed over—Dad, Grandma Ada, and Brother; my dear friend Dr. Small, who was always there for me if I couldn't pay the medical bills for my children; Bob Williams, my mentor, friend, and teacher whom I dearly loved; Joe, who was one of my first loves; Abass, who was my friend and tour guide in Egypt (and when I was going through my last divorce would call me every day and ask, "How are you doing, Queenie?" [his nickname for me]); and myriad other souls who have passed on. I know that they're all there with Francine and the angels, and the room fills up with love. That's when I tell myself, "This is your heaven right here, Sylvia."

How Can This Tenet Help You?

As Milton said, "The mind is its own place, and in itself can make a Heav'n of Hell." When things used to happen to my children and me that were wonderful, I'd always say, "Close your eyes and save it, because when things go wrong on that awful, dark, rainy day that life gives you, you can take this out—like a scrapbook of your life. Cherish this moment, and it will brighten even your darkest hour."

Sometimes it's better not to act at all during the hard times—instead, stay in your quiet, spiritual place, and reach for God's hand that's always there. Can you look at yourself in the mirror? Can you sleep at night? If so, then you're okay. I don't mean that you won't lose sleep over the pain, grief, and whys of life, but did you pull the bow that sent the arrow? I doubt it—or you wouldn't be reading this (or any other) spiritual commentary or text because you wouldn't care. It's only good people who worry whether they're on track—the bad ones never do.

Take the people you know who are rich or famous, only to find out that they have substance-abuse problems, broken marriages, eating disorders, and so forth. Money and fame don't exempt you from problems. Look at Martha Stewart: Right or wrong, she stumbled, and created a hell for herself. Then again, Montel Williams, one of the guardian angels of my life, battles multiple sclerosis (MS), but he keeps on going and finds joy. He goes snowboarding, travels, helps people, started an MS foundation, and is proactive. He's stumbled but hasn't fallen. There was a time, which he himself even wrote about, when he found himself in his own hell and wanted to end it all, but from deep in his soul came the strength to live, love, and enjoy every day.

How can we take for granted the feeling of capturing a child's hand in ours, looking into a baby's eyes, or seeing the joy on our pets' faces when we come home? What about the ardent kiss of a lover, a sunset or sunrise, a bird's song . . . there's so much beauty that we don't even notice because we get rooted in our own hell. Remember that there's always going to be a hole in the prison walls that you construct for yourself—why do you think you have the desire if your chart didn't put it there? Stop with the "I'm too old, too young, not equipped, not smart enough," for then you'll create your own hell. It's not your dreams that you're worried about following, but your destiny!

Not only do you need passion as you realize your path, but you've also got to prepare and steel yourself against the "slings and arrows of outrageous fortune." It's true that bravery comes with a price, but know that you're building on your mistakes and heartaches. Rejoice that you're not only climbing the mountain of self, but you're also learning to love unconditionally—as well as giving yourself to an all-loving God. And *that's* where you'll find your heaven on Earth.

* * * * * *

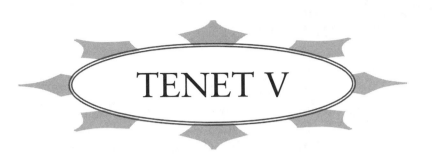

TENET V

*Turn thy power outward, not inward,
for therein shines the light and the way.*

As opposed to the last tenet, which was internal (creating heaven instead of hell), this one is proactive and
more external. Of course, power must start inside—if there
isn't anything in there, it's pretty difficult to turn the "power
light" on, especially when the cord isn't plugged into anything. Sometimes it's best to just take a moment and decide if
we're feeling happy or dull, with no passion that can propel
us outward in our lives. Think about it rationally: Our eyes
don't turn inward but outward to see; our bodies even fit into
other bodies. In other words, we weren't built as mere receiving tubes, but as entities that were made to focus out.

When we turn outward, then as the tenet says, therein
shines the light and the way. The light means spiritual
enlightenment, while the way is following the teachings of
Christ. As our Lord said, "I am the light of the world." He, of
course, was very spiritually enlightened and certainly didn't

sit around—rather, he chose to focus his power outward. He walked and talked, taught and healed.

Now Francine has always said that we all have more power than we could ever realize or know until we use it. At first this made me crazy. "Okay, then," I asked her, "where is it and how do we use it?" When she told me to look at the concept deeper, it became clear that it was related to miracles.

For example, I know of a mother and two children who were wedged in a car after an accident, and the car caught fire. There was no way that anyone could see how the fire department with their "jaws of life" could get there in time before they'd be engulfed by flames. As everyone stood around screaming, a beautiful black man came out of the crowd, approached the car, and with one hand ripped the door off its hinges and saved the mother and children. Everyone there reported that the man had a trancelike look on his face the whole time he was executing the rescue. I stated at one point that this man was an angel, but I now believe that the angels actually propelled his power outward instead. When the man was subsequently found after a long, intensive search, he had no recollection of the episode—but even more startling was the discovery that four years prior to that episode (almost to the day), he'd lost his wife and two children in a house fire and felt helpless because he wasn't home to save them.

Then there's the story of the 90-pound mother who actually lifted a huge SUV off of her son, who was pinned underneath it. He came out with just a concussion and a broken leg, but authorities said that if the SUV had been left on top of the boy, he would have suffered internal injuries due to the weight of the vehicle. Many say that the woman's strength came from a rush of adrenaline, but it doesn't matter—there was a surge of power that defied all explanation. You can call this the energy that always comes from God, but it's actually lying beneath the surface in all of us and can be used when called upon by a desperate need to save, heal, or simply make a situation better.

The power that we can exude physically when needed is truly a miracle in itself. I remember about 40 years ago when a friend and her four-year-old daughter, Sally, were visiting. My kids were playing with the little girl and were just coming down the stairs when out of the corner of my eye I saw Sally fall. I was on the couch, which was far away from the steps. Without thinking, I jumped up and with one leap managed to catch her head before it hit the last step. In wide-eyed disbelief, Sally's mother proclaimed, "I never saw anything like that! You were like a blur of motion, and your reflexes were miraculous." I'm not being heroic or humble here—I'm sure I was simply propelled by a primordial God-given reflex to save this child from possible brain damage, which surely would have occurred had she hit her head at the rate she was falling.

I happened recently to tune in to a show called *Extreme Makeover: Home Edition,* in which a home was remodeled for a family that had two deaf parents and two sons, one of whom was blind. After the house was completed, the blind son was lifted up so that he could ring the wind chimes, which brought him such joy to hear. The other son was given money for the college education he so dearly wanted.

The family was in tears, and the show's host said, "It gave me such a sense of power and grace from God." This coming from someone on a reality show! I thought, *We're finally getting it. It's even sinking into mainstream America that we do have the power to change lives.* Sure, we don't all have that kind of money on a grand scale or the physical powers, but we do have the power to heal. Maybe we won't attain the level of Padre Pio, a famous priest who was known for his healing ability, but we all hold the potential.

* * *

How can we "ordinary people" do outward healing? Well, each and every one of us has the energy to do it—and it can be physical as well as mental. For example, the prefect of our church had a daughter named Kathy who had a very advanced case of multiple sclerosis. Since she was also one of our ministers, many naysayers would ask Kathy, "Why are you not healed?"

I'll never forget her response: "What you don't understand is that I have been. Just because my body has MS doesn't mean that my soul isn't at peace or that I don't know the truth of where I'm going and why I came here." In other words, Kathy *was* healed.

Now don't get me wrong: It's important to address physical concerns, but when the mind and soul are convinced of its spiritual path and light, it *is* healed. Just as we aren't the car we drive—we just operate and then exit it—we aren't the physical shell we inhabit.

Think of the power of any emotion, and watch what it can accomplish. Love can almost move mountains; unfortunately, so can hate and vengeance. I truly love my life now, even though it took many years to keep that power steady. There were periods when I loved it and times that were heartbreaking and dismal with death, divorce, and betrayal, but you know what? I found out that as we constantly reach toward our passion, our power gets stronger, and it's that power that's turned outward.

When I was 18 years old and doing readings, I was happy. And when I was teaching and raising my children, I was happy. It was in those other outside things like holding on to negative memories of my childhood, a bad marriage, or the death of a loved one (which has happened to me many times), that my light would dim because it was focused inside on the deadly trap of "poor me." One day I finally told myself, "You can stay in this comfortable circle, or you can go for broke. If you don't go for it, how will you ever know what you can accomplish?"

So with trepidation I started to go public. The same thing happened when I wanted to start Novus Spiritus—my family just sat in stunned silence. My boys spoke up first and said, "Mom, it's always been your ball game, so play it." It was hard, and the criticism was even harder, but I kept putting one foot in front of the other and praying that this was what God wanted.

I gain power from writing and from all of you—fans of my books, those who come to my lectures, the people I read for—as well as from doing shows for Montel or Larry King (who is a prince and the best interviewer in the world). Whenever Larry sees me, he starts to quote Shakespeare: "Who is Sylvia? What is she? That all our swains commend her . . ."

Will I ever retire? Never! It really sounds disgusting to me that the root of that word is *tire*. Plus, what do we really do when we retire? People say, "I'll do all the things I always wanted to do," and then I ask, "Such as . . . ?" knowing full well what's coming. "Oh, I'll sleep as late as I want, watch all the TV shows I've missed, read, visit with friends," is the response I typically get. Well, then what? How many books can you read? I read and write all the time—in fact, I usually have three books going at once. I also watch my favorite shows on A&E or the Discovery and History Channels, and I love to needlepoint. I do all of these things and still go out and do what I love with all of you.

I think we should get rid of the four-letter word *work*. The idea of work is what causes us to lose our power and passion to turn outward. If it turns inward, it lies dormant, is useless, and doesn't go anywhere.

Take, for example, my dear friend Lindsay's mother. She's in her late 80s, yet she teaches a children's Bible class, takes kids on educational field trips, and was recently honored for her contribution to society. She hurt her back a few years ago and couldn't wait to get better so that she could get back to her "little people" (which is what I used to call my students when I taught). Then she got pneumonia, but she willed herself to get better and was up faster than any doctor could predict at her age. She didn't fall into the pit of "pneumonia is the old people's friend"; instead, her one focus was to get to her children. Her passion—that is, her power going outward—healed her.

* * *

I don't think that we can leave this tenet without the actual extension of righteousness and justice that it deserves. A perfect example of this happened when I was 16. My father had a mistress named Virginia who lived just a few blocks from us. My mother knew about it, but because she liked the economic lifestyle she was getting used to, she closed her mind to it. I know that I've said that "it takes two," but I'd been an unhappy witness to my mother's castrating ways. She was very moody and stayed in her room for days, where she'd usually lie around in a leopard-skin robe and read. My sister, Sharon, was left with me and our maid, Rosie, who had been with us for years. Poor Rosie was hardly ever paid—yes, my mother gave her carfare and food, but she always told my father that she paid her. My dad would end up paying Rosie when he would get home from business trips—each time he usually had to give her back pay as well.

Anyway, Daddy said that he was going to leave and when he got settled he'd send for me. As much as I loved my father, I couldn't leave Sharon or Grandma Ada and Brother. The thought of either being with my father and Virginia or of staying with my mother and being relegated to the keeper of the household was more than I could bear.

At the time I was dating one of the sweetest guys in the world, and I confided to him how torn up I was. Joe looked at me for a long time and said, "Why don't we get married? Then I could stay and help you." I thought it was the perfect solution! I'd be married; even at his age he was working two jobs, so I felt I'd be taken care of. (And we loved each other.) We were too young to get married in Missouri or Kansas, but I had a brainstorm: If I doctored up our birth certificates, we could go to Kansas and finish our senior year, and no one would be the wiser.

It was September 16th (I'll never forget the day!), and I dressed in a white pinafore with matching white sandals. Joe met me at the streetcar, with two of our friends whom we'd sworn to secrecy. We got off in Kansas City, Kansas, and Joe and I had to get a blood test, which resulted in me almost fainting. Nevertheless, we marched to the courthouse and got married.

As soon as we were done, I became physically ill—not because I didn't love him, but thanks to that gut-level feeling of *What have I done, and really, what was the reason I did it?* Yet Francine assured me, "You'll see how this will play out for the best."

I got home at around 3:30 in the afternoon and was going to change because Joe was going to pick me up as if we were going on a date. We'd then "consummate our marriage" . . . which hadn't dawned on me until later when I thought about all the other parts of what being married meant. Well, I walked in the house, and my mother, who never seemed to care about my comings and goings before, asked me where I'd been.

It was almost as if a silent signal had been sent out. This isn't because I'm so good, but I just couldn't lie. Would you believe I opened my mouth and blurted out, "I just married Joe"?

My mother went into hysterics and went to track down my father. I couldn't face that, so I took a few dollars out of my drawer, caught the streetcar, and went to the local Katz drugstore. I must have sat there for hours drinking Coke after Coke and crying. I kept wondering, *What did I do? How many people have I hurt? What was I thinking?*

I decided to get back on the streetcar and go see my grandmother. I remember it as if it were yesterday: I ran in the door and knelt on the floor with my head in her generous lap, and in between hiccups and crying my eyes out, I told her what I'd done. She didn't say anything for a while— she just listened and rubbed my face and stroked my hair. Sounding like Francine, she kept saying, "It will all turn out all right—nothing ventured, nothing gained."

Finally, the door opened and there was my mother, looking like the mad Lady of Shalott. She looked at me and then at my grandmother, and then she screamed, "Mama, what are we going to do with Sylvia?!"

Without missing a beat, Grandma Ada shot back, "That's not really the question. The question is what are we going to do with *you?*" Apparently this was one of the few times that my grandmother had ever spoken to my mother like that, so Mama just stood there with her mouth open. My grandmother continued, "Celeste, get your house in order, and for once look outside of yourself," which, of course, goes right back to this tenet we've been discussing.

Well, I didn't know whether I was still upset by what I'd done or more dumbfounded by what I'd witnessed, but I rode home with my mother in silence. When we arrived, my father was there. He had his head in his hands and had been crying. "Daddy," I wailed, "I'm so sorry!"

All he did was ask, "Why, Sylvia?" At this point, I really didn't know why I'd done it. What seemed so clear to me at the time was now just a mishmash of pain, and I felt that I'd been incredibly selfish.

My father promptly got on the phone and called an attorney to have the marriage annulled. This was on a Friday, and I went through Saturday and wouldn't take Joe's calls. On Sunday, I finally told him what had happened. He said, "Where do we go from here?" I truly didn't know. I was so full of shame.

Wouldn't you know that even though Joe and I had gotten married in another state, it had showed up that Sunday in our city's newspaper? I had to go to school the next day, but I didn't sleep all night. After all, this was the early 1950s, and good girls, especially Catholic ones, didn't do this sort of thing.

I'll never forget entering the school—of course, my locker had to be at the end of the hall. Joe hadn't shown up (I found out later he was sick with a high fever), but my dear friend Warren walked right up to me and took my hand. He said, "Walk with me with your head high, and just take one step at a time." The silence was deafening—there were whispers and backs turned. Shaking like a leaf all the way, I made it to my locker. I blindly went to my first class and sat down. Sister Delores quietly said, "Sister Teresa Marie and Father Hicks want to see you in the office."

Here it comes, I thought. I went in repeating to myself, "Within your weakness—or, in this case, your silly selfishness—lies your strength sleeping." First, Father told me to ask forgiveness for what I'd done, and I did. Then Sister Teresa Marie said, "We've decided to keep you, but we're going to send Joe to another school." I pleaded, "No, please don't! I'll go—it wasn't his fault. I more or less talked him into it because of a problem I was having."

"Are you pregnant?" Sister asked.

"Of course not!" I replied, horrified (but now I see why that would have been a logical assumption).

"We'll keep him then if you promise you won't date or hang around him anymore."

"I promise," I said. It hurt so bad because puppy love or not, I really cared about him. I never told Joe that they wanted him out, but if he reads this he'll understand.

Time heals. . . . Daddy found out that Virginia was having an affair with another man, and for whatever reason, the family sort of hung together. My father never played around again, and I'm sure he settled into a life of quiet desperation, but we did have some good times and great vacations in California. Grandma Ada was the rock, of course, and by her telling my mother to turn outward, she did try in her own way. It was a moment in time in which my motive was (I thought) pure. At least I tried to do something, and Francine was right . . . everything turned out okay.

I saw Joe again at our 50th class reunion. He walked right up to me, just as he has many times over the years. He's now been married five times and has six kids (I think that, like me, he has a penchant for trying to make people better), and his present wife is an angel and I love her.

Anyway, when he walked up, he kissed me and said, "I'll always remember you, sweetheart—you were my first love." I kissed him back and said, "And you were mine." [**Note:** This isn't the Joe who was my boyfriend later on and recently died, whom I mentioned in the Introduction.]

Before we go on to the next tenet, I hope that you can see how life takes its turns, and if you keep going, things do get better—if, that is, you turn outward rather than go in and hide. Just think of my grandmother's words to my mother: *Look outside of yourself.* Sometimes you won't always do the right thing, but if your heart is in the right place, it usually does come out okay.

How Can This Tenet Help You?

Is your power genetic, environmental, or just in your chart? Well, it's a little of all three, but I believe that it's in every human soul to succeed, whether it's a primitive people's need for survival or Dr. Jonas Salk's discovery of the polio vaccine. Let's examine your chart again, as it still might be causing you some confusion. You've written all the major and minor points you need to learn—the bad, the ugly, and the beautiful—but you may not realize that it all comes down to what you make of it. Say that you've written in (as horrible as it sounds) that you lose a child or loved one. While you may have fulfilled that horrendous learning curve, it's what you do with it that brings about spirituality.

So even with your chart, you still can create miracles or make your schooling here so much more enjoyable by literally "putting on a happy soul" and projecting your power outward. You can make yourself as well as you wish to be and have even more physical strength by doing the right things for your body. Physically, it's best to eat healthfully, exercise, and take vitamin supplements; get regular facials or massages; and avoid drugs, alcohol, and nicotine. But what's vitally important—no matter what age you are—is that you believe you're strong, not sickly, fragile, or frail.

Now that we've addressed the outward manifestation of strength and power, I'd like you to realize that not everything comes down to your instinct and survival—it also comes from your soul and even from life, which has hopefully given you the strength to get through any hurdles and sorrows . . . even if your power isn't psychic. Maybe it lies in building a boat or running a small business. The world is filled with options, but we seem to be infected by a type of malaise that threatens our health and creates more mental stress. Every time I hear "I'd like to do it, but I haven't gotten around to it," I always respond, "Do it now! Make the time."

Just keep in mind that when I started to write and share my research, I endured years of scoffing and critical and cruel rhetoric. But if you're full of conviction and walk in truth, you're going to make it, just like I did. So many people can't get out of the box—all I ask is that you try. Believe me, if you do, you'll notice that there's sunshine, fresh air, and blessings all around!

* * * * *

TENET VI

In faith be like the wind chimes: Hold steady until faith, like the wind, moves you to joy.

I've often mentioned the desert period in life, which happens to all of us—whether we live in an actual arid region or not. It can happen at the beginning, middle, or end of our days, although most individuals choose the early or middle years because these times are confusing to begin with. We might call it puberty or a midlife crisis, but a desert period can hit whenever we chart it. This is how it operates: We feel that we're just existing or are in a rut. We get up, go to work (or do whatever we have to do) without joy, and then we go to bed.

"What am I going to be?" "Where am I going?" and "What does it all mean?" are common sayings for our early days; and "What have I done?" "What have I accomplished?" "Am I on track?" and "Have I failed?" are common threads of middle age.

Life themes have been written about many times in my

books, but it should be explained that these are actually subjects that we choose to learn from in order to become what God wants us to be. (For a detailed description of our themes, please see my book *Soul's Perfection*.) We don't tend to pick the same themes for each life; rather, we choose different ones that will help us expand our knowledge for God and ourselves. For example, we don't want to become a victim, so we conquer it. Some themes are negative and can belong to the dark side, but we need the negative to accentuate the positive, so to speak: A poverty theme can mean that you can beat it by not succumbing to it. Usually all the themes are for us to learn from and overcome, and within that process we have our desert periods.

Faith to us Gnostics is synonymous with *knowing*, which is really important during the desert period . . . and Lord knows I understand this. When I was around 50, I went through a bad one of these. I'd been doing readings and teaching for years, and although I enjoyed it, it was the sameness of it that was getting me down. I wanted to break out—and that's when Hay House picked up *My Guide, Myself*. I tinkered with it; added to, deleted, and updated it; and renamed it. You might know it as *Adventures of a Psychic* . . . a book that went on *The New York Times* bestseller list and stayed there for more than a year. I then got on the *Montel Williams Show* a few years later, and I've never looked back. When I did feel that I was in the proverbial vicious cycle, I went on the road and lectured, which I still do today because I love it so much. Now I'm taking cruises and lecturing on them, too.

So many times, especially in this day and age, we look at times of inactivity as depression. I'm not talking about people who need pharmaceuticals here, since many of us have chemical imbalances that physiologically as well as biologically cause depression, but we often run for a fast fix instead of realizing that we charted this for ourselves. The word *depressed* means to "press down," and many times it's nature's way of getting us to stop and take stock of our life.

Even what we call "accidents" can be written in our charts to slow us down.

I remember about 15 years ago, for example, when I was running up the steps to my front door and just nicked my right foot on one of the bricks. The next day my foot was twice its size. I went to the doctor and found out I had blood poisoning and cellulitis (all over a little nick in my foot!). I came home with pills and poultices and was relegated to soaking my foot. Thoroughly aggravated, I sat down on the couch and said, "What in the hell is this about?" The message that came in loud and clear was: "You're running too fast—you have to slow down."

So when I find my clients in a desert period, I explain that to have faith, they have to be quiet and hold steady because this truly is the time when they can learn all those miserable lessons they don't want to—the tolerance, the patience, the endurance, and the survival that they never would have learned during the frenzied times. Instead of looking at a desert period as a bad thing, I tell my clients to be still and go through it like a cleansing. This way, when their faith and knowing, like the wind, not only moves them to the joy of what they've accomplished, they'll also be moved to activation.

When unexpected negative change hits, which it does in all lives, we have a tendency to go on hold. The desert period is called this because it can seem like no matter where we look, there's only sand as far as the eye can see. Sometimes we might see a mirage—which is even worse, for it takes the form of a false solution that only sinks us deeper into the sand. So what can we do? We can only keep walking . . . eventually, the heat will subside, and before we know it, we will have reached the oasis.

We always have a choice: We can gripe and cry and shake our fists at the sky and wonder what we've ever done to deserve this long "nothing" period, or we can use it to advance our soul. Think for a moment about how the pioneers felt coming from my area of St. Joseph, Missouri, to

Oregon and California. Now that was a real, living desert period—I mean, think of the heat, the lack of conveniences, the Indian raids, and so forth.

When I was in Egypt, talking to about 250 people in front of the Sphinx and the Great Pyramid, I contemplated what it must be like for the Bedouins who really do live in this rocky wasteland. Then I pictured the ancient caravans that followed the trade routes in the heat and unforgiving sun, while fighting with the bugs, scorpions, and unruly camels (which are amazing and wonderful animals, but God, they smell bad!).

You can say of the Bedouins that they're used to it—well, that's not exactly true. I was privileged to talk to a large group of Arabs near the tomb of Seti I and asked them if they loved their life. In very good English they answered, "Madam, it is a life. It is very hard and many get sick and die, but it is what we know—and *all* we know—and we respect the desert because it can be cruel and unforgiving."

There's something innate in the human spirit that knows what's difficult and what's easy, but the Arab people are to be admired. They make it through a *real* desert period, and they give honor to Allah for giving them abundance when they have it, and when they don't, they forge on anyway.

You can't tell me that the peasant doesn't know he has it hard or the pioneer woman didn't know her life wasn't easy. The desert period in our culture can be outside as well as inside, but again, it's what we make of or learn from it. It goes along with that ancient expression: "I cried because I didn't have shoes until I saw a man who didn't have any feet."

How Can This Tenet Help You?

Whereas the previous tenets have been action-oriented, it may seem that this one suggests you stay steady or seemingly quiet, but look deeper. . . . To hold steady means to stay firm in your convictions and be witness to your beliefs. *Faith* is a harsh word because you have to go on supposition. If you hold on to your beliefs in a loving God, you'll find that your faith turns into an unshakable knowing.

You see, there comes a time in every life that fits the ancient Asian proverb "When in doubt, do nothing." This means that you keep still inside as well as out when those desert periods hit. It will seem as if your life has come to a standstill and you can't seem to lurch out of it, but remember that it's all in the pattern of perfection. Think of this: No matter how diversified your life is, isn't it one that still has a lot of sameness to it? Mine certainly does. I travel, do readings, do Montel's show and other media, lecture, and write . . . over and over again. Sure I see my family, play with my grandchildren, and love my animals, but it's all the same for each and every one us—the survival of life!

Just to survive this hell on Earth is a tremendous accomplishment for anybody. The survival period can be boring, and I know that sometimes you feel so stressed and overdone that living ceases to have any joy. That's when you've got to change, no matter how hard that is to do. Yet please understand that survival can be quite different from the nothingness of the desert period. That's when you're really not doing that much and you don't know what to do, and it seems that the air of life has gone out of you. But remember, this is all a charted period that you can (like any period) use for good or ill.

Even though you chose your chart, keep in mind that you can make all things better by how you perceive them. So you hold steady and make it through with what you've learned through the desperate periods, the grief periods, and the holding (desert) periods; after all, if you stay quiet and steady, the breeze of God will come in and move you. There's always another day, a telephone call, a new friend, and episodes that will change your life to joy.

Sure, you can take the path of least resistance, but that doesn't get you anywhere except to the cardinal sins that we hear so much about. I think they should be listed as *apathy, self-indulgence,* and *spiritual bankruptcy.* Yet these aren't so much sins as roadblocks. To have apathy is deadly because there's no feeling or sympathy (Lord knows I'd rather be empathetic than have no feeling). Many times apathy is the armor we wear so that we won't be hurt, but then we feel no joy *or* pain—it's truly the "nothingness" of mere blind existence. We could learn from the love and unconditional loyalty animals give without asking for anything in return.

Self-indulgence is a case of "It's all for me, not for you" . . . what a lonely life that must be. Everything to these poor souls revolves around them and what makes them feel good. Spiritual bankruptcy is also sad because it encompasses the ones who've given up or chosen to ignore what's going on. The emptiness that fills these souls must be very dark and depressing. God is *always* there for you to just lift one little finger of hope or a "maybe" of realization to let the floodgates of grace and knowledge come in.

Note that some desert periods are short, while others are long, but everyone gets them. I'd advise that instead of looking at them as negative times, look at them as if you're a marathon runner: The race can be boring, but you're strengthening your soul. So use this desert period to take stock and learn and be like the wind chimes—God's "wind" will move you to joy at what you've learned.

* * * * * *

TENET VII

Know that each life is a path winding toward perfection. It is the step after step that is hard, not the whole of the journey.

We're supposed to modify our charts without changing the ultimate learning process. Now, while they give us an overall map of life, there are many ways to get to, let's say, Miami. We can take a bus, train, car, or plane (or we can just walk or crawl if need be), but the outcome is the same: We get there and, hopefully, arrive better off than we were before we started.

Of course, if we expected life to be fair and just, then we shouldn't have come here. I'm reminded of a rock climber I once read for. He'd scaled El Capitan, a sheer cliff in Yosemite National Park, and said, "It looked great from below. Yeah, I knew it would be difficult, but I was fit for it and had been training and practicing for a year. Halfway to the top, I wanted to give up because it was so hard, but I kept going—cursing myself the whole time as I did." So it is with life. We look at our proposed chart and say, "No problem,

I can handle that!" Then we get into it and wonder what in the world we were thinking. Nevertheless, we forge ahead and hopefully are better for it.

If we look at our life in one fell swoop, it can be very daunting. As I've said so many times (and I'm not trying to be negative), life isn't too short—it's too long. Like you, in the 69 years I've lived I feel that I've actually endured many lifetimes. Even in childhood, we take steps on many paths depending on our themes and charts. Yet to look at our lives as a series of small steps can make things seem easier, for we can then analyze how we've gotten where we are now. I'm going to show you what I mean by using the example of my own life. (Those of you who have read *Adventures of a Psychic* may find some of this familiar, but it bears repeating here, so stick with me.)

The tiny steps of our childhood can be looked at (for better or worse) as the first ones on our journey of learning. My early life was fraught with an absentee and critical mother. Maybe you had a miserable father, were raised in a foster home, or were even fortunate enough to have a great home life (congratulations—few do). Even if the outward scenario is all right, sometimes we don't feel good about ourselves internally when we're very young. Either way, it's one of the steps of the journey that we can't see at the time, but which helps form who we're going to become.

The next steps are the beginnings of our schooling and levels of social interaction. Our younger years are more formative than we realize—here we begin to forge our own self-image along with the way others make us feel. Unlike my sister, I couldn't wait to get out and mingle with people. Sharon, unfortunately, was under my mother's neurotic wing and was therefore programmed to be frail, so she hid inside. This isn't meant to be critical—it's just a fact of our charts, along with the way brainwashing and apathy can work on us.

We then get into young adulthood and hopefully finish our schooling or get a job. Every part of these phases, as you know, contains both dark and light. For instance, my high school years were good, but my college years were just golden. I went to the College of St. Teresa (now known as Avila University) in Kansas City, Missouri. I had friends and parties and loved my classes. I remember when I was in the annual College Day parade as the "mad scientist." Each float had a subject, some serious and some funny (I always chose to be on a funny one—the year before I'd been a cavewoman). I had my hair sprayed white and sticking out in all directions, wore kooky glasses and a white lab coat, and I'd pasted a false eye to my cheek.

As I passed the gaggle of nuns that had gathered to watch, Sister Marcella Marie walked up to the float and asked, "Sylvia, why do you always make yourself so ugly when you're so pretty?"

I was shocked by this because my mother had often announced that "Sharon is the pretty one, but oh well . . . Sylvia *does* have somewhat of a personality." I'd never had much of a sense of my outer self (which I attribute to my grandmother), but to hear from a nun that I was pretty was mind-boggling. Later as I was telling my best friend how surprised I was, she just looked at me and said, "We thought you must know. I mean, you have a mirror don't you?" Now, this has nothing to do with my level of attractiveness, it's just an example of how we can be programmed by the reflection of others.

Anyway, back to college. My time was filled with learning, which I dearly loved. I was studying to be a teacher (in those days, girls became nurses, secretaries, or teachers—everything else was unacceptable). I took theology courses along with my education classes because I couldn't reconcile what I was taught with an all-loving God.

I used to throw these legendary parties every Saturday night with my father's consent (because it kept me home), and it was at one of these that I met Ski. Francine had said that this would be one of my biggest steps to date. I fell madly in love with him, and I interpreted Francine's message to mean that we'd be married, have children, and enjoy love everlasting.

Looking back now, I can see that I measured every male I met afterward with how I felt about Ski. He was educated and loved poetry, was fun and kind, and was like no one I'd met before—after all, he'd traveled the world as a sailor, and I was a simple Kansas City girl. The first time he kissed me, it was just like the movies: The world faded, and I said to myself, "So *this* is what all the poems and songs are written about!"

However, it turns out that he was married (although separated) with two kids. I found out from a friend of his, and then his wife wrote the college and named me the "other woman." I was called into Father Nadeux's office (God rest his loving soul), and given the news. To say that it broke my heart is an understatement.

I ended things with Ski, although how I did it or where any of the courage came from I don't know. I do remember thinking of the heartache his wife must be going through, and of those two little children. Ski professed that it was over with his wife, but I was also Catholic and couldn't marry a divorced man. Before we parted for the last time, he told me, "See that bright star on the right? When this life is over, I'll meet you on that one."

My heart was in shreds. For a while, the world went black, and everything seemed far away. Life looked ugly and dirty for a long time—I noticed trash on the streets and flowers that were dead rather than blooming—yet I went on having parties. Within a year, I married a policeman whom I can't say I loved, but he did seem to love me.

Francine has said to me often in my life that things happen for a reason, usually after something bad has taken place. Looking back, as much of a rebound as this marriage seemed to be, I never would have my sons and would never have gotten to California if it had not taken place. So as you can see, sometimes these crazy and seemingly unpredictable steps lead us onto the path we should be on.

My husband, Gary, had lost his job over mysterious circumstances. When a friend told him of a good offer in Sunnyvale, California, we decided to move. Consequently, I had to leave my hometown, my family, and all my friends and go to a strange place. Even though I had a job waiting for me as a teacher, I was very frightened and feeling alone—my baby, Paul, was my only comfort. I was 27 and had just recovered from a severe operation in which I'd almost died, and I was even afraid to leave the doctor who'd seen me through the whole ordeal.

In 1964, with $2,000 and a 1958 Chevrolet Impala convertible holding only what we could fit into it (which wasn't much), Gary, Paul, and I moved west. I tried to tell myself that it was an adventure, but I was so very homesick. We rented a house filled with earwigs, and that first night, I sat there on the floor with a blanket over Paul and me as the bugs dropped from a recently painted ceiling around us like rain. "I'll pretend I'm in a rain forest," I kept telling myself. It turns out that my husband's "great opportunity" turned out to be like so much smoke, so he spent the next several months halfheartedly looking for a job.

About a month after we'd arrived, my father, mother, and Sharon drove up and said, "Surprise! We've sold our house and have come to stay with you!" My father, bless his heart, wanted to be with his eldest daughter. "Besides," he said, "I hate the winters." He'd been a vice president in a large firm back in Kansas City, but he'd quit that lucrative job. For months I was the only one working, teaching at St. Albert the Great making $275 a month. Daddy did get a job selling cars, while my mother went into substitute teaching—and Gary finally became a security guard. Regardless of how much you love your folks, two families in one house is hard, but here again you learn patience and tolerance.

Although it was hell at times, being married to Gary made me grow in ways I never believed possible. Being raised with a strong father, I always felt that you did everything for the man and your life would be happy. I guess for the right person it might or should be reciprocated, but not so in my case. Perhaps if I hadn't been raised the way I was, I could have stood up for myself, but the steps of survival are truly marvelous. . . .

One day I told myself that I'd had enough. I didn't want my children (especially *male* children) to grow up and disrespect women, so I left Gary and filed for divorce. I had no money except a measly teacher's salary—although it was now up to $500 per month, even in the '70s that wasn't anything to speak of. I just couldn't go to my parents, so I moved the kids into the cheapest apartment I could find.

As I look back on my first marriage, which contained a lot of abuse and pain, there *were* good times, some laughs, the birth of our children, and even some fairly intellectual talks. So you can choose to remember the days that weren't all bad. I smile when I hear now that Gary is a born-again Christian, which I think is great as long as he stops judging everyone. When I met him in 1958, he was an atheist—how ironic life can be! Of course, I don't believe that anyone really is an atheist deep inside. I'm convinced that such people are actually driven by fear, false ego, or just plain fatalism.

Anyway, I'd known at the beginning that it was wrong to marry Gary, as my best pal of 61 years, Mary Margaret, will tell you. Nevertheless, I felt driven and compelled to do so—which was probably in my chart. We come into life with a road map, a chart we wrote to learn by. But life can be a false seductress, and sometimes we feel that we've missed out and should have followed a different path. No, the chart will have its way with us . . . just as it has with me. So we can make the best of it and enjoy the ride, or get caught up in our own doubts and fears and spend our whole life feeling as if we missed the boat. Perhaps I could have taken a less painful route to get to California . . . but I got here nonetheless. We'll always fulfill our charts, but often out of poor judgment we delay it or take the bumpy road rather than the easier one. In the long run, though, we learn. (Incidentally, Mary Margaret sends me a condolence card every April 2 because that's when Gary and I got married, and she's always said that she had guilt because she introduced us. I told her to give that up, for I was supposed to get to where I ended up.)

When I started doing readings in California, I fought it like a cornered tiger. I'd vowed after I left Kansas City that no one would know I was psychic, which certainly included my not doing readings. Sure, my friends in Missouri knew and accepted me, but there I was comfortable using my psychic abilities. Now I was going to a strange land with strange people, and I was going to keep quiet about this psychic stuff no matter what.

I remember driving up and down a boulevard in the San Francisco area and having Francine tell me that I couldn't and wouldn't stop. In fact, I'd eventually be interviewed on TV by a blonde woman, and my career would start publicly—it wouldn't be just for friends in school or women's groups like it was in Kansas City. I remember beating my hands on the steering wheel, crying, "No, I won't!" Sharon was with me at the time, and I asked her, "I don't have to if I don't want to . . . do I?"

"Of course not," she said, and we both went silent, knowing that my destiny was set as surely as the road we were on.

＊ ＊ ＊

I started taking night-school classes to get my master's degree, and that's where I met Bob Williams, a professor who was to become one of my dearest friends. We immediately hit it off and became very close. Since Bob was my teacher, we talked about literature a lot, but eventually I confided in him about my psychic abilities. He wanted me to use my talent, but I remained adamant about keeping it quiet. I was just into my second semester of his class and we were studying George Eliot's *Daniel Deronda*—particularly a part in the novel about spiritualism—when Bob suddenly announced to the entire class, "Next week Sylvia will show the class what true spiritualism is about by doing readings."

I had visions of how I was going to strangle him. But because I loved him so much, I finally consoled myself with the thought, *So what . . . it's only 40 people in the class—how far can that go?*

The next week I very nervously got up and went through my explanation of how I was born this way. Then I began to tell the students about their lives, and the ensuing uproar almost turned chaotic. During a break, I went to a small coffee bar on campus, and to my surprise, almost everyone from class was lined up for a reading. I just wanted to have a cup of coffee, but ended up answering more than 100 questions. As fate would have it, one of the women in the class was the head of a local woman's group, and she asked if I'd come and talk. I declined, she persisted, and I finally gave in. (Oh, what fools we are when we try to deceive ourselves!) I did a talk for that group and then another, and on and on it went. . . .

After I divorced Gary and remarried, my new husband, Dal, encouraged me to go public and start a foundation. I was still teaching and doing readings for the nuns and priests, and my popularity grew by word of mouth. By the end of 1972, I'd begun to do readings for five dollars and have small group lectures in our apartment. I was still teaching school as well and lived with Dal, my two boys, and Mary in a small two-bedroom apartment in a poorer part of town.

Bob had gone to Australia, where he died, leaving a huge hole in my heart. So, because he was so instrumental in my going public, I started a foundation in his honor. It was first called the Nirvana Foundation for Psychic Research, and along with readings and hypnosis, we researched everything related to the paranormal. Thank God, because so much material in my books has come from more than 30 years of research by the foundation and subsequent organizations.

It got to be too much in our small apartment, so we

moved into a townhouse. Soon after, my clientele became too disruptive for that home, too, so we found a tiny two-room commercial venue in Campbell, California. It was in the back of a building, so we didn't even have a front entrance with a sign. We had an old couch in one room that had lost its legs and was supported by bricks—this was the hypnosis room and waiting area. I was in the other room, which was like a closet with no windows. I was so claustrophobic that I hung a curtain rod with drapes on a blank wall. Many people just stared at me when they tried to look out, but it helped alleviate my closed-in feeling.

People seemed to find me. It was like the movie *Field of Dreams*: "If you build it, they will come"—and come they did. My dad worked with me at first; then, as business grew and more assistance was needed, I was fortunate to get volunteer help from some of the attendees of my study groups (which I still held in my home). The first were Larry, Laurie, and Pam and Gene Meyer (a married couple who are still with me today).

I was called by a producer from KPIX, the local CBS affiliate in San Francisco, and was asked to appear on a local television show called *People Are Talking*. It was hosted by Ann Fraser, a petite blonde (Francine scores again) with a marvelous and bubbly personality whom I'm still friends with to this day. She was later joined by Ross McGowan, a local host and personality and also a dear friend, and I spent the next ten years or so appearing frequently on their program. I made so many friends from that show, such as Bob George, Ann Miller, Steve Ober, and others—that they spread out and produced their own shows and then remembered me and gave boosts to my career later on.

How Can This Tenet Help You?

As you can see, each step of my life may not have seemed like much at the time, but when you put the entire journey together, it's not too shabby. The same holds true for *your* life's path. As I tell my clients, things can change in a second. Each step helps us to move forward and survive pitfalls—even the loves lost, the divorces, the deaths, and the illnesses. But no one can convince me that life is one long, agonizing, painful journey unless a particular individual chooses to put rocks in their own shoes.

The whole of the journey is the legacy we leave behind. After all, when I started so many years ago, they didn't know whether to bless me or burn me, but if your motive is truly to purely help and you're sincere in your soul, people will see it.

Look at the entirety of your life—not just the cracks and flaws, but each step you've taken. Of course you have your themes and your blocks to overcome—even if you try to hide from them, they'll circle around until you face them and scale that mountain of self. Now it's one thing to plod along a dusty old road as you fulfill your destiny, and it's another to be on a superhighway that goes along with speed *and* ease. So try, if you can, to find a road that has rest stops, eating places, and nice hotels—in other words, one in which God is present—it will still get you to the same place, but it will be much more comfortable.

Also, keep in mind that you've had many lives, and in each one you've learned a different facet of yourself. I've never talked much about my lives, but I'll cover a few here to show you how they build on each other.

I had a life in Kenya, which is probably why I love that country so much. I carried water, cooked for the tribe, and died early. I had a life in Austria where I wanted children but couldn't have them, and my husband left me. I had a life as an empress in Asia in which I lasted 27 days before I was poisoned. I had a life as a wife of a Crusader; he died, and I went on to teach Gnosis. There are 54 of these lives, but what comes through many of them is the will to help—in the lives that I didn't assist others, I wasn't happy. I've seemed (as we all have) to have taken steps to be better:

I've fallen and gotten up, just as you have at one time or another.

We can take detours, but we always live our charts and our destiny. We are what we are and what we're meant to be. We all end up taking the steps we must complete to finish our journey. It takes time, and it's quite a journey, but you're perfecting by the sheer fact that you come here to Earth in the first place.

＊ ＊ ＊ ＊ ＊

TENET VIII

Be simple. Allow no man to judge you, not even yourself, for you cannot judge God.

Despite this tenet's advice, I do have a tendency to judge *people* who judge. When I was raising my children alone (that was in the days when most women didn't work), for example, I was told that they were going to grow up lopsided because they didn't have a father figure. I didn't buy that one, but what I did do was ensure that my blessed dad was an integral part of my boys' life. I realized early on that their father wasn't the paternal type—so, wrong or right, I took on that mantle of motherhood with a vengeance.

People who have worked with me for 30-some-odd years will attest to the fact that I never bring my personal life into my work, but if my children or grandchildren are in trouble, my world comes to a halt. I've worked through my own grief and divorces, but if my loved ones are hurt, I'm there for them and that's it. I've been judged for being so involved, but I never push . . . I'm always asked. I guess my sons and I must have formed a silent pact to be like the Three Muske-teers. Do I interfere in their relationships or in the raising of their children? Never, for that's judgment.

I feel that's part of my being psychic, for I really try to refrain from forming an opinion of human behavior unless it's evil—then, of course, all bets are off. You don't hurt peo-ple out of spite and cruelty or for the sport of it and not reap what you've sown. I'm a great believer in karma—and not the insane type that never lets you breathe without wor-rying. I mean that if you perform actions with malicious intentions, it's going to come back to you in one way or another. (I talk more about this concept in Tenet XIV.)

Now, when some members of humankind first came into form, they decided that they'd go on their own track away from God—these are the misguided souls we call "dark entities." Dark entities are much like bad children whose behavior doesn't reflect that they had great parents who did everything right. I have visions of Mrs. Hitler walking around saying, "What did I do wrong?" After all, not all of history's evil figures came from horrible homes.

I'm sure that we've all had run-ins with these dark souls (as I explain in my book *The Nature of Good and Evil*). There are no devils—there are just these entities from the Begin-ning that separated from God and decided to be missiles of destruction. In all fairness, they can give our souls fodder by being the opposite of them. I don't believe that a person who's abused has to become an abuser (unless it's in their chart to do so), but in God's plan, we can learn from these people. It's like "There but for the grace of God, go I." For example, in my early years I loved my mother, then I tried to love her, and then I couldn't love her. Sadly, she didn't love me or my sister or my dear father. It may seem shock-ing to say, but she was one of those misplaced dark entities who *couldn't* love. I guess I could have tried to have pity and compassion for her if she hadn't been so venomous up till the day she died.

The way you can tell a dark entity is more simple than

you might realize. At first, they come on very kind and sweet, and they seem to be everything that you've been looking for (male or female). But it doesn't take long for them to turn—no matter what happens, it's always your fault as far as they're concerned. I always say that they could stab you and then blame you for running into the knife. This may be a little excessive, but it's true. Ted Bundy and Jeffrey Dahmer didn't show remorse; neither has Scott Peterson or Charles Manson—it's always someone else's fault.

Dark entities leave destruction in their wake. They can wreak havoc on their loved ones, which they justify by their own track that only runs one way and causes devastation. They also don't have angels around them and seem to be devoid of a spirit guide. (If they do have one, the guide is also dark.)

All bets are off when it comes to judging dark entities. After all, no one who has any conscience or God-loving sense would refrain from judging Adolf Hitler or Osama bin Laden—our assessment of such individuals may actually be a means of survival—but God will ultimately have the final say as far as evil is concerned. Here again, in the perfection that is God, He/She doesn't judge the evildoers, but ultimately removes them. Just as on the Other Side, where we have our Home and live for eternity, all evildoers will ultimately be removed at the end of this reincarnation schematic that we're in now. They'll be reabsorbed back into God's mass and no longer be a part of creation, thus losing their individuality. (Those of us in creation keep our individuality as one of the multiple facets of God.)

The concept that "God judges" has confused theologians for years. It's just not so, for here again that makes God humanized. You see, God allowed these entities to utilize their own free will to not only separate from Him/Her, but to also incarnate as we do on this planet. Their continued existence is allowed by God in this schematic so that we can learn by incarnating in a plane of existence that contains negativity and evil.

All religions seem to have some type of war with good against evil in their dogma, as if they were trying to describe the inequities of life—yet they're neglecting the simple fact that Earth is the hardest school there is. As my guide Francine has always said, "This planet is the insane asylum of the universe. Those who come here are the bravest and want to perfect their souls faster than they would on another planet—one that is not so inundated by every type of hate and cruelty."

Think about this: It's much more difficult to learn in a perfect environment. All of us are faced with negativity each day that we live on Earth, but from this constant barrage we learn endurance, patience, and survival. And strangely enough, we learn a great deal from these dark entities—namely, how not to be. When we observe and hear about the actions of evil every day in the news, most of us turn away from it and strive to be better. As our spirituality deepens, we even fight against evil by doing good deeds, helping others, donating to charities, and giving our time and effort to causes for good.

The eighth tenet basically says that *we* are God, because we're the genetic part of God, made by God, and we carry that spark of the Divine within us. (Granted, there are some who seem to have a larger spark than others, but it's a spark nevertheless.) So we don't have the right to judge someone who doesn't measure up to what we think our standards are. Even our Lord said, "Judge not, lest ye be judged" (which I find that some people who profess to be spiritual conveniently forget) and "You without sin cast the first stone."

It's interesting how it's only taken 2,000 years for some of humankind to feel that they can judge with only half-truths. Fortunately, it's just a portion of society that acts like they have too much time on their hands—to that end, they take up causes to persecute people of different creeds, ethnic backgrounds, sexual orientation, and what have you. People are even judged by the money they make, where they live, or what their heritage is.

Many times bigotry can actually be explained by actions from a past life. For example, a woman came to our foundation years ago who seemingly hated Asians. We found out through hypnotic regression that in a past life she'd been raped by some renegade Asian men, which had tainted her present life. Once this was consciously known and released, the woman softened her racism; today, she even has an Asian best friend.

These days, we see white women with black men where I grew up in Missouri. I remember the terrible days where if you were walking on the sidewalk and a black person approached, they had to get off the sidewalk and walk in the gutter. African Americans also couldn't drink out of the same water fountains, use the same public restrooms, or eat in the same restaurants as white people, and they were forced to sit at the back of the bus. My grandmother voiced her feelings on this to anyone who would listen, but in those days it was like whistling in the wind.

At least now we can see people of color with a white person without fear of the lynching posse. Yet even though things are somewhat better, we're not totally there yet—not with Latinos, Middle Easterners, Jews, and gays, among others, still being targeted for discrimination. I guess I'll just never understand. . . . But even if you forget what bigoted issues people have, why wouldn't logic dictate that God made everyone and everything? Who do some people think they are to sit in judgment—or even propose to know the omnipotence of God—of a person's creed, sexuality, or color? You can never attain true spirituality when you have bigotry in any form in your heart.

With judging also comes hate and violence, so it has a long tail like a serpent that can recoil and turn on you. I cannot understand how, for instance, some so-called Christians can preach about Jesus and then turn around and evaluate others to the point of creating hatred and dissent among humankind. They use the parts of the Bible that are fearful in nature, which have nothing to do with Christ's teachings of love and tolerance, and call themselves "Christians." They slam other religions and even churches within the same faith, lambasting Catholics or other Protestant sects; they condemn homosexuality, mixed marriages, certain ethnic groups, and the list goes on and on. How on earth is this Christian? Jesus taught us to love one another, be tolerant and peaceful toward others, and to help one another.

It's fine for these people to be intolerant if they must, but they should at least be honest about it and not put up the sham of being kind people who love all of humanity. We've seen several instances where a religious figure in the public eye has been hurt or brought down by that "serpent of judging," and their hypocrisy was there for all to see.

In fact, it's well known that Christianity, which was based on a messiah who preached love and kindness, is one of the most intolerant religions on the face of this planet. The many wars started in the name of Jesus are proof of this. I've also heard many so-called Christian leaders say that unless the natives of Africa accept Jesus, they won't go to heaven (or, as they put it, "be saved"). To some of these people who have been "vaccinated by ignorance," I've said, "If you feel so strongly, then go into the bush and convert them yourself." I haven't seen any takers among these bigoted armchair or rocking-chair philosophers.

I've been to Kenya at least a dozen times, and people have asked me, "So what did you think about all the black people?" Each time, I've replied to this with complete honesty: "I didn't see any. I just saw *people*—kind, loving, and giving people." Men even walk down the roads holding hands together, and no one says anything. Kenyans all have the philosophy of living day to day: If they have a few shillings, they'll invite guests over and have a party all night, not caring that there may be nothing tomorrow. They live so much in the moment that if you put a Masai in jail, he'll give up and die because his "now" is forever. This is extreme, but wouldn't it be great if we just had some of that living in the now instead of running around judging everyone?

I don't want to pick on just the Christians, for most of them are loving and kind people, but the fanatics of any religion are becoming the bane of humankind. Extremists' viewpoints are fertile ground for dark entities to operate in, for they can then vent their hatred, bigotry, and destruction on the world under the guise of a religion or faith. Even the words *extreme* and *fanatic* suggest an unbending intolerance toward others who don't believe the way these people do. Of course, Jesus never did this.

We're all human and make mistakes, and by no means am I a saint. I've made a lot of blunders in my life and have never set myself up as a paragon of virtue. Like everyone else, I've stepped into many a pile of you know what. I've made some bad choices in husbands and friends. I can't drink to speak of because I get sick and vomit—not pleasant, but true (I really thank God for this intolerance). And I've been judged by many, as I'm sure all people in public life are.

That doesn't mean that celebrities should ever be above reproach, but to be knocked around by complete strangers who accuse you of being greedy; a fake or a charlatan who bilks people; fat, ugly, cruel, and having a voice that sounds like a man (yes, I've been accused of all these things) does affect you, no matter how spiritual you are. I know that I'm bluntly honest and forthright at times and can become impatient with some people, but I still love them. I'm constantly working on trying to be a better human being—and the more spiritual I get, the more I have to put the skids on myself as far as judging goes. I try to be the best person I can possibly be—and that's what I believe God wants for all of us.

Remember that God also allows us the tools of discernment and laws for social order; otherwise, we'd have anarchy running rampant, and innocent people would be taken advantage of by immoral scoundrels. As it is, new victims are enveloped by evil every day with wars, acts of terrorism, and genocide; not to mention the individual or group acts of murder, rape, child abuse, bigotry, and so on. Yet don't you find it somewhat amazing that the symbol for justice in front of most courthouses is a statue of a woman with scales (that, by the way, is the symbol for the astrological sign of Libra, which I am) in her hand—but she's blindfolded? Does this mean that justice is blind or doesn't choose to see, or that if she did see she couldn't stand what she saw?

In all seriousness, it seems that we don't want to see justice these days—not in small enclaves of society or larger scenarios that play out in the media. We see the perpetrators of crime sometimes being brought to justice, while other times we see criminals go free over some technicality. But know that, even if we don't see it, God's justice *always* comes into play. Look at Jeffrey Dahmer, who was murdered in prison—I'll never say that I wish anyone harm, but it's the way the Divine system operates.

Unfortunately, I don't think that anyone gets justice or closure in situations like this. Yes, the perpetrator may be caught and punished, but the family is still left with the loss. The only real comfort here is that, like I've said, this is a transient place—like a play, we act out our parts, then exit stage right and go Home to God.

Regardless of all the negativity I've listed in this section, I haven't meant to elicit fear but to just show you that all of us chose to come to this planet to learn faster than we would anywhere else. We only have one way to go about being happy, and that is to know that we're doing our part for peace—both out in the world and within ourselves. Please realize that we did pick this for our own perfection. After all, for the greatest education, you go to the most demanding college . . . or in this case, life on this planet.

How Can This Tenet Help You?

I've found that judging yourself can often be the worst thing you can do. (I cover some of this in my book *Sylvia Browne's Lessons for Life*, but I'd like to address it from another area here.) You learn to "judge" from your environment, even from your religious instruction that many times also teaches guilt. Nine times out of ten you've been taught that you're "bad" or did bad things, and then the conclusive result is guilt. Now you have a triple whammy—judging yourself, believing that others are doing the same, and feeling that God is, too. This tenet says to lighten up on yourself! Don't be overly concerned with judgment, because if you live the best you can and try not to hurt others, you'll be fine, especially in the eyes of God.

Now I must confess that I come down pretty hard when I see myself on TV (not the content, because I know that doesn't come from me, but my mannerisms). Once Angelia and I were sitting in my front room when I came on *Montel*. Angelia was watching, and I was trying to do some needlepoint. Out of the blue she asked, "Bagdah, why don't you keep your hands still?"

"I know," I replied. "It's either a nervous habit or I'm concentrating and don't know what I'm doing." Even so, I've got to let things like this go. I'm working on it.

It's also easy to judge situations. For example, while I'm writing this I'm in Hawaii, because my son sometimes brings me here. The first day he wanted to take me deep-sea fishing. *Damn*, I thought, *I'm going to hate this*. It wasn't because of the water, which I love—I didn't want to take time away from my writing, nor did I relish getting seasick. I went, certain of how bad it was going to be . . . and ended up having a great time.

The judgment of society can be really tough (boy, do I know!). If you keep time to a different drummer, putting forth new ideas and concepts, many times society will try to put you down. Look at the scientists who were called crazy, such as Thomas Edison. He was constantly laughed at, yet he never gave up—and, of course, he turned out to be one of the greatest inventors of all time.

Edgar Cayce was tried in a New York court for practicing medicine without a license. He won, but the headlines read

"Seer Gets Seared"—what an awful humiliation for someone who was only trying to do good. And how about our Lord, who preached love and right behavior and was then crucified for it? It can seem that people who come up with goodness, love, and truth can be judged along with the criminal . . . sometimes harsher. Nevertheless, keep in mind that you're definitely a part of the Divine, so don't let anyone judge you.

Also, remember that bad entities never judge themselves and are impervious to any criticism—in fact, they think they're perfect. So if you ever worry about being on track, you are. It's easy to do so: Just simply ask God every day to help you and love others, and you're fulfilling your programmed chart for God. In addition, there's a difference between justifiable anger and judgment without any knowledge, research, logic, or just common sense. Sometimes your judgment fails, but if you listen to that inner voice (not some preconceived notion), you'll become more psychic.

Life has holes in it, so fill them up. Worrying about your appearance wastes time, so if you don't have the looks you want, concentrate on the "inner" you. And don't listen to others' judgments—after all, at the final tally it's just you and God. As Jesus said in Matthew 5:45: "That you may be sons of your Father in heaven: for He makes His sun rise on the evil and on the good, and sends rain on the just and the unjust." So you see that to God, all are equal. That doesn't mean the unjust won't get theirs; it simply means that you can't judge except for evil. And when you *do* judge evil, be careful, because you don't know the path these people have chosen. It really boils down to this: *When in doubt, don't judge at all.*

* * * * * *

TENET IX

*You are a light in a lonely, dark
desert who enlightens many.*

All right . . . it's time to take a long, hard look at the world we live in. Most enlightened messengers have recognized that this planet we inhabit in a physical body is not just a desert, but it's also a place of illusion and many times *de*lusion.

For example, in *The Teaching of Buddha*, Bukkyo Dendo Kyokai states: "To adhere to a thing because of its form is the source of delusion. If the form is not grasped and adhered to, this false imagination and absurd delusion will not occur. Enlightenment is seeing the truth and being free from such a foolish delusion."

He also says that "since everything in this world is brought about by causes and conditions, there can be no fundamental distinctions among things. The apparent distinctions exist because of people's absurd and discriminating thoughts. In the sky there is no distinction of east and west; people create the distinctions out of their own minds and then believe them to be true."

So once we understand and embrace the world for what it is—and realize that the oasis for this desert resides on the Other Side—all of life becomes easier (especially when we realize that this planet is a learning plane that contains evil and negativity). T. S. Eliot wrote about the "wasteland," and I don't want to belabor the point and seem overly negative, but this world *is* a wasteland. In all fairness, it's also a place of beauty, joy, goodness, and even propriety. There are people to love, families to be close to, and an abundance of kindness to share. Look at Martin Luther King, Jr., or Mother Teresa, both of whom tried to make this world a better place with a dream: One had a vision of an ecumenical world where everyone would love each other regardless of color; while the other aspired to save the poor from sickness and dying.

We should also keep in mind that this world is what we make it. While we're here, why not light our lamp of enlightenment? When we do, we find that we inspire and attract others.

Someone asked me just the other day, "What if I love and I'm hurt?" Well, Tennyson said it better than anyone with this: "'Tis better to have loved and lost than never to have loved at all." In other words, loving and giving a person a light in their soul actually makes *our* souls deeper and fuller. Even if it doesn't work out, then we'll go on to love again and light another soul—provided that we don't become callous and close ourselves off and never feel again. If we do that, then we only end up hurting ourselves . . . along with the countless others who would have loved us back.

I've loved and lost (and gained), but I've always recognized that spiritually I can't live in a desert of my own making. Now you may prefer to platonically love children or animals or friends (or God)—no matter, you're putting out a light from your soul. I've heard people wonder, "Why should I help anyone? I mean, what have they done for me?" Well, probably nothing. After all, the type of person who would say such a thing hasn't taken the time to love; consequently, not many will love them back. Their only existence is themselves, and that's all they care about. I know *you* don't want to be this type of person!

When we make baskets for the poor, do we need to know each family that a toy or turkey was given to? Of course not—we just send it out! So should light and love be packaged up and sent wherever it needs to go. Love is the water on a dry desert that enables the flowers of joy to grow.

Los Angeles is a desert, yet look at how the foliage has grown up and made the area lush. So does the love we send out to others: It may not hit the mark it was intended for, but it will hit *some* mark, somewhere, sometime—and even if *you* don't know it, God does. It's also written in gold in the Hall of Records (this is where the phylum of angels known as the Dominions records our deeds in our charts), and a light will go on in someone's lonely desert of a soul because of this good deed or action.

* * *

I'd like you to remember one very important thing: Don't leave *yourself* in a desert or forget to light your own candle, because if you don't have a light, you can't spark anyone else's. Our Lord even makes it very clear that you should never hide your light under a bushel. In other words, bring it out into the open! Each time you love and give to others, you give water to the desert of your own soul, which may need compassion, love, advice, or sympathy just as much as—or more than—the people you're helping.

When I think of lights in a desert, I automatically think of Grandma Ada. She was so self-sufficient, yet her light inspired everyone around her. For example, when she was 81, there was a large broken branch on a tree that was threatening to fall on her tomatoes (this was when she lived in a little cottage, before she was relegated to the flophouse). My boyfriend at the time was going to get on a ladder and saw the branch off. She looked up and said, "That's ridiculous," and with one hand reached up and ripped it off. Much later, we'd laugh about this, and he'd say, "Never let me get into a fight with your grandmother!"

Then when Grandma Ada was 84 she broke her hip (which, as you probably know, can be deadly for the elderly). She went to the hospital, where they put her in a cast and placed her in a bed. As soon as all the medical personnel had left her alone, she promptly got up, got dressed, hobbled out the door, got a cab, and went home. I got the call from the doctor who was frantic that they'd lost Ada Coil. For a moment I was concerned, but then I realized exactly what she'd done and where she was.

I went over to her little house, and there she was: cleaning and fixing dinner for Brother. I asked her why she left, since she had everyone at the hospital worried sick. She looked at me with surprise and said, "Well, I just felt that they'd done all they could do for me, so I left. Besides, who would take care of Brother?" She recovered just fine, and when asked about her hip, she'd wave it off as just a foolish mistake, and that was the end of it. Talk about your lights in the desert! She truly was the one that my entire family looked up to.

How many times have we heard that a parent dies and the entire family falls apart? Unfortunately, it's because that person was holding the only light, and the rest circled around it like moths to a flame. When that person dies, no one else knows how to carry the torch, so to speak. Sometimes it's easier to let someone else carry the light, but if you never pick it up, you'll never know what you're missing. To be the torchbearer who sparks other people's lights is really the bottom line of what life is about. We all contribute to making this world what it is, so let's all make a concerted effort to be a light and make the world a brighter and more loving one.

If you're having trouble finding your own light, try the

meditation below. It will take you through a long, lonely desert and then into a beautiful meadow.

You are in an arid desert, and your feelings of loneliness and even isolation are rising to the surface. Soon, even as tired as you are, you come to the top of a sandy hill, and below you see a beautiful meadow with grass and flowers. The colors are so bright that you can barely stand to look at the scene at first.

With a renewed energy, you run down the hill and into the meadow. When you arrive, you begin to see loved ones who have passed gathering around you. (Even your pets are there!) All of a sudden, a pillar of light descends— seeming to come right through the top of your head—and spreads through your entire body. You immediately feel refreshed and realize that without the desert of life, you would never be able to enjoy the light of your own spirituality.

During this relaxation period, think of yourself as a giant pop-it bead of gold who's pushing your individual energy of love to the person or fellow bead on your right. (When several people have done this in my presence, I've seen the whole room light up with a golden light that then forms a giant pyramid.) Then send this love and energy out to anyone who needs it. Maybe someone in a dark alley will get a bit of your golden light and never know who sent it. Or perhaps a sick or dying person will have their suffering lifted, or someone on drugs will become enlightened.

Haven't you ever heard somebody say, "One day the pain just went away," "For some unknown reason I just decided to stop drinking," or "I got tired of feeling sorry for myself and went out and began to help others"? How do you know where this remote healing goes? It doesn't matter, nor should it—it will go through the desert. Maybe you won't know until you reach the Other Side where it went, but know that it will go where it's needed.

How Can This Tenet Help You?

Tenet IX seems to mirror some of the others, but when you look at it more deeply, you'll see that it's referring to the personal you—that is, the essence of who you are.

Now, how can you become a light? I asked myself this when I was very young and started out really wanting to save the world (not ostentatiously, but to bring about some sort of order and peace). Even in my writings or lectures, the amount of people I reach is small compared to the world, but I began to realize that if you can light just one candle, that candle will spark another and another. That's where you come in, for if I can light your candle, then I know that you'll illuminate another candle and another, and then you'll become a light yourself (if you're not already one).

When I started my readings and lectures in my home, I often wondered where my light would go—but I kept telling myself to just keep going one step at a time and see what happened. I decided to hone it down to what I wanted to get across against all odds. After sifting through many things, I was led to the logical conclusion that we have an all-loving Father and Mother God, and we live many lives to perfect and follow Christ's teachings. Was it easy? Hell no! I was bucking years of political and religious dogma, but I kept telling myself what my professor Bob Williams always said: "They can hurt your feelings, but they can't eat you."

To that end, know that you're going to question yourself during this process, and even on a few dark nights you'll wonder why you're doing what you're doing, but that's the dark side trying to attack you and make you despair. When this happens, just "eject that tape" and shine that light of yours that gives solace to others, a shoulder to cry on, or someone to listen or sit with in times of grief. Even helping people pass over is a blessed thing to do.

Whatever you do, in whatever manner you do it, do it with love. Is it hard? Sure it is! I mean, do you think that every morning I get up dancing and singing? Some days are tiring and others are gut-wrenching, but overall, the key is that I love what I do. I wouldn't want to do anything else but be with you and around you and talk to you. That's my love affair.

And let's face it: If we humans don't get it right this time (I feel that we only have 100 years or so left on this planet), maybe it will never get done. We have to learn to get over ourselves and help others as Jesus taught—after all, he wouldn't have said to love your neighbor as yourself just to be saying it. All the "messengers" such as Buddha, Christ, and Mohammed taught the same thing, and all of their work will be for nothing if we all don't "get it," and even more important, "practice it."

It's just like the cross: Pieces of it are religious relics and a substantiation of many people's faith. Most of us, however, carry our faith inside our heart. Yes, I wear a cross, but it's because of what I feel it represents for me. We love God in our own way—when we do so, we don't have to keep obsessing about our so-called ego. After all, *ego* only means "the I am." And when you get down to it, who I am and what I've accomplished through life after life simply comes down to loving others. This is where the light for each and every one of us comes from. We must never forget this.

✳ ✳ ✳ ✳ ✳ ✳

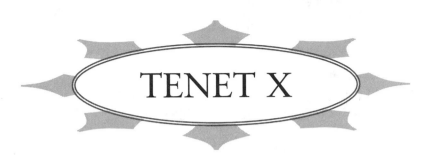

TENET X

Let no one convince you that you are less than a God. Do not let fear imprison your spiritual growth.

I have to tell you that when I heard first heard this tenet, it really threw me. Me, a God . . . come on! Give me a break— let's put our ego in perspective! But then as I researched, I began to see what this tenet really means. We're the true genetic offspring of our Divine Creators, just as we are of our parents and grandparents. So, in other words, if I can say that I got my philosophy and strength from my grandmother, my drive from my father, or my tenacity from my grandfather, then why can't I go further and realize that I'm part and parcel of the Divine? Nevertheless, it seems so difficult for us to accept this fact, and that's where the fear comes in.

Two emotions cannot occupy the mind at the same time, so if we're full of fear, we can't love; by the same token, if we're full of love, we can't fear or hate. While *hate* is a harsh word, I've found that people who are fearful do indeed hate

343

being that way. They often try to change themselves to cope with (or do other things to take their mind from) their fears, but without spiritual help, it usually ends in failure—and the fears loom ever larger.

The dictionary describes *fear* as "a feeling of agitation and anxiety caused by the presence of the imminence of danger." Sometimes this can be *imagined* danger, but it doesn't matter—the adrenaline kicks in for fight or flight. Fear is a normal part of life, usually boiling down to the feeling that we're helpless and out of control. I can't tell you the times when I've told people who were afraid of flying that if they could pilot the plane themselves they'd feel better, and nine times out of ten they agree.

In this day and age, our entire society seems to feel out of control. We live with the ever-present danger of terrorism, especially after 9/11, and most of us don't feel safe. And that collective fear is a powerful emotion that seems to have tentacles like an octopus—it starts out small, but as it grows, its arms go out to many things instead of one. Take heart, though: No matter how many arms your personal concern may have, it usually goes back to one event, whether from this life or a past one.

For example, I recently spoke with a woman who had four boys. Strangely, she didn't worry about the youngest three, but with her oldest, it was getting to the point where she was obsessed with where he was every moment—she was completely convinced that she was going to lose him. Looking at her chart, I saw that she'd had four children in a past life in Poland. The family's house had caught fire, and she was able to save three of her children, but the oldest died. The woman had carried over the fear of this loss to her current life—but once she was able to face and release it, her dread disappeared.

Then there was the woman who was deathly afraid of snakes, especially cobras. Now, she lived in a brownstone in New York City, hardly the place where you'd find a cobra under the bed, but she was paralyzed by this fear nonetheless.

She was told by therapists that it was an unfounded fear and she should just get over it.

The woman scheduled a reading with me, and I picked up that in a past life an irate husband who was convinced that she'd been unfaithful had pushed her into a cave with cobras. Of course they bit her, and she died a painful death. She'd carried this fear over, and it became more acute the closer she came to the age she'd been when it had occurred. (In my research, I've found that this is not uncommon; various triggers such as age, similar incidents, and so forth can activate a fear or memory from a past life.) Once this became known to her conscious mind, the fear dissipated.

Now some may say that these are just healing stories for the mind. Well, even if they were (which they in no way, shape, or form were), if it works, who cares? The truth always connects with the subconscious, and even the best hypnotist or psychologist will tell you that you can't lie to the subconscious (or what I like to call "the super-conscious"), where all memory exists. Sometimes because of this, people just get over a fear that they had most of their life, and they never know why. It can also happen in reverse, in which a person who never had a fear of something has it suddenly come upon them out of the blue—for example, the man who was never afraid of heights until he reached the age of 26, which coincided with the exact time that he was pushed into a volcano as a sacrifice to the gods in an Aztec life.

Most of us have heard about the cases in which some idiot therapist implants a memory in his or her patient, such as, "You were molested." An implanted memory is a Band-Aid—and a fake one at that—which eventually falls off, showing the still-festering wound. However, many children have all-too-real night terrors, which are left over from past lives.

The best way to deal with this is to go into their room, hold them, and tell them that this is not happening *now,* but it's something that's coming from another time and place. I guarantee this will work. I've done it (or had my sons and daughters-in-law do it) with my grandkids, and it stops immediately. Strangely enough, I could even break my sons' fevers by going in and telling them that it would be gone and they would be well. Their systems, with God's help, would fight the illness, and in the morning they'd be running around like wild deer, wearing me out. Thank God, though—that was better than sick boys.

* * *

Sometimes fear is so strong that it can be paralyzing. The only difference between a fear and a phobia is that phobias can be more irrational—which doesn't help someone who's suffering from them. Again looking to the dictionary, a phobia is described as an "abnormal and irrational fear of a specific thing or situation that compels one to avoid it, despite the awareness and reassurance that it is not dangerous. A strong, unreasonable fear, dislike, or aversion."

The problem with these negative emotions is that they stop spiritual growth. There are some universal fears that scientists and doctors agree on, such as the fear of falling and darkness that we're supposedly born with. I never found this to be true with the children I raised, however. The universal concerns that much of society obsesses over are prodigious in length, but here are a few of them: fear of exposure, death, pain, loss, rejection, loneliness, abandonment, rape, burning, drowning, heights, crowds, outward appearances, cancer, blindness, and becoming homeless. I feel that I've heard most of them from my readers and clients—of course, as soon as I say this, I'll hear of another one.

Ancient Indian beliefs state that a snake may not kill you, but the *fear* of a snake might. How many times do we conjure up our own worries that are unfounded, only to have them gradually take over our mind? I can remember as a young girl that I heard so much about hell that I became almost sick with guilt over any little thing. Even looking at a pair of underpants hanging on a clothesline, thinking that they covered "naughty parts," would give me sweaty palms. In those days, to just think a bad thought was a sin, so guess what? We thought bad thoughts! It's like saying, "Don't think of a pink elephant." Naturally, a pink elephant is the first thing that appears in your mind.

My father, bless his heart, could see that I was suffering, so one night he came in my room to ask me what was wrong. In between spasms of tears, I managed to get out that I was thinking bad thoughts and was going to hell. "There isn't any hell, baby—it's only in our own mind," he gently said. "But go ahead and think all the bad thoughts you want, and then you'll be done with it."

Presto! Just those wise words of consent drove the so-called demons of fear away, and even at nine years of age I felt what I realize now was grace being allowed to come in.

What upsets me is that our religious beliefs tend to add to our fears instead of quieting them. We're afraid of hell or retribution by a capricious God who plays favorites. This, of course, is a powerful emotion that keeps people controlled and in line. I hate the expression "Fear God." Why should we fear not only what we're part of, but an all-loving Creator and Parent? I prefer the Sikh doctrine, which resonates with the belief that all people have the right to follow their own path to God without condemnation from others. The Gnostics believe the same thing, which is probably why Christ was of the Essene sect.

There's an old saying that goes, "Fear is a great enemy of mankind. It is the enemy of his progress. It disturbs his peace and harmony. It sucks or saps his vitality and energy. It drains the nervous system of its reserve of energy. It produces weakness." And one of my favorite sayings, "A coward dies many times before his death," says a lot, too. In other words, the brave know what they're afraid of, but cowards live in abject fear and imagine all the ways they can die. This is disabling and stunts spiritual growth.

We're all sons and daughters of God—even the dark entities who will eventually be absorbed back into His/Her uncreated mass. You may wonder, "Well, if we're so Divine, then how can we make so many mistakes?" Francine told me years ago that the human form makes us stupid. I thought, *Boy, in my case that's true—I certainly wouldn't have picked some of the people in my life that I did!* Yet later I realized, *Yes, I would. Even an evil mother teaches us how not to be. A bad marriage can teach us how to rely on ourselves. Loneliness is a state of mind. My writing is self-imposed aloneness, but it's what I enjoy.*

I'm not saying that when life gets too debilitating we shouldn't seek counseling. In extreme cases, it's even okay to take pharmaceuticals—but it's not okay to immediately rely on them because you have an anxious moment here and there, are experiencing natural fears, or are stricken by grief. When I lost nine people who were very close to me in three months, for instance, the doctor said, "Sylvia, you're depressed. I'm going to prescribe an antidepressant."

"I'm in grief," I replied, "and you don't have a pill for that."

Now that doesn't mean that those who can't pull themselves out of a hole for a reasonable amount of time (for each person it's different) shouldn't seek medical help. If you become incapacitated, then realize that God made doctors, too.

Most of us at one time or another think that we're going crazy. So many people who saw things like I do or heard things like I do used to be dubbed crazy, while people who astrally projected were locked up. I tend to feel that crazy people don't know that they are, so they don't worry about it. They think that they're normal! That doesn't mean we shouldn't be tested or see a doctor like I did, but we really must accept that there are so many things on this planet that we will never know or understand.

How Can This Tenet Help You?

The East Indian belief, which is identical to our Gnostic one, is that ignorance is the cause of fear. Sometimes I despise the word *ignorance* because it makes us feel stupid. It actually means "disregarding a truth that's available," but many times we don't even know where to go to look for the answers, so it can be like trying to find the proverbial needle in a giant haystack.

Don't mistake being nervous or anxious as not being normal. Being obligated to go to court, see a doctor, attend an important meeting, or face an ex-love—these are all normal types of situations in which you might feel trepidation. It's only when it rules your life that it becomes a problem. And don't confuse foolhardiness with lack of fear. Sensible people can take chances, but those who venture out of the realm of reason can become daredevil types who cause great danger to themselves and others. We can't always judge these kinds of people, though, as some individuals get an adrenaline rush from testing fate. I like the expression "Don't try this at home."

Of course, normal fears of losing our loved ones or having our family harmed are natural and come with a human body. Jesus' kingdom was not of this world and neither is yours, but you can't stop the grief or fear of loss—it comes with the territory. Yes, we know that our loved ones went Home and are happy, but we're stuck here missing them.

As your knowledge gained through reading, research, and working with people expands, fear does diminish. First of all, you become more Godlike and not so rooted in your own transient, mortal body. To know that you're not alone in your fears is also a great cure.

There are many moments when I experience anxiety (I pretty much stomp fear down), such as before every lecture, Montel or Larry King's shows, a pay-per-view special, and so forth—I'm not so concerned for myself, but for all the people I love. I don't want to embarrass them, and I only want to give out the right information and be a pure prophet for God.

I so clearly remember the first pay-per-view special I did: I was beside myself because Montel and my publisher, Hay House, had their money riding on me. (If it had been my own money backing the show, I would have been uneasy, but not fearful.) Anyway, I obsessed about it for a solid week. Not even Montel's kind words—"You're going to be great, girlfriend"—or anyone else's words, for that matter, helped. *What if I freeze up?* I worried. *After all, it's live!* (I won't work with a TelePrompTer or script, so I always fly by the seat of my pants.) *What if I go numb and just stare into the camera or say something stupid? Maybe I'll just break a leg, but that won't work because the time slot's already paid for.*

Of course when the time came, it worked out all right, and everyone got their investment back. I've been on TV for 30 years, but to have people put their money on me just frightened me. I worked through the fear, and the second and third pay-per-views I did were fine—but that first one was grueling.

Through our massive statistical references of past-life regressions, my ministers and I have seen cure after cure of fear-related problems. True, many problems with fear can come from this life. A fear of drowning because some dumb parent threw a child in the water and said, "Swim," thus causing a terrible fear of water, can be an example. But more times than can be counted it comes from a past life, and that's why people can't trace it in a therapy that just covers *this* life.

So, going back to my own regression, I had a life in England where I'd been given money collected by the villagers to release a prisoner. In my hectic travels, I'd lost it, and a fear of losing money resulted. This is why I was so frightened about the pay-per-view (cell memory returns in the strangest ways). So, as they say, to face your fears sometimes doesn't help, but having knowledge of where the phobic reaction comes from can, because understanding releases us from the unknown "boogie man" that hides in the closet of our minds. As this tenet says, you are nothing less than a God, and in truly believing this you can learn from your fears. You don't have to keep them, however, because they will imprison your soul so that it can't grow.

For those of you with phobias and physical maladies that don't seem to respond to medicine, you might want to try this on yourself: Ask God to take you out of that past-life groove and put you in *this* time frame—and to see that the past is gone and has nothing to do with now. You might be surprised by the results.

You can also check when your fear first started and try to meditate yourself back to a life in which it could have begun. What were the circumstances that led up to it? What were you doing? What was happening or what did someone say right before the phobia or anxiety happened? Then go to a reputable therapist or certified hypnotherapist and ask God at night to take it away. It will go, your life won't be filled with the emotion of fear, and you'll get your God-center back. It's there if you find it (as I did) by reading, researching, and questioning.

An East Indian proverb says: "Imagining fears causes diseases." That is to say that fear can make you immobile and stressed and consequently can make you ill. If we truly believe that fear is illusionary or if we say that it comes from a real point of entry and then light is shined upon it, it cannot live. Another proverb says: "Courage is eternal, it will not die, but the thrusting of fear is a terror in the soul and blocks out our Godliness."

You are a God and carry that light. Like our Lord said in Matthew 7:12, "Therefore, whatever you want men to do to you, do also to them, for this is the law and the prophets." I've tried to always live by this "golden rule," and knowing this—and that we're human vehicles—has alleviated fear from my life a great deal. Spirituality then pours in, and by going through it, your soul will have learned and be more open to grace.

* * * * * *

*Do not allow the unfounded belief in demons
to block your communion with God.*

Demons haven't always been around. You see, at one time humankind didn't know how to explain the horrors or inequities of life, so they figured that a God Who had to be appeased was behind everything. Then they graduated to trying to explain the negative aspects of life by coming up with evil entities or demons.

All religious texts refer to evil. Our ancestors not only couldn't come to the logical deduction of a perfect, loving God, but they also couldn't believe that evil was nothing more than a by-product of God's creations, not God.

Several documentaries and writings on the historical life of Jesus said that during his "lost years" he visited India, Tibet, and several other countries in the Near and Middle East. (My spirit guide Francine has confirmed this, too.) It was during this time that Christ learned about other religious philosophies and practices, including healing. The "casting out of demons" phraseology that's mentioned many times in the Bible when Jesus did a healing is in fact a direct reference to the Indian belief that demons caused illnesses. Christ realized that a mostly unlearned population had to be related to in terms that they'd understand.

Take the following, for instance:

> Now when the sun was setting, all who had persons sick with various diseases brought them to him. And he laid his hands upon each of them and cured them. And devils also came forth from many, crying out and saying, "Thou art the Son of God." And he rebuked them, and did not permit them to speak, because they knew that he was the Christ. . . . (Luke 4:40–41)
>
> And it came to pass, while he was in one of the towns, that, behold, there was a man full of leprosy. And when he saw Jesus he fell on his face and besought him, saying, "Lord, if thou wilt, thou canst make me clean." And stretching forth his hand he touched him, saying, "I will; be thou made clean." And immediately the leprosy left him. And he charged him to tell no man, but, "Go, show thyself to the priest, and offer the gift for thy purification, as Moses commanded, for a witness to them." But so much the more the tidings spread concerning him, and great crowds gathered together to hear him and to be cured of their sicknesses. But he himself was in retirement in the desert, and in prayer. (Luke 5:12–16)

Now several things or concepts are happening here. First, you don't need a long procedure to heal, since it's the laying on of hands in the name of God or our Lord that does it. Second, in all four of the Gospels (of Matthew, Mark, Luke, and John), our Lord states that when you do a good deed you don't need to have it told to everyone—it really is between you and God. If you did get all your rewards here, then what lesson would you have learned?

Next, when the "devil" was trying to seduce Jesus in the

desert, through logic and reading the text, we can see that the meaning is allegorical. The following is from Luke 4:1–13, and I've included commentary in parentheses and italics:

Then Jesus, being filled with the Holy Spirit, returned from the Jordan and was led by the Spirit into the wilderness *(How many times, just like Tenet IX says, must we go to the desert period to learn by temptation or just loneliness—or finding it in our soul not to fall into despair and negate evil or depression?)* . . . being tempted forty days by the devil. And in those days he ate nothing, and afterward, when they had ended, he was hungry. *(How many times in our darkest time do we hunger not just for food, but for enlightenment?)* And the devil said to him, "If you are the son of God, command this stone to become bread." *(It's heartening for me to read here that in the toil to bring truth, we're always going to be challenged by naysayers.)* But Jesus answered him, saying, "It is written, man shall not live by bread alone, but by every word of God." *(It's true we need sustenance for the body, but if the soul is in despair, the body will go into stress and even illness.)*

Then the devil, taking him up on a high mountain, showed him all the kingdoms of the world in a moment of time. And the devil said to him, "All this authority I will give to you, and their glory; for this has been delivered to me, and I give it to whomever I wish." *(This is interesting because our planet doesn't belong to the devil per se, but to negativity. It's ruled by hatred, prejudice, and all the other hardships we've experienced in this life or even other lives.)* "Therefore, if you will worship before me, all will be yours." *(This asks what it profits a man to gain the whole world, if he loses his soul. Now does this mean that we can't enjoy comfort and some luxury in life? Of course not, but if you're bound by the evils of the world and use it for your own gain or fame, you're headed for spiritual bankruptcy.)*

And Jesus answered and said to him, "Get behind me, Satan! For it is written, you shall worship the Lord your

God, and him only you shall serve." Then he brought him to Jerusalem, set him on the pinnacle of the temple, and said to him, "If you are the Son of God, throw yourself down from here. For it is written: 'He shall give His angels charge over you, to keep you,' and 'In their hands they shall bear you up, lest you dash your foot against a stone.'" And Jesus answered and said to him, "It has been said, 'You shall not tempt the Lord your God.'"

Now when the devil had ended every temptation, he departed from him until an opportune time.

So we can see that this is an analogy of life and its trials and temptations. The main principle here isn't the devil at all—instead, the story points to what life throws at us and what the outcome will be if we lend our life, our soul, or even our name or power to evil. We'll become miserable, because I believe that in good souls there's an innate guardianship that screams "No!" when things are tainted. All that glitters is not gold, so look at the devils or demons as a type of ancient litany constructed by human beings to understand the hell of this planet.

Like Jesus, Buddha also used demons as metaphors for evil in order to communicate to the uneducated masses. If you've read as many religious texts as I have, you'll swiftly come to the conclusion that any so-called demon is just a ruse. Yet the fear of hell or the devil has built so many ornate edifices. Not that I don't think we should honor God, but I wonder why people don't realize that God exists everywhere. Don't get me wrong; I love to go into temples and churches (when I'm in New York, I love to visit St. Patrick's Cathedral, especially when it's quiet), but we also have to remember that Buddha, Mohammed, and Christ didn't teach in such places of worship—they happened after the fact. Instead, these wise prophets went to the people of the land and delivered their messages of love and peace.

With so many messengers preaching love and right actions, why has humankind gone so far to the negative side? Well, as I've explained, they just didn't know how to explain the inequities of life, so they came up with demons and hell. Such dogma also gave early religions a way to control people with fear, which in turn gave them a lot of money to keep their religions going. (Don't you find it amazing that the fear that was utilized to control the uneducated masses of the past is still successful today with the "educated" masses? Today, many so-called religious people interpret the stories literally, which constitutes confusion because their illogical and literal interpretation also makes them lose their original meanings. This is a case of tradition and history—which, I might add, was written by the winners—overcoming education and logic. How tragic.)

Humankind has a primordial fear of the unknown, so when bad things keep happening, it seems that we slip back into an ancient belief that's in our DNA, which says that there has to be some outside force responsible, such as a devil. I find it funny that we've spent so much time on worrying and talking about the devil that this concept has become stronger and larger than God. If we adhere to a good life and avoid evil, why do we have to dwell on all the negative? If we're continually worried about demons, we've not only negated a loving, merciful God, but we'll become so preoccupied with fear that it takes over our thoughts and minds. Consequently, love, harmony, and peace—along with the communion with God—are blocked here, which begets ego and self-importance.

Human beings who have separated from God out of their own ego and then took on a chart or direction of destruction can also render good people impotent. They do so by using us and playing on our weaknesses; by hurting, rejecting, and abandoning us; and by coming in a very seductive face and utilizing charm and other means to suck us in. Yet such dark entities know that they can't possess us, for there's a primary link between God and ourselves that won't allow it. If a spirit guide can't read our minds or force us to do something, then why would a lower form of entity be able to take hold of our life, actions, and mind?

The courts don't even buy this "devil made me do it" type of syndrome. Ronald DeFeo, Jr., the young man who killed his family several years ago, tried that absurd defense after "the Amityville horror" occurred. He even had two so-called paranormal investigators trying to come to his defense. It didn't work, thank God. Can you imagine? With all the injustices we see, all we need is everyone who commits a horrendous act claiming that the devil made him do it. (Of course, this doesn't apply to the truly mentally deranged.)

Another fallacy is that in some cultures, people who go crazy are thought to be possessed. This is actual ignorance because these societies are uneducated about illness, heredity, post-traumatic stress disorder, mental breakdowns, and so forth, all of which can lead to real forms of mental illness. In other words, the mind is just an organ that can be affected—or infected—the same as any other organ.

And as I've said so many times, there's no such thing as an evil ghost either. Such entities are confused and sometimes deranged, but they're mainly just aggravated that you're in their territory. You can usually release them by telling them that they're dead and they need to go to the brilliant white light. (It can also be helpful to use holy water and a crucifix in every room, open up your home, and surround it with salt.) I know that some of these spirits can be tenacious—I've personally encountered a few who won't listen, so you either have to move or put up with it. But know that they'll eventually be picked up by someone from the Other Side who will convince them that they need to come Home.

Finally, at least once a week I hear that someone put a curse on a person's family. This is ridiculous . . . but not to the person going through it. If anyone would have a curse on them, it would be me. All of the charlatans I've turned in or called and then reported to the authorities would have hundreds of Sylvia dolls out there full of pins. But the only way "black magic" works is because certain cultures have been conditioned by years of belief. Remember that the mind is a powerful mechanism, which can be the healer of your body or the faculty that makes you sick. I have great respect for Vodun (also known as Voodoo), the true religion that has its roots in Africa *and* Catholicism, and their own ancestral gods that protect them from evil, but you always find the renegades in any religion. Satanic cults, on the other hand, practice no true religion; instead, they contain the dregs of the earth, which have no spirituality and merely want the thrill of flirting with the rituals (and sex) that accompany such endeavors.

How Can This Tenet Help You?

I'm sure you've figured out by now that *there is no devil*—there is only humankind's construction of evil, and the devil is its figurehead, so to speak. It was devised out of ignorance to explain the inequities of life on this hellhole of a planet.

Nevertheless, even in this day and age I still hear from people on practically a daily basis who feel that they've been cursed or tortured by the devil. In the first place, if there was such a creature, what makes you or me so important that he'd bother with us? Wouldn't he go after Billy Graham or someone else who's important and doing God's work? The whole concept of a devil is just not true.

A woman once told me that she thought getting old was evil. I replied, "No, but you can hate it enough to fight it all the way down to your heels." People are afraid to use the word *hate*, and I don't know why. After all, I hate hunger and strife, and I hate child abuse and molestation . . . I certainly don't want to love that evil! So instead of worrying about these silly demons, fight negativity, ignorance, and bigotry by standing up for human rights, and for the needs of children and the aged. That's what will keep your communion with God alive.

The logo for Novus Spiritus connects the three circles of gratitude, loyalty, and commitment like the trinity, and then interlocks them with a dove that can be the Holy Spirit or the ancient symbol of the Mother God. I have jewelry with this logo on it, and a good portion of the proceeds from the sale of it (which is available on my Website, **www.sylvia.org**), goes to multiple-sclerosis charities. Our church also adopts children from the Christian Children's Fund, gives to a home for the elderly as well as one for children, and donates free spiritual counseling through our ministry. It's not because we're so great, but it's what we can do right now. Even so, it never seems like enough, but as we say, "It's better to light one little candle than none at all."

Sometimes the best way to battle negativity is to simply give of yourself—for instance, go out to the elderly and talk to them, which will greatly help remove their fear and loneliness. It's heartbreaking to see so many of our elders put in homes—in fact, I want to have enough money to start my own place for the aged (ideally for children, too)—but sometimes we can't physically or medically take care of them. It's worst for those who are alone every day with no one to come and visit them. In other cultures this is unheard of—they think that we Americans are uncaring and even evil for neglecting our elderly. In many cases, the problem has to do with lifestyle, because so many families now have both parents working, and they don't have the time and energy it takes to care for their elders. If you're in this type of situation, then *make* the time to visit as often as you can because it will help a great deal.

I absolutely hate getting older—not out of vanity but because the body wasn't supposed to last this long anyway. It's the bounce that goes out of the step and the funny aches and pains that go with it. I'm looking at my 70th birthday this year, and I keep hearing my grandmother's words coming back to haunt me: "Someday you'll know what it's like to be a young woman trapped in an old body." Well, dearest love of my life, I'm beginning to. In fact, I just had a physical, and the doctor said, "You're in great shape." And I added, "For the shape I'm in."

I know that God loves me—and you—unconditionally, but before I started my church I went into a slump. "Who do you think you are?" I asked myself. "You should just give it up and stay in your quiet corner of the world." As soon as I realized that I was being torn, I got rid of my fears and went straight ahead. In other words, our own emotions take over our intellect and take on any form we fear—it's got nothing to do with demons.

Such fear also points to a misplaced ego. For example, as I once asked a friend who was convinced that the devil was always torturing her, "Why are you so important that the devil would want to torture you?" After a moment she said, "You know, you could be right."

"Just get involved with others and forget about this devil," I replied.

Of course, many so-called fortune-tellers would tell my friend that her "demonic possession" could be cured for the right sum. A client once told me that she'd been told by a "psychic" to hand over her Mercedes-Benz because it was possessed. I asked her, "If it was so possessed, then why did she want it?"

I try to get the names of these individuals to turn them in to the local district attorney's office, but most of the time superstition runs high and people are too afraid of being cursed to give me this information—sad but true. Before you visit *any* psychic, see who knows them, what they've done, and what licenses they hold. Are they registered with the Better Business Bureau, or do they even have a business license? How far ahead are they booked? If you can see them right away, chances are they're not so good. After all, would you go to a doctor just because he or she has a flashing scalpel on a sign?

I'm reminded of the time several years ago when I was approached by a big producer to do a psychic hotline. The money would have been $40,000 a week to start, with an additional upward scale on every call that came in—which could have meant thousands of extra dollars per week depending on call volume.

I naïvely asked, "How can I answer all those phones and give the people enough time?"

He smiled like I was a dope. "You won't be doing that—you'll just write a script and lend your name to hundreds of people answering the phone."

I thought he was kidding, but quickly realized that he was dead serious. Now I'm not telling this because I need kudos, but in a split second, I saw all the people who believed in me and how hard it was to try to make this spiritual psychic journey authentic and for God. And then I saw the faces of my ministers and Grandma Ada. It was a time when I was barely making staff payroll, but what would it have ended up costing me to sink to that level? I couldn't say no fast enough (as my eldest son will attest to because he was with me), and felt lucky to have narrowly avoided this psychic attack.

Speaking of which, psychic attacks are more bad energy than actual attacks. For example, there are people out there who can drain you or make you feel uneasy. Take your first impression and run, or at least avoid them. They may not want to overtly hurt you, but in all probability, they wouldn't be good for you. I've been subjected to such attacks, and they can hit before you realize it. It's that what's-the-use feeling, the worthlessness and even depression that can come over you. As soon as you feel this, it can be like a tape that plays and plays—so eject it. Just place it, along with your so-called demons, in a box and blow it up . . . your soul will soar.

* * * * * *

TENET XII

The body is a living temple unto God, wherein we worship the spark of the Divine.

Jesus, Buddha, Mohammed, and other religious leaders have all stated that the body is a temple. At Novus Spiritus, we believe that the body houses the soul, and what seems to be so temporary and fragile is probably one of the biggest miracles that God has created. People who don't believe in God need only look at this wonderful creation that comes from *a single* egg and sperm and becomes this perfect machine (as it were).

Even if science discovers how to clone the human body, they'll only be copying what's already been created by God. Personally, I'm not thrilled about the cloning aspect, but I know that if God doesn't want it, it will fail. It almost seems as if humankind wants to *be* God, not be part of Him/Her. And as for stem-cell research, I favor it, but why not use the umbilical cords? There are certainly enough of them without harvesting embryos.

Anyway, we should honor and care for this temple we live in because life is a miracle. Yet when we become addicted to harmful substances (which seems to be an astronomically growing problem), we defile our temple. Now there are probably as many reasons for addiction as there are substances to be addicted to. It can strike anywhere, and we all probably know someone who has such a problem. In fact, we all have some kind of addiction ourselves—for example, mine is coffee, which I've had to cut down on (too much acid—damn!); other people find themselves continually craving chocolate or soda. These are the "lesser addictions," which I'll address in a bit. Right now I'd like to tackle the really lethal addictions: those related to alcohol and drugs.

Drugs and alcohol have been with us in some form as far back as recorded history—and beyond. For example, hashish and peyote have been used by witch doctors and shamans for centuries to put them in an altered state (yet they tended to only be used at certain times for tribal rituals). Many workers in South America are given coca leaves or beans, which is where cocaine comes from, so they'll work harder and longer with no sleep. And in America, we've dealt with all kinds of drugs, including LSD. Originally concocted by doctors to explore the recesses of the mind, LSD somehow got into the mainstream and was used widely in the hippie days. It started out as peace and love, but like all things taken to excess, by the 1970s it had begun to spread like a cancer (along with cocaine abuse). Dr. Timothy Leary didn't help matters any by extolling the virtues of mind-altering drugs.

It was almost as if we were trying to escape the horrors of our society (at that time we were dealing with Vietnam). I'm sure that there have always been pockets of substance abusers all across the country, but mainstream-media attention was soon focused on drugs . . . and has yet to let up.

Substance abuse used to be hushed up among the upper crust and the rich and famous, but even that eventually became news—especially now that we hear so much about celebrities and their addictions. Rush Limbaugh; Nick Nolte; Bobby Brown; Whitney Houston; Courtney Love; Robert Downey, Jr.; and others have generated headlines in recent years, and that was just the tip of the iceberg. Even Ray Charles, who was a wonderful talent, was bedeviled by heroin—but fortunately was able to kick the habit long before he died. Sadly, the same cannot be said for John Belushi, River Phoenix, Judy Garland, Marilyn Monroe, Jerry Garcia, Kurt Cobain, Jimi Hendrix, Janis Joplin, Chris Farley, or Elvis Presley . . . and the list goes on.

We're in the process of making our way through this world, and if we don't face life full on, we'll just have to come back and repeat the whole process. Whether people realize it or not, addiction to alcohol and drugs is a type of subliminal suicide. I know that life isn't easy, but it can't be any harder than having the proverbial monkey on your back as you wait for that next drink or fix.

Peer pressure is very strong, especially among our youth. Some of us remember when beer was the only choice—now we have drugs on the street that we can't even pronounce. But it's not just kids who are in danger. I talk to men and women every day who are hooked on painkillers, uppers, downers, and on and on it goes. And I know about this silent, creeping cancer firsthand because my mother was a prescription-drug addict (and I'm not blaming her doctors for this, since she went "doctor shopping"). Yet I do thank God for the one good thing I got out of this: I hate drugs and can't drink!

Think of it this way—why would anyone want to live in a filthy house with mold and scum? Yet that's essentially how many of us treat our temples. As my grandmother used to say, you can be poor, but you don't have to be dirty. And our outward living conditions do tend to be an example of what's going on inside. As I mentioned earlier, Grandma Ada lived in one room of a condemned building, yet it was spotless. She bought paint and fixed up the rusted iron bed; she also made doilies for the dresser, and dyed sheets to make curtains. Her space was sparsely furnished, but it was clean and cozy. My son Chris takes after her in this way. His house is immaculate, and I think I drive him crazy because I'm a collector and have knickknacks all over my home. And my son Paul is also clean, but he's more laid-back about it.

Then I have a dear friend who's spotless about her person, but her house is a pigsty. I find it phenomenal that she can reside in a place that has no semblance of order. Of course, I have to admit that I can be the opposite. As my dad used to tease me, "Why don't you have a mop tied to your butt so that you can do two things at once?" I've gotten better, especially when I realized that people didn't necessarily feel comfortable in my home. If they smoked, for example, I was immediately cleaning their ashtrays—it's a wonder I wasn't dusting my guests off, too.

After I divorced my first husband, my neat-freak tendencies calmed down. I now see that I was trying to bring order to my marriage, which was completely in chaos. I tried to at least have some control over my outward environment, if not my internal sadness. So it can be easy to keep the outward temple in order, but the real test is the inner temple.

Now don't get me wrong—there's nothing wrong with taking prescription drugs as long as they're not abused. I mean, who would deny that a diabetic needs insulin or that all manner of illnesses have been treated with medications that have saved countless lives? I'm talking about the *abuse* of substances here. For example, I saw a housewife on Dr. Phil's show who took 30 to 40 painkillers *a day,* and she was forced to sell her possessions to feed her habit. (Meanwhile, I threw up and came down with a horrible rash after taking one single Vicodin!) Someone who's taking this many pills is hiding from herself and trying to cope with a world or situation, past or present, that she feels she can't deal with . . . and she's not alone.

Countless people abuse themselves with drugs or alcohol, regardless of what it does to their brains or organs, or what laws they have to break in the process. The substance becomes the master; and the addict has to steal, prostitute themselves, or do any manner of illegal activity to get what their system cries out for. But it doesn't last . . . the fix wears off, and the vicious cycle begins all over again. Addicts like to say, "Just one more time and then I'm done." Then the guilt sets in; and they feel hopeless, helpless, and debased because of their weakness.

Addiction can also bring about changes in behavior. How many times have you heard a person say, "He's a completely different person when he drinks"? Addicts commit acts that they'd never do if they were sober, such as abusing their spouses or children. Some don't care, but the majority really do hate their lifestyle yet feel trapped by their addictions. Often addicts will say that they're embarrassed by their weakness—well, there's nothing weak about sitting through an intervention from family and friends, checking into a rehab facility, or going to see a doctor who can provide the right treatment. Substance abusers not only need help from friends and family, they need medical attention, too.

If you're involved with an addict who doesn't accept your help, keep in mind that there are so many out there who *do* need and want your assistance, so don't waste your time and energy on those who can't or won't be helped . . . no matter how much you love them. I'm reminded of a woman I talked to once who was half-crazy because she'd put her son in rehab ten times, only to have him come out and get back on heroin—the same day—every time. This was an incredibly sad situation, but I had to gently tell her that there comes a time when we realize that we have to give up because the drug has beaten not only our loved one, but us, too.

And then there's St. Monica, who prayed for 17 years that her son, the future St. Augustine, would give up his ways of debauchery. I don't mean to seem hateful, but it seemed that he finally did so when he was too old to party anymore—and then he wrote about how putrid mankind was. I admire the fact that he gave up his lifestyle, but I wish that he would have come out of his darkness to give hope instead of telling us that our temple was rotten. Certainly we get old and things break down—sure, a rose doesn't last forever, but at least while it does, it brings beauty, joy, and fragrance. Better to be of an ephemeral use than crabgrass that kills off the lawn, I say.

* * *

Now I'd like to shift the focus to those addictions that don't center around drugs or alcohol. For example, many people have obsessions with sex and pornography, which cause widespread infidelity. Such behavior not only disrespects the person you've chosen to be with, it also debases the very essence of *your* being.

Our Lord is very specific on this in Matthew 19:3–5: "And there came to him the Pharisees tempting him, and saying: 'Is it lawful for a man to put away his wife for every cause?' Who answering, said to them: 'Have ye not read, that He who made man from the beginning, made them male and female?' And he said: 'For this cause shall a man leave father and mother, and shall cleave to his wife, and they two shall be in one flesh.'"

Jesus later states that the only reason for divorce is sexual infidelity. Even back then he was trying to keep families together and wasn't accepting divorce. (Moses, on the other hand, did believe in putting away a bad spouse by divorce.) I divorced my first husband because after 13 years I couldn't stand the physical and mental abuse. I felt my own temple was crumbling, so I went to see a priest at the Queen of Apostles Church, where I was working as a schoolteacher. I was wringing my hands out of panic, yet I told him about the abuse and my desire to divorce—which, of course, was not allowed by the Catholic Church except under extreme circumstances.

The priest looked at me long and hard and gravely said, "Sylvia, you have to leave for yourself, as well as your boys—

or they're going to believe that it is right for a man to treat a woman like this."

I just stared back at him, for that was the last thing I thought I'd hear. I did leave with my kids in tow, and even though Gary threatened to kill us, I held firm and got my divorce. I will be forever grateful to that priest for giving me the courage to leave and go on with my life. I had to get away for survival, but the key phrase was not just for me, but *for my children*. After all, a lioness will protect her cubs at all costs.

Food can also be an addiction for some people, and we've all heard the statistics about the frightening increase in obesity levels in this country. I feel that people are just eating more these days to fill the empty hole inside that only spirituality can address, and also I feel that this hole is homesickness for the Other Side. It doesn't take a rocket scientist to see that as the world gets more hectic, people find relief in what they call "comfort food."

Personally, I prefer a high-protein diet. In fact, long before Atkins ever wrote his book, Francine told me that if I didn't start to feed my body what it's made of, I'd get all types of immune diseases. Now that doesn't mean that we can't eat soy or protein substitutes, but remember—we have canine teeth, not flat teeth like herbivores. People tell me that they can't eat any living creature because it's "cruel," but let me tell you, plants literally scream when you cut them! Then we have the fanatics who only eat sprouts, exercise six hours a day, meditate for another three, and take everything to the extreme. It's much better if you just *do everything in moderation*. Eat right, sleep well, exercise, and fill your mind with good thoughts, and illness won't get in.

I've never been a fanatic about my body, but I do try to look and feel as good as my age—or any age—allows me to. Yes, I've had a facial peel and veneers put on my teeth. I get massages and facials when I can, and I try to walk daily (as if I'm not running through every airport!). I get my hair and nails done regularly, which might be considered vanity, but

I just feel better if I outwardly can show what I feel inside. I have low blood pressure and low blood sugar, so I have to eat often. I stay pretty much on protein—not a lot of red meat, but fish, turkey, eggs, and chicken—and vegetables. Starches could be my downfall, but I try to stay away from them. I have an occasional glass of wine, but I really don't drink because I get sick and don't like the smell of booze. That's probably a blessing, as so many psychics have been addicted to alcohol. I'm not judging here, as I'm sure it comes from the tension of their lives.

It does make me crazy when people tell me that I look tired or sick or that my voice sounds like I have an upper-respiratory disease. I guess that means all the women in my family did, for they had similar voices and lived to be in their 80s and 90s. It's funny, though—my dad used to call when he was out of town, and if I answered instead of my sister or mother, he'd ask, "Who is this?"

I'd reply in my girlish and docile way, "Who in the hell do you think it is?" And he'd laugh and say, "Oh, it's you, Sylvia."

Those who know me or have seen me on TV for years never ask if I'm feeling well, it's just well-meaning strangers who do so. But remember, it's just as easy to say, not only to me but to everyone, that someone looks good instead of planting a negative thought—no matter how well-meaning you might think it is.

How Can This Tenet Help You?

Buddha said, "Worldly desires are always seeking chances to deceive the mind. If a viper lives in your room and you wish to have a peaceful sleep, you must first chase it out. You must break the bonds of worldly passions and drive them away, as you would a viper. You must protect your mind." Or, as Nancy Reagan said, "Just say no."

There has to be some control learned here. We're all

subjected to the temptations of this feel-good society, yet the abuse can crumble our temple. We tell ourselves, "I'm stronger than this; I can try it and then give it up when I choose." Wrong! As any drug addict or alcoholic will tell you, it's like a viper that not only lives in your room, but in your mind and soul as well. No matter if it's a drink, a puff, a pill, or a snort, you'll always want another one if you're prone to addiction. Don't be fooled by the few who can take a substance once and not be affected. Why take the chance?

You may be using any number of the excuses (which number in the thousands) that addicts trot out to explain the abuse of their bodies with drugs and alcohol: "I started drinking to impress my friends, and then I couldn't stop," "It runs in my family," "I was abused at an early age," "I wanted to be cool," "I was socially afraid, but drugs/drinking made me more outgoing," "The stress of my life drove me to it," "I couldn't sleep at night," "I couldn't get up and do my job," "I couldn't get along with my partner," and so on—the list is endless. Well, these are just crutches you're using to try to salvage the knowledge of the soul that knows that if you abuse your temple, you block grace.

Go back again and find when you took your first drink, puff, pill, or snort and recall what you were doing or feeling. I'm not talking about your saying "I just wanted to experiment" here. Go deeper . . . what was going on in your internal or external life that made you feel you needed it? What made you keep chasing that elusive high? Remember, the temple you've been defiling all these years doesn't just belong to you, but to God. If you had a beautiful home and rented it to tenants who destroyed it, how would you feel? Also, they'd be legally bound to make it right. So it is with your body: Spiritually, you must make it right.

The addictions of life—including the gratification of gambling, drinking, drugs, sexual infidelity, and anything else that debases or affects our temples or those of our loved ones—stop spiritual growth. I don't mean that you have to live like a monk, but any type of excess will cause damage in one way or another. You don't need a pill to expand your mind—the highs of life are found in love and joy, marriage, the birth of a child, a new puppy, the hand of a friend, or a kind word in the dark.

Go back and unplug the reasons for feelings of unworthiness, despair, guilt, remorse, or just foolhardiness, and ask God (with the help of your friends and family and trained professionals) to regain your temple. Start *today*, not just at the beginning of a new year or some far-off, never-to-happen time. Do it now before you lay waste to this beautiful edifice that God made for you. After all, who are you to deform not only yourself, but your God within? And remember to keep your temple pure and in good condition by doing everything in moderation.

* * * * * *

TENET XIII

God does not create the adversities in life. By your own choice they exist to aid in your perfection.

Hindus don't dread death, nor do they believe in an external hell (unlike many Christians, unfortunately). However, they *do* believe in hellish states of mind brought on by fear, hate, jealousy, bigotry, anger, and the like . . . which brings us to this tenet.

Sikhism, which is an offshoot of Hinduism, advocates holistic life experiences—in work, worship, and service—in order to attain a perpetual union with God, while also creating a just social order in this world. Sikhs are enjoined to lead a wholesome lifestyle; and they have a long, celebrated heritage of speaking out against injustice and for the defenseless. Sikh doctrine dictates that all people have the right to follow their own path to God without condemnation or coercion from others. They're profoundly democratic and believe in civil rights and freedom of religion.

Gnosticism, which is one of the world's oldest philosophies, feels the same way and is very tolerant of the beliefs of others. It believes that everyone has to find their own way to an all-loving, perfect God. In fact, when you analyze the world's main religions, you see so many similarities. Most of them, for instance, teach no prejudice and concentrate on right actions. The Dharma Wheel, which represents the major belief of Buddha's Eightfold Path (encompassing right views, right intent, right speech, right conduct, right livelihood, right effort, right mindfulness, and right concentration), is a prime example.

Gnosticism goes a little further and addresses all these "right actions" by their motive or intent. After all, it does no good to do something without love and understanding. Gnosticism also explores the reason that we're all living such harsh lives—namely, we're honing our souls and learning to ascend to God with knowledge. If we feel that we're just pawns or victims of our lives, then we haven't gained knowledge the way we should. Sure, we learn, but doing so without understanding falls somewhat flat. It's so much more glorious to really *know* that we're perfecting our souls.

As I've mentioned before, Earth is the only "hell" there is. My spirit guide Francine says that there are millions of planets that are inhabited, but this is the only one that has evil and negativity in such abundance—and only the bravest of the brave incarnate here to face this planet's adversities. Earth is the toughest school in the universe, which is why so many of us come here.

We may often wonder why, if God is all-loving, He/She allows this planet and all of its suffering to exist. When Jesus went to the garden of Gethsemane and asked God to remove the pain of the crucifixion that he knew was coming, God essentially told him, "No—you chose it to be this way in your contract, so you have to see it through." We're fairly confident that this took place because we hear our Lord say with resignation and almost despair, "Thy will be done." Meaning that he knew he chose it, but he wasn't happy about it. It was his contract with God, which contained his messianic legacy to fulfill his chart. And if *he* couldn't get out of his contract, what hope do we have?

You see, what happens is when we're on the Other Side, we say, "Oh, I can handle that." We end up picking all sorts of hardships that, in this state of bliss, we feel we can handle to spiritually advance for God. Then we get down here and want to change the chart. Yes, we can modify it in minor ways, but its major attributes can never be altered.

We end up picking a contract for a loving God without human qualities Who gives us a chance to learn what He/ She already knows. It's very much like the symbology in Genesis when God declares that we learn by coming down and tilling the field and bearing our children in hardship after Adam and Eve eat from the apple of the Tree of Knowledge. Unfortunately, negativity is part of that knowledge, whether we like it or not. If we don't have any adversity, then we don't know what we're made of and can't advance our knowledge and soul.

This temporal plane of existence exists because God allows it to. As our Creator, God is also our Father and Mother. We who are parents can attest to letting our children venture out from home to learn, and it follows that our Creator would do the same thing, since He/She wants us to acquire knowledge.

Our kids are part of us, just as we're a part of God. Loving them, suffering for them when they make mistakes, and having empathy for their pain all comes with the territory of being a parent. And Shakespeare hit the nail on the head when he said, "How sharper than a serpent's tooth it is / To have a thankless child!" Speaking of this (and it's not just because I'm a mother), why is it that when a child goes off track, the first person the therapist looks at is the mother? True, she's the heart of the home, but what about a cruel, neglectful father?

Anyway, we parents try to make a home for our children that's secure, loving, and safe; and we try to protect them as much as possible, but we can't live their lives for them. Why would our Creator be any different? That's why the earthly plane is only a temporary stopover in our existence. The real reality is our Home on the Other Side, where it's a safe environment filled with nothing but love. There's no negativity or evil on the Other Side, and our Creator loves us so much that He/She makes *that* the real plane of existence for our souls.

Of course we've been told from ancient times that if the gods aren't appeased by sacrifice or penance (following human-made rules, I'd just like to add), we'll have all manner of strife befall us, from crops failing, pestilence, and war to having our loved ones being taken from us. In fact, in the not-so-distant past, you couldn't compliment a baby for fear that either God or a so-called demon would be jealous and take it. And my grandmother used to tell me that when she was a child, she was told that if you love something too much it will be taken from you. Naturally, she knew this was nonsense, but it illustrates how ignorance can poison us all. I cannot stress enough that God does not create the negativity in our lives—*we do.*

We've all experienced joyous births, heart-wrenching deaths, lost friendships, being defamed or deceived by others, hardship, pain, illness, surgery, getting old, and myriad other facets of life . . . yet all are part of the learning process. Often it can feel like giving birth: My son Christopher, for instance, was an eight-pound, premature baby who took 36 hours to deliver. Believe me, I wasn't having a good time. Nevertheless, as soon as I saw him, I forgot all about the pain and found joy in what I'd gone through to get this prize. So life goes.

I have two wonderful sons and three amazing grandkids . . . and terrible taste in men. I've lost so many I love to the Other Side, and it seems that the number grows each day. My sons and I even went through divorces almost simultaneously—Chris's was first, and then Paul's and mine happened at about the same time. This was all as recent as three years ago, and there were days when I was seeing all parties suffer so much that I thought I couldn't bear it. It was one of those times when you want to scream, "What next?!" But now the grandchildren are fine and very well adjusted. My boys have wonderful partners now, and I still love and see both of my former daughters-in-law.

So many times we wonder why, if we're following our path correctly, it can't be easier. The bumps in my road have certainly aggravated me—after all, I'm human. At such "lost moments" I've even told God, "Okay, that's enough . . . I got it! Maybe I charted for rain, but I didn't expect a flood!" But then Francine will say, "Well, if you're going to learn it, Sylvia, learn it right." She can really be aggravating at times. Yes, she's right, and I love her, but I'm like anyone else and don't always like the truth.

When tragedies happen, it's natural to ask, "Why me?" Well, why not you? Each one of us wrote our charts in order to perfect. It's just that when we get into it, we decide that we don't want to do it. I find it really interesting, though, that humankind doesn't seem to want to take responsibility for any part of our lives and would rather blame things on God. We give our souls to dogma, entrust our bodies to doctors, and put our finances in others' hands. Some people even have their own personal shoppers! We can't seem to do anything for ourselves anymore—no wonder we often feel helpless and useless.

I purposely tend my own garden and do my own sewing—along with all the other things I've always done. I had my grandkids at Wal-Mart recently, and at least ten people approached me and said, "I can't believe you're here!" Why? I have to be somewhere. (I've also gotten that same response at Denny's.) I don't have to be at Spago or Louis Vuitton. I'm not against anyone who does frequent those places, but I happen to love the bargains at Wal-Mart, and my grandchildren enjoy it there, too. And I buy a lot of my clothes at a little shop in Santa Monica called Gioia where Laura, the owner, saves what she thinks I'll like, and I usually do.

I'm including these little vignettes to show you how "average" minutes, hours, and days stack up to make a life. Remember, your motive for how you handle your life is always and forever between you and God. Every minute of our lives is meant to improve us—we just have to remember to look at it that way.

The one facet of my personality I've really had to work on is my temper. I was perenially in the principal's office, especially in grade school. I'm sure that today they'd say I had ADD or ADHD, since I wasn't much for sitting still. Although I always got good grades, I preferred to pass the time in class passing notes, talking, and telling stories to everyone. God bless the nuns—they'd roll their eyes and do the best they could with me.

Getting back to my temper, I remember when I was in the sixth grade and my sister was in kindergarten—she came crying to me about a girl named Sheila who'd taken her lunch money. Well, I caught Sheila after school and smashed inchworms (which hung off trees in Missouri) in her hair. Back to the principal's office I went. And when I was in the seventh grade, I was on the girls' softball team. A player from another team called me a "Jew bitch," and before I knew it I had her on the ground and the battle was on.

I did learn over the years, with my grandmother's admonitions, that nothing is accomplished by physical retaliation, even though I certainly felt that justice had been served with inchworms and fists. Usually my ire comes to the foreground when someone I love is hurt. Touch what I love and my mouth lets loose.

Speaking of my mouth, I've been criticized for being a little too "colorful" in my language. Some would like me to be saintlier in my speech when I lecture or answer questions, while others love the way that I tell it like it is. No matter if you love me or hate me, I am who I am, and I just don't believe that God is going to fault me for speaking the way I do—after all, it doesn't take away from my spirituality.

Some people have mistaken my honesty for sarcasm. Now this doesn't mean that I'm never sarcastic, but I don't use such a tone in my psychic work. I give no excuses, but I've run several businesses as a woman alone, so I've had to live by my wits. It's enough to be stereotyped in business, but I'm blonde and have an endowed chest, so does that make me dumb?

Nevertheless, all of the put-downs I've received over the years—along with all of the good words and love—have helped me fulfill my chart. No matter how small or large an incident may be, it serves to bring us the lessons we need. The road is filled with heartaches and adversities that we've chosen, but there are also so many moments of love and happiness.

In school we can't just go and bitch to the counselor, especially when we picked the classes to graduate. Life is the same way: Why blame God for what *we* chose to complete? If we take a more optimistic view of our perception of life, we'll find that the world becomes less adversarial. Yet some individuals can't enjoy the good times and keep waiting for the other shoe to drop.

It's amazing how many people can't savor the precious moments of life, especially those spent with loved ones. These are so much more valuable than any material thing. I'm immediately reminded of the time I was sitting with my granddaughter about four years ago after we'd spent the day shopping (we even got a rabbit!). We were sitting at the kitchen table eating our favorite salad, when Angelia looked at me and said, "This was a perfect day."

I said, "Yes, it was, darling. Save it in your mind because when life gets hard, you can take it out and it will make your heart glow." *Good God,* I realized, *I've become Grandma Ada!* Yet these are the memories and treasures that we take with us.

* * *

The hardest thing for you and me to swallow is that we're the ones responsible for our charts, especially if they seem really rotten. We may wonder, *Why did I write one thing and want another?* Well, some of us recall a past time when we were happier, or we remember the Other Side where things are perfect. This leaks through and makes us homesick.

I really thought that I just wanted to have children, stay home, and have a man take care of me. Things didn't turn out exactly as I planned, but then would I have been really happy? Probably not. Would I have liked to have given my children more time? Yes, but the time I gave them was quality. Did my dream of being taken care of come true? No, I always supported everyone, even my husbands. Yet do I regret that? No. As I look back, I remember what my ex-boyfriend Joe once told me: "The world called." The need to support has also given me the impetus and will to continue.

With much gut-wrenching work, I've made baby steps to find what Sylvia wants. Yes, I have to live by my chart, but I also try to be good to *me* in the process. I won't say that I've always been thrilled with my fate, but I did have choices (not so much externally, but internally), and so do you.

How Can This Tenet Help You?

Life is circles within circles: You come in and go back and make the rounds again until you go Home and stay there. I know that you've probably felt abandoned like Job in the Bible—you feel that God has ignored you, let things happen to you, or created them to happen. None of that is true. So instead of blaming God for the adversity you picked, blame *yourself* for not handling it with grace and dignity. Even if you have to grit your teeth and bear it at times, at least when you get to the Other Side you can know that you did give it your all.

The "poor me" syndrome just brings more negativity to your doorstep. It builds upon itself until you're buried in a sea of self-pity or the feeling of "Why has God done this to me?" Until you break this pattern, you'll always feel self-defeated, and the strength God gave you will diminish in your soul. You'll feel abandoned and alone and will be apt to say something like, "What did I ever do in this life, or any other life, to be punished like this?" You haven't done anything—except perhaps take on a difficult chart to learn and graduate and advance your soul, which is in a very temporary body.

Now, just as I'm working to improve my temper, you also have facets of your personality that you must overcome. In other words, it isn't just the adversities of life you must face, but also those inside *yourself*. It's truly not only what you go through, but how you handle it, too. The outward world is just a proving ground, but you're the one who's here to test your inner essence or soul to see how you overcome such obstacles.

It's true that now I find more people on their last lives than I have in the last 20 years—and I'm one of them. There could be two reasons for this. One is that people are merely finished—that is, they're tired of this world that has beauty, but which also has so much hate, war, stress, cruelty, and so forth. So many people whom I talk to on the phone, when I tell them it's their last life, say in one form or another, "Oh, thank God! I just knew it, and I don't want to come here again." I myself have frequently said that we're coming to the end of days.

The other reason is that I think many people have had a lot of lives and feel ready to graduate. It's like school: You may find it hard at times. You may enjoy some classes, but others you hate or fail and have to take over again; or you feel that your grade wasn't an accurate indicator of what you can do, so you try harder. I hated math, especially algebra, but with tutoring I got through it. I never used it and didn't really master it, but by sheer determination I passed the damn course. School was a test of agony, tenacity, and patience, but there were wonderful classes, too: English, drama, humanities, and history were all stimulating for me. When you're ready to graduate, just like in life, you're anxious to start another facet of your true existence (like going Home). Your lessons have been learned, and reality begins.

It's said that we should seize the day. Well, I say seize the *moment*. There really is so much beauty, glory, and love around you, but you're passing it up by focusing on self-pity. It's all so simple: God is truly in His/Her heaven (and ours), and everything will ultimately be all right in your world. If it isn't so externally, then make sure that it is internally. When you take your adversity and stare it down, you'll come out the winner—especially if you keep telling yourself, as all the prophets and messengers have, that this is a transient place, and you'll soon be going Home.

So stand tall, muster up some courage and dignity, and face this difficult world with your chin high. Know that you *are* going to get through it!

* * * * * *

TENET XIV

Karma is nothing more than
honing the wheel of evolvement.
It is not retribution, but merely
a balancing of experiences.

*K*arma is a word that has been so bandied about that its true meaning has become muddled. It actually just means to experience for your soul in this life and many others . . . no more, no less. Yet the word was subsequently interpreted by Eastern religions to mean that whatever you put out (especially if it's negative) will come back to you many-fold—and they didn't go further to explain that bad actions only come back *when they're done with malice.* Finally, as the New Age (I hate that expression) arrived, "karma" seemed to be adopted by neophytes who thought that they truly knew what the word meant and carried it to the extreme. *Everything* seemed to be laced with karmic over- or undertones.

I remember one time, for instance, when I was invited by a spiritual group to present some pointers on healing and meditation. After sitting on the floor for a long time, I said, "Oh, I'm so stiff I can barely get up!"

The man next to me was named Charles, and he quickly responded, "Don't put that out in the ethers [atmosphere] or it will karmically come true!"

"Get real, Charles," I shot back. "That's silly. I'm not going to monitor every word I say for some definition of *karma* that's totally erroneous." It's no wonder that some of these New Age groups are considered strange!

People get so bound up in dogma or some type of false spiritual decorum that they forget that God knows their hearts and intentions. In fact, sin and karma seem to be sisters. The origin of the word *sin* means to just miss the mark; while if you miss the experience of learning, karma will make sure that it comes again. Consider this: It's the realization that we've missed the learning experience that makes us go back to try to fix something or make up for it. If we can't mend that particular situation, then we tend to pick the one closest to it and address that. For example, I couldn't fix my mother no matter what I did, but I used her example to fix *me* so that I wouldn't ever be like her.

I'm sure you've noticed that if you try to dodge the bullet of learning, it will come again. As I've said before, life is circles within circles, and many times we end up where we started—but hopefully we're wiser and have gained more grace and spirituality. In many East Indian religions, the wheel of karma never seems to stop: Some Hindus and Buddhists, for instance, believe that the wheel of life keeps turning to the point that some people live thousands of lives.

All I can say (not to be critical or disparaging) is that logically you'd have to always come back into life immediately after death, and no one would be able to get you on the Other Side. You'd always be on a journey of coming and going, so you'd never be able to reside at the Home from whence you came. You wouldn't even have the time to regroup and see what you wanted to accomplish next time.

Now in all my 50 years of research, in which my ministers and I have personally done thousands of past-life regressions (including many on individuals from Eastern religions), never once have we found anyone who has lived thousands and thousands of lives.

During these regressions, I've also failed to find anyone who has experienced the transmigration of their soul. Many Eastern religions believe in this concept, which is basically living a life (or lives) in the body of another living creature, such as a cow, insect, dog, cat, rat, or what have you. This belief has direct tie-ins not only to karma, but also to the caste system that was in place just decades ago (and is still practiced unofficially in many places).

To try to simplify it as much as possible, this goes back to the belief that karma dictates how you're going to live your next life: If you lead a good one, you'll go upward in the caste system in your next life; but if you don't, you're going to go downward to possibly become an "untouchable" (lowest caste of human life) or even an animal or insect in your next life. This is one of the reasons why animals and insects are never killed intentionally in countries such as India. Citizens believe that they might be killing a soul who's trying to get to the point of perfection in which they can live a human life—thus, they'd incur their own karma for interfering. These people seem to take karma to its extreme definition, just as they do reincarnation.

Well, I'm here to tell you that an animal has no agenda except to live by pure instinct, love, and even honor. Yes, it's a shame that we don't come back as cats or dogs and learn what pure, uncomplicated survival means, but God created animals without any karma. In fact, they're a separate species unto themselves for humankind, both as a help (food, balance of nature, pollination, and so forth) and a hindrance (disease, crop destruction, and the like) to help us perfect our souls. Just as angels are separate creations from spirit guides or ghosts, the animal kingdom was created to help in the evolution of the planet and humankind—not as vehicles for us to live lives in.

We only incarnate in human form, but many times society has its way of forming barriers due to religious practices.

Taking the aforementioned caste system as an example, religious belief dictated that those in the lower classes wouldn't be as evolved as those in the upper classes. The untouchables were considered to be very unevolved souls in comparison to the upper castes, so they were relegated to the harshest menial labor and its subsequent outcome: poverty. Hinduism is considered to be one of the world's oldest active religions, and its teachings have influenced every major religion today—but it has also influenced today's society. The caste system (which was outlawed a few decades ago due to pressure from human-rights activists) is really no different from the delineation of classes of people today, as we have the poor, the middle class, and the rich . . . and that's it.

It's so wrong for people to always use karma as an excuse for everything—especially when past lives and cell memory more often come into play. Many times in a past life we'll have had a negative experience with drowning, snakes, heights, choking, closed-in places, and so forth; consequently, they become left over in our cell memory. Then, when we come into this life, that cell memory is often still active and affects us, but it has nothing to do with being punished for a bad action.

For example, in one of my past lives I was an empress who was poisoned. This memory had invaded my cells to the point that when I was very tiny, I wouldn't eat anything my mother gave me until my dad or someone else tasted it first. I haven't investigated it, but perhaps my mother or someone close poisoned me in that life and it was a carry-over. I eventually got over this fear with my grandma's help, when she very matter-of-factly explained that that was then and this is now.

Also, six lives before this one, I didn't have any children because I was an oracle who couldn't marry. In other lives, I was a spinster in Poland who was the last daughter and had to take care of aging parents, a young girl in Kenya who died early, and a nun. So in this life, I wanted children more than anything—it was my need and karmic experience to do so.

On the other hand, I have two friends who had so many children in past lives that this is the last thing they want in this life.

Now the reason we pick so many lives (and we white entities usually do) is *not* because we've done something terrible or have incurred karma. Instead, we usually feel that we could have handled a situation much better, so we try it again to make sure that we've gotten out of it what we needed. We also might feel that we have to learn a certain hardship or experience sorrow or even violence to perfect our soul. Maybe we choose an early death to bring others to spirituality and awareness, or we want to be kinder and more patient—the list could go on endlessly. Unlike this life, when we say, "If I had it to do over again, I would have done such and such," reincarnation allows us many chances to do what we didn't do according to our own karmic experience for God.

So when life gets bad, we shouldn't immediately jump to the false conclusion that "I must have been terrible in a past life." It's more that we're just working out a balancing of our experience and knowledge. And as hard as it is to understand, people do karmically come down to create a greater good through suffering. The incident of 9/11 was an example of that. Those incredible people didn't die in vain; rather, they were like saints who chose to show us that this country was far too complacent. They were like a type of Paul Revere, warning that the enemy was coming in the form of terrorism. In Hitler's time, the blessed souls who died in concentration camps made the world turn their attention not only to the Nazis' atrocities, but also to what horror can be done in the name of bigotry and insane prejudice.

On the Other Side, when we're happy and in "bliss" (a term often used by Joseph Campbell), we feel so good that we pick all types of charts for the realization and betterment of the whole human race. Those who choose charts full of suffering are truly our saintly martyrs. The countless people who were either burned at the stake or tortured and killed in the Inquisition by the Catholic Church are examples of those who died in martyrdom and innocence. (It's no wonder why anyone with any type of healing ability or second sight kept it hidden!) Everyone, no matter who they are, has their own experience to fulfill their chart for God. It seems senseless to us here because we sometimes forget (myself included) to look at the bigger picture. We all come into life for a very short period of time in comparison to eternity, and we choose different lessons to bring about a better and greater good.

* * *

Kenyans are firm believers in the type of karma in which what is sent out comes back, even though most of them are practicing Christians. And here I'd like to digress for a moment.

It's true that there are places in the world that if we're fortunate to find them, they'll help bring peace to our soul. For me, that place is Kenya, which is a spiritual home for me. I've been there many times, but the world and my work has crowded in so much that I can't take the time to go back as much as I'd like. Nevertheless, that country is forever with me. When I stepped off the plane on my first visit in 1981, I said, "Oh God, I'm home."

The smells, the dear animals, and the smiling faces of everyone you see are unbelievable. They have the most incredible sky there . . . you can actually touch the clouds. The light at sunset is a golden orange, with the animals silhouetted against the growing night sky. Even if you're having tea at the old Norfolk Hotel, as I was with Christina Kenyatta (daughter of the first president of Kenya), and have a serious expression on your face, you're apt to have an attendant come up and say, "Mama, are you not happy? Can I make you happy?"

I often half-jokingly say that the problem is that God *lives* in Africa and only *visits* other places. So when I get a little down, I think of when I was sitting under a baobab tree writing with Samson, a German shepherd, sitting at my feet—I think that this is as close to the Other Side as I will get on this earth.

I also try to remind myself that to be in a state of stupor doesn't allow us to perfect anything. There's an old saying that's trite but true: "What comes too easy probably shouldn't be trusted." I found this to be reliable in my life, as I'm sure you have. That's not to say that opportunity will never drop in your lap, but generally it will be because prior to this, you paid your dues.

For example, let's look at the "overnight success." Usually this person has toiled for years before he or she gets noticed. For example, I was 36 before I got my first TV interview and didn't write my first book until I was 50—but I'd been doing readings and oftentimes was the local oddity since I was 18 years old. So you see what it takes to become an overnight success. Of course, some of the younger stars who quickly do become sensations often have their lives turn upside down later. They live as if their fame and fortune will go on forever, and it doesn't. So many become penniless, addicted to drugs or alcohol, have run-ins with the law, and so on.

Step-by-step, we all make it to the top of our karmic or experiencing ladder, and the hardships of that journey can often be what save us when we finally get there. Our karmic path will get us to our appointed destiny if we just take it with slow strides and never demean or step on anyone, or use them to get ahead. We can never put ourselves above others, because we're all on the same journey and have all had a chance to be someone of importance. Even if we live a simple life, we're all famous in God's eyes.

There can also be group karma, in which many people experience for a cause or truth together. More than once, members of my study groups—and all of my ministers—have jokingly told me, "I know you talked us into this Gnostic mission on the Other Side, and you were so persuasive that we went along with you." They've even threatened to run from me when we all get back Home, just in case I get it into my head to come back and make sure that what we started continues properly!

It's true I always fear that after I'm gone my words will get misinterpreted, as those from so many messengers from God have over time. But I know that Chris, my youngest, will carry on just like Hugh Lynn Cayce did after his dad, Edgar, passed on.

The group-karma experience is usually wider in scope than the individual experience, but it's not a lesser or greater one. We truly are our brother's keeper, which means that we're all tied together in a great "karmic jigsaw." In other words, what you think is unfair is actually fair, and what injustices you see have been chosen by the brave souls who've come to show us what the human spirit can survive and learn from. People on the Other Side are also learning by watching us go through our tribulations, so when we get back Home we'll share our experiences and will even help others write their charts accordingly.

Now, as I've already mentioned, sometimes we choose too much because we're so enthusiastic on the Other Side— then we come down here and the full impact of what we've chosen hits us like a two-by-four. I know that I've certainly felt like this a time or two. "If you live long enough," my grandmother used to say, "you'll see it all." That's so true.

We may think that we have a choice when these deaths, deceptions, divorces, and illnesses happen, but we don't. So we pick up the pieces of our lives and superglue them back together with every spiritual part of our being, and we get up and (for a while) painfully go on until time heals the wounds. While nothing may be able to give us solace at this time, one day we wake up and the lights go on again. We may never truly stop the pain of the loss, but we can eventually turn it into sympathy and understanding for others and a deeper understanding of ourselves and the strength we have.

We all share the experience of karma and learning . . .

hopefully, we can do it with dignity and spiritual strength. I know that I work toward it every day, knowing that total understanding and peace is not for here, but for our heavenly Home. And I also know that our Creator never says that He/She is disappointed in us, but it's the God within all of us that stretches for perfection in this life—and can sometimes be our harshest critic. Of course we fall at times, but we'll get up and make it better, in this life or the next. Most entities are on their last life or two, so that's why we're seeing such a search for truth today.

To release karma, we don't need to use sage, crystals, or cards; meditate for hours; or cleanse ourselves through various methods. We simply need to do the best we can and make it through the adversities and good times of life. And remember, we never stop learning—not even on the Other Side.

How Can This Tenet Help You?

I started this book in Hawaii, and now I'm on the *Mississippi Queen* riverboat giving lectures and readings and continuing my writing. I love to see the different cultures within our own country, but one thing I've found in all my travels here and abroad is that people are searching for spirituality, and it's as individual as our looks. I had someone on the river cruise, for instance, come up to me and say, "The Bible doesn't mention 'karma.'"

I politely replied, "I beg to differ, but there is no finer example of karma then when our Lord said, 'Do unto others as you would have them do unto you.'"

I hardly ever get aggravated with people because (and I'm not trying to sound like Bill Clinton here) I feel their pain, but once in a while, I'm human and my nerves just go. And there are some people I simply can't please or give enough to, so it's better to just let it go. Now you might feel karmically attached to your family, friends, and co-workers and try and try to please them. Well, if they can't accept all that you do or have done, then just go, or let them go because this isn't your karma, it's theirs.

Now to truly comprehend the concept of karma, you have to understand its universal rule: to live life to the fullest and care about others *as well as yourself.* Don't let the past cripple you, don't let guilt overcome you, and quit obsessing about what you did or didn't do—it's dead, wasted energy. Then you start carrying around your own heavy armor of karma that you've forged in the fire of your personal fears and misgivings. This will make you sick, depressed, and tired . . . and your life will hold no joy at all.

Karma simply means that you're completing the themes you chose for learning, so stop with "What did I do so terribly wrong that I'm being punished this time?" In the first place, only good people say this—dark souls never give it a thought because they think they're perfect. Also, dark-soul entities have to keep coming back to this hellhole and never get to the Other Side like we do. To me, that's the best karma of all.

Francine says that it usually takes five years for karma to enact, especially when something has been done to you out of maliciousness and premeditated intent. Now some of you will say, "I've waited 10 or 20 years for a crime to be solved, or for someone who has hurt me or my family to receive their just due, so what gives?" Well, many times you won't hear about what's happened to these people; or, from the outside things may look great for them, but inside I can tell you that they're definitely not.

Don't be concerned if you think negative thoughts about the individual who hurt you, because it's a human reaction that has no effect on him or her. Remember, curses don't work. Don't get me wrong—anyone can absorb negative and positive energy emanating from someone in close proximity, and thoughts are things that have energy, but the average human being doesn't have the time, power, or concentration to project thoughts that harm another.

However, God has given all of us an innate defensive system that wards off most negativity—unless you leave yourself open to receive it. This accounts for the rare and isolated cases in certain cultures in which a person believes that they're cursed (making them open to negativity), and then they get sick or die as a result of that belief.

Yes, the mind is very powerful, and you can heal or hurt yourself depending on the power of your belief. In either case, *you're* the one doing it, not anyone else. Keep in mind that what is purposely sent out comes back. If you've lost your husband to another woman, you might want them both dead, but that is an emotional human reaction—with time, it will cool. Now if you hire a hit man to take care of the wayward spouse, that would incur karma coming back to *you*.

I know that karma can sometimes be a fine line to understand, but we *are* allowed to hate evil and evil actions. When this world ends, God in His/Her mercy and love will absorb all of the dark entities back into His/Her mass, while we will stay as ourselves and reap the rewards from the Other Side. That certainly sounds like good karma to me.

✳ ✳ ✳ ✳ ✳

TENET XV

God allows each person the opportunity for perfection, whether you need one life or a hundred lives to reach your level of perfection.

Just as we choose different themes or lessons that we're going to learn, we also pick the number of lives (and even the years, months, days, and hours) that we're going to exist on this planet in order to complete our mission or education. After all, how could Mozart compose at three years old? We see prodigies all the time who have no genetic predisposition, so why not believe that they chose to come into families that would benefit from their particular gifts?

This is also the explanation for why some seem to be taken before what we feel is their time. We say, "They went too soon," "They never really got to live," or "It was an accident, and they went too young." Yet their charted time may be entirely different from our own. As simplistic as this sounds, we each have our own allotted time, or "curfew," in each life. Much like when I was in my late teens, midnight was my time to come home, but some of my peers could stay out later.

To show you how conditioned I am, before my dad died, we all took a trip back to Kansas City. I was about 49 years old at the time, and had gone out for the evening with my dear lifelong friend Mary Margaret. It got to be around 11:30, and I told her that I had to get back because my family was staying at a friend's house. At the same time, my father announced to our host that I'd be back by midnight. Everyone laughed and said, "For God's sake, Bill, she's close to 50! Certainly she'll be out later than that."

My dad was adamant. "No, she'll be here."

When Mary Margaret and I drove up at 11:50, Daddy was standing outside with a huge grin. As I walked up to the house, I asked, "Why are you smiling?"

He replied, "I just know you, sweetheart."

This is how it is with our chart: We're programmed to know when we're done. Even if others looking on through their narrow scope see what we didn't fulfill, *we* know that we did all we could—and we have other opportunities to come back and try again.

Some people without any discrimination will pick 10, 25, 40, 50, or more lives—whatever it takes for them to reach their own particular goal of perfection. I've never seen anyone with 100 lives, but I did meet one person who'd lived 99. "Boy," you might say, "they must have been really advanced." Well, they were as advanced as their soul needed to be. Certain individuals just want a high-school education, so to speak, while others want a Ph.D.; but no one on the Other Side looks askance at an individual's level of evolvement. No one carries a badge that proclaims what level they're on or how much better they are—it's only in this hellhole that people are so critically discerning.

Each and every one of our lives is set out in a gigantic pattern. We have the large pattern that encompasses everyone's existence as a whole, and then we have the smaller patterns of each individual life—which is reworked and defined as much as possible to perfect for God. It just makes logical sense that no one can complete everything in one life; if an entity does choose just one, then they have to complete their education by serving as a guide or doing some kind of service on the Other Side. *Everyone* keeps on learning and perfecting until they graduate.

Now, many historians and theologians claim that the concept of reincarnation was brought to light by the Egyptians, but that's not really true. Yes, they contributed in a limited way: They were the first, at least in recorded history, to believe that the soul existed after death—thus the burial chambers filled with food and artifacts that they'd use in the afterlife. Previous to this belief, especially in the ancient Judaic tradition, life after death didn't exist or was unknown. Even Christ's "resurrection" had him coming into flesh.

The real beginning of the belief in reincarnation comes from the ancient East Indian religions, which are also the world's oldest. Their belief in having many lives to perfect the soul was carried over from Lemuria and resides in ancient Sanskrit texts that are thousands of years old. (For more on Lemuria, please see my book *Secrets & Mysteries of the World.*) These texts claim without any complicated dogma that human beings live many lives to fulfill our perfection and to learn our lessons. In other words, one life does not and cannot produce perfection, not only for God but the God within.

Reincarnation as a belief has always been labeled an "Eastern" one; consequently, it wasn't adopted by the Western world and was even suppressed by early Christian leaders. Today, it's estimated that approximately two-thirds of the world believes in reincarnation in one form or another, but it's really only come to the foreground of Western public acknowledgment in the last 20 or 30 years—and is growing in belief as I write these words.

The Gnostics have always believed in reincarnation, but kept silent because they were afraid of being branded heretics. The premise is mentioned frequently in texts such as the Manichaean *Hymn Exhorting the Soul to Remembrance*, from which the following comes: "Remember the cycle of rebirths and the torture of Hell [Earth], where souls are hurt and oppressed. Maintain the fervor of the soul and the treasure of the word, so that you may enter the Paradise of Light."

Gnostic texts such as the Apocrypha, the Nag Hammadi codices, and the Dead Sea Scrolls; as well as the numerous writings of the Valentinians, Manichaeans, Cathars, and Templars, all support ancient texts about reincarnation. And in Buddhism, the Noble Truth regarding the origin of suffering centers around the thirst to gratify the senses or the cravings for material gains. Too much of this thirst leads to rebirth after rebirth in multiple lives. To reach Nirvana is to attain the level in which you're released from the "rebirth cycle," as well as from the bondage of the endless cycle of birth, death, pain, sorrow, and all the other human conditions of life.

Gnostics don't believe that one must be uncomfortable, but think that making only material gain one's entire aim leads to an empty life. Also, Hindus and Buddhists differ from the Gnostics on reincarnation in their unspoken philosophy that humans were sent on this journey to perfect because we weren't good enough to reach God, while Gnostics believe that we choose to come into life to learn and perfect for God with a purpose—not to be just "thrown into it," so to speak.

Reincarnation became a prevalent belief in early Christian dogma thanks to the influence of Greek and Roman thought. St. Gregory, the Bishop of Nyssa, gave words to that effect: "It is absolutely necessary that the soul shall be healed and purified, and if it doesn't take place in one life on Earth, it must be accomplished in future lives." Nevertheless, in A.D. 533, belief in reincarnation was declared a heresy by the Council of Constantinople.

The reason for this was twofold: (1) The Church believed that such a belief detracted from their teachings of death and judgment, which were clearly established in basic Christian doctrine; and (2) the Church believed that it took away a control issue. That is, they realized that if people knew they only had one life in which to make it to the kingdom of heaven, then the Church could exert more control and dictate how people lived their lives. Out of this mentality, stricter dogma came forth that eventually led to the Inquisition. This was also one of the primary reasons behind the Reformation, as rich people were buying indulgences from the Church to assure themselves a place in heaven.

Most Christian churches today don't believe in reincarnation because it conflicts with their dogma of one life, death, and then judgment from God—after all, that's what the Bible says. What they have a hard time explaining, however, is the early deaths of children and the obvious inequities of life that stare that dogma straight in the eye and tear it to shreds. Then they start backpedaling and putting forth exceptions, such as "a child is innocent and can't be judged." Yet a one-life philosophy doesn't begin to explain life's unfairness, and the whole judgment philosophy contradicts an all-loving God. As Huston Smith said in his book *The World's Religions:* "Everything that came from his [Christ's] lips formed the surface of a burning glass to focus human awareness on the two most important facts about life: God's overwhelming love of humanity, and the need for people to accept that love and let it flow through them to others."

I'm constantly amazed at how people can believe that they'll be judged by God, and if found lacking will be thrown into a fiery pit of damnation forever. I'm not condemning their right to believe in any way they want, I'm just astonished that they can swallow that gunk that so many Christian churches put out and believe it. But then, I'm not looking at the economics of the situation—that is, if there's no fear, there won't be any money for more churches.

It's sometimes a sight to behold when you look at the beliefs and values of humankind, along with their inconsistencies. Again, Huston Smith points this out in *The World's Religions* when he writes about how Christ's teachings shocked the populace of his day by giving "hard sayings" that countered the usual prevalent thought and rocked us like an earthquake:

> We are told that we are not to resist evil but to turn the other cheek. The world assumes that evil must be resisted by every means available. We are told to love our enemies and bless those who curse us. The world assumes that friends are to be loved and enemies hated. We are told that the sun rises on the just and the unjust alike. The world considers this undiscriminating; it would like to see clouds over evil people and is offended when they go unpunished. We are told that outcasts and harlots enter the kingdom of God before many who are perfunctorily righteous. Again unfair, the world thinks; respectable people should head the procession. We are told that the gate to salvation is narrow. The world would prefer it to be broad. We are told to be as carefree as birds and flowers. The world counsels prudence. We are told that it is more difficult for the rich to enter the Kingdom than for a camel to pass through a needle's eye. The world admires wealth. We are told that the happy people are those who are meek, who weep, who are merciful and pure in heart. The world assumes that it is the rich, the powerful, and the wellborn who are happy.

Smith then goes on to paraphrase H. G. Wells, who said something to the effect that either there was something mad about Jesus, or our hearts are still too small for his message.

※ ※ ※

I'd like to take a moment here to talk about my great-uncle Henry Kaufholz, who died when I was 13. He was Grandma Ada's only brother, and they both inherited their psychic gifts from their mother, who came from Prussian royalty. Henry, who was named after his father, was 6'6", a large blonde, blue-eyed man who was very adventurous with his ability. He even left Springfield, Missouri (where the family settled after a brief stay in Texas), to join the old Florida Chesterfield (Spiritualist) camps.

Uncle Henry was not only a psychic medium, but he also loved to do research—just like me. He was a great proponent of the soul's timeline, which I wasn't aware of until my granddaughter pulled out his scrapbook one day. (It's amazing that I've had this bound book all these years and never really read what he'd written.) In it, he talks brilliantly about reincarnation and the allotted time people had . . . and please keep in mind that we're talking about a scrapbook that dates from the early 1900s here.

He states that some of the material was acquired from his grandmother, who was also a psychic and a doctor in Germany (which was quite a feat in those days). The one thing I'm proud of is that those in my family are and were bona-fide, documented psychics—genetic or not. Even Paul, my grandmother's son who died so young, had a spiritual relationship with God that was awe inspiring. The only one I know about who fell through the cracks was my mother, but that's another story. . . .

My great-uncle never called himself a Gnostic Christian, but the one refrain that runs through his writings is: "Find your own power and your own God-center." He didn't subscribe to any particular organized religion, although he had some background in the Lutheran faith, as many German families did. Grandma Ada, on the other hand, leaned more toward Catholicism and loved Fulton J. Sheen (a great bishop who was very popular on TV in the '50s).

The poetry, letters, and articles that Uncle Henry both wrote and collected are priceless—not just because of their age, but because of when they were written. True, this was the time of Sir Arthur Conan Doyle and Harry Houdini, both of whom were devout researchers of the paranormal; and Spiritualism was enjoying a great revival, especially in Europe—however, it diminished as the new century progressed, thanks to the work of so many charlatans.

As I went through these scrapbooks, I noticed Uncle Henry's detailed research on death and dying and the soul's progression through lives. His view was very similar to mine in that he said we all make a contract with God that's completed through many lives. He'd incorporated many articles and essays on the subject, such as the following, which was written in 1912:

> The spiritualistic answers agree as to the revival of the individual after the death of the body, and a mass of evidence is proffered which, in the opinion of all those who have carefully studied it, places the fact of revival beyond dispute. When every possible deduction has been made for fraud, hallucination, [and] self-deception, there remains an irreducible minimum of evidence, which is sufficient to prove that man survives on the other side of death. The evidence, as is well known, is obtained through the class of sensitives known as "mediums," and is of the most varied kinds—writing, materializing under trance conditions, or otherwise.
>
> The greater part of man's consciousness is outside man's physical body, and can manifest itself through the medium of the astral and mental bodies in the astral and mental worlds. In "waking consciousness," the activity is shown through the physical body; but man is not "awake" all the time.
>
> Consciousness is active when the body sleeps, and psychologists have investigated the "dream consciousness," and by the study of dreams, of trance conditions, hypnotic and mesmeric, they have accumulated a number of facts which show when the senses are deadened and the brain is inactive, the consciousness manifests certain powers more extensive than it can show during the use of its ordinary physical apparatus. To put it into other words, the consciousness which works in the waking body is largely withdrawn from the body when it sleeps, and

consciousness is less impeded in the exercise of its powers when it is working outside the dense and comparatively sluggish matter of the physical body.

In certain conditions of very deep trance the consciousness is almost withdrawn from the astral as well as the physical body, and then it works in still rarer regions, and we can have visions of the saints or passed loved ones.

Many an experience of happiness and of suffering are engraven by the consciousness of the spirit's memory [cell memory] and appear as "conscience or knowing" from a subsequent life, as the impulse to do the right and abstain from wrong.

Our future is in our own hands, for the Spirit who is "man" [God] is the inner ruler immortal. We create our future [making our chart] by our present [learning lessons], for we live in a world of law and for him that lives nobly death is but the entrance to a larger consciousness of knowledge and another life.

I included this here because even 100 years ago, people seemed to grasp the meaning of bringing over past memories—and the acknowledgment of cell memory is astounding. Even back then, we had knowledge of it all, and the only thing we lacked was the gigantic statistical findings.

As soon as I read this article, I wondered why it had taken me so long to go through my uncle's book, but then I thought, *How stupid . . . things come when they're supposed to.*

Henry lived to the ripe old age of 96, and his entire life was spent helping people by being a trance medium, and the reason I wanted to talk about him here is partly because he was such a force of spirituality, yet no one really knew about him. I think he deserves some recognition for his great research after almost a century of toiling in a world that was less than sympathetic to his beliefs. Since he was born in the mid-1800s, he must have gone through his own times with skeptics, but from what I heard, nothing bothered him—he persevered even to his death. Until the day he died, he did readings for everyone and anyone, just like my grandmother, and like her, he was also an avid reincarnationist. What's funny is that in the beginning, I wasn't. Oh, I thought it was possible, but truthfully I wasn't going in that direction until I got into hypnosis. It was after many sessions that I finally found irrefutable proof that we live multiple lives; then I went even further to research what we bring over—good *and* bad—from those lives. So through my research, I became a believer.

Today, we're seeing new information come to light in books such as Elaine Pagels's *Gnostic Gospels; The Messianic Legacy* and *Holy Blood, Holy Grail* by Michael Baigent, Richard Leigh, and Henry Lincoln; or Dan Brown's *The Da Vinci Code,* which has become one of the most talked-about books in decades. It's exciting that so much hidden information, which we've been denied for so long, is now coming to light.

How Can This Tenet Help You?

Francine says that I've had 40 lives being psychic (oh, joy). I've also been a Bedouin girl who learned what isolation was like in the desert. When I was an empress, I learned that fame is fleeting; when I was an oracle, I learned how to read for people; and in Atlantis, I learned to write. As a Chinese girl, I learned poverty; in Kenya, I learned to love nature and animals and the pureness of human life; and in Poland, I learned how to care for my sick loved ones. I've learned to be without children, to be humbled, elated, poor, rich, sick, rejected, and on and on it goes. Each of my lives built on the next and taught me different things . . . and so it is with you.

Just as I was never a baby killer or a tyrant, neither were you. You're not dark or you wouldn't care about finding truth (even if you were curious). So, if you can release ills and phobias—which I've done—by talking to the soul mind and releasing the carryover from a past life, how can that be just a healing story? The mind is too clever to be fooled by some tale that doesn't ring true to the soul.

I'm also convinced (after obsessing about the fact that I can't see more than about 100 years from now) that it's absolutely true that humankind only has that much time left on this planet. It was right in front of me, yet I didn't see it. How many times have I said that I've never seen so many people who are on their last lives—*duh!* On that last life, which many of us are already living, we'll go through all of these experiences and many more to make our souls strong. We may not like it—like me, we can sometimes gripe and bitch through it—but we'll get up, dust ourselves off, and keep on going.

Now while I'm sure that the final days are coming, I'm not like all those soothsayers who have predicted doom—I'm just convinced that after millions of years on this planet, in which we've learned through many lifetimes for God, this schematic will end.

Don't worry, though—there will be other plans for us: We'll either stay on the Other Side and learn, or we'll wait for another planet to swing into place and possibly explore life there. Regardless, life will never end, but I can assure you that nothing *anywhere* will be like it's been here. I'm convinced that that's why our Lord and the other messengers came here—to try to nurture a truly hellish planet. Tragically, every time they did, they were punished for it.

Even Martin Luther, the founder of the Lutheran Church who tried to bring about love and peace and quell corruption, was branded a heretic. His whole stance was that the scriptures didn't support much of the politics of the Church at that time—in much the same way that human-made doctrine ruled out the reincarnation that was in the original books because they felt it took away from Christianity.

I've always wondered how a merciful and all-loving God wouldn't give us as many tries as we needed for our own souls to live and advance. Yet if anyone tries to bring the reality of hope, logic, and love to the table, they're condemned because they don't fear God or get caught up in a devil (which, as we know, doesn't exist anyway). Much of the dogma in Christianity today is such that you sit back and wonder, *Where did that church law come from?* Humans, that's who!

No matter if you believe in one life or many, be assured that God is all-knowing, forever loves you, and will never abandon you. After all, if Jesus promised that he would be with us always, why wouldn't his Father do likewise through our life-after-life journeys? As Christ said in Matthew 5:45–48: "So that you may be children of your Father in heaven; for he makes his sun rise on the evil and on the good, and sends rain on the righteous and the unrighteous. . . . Be perfect, therefore, as your heavenly father is perfect."

✳ ✳ ✳ ✳ ✳ ✳

TENET XVI

*Devote your life, your soul, your very
existence, to the service of God. For
only there will you find meaning in life.*

I've shared what this tenet relates in many ways over the
years, but sometimes people are confused as to how they
should really devote their lives to God. They think that they
have to be saintly, when the truth is that most of us already
have the calling to live the best we can. And I'm not trying to be pessimistic when I say that so many people are
enduring lives of quiet desperation or futility, are in a desert period, or are just surviving—and they don't realize that
this, too, can be a glory to God.

Think about it—if life wasn't hard, we wouldn't learn.
After all, we can't master algebra if we're not subjected to its
equations. The worst thing we can do, however, is despair
and go into apathetic thinking, such as, *What difference can I
make? I'm only one person.* Unfortunately, because of the way
the world is, we're going to feel overwhelmed—that's just
the way it is—but that's no reason for giving up either.

So many times in readings, people are worried that they're not on track, that God won't forgive or is mad at them, or that they haven't done enough to perfect. None of us should be worrying about these things—as I've said so often, individuals who are bad or dark don't care—and I'd like to see us all become more optimistic instead of constantly dwelling on pain and suffering.

I don't talk to, or do readings for, too many happy people, so a lot of folks ask me, "How do you, your son, and your staff stay positive with all the pain and suffering you hear?" Well, it comes down to the belief that God is good and we're here to learn. It's true that, like a doctor, I don't tend to see well people, but I try to give truth and help or even help make their pain stop.

This reminds me of a beautiful meditative prayer I once read, called "Enlightened Buddha":

> *Beyond the beliefs of any one religion,*
> *there is truth of the human spirit.*
> *Beyond the power of nations, there*
> *is the power of the human heart.*
> *Beyond the ordinary mind, the*
> *power of wisdom, love, and healing*
> *energy are at work in the universe.*
> *When we find peace within our hearts,*
> *we contact these universal powers.*
> *This is our only hope.*

In all the major religions, the basic themes of love, giving, and peace are pervasive. So if we go through life as the various messengers have told us to, then we've devoted our existence to the service of God. It's as simple as that.

So many times we note the lives of the saints, clerics, and holy people; along with the Gandhis, Mother Teresas, and Martin Luther Kings of this world; and we feel inferior compared to what they've sacrificed and accomplished because they really seem to have lived their lives totally for

God. Well, we don't have to be canonized or written up in history books—it's what we do in our everyday lives that puts notches in our spiritual belt.

My guide Francine also says that *everyone* has had a life in which they worked and gained some noteworthy spiritual knowledge—but not every person who gave up their lives to work tirelessly for a spiritual movement got headlines. After all, we didn't always have TV and newspapers to follow every human-interest story. Take Mohammed, Buddha, and Jesus, for example: Who interviewed them? Who would have known about my grandmother, who died in 1954, if it weren't for me? Yes, there are a few people in Kansas City who remember her, but if I hadn't written about her, who would know?

It's our actions that change our circle of influence and impact the world. So when we feel that what we've done isn't enough, we just need to remember that our lights are in heaven, and angels are writing down our deeds in golden script in their scrolls. (Many times it's actually *better* to do our good works in comparative obscurity.)

Devoting our lives to God and our own family and friends, and just treating others as we want to be treated is so simple and so wonderful. Yet we can oftentimes take this too far and get too scrupulous. We become afraid that if we have negative thoughts, get angry, lash out or get cranky at a loved one, speak sarcastically to a grocery clerk, or what have you, then that means we aren't living a life devoted to God and good works. Well, take comfort—these are stress-related *human* emotions, and we've got to allow ourselves to be human. Personally, I don't trust people who are too goody-goody and thus never stand up for themselves.

For more than 30 years, I've told my staff to always be courteous, but they're not on the phone to put up with someone who's rude or insulting. The customer is always right when they have an honest and courteous complaint . . . however, I remember that we had this guy who used to call at least once a week and berate anyone who answered

the phone. He'd say things like, "You people are all pho-
nies—you just want money, and you're all a bunch of scam
artists."

I happened to be walking through the office one day
and heard Michael (my secretary of 18 years) saying, "I'm
sorry you feel this way, sir, but I can assure you that we're
accredited and never entrap anyone. No one is forced to call
us, and we don't solicit anyone."

I asked Pam, who's been with me for 30 years, "What's
this about?"

Warily, she said, "It's just some guy who calls once a
week and reads us the riot act."

I marched in there and took the phone out of Michael's
hand. "Who is this?" I asked the caller, knowing already
that his name was Richard.

He responded, "Is this Sylvia?"

I said, "Yes, it is, and I'd like to hear your complaints!"

He stammered that he thought we were in the business for the money, and I replied, "You're right, we *do* need
money because we have ministers and an office staff of 22,
overhead, a phone bill that would floor most people, Workers' Comp, taxes, and leased computers and office equipment." Then, as if it mattered, I continued, "And as for me,
I'm on salary, I don't own a house, and I lease my car." I
wondered why I was going through this with a clearly ignorant person, so I ended the conversation with, "Apparently
you have too much time on your hands, and if you call back
here again, no one will be allowed to talk to you."

There was a long pause, and then I heard, "I'm sorry, I
didn't know."

Remember that before you go into a fight, you should
at least go in with knowledge. As I told this Richard, "If you
didn't know," I replied, "then you don't need to spread your
hateful accusations."

He called back a week later to apologize again, and he
even sent us flowers.

Now I'm not telling you this story to be a martyr, because

I do live very well. I have a nice home, a great Ford van, a wonderful family, and plenty to eat—but I think that we all get too tied into what our economic status is. It's true that the economy goes up and down nationwide; while individually it seems that if people have money they're afraid they're going to lose it, and if they don't have it, they're afraid they'll end up homeless. I'm not saying that these aren't valid concerns, but if we shove down our expectations and also believe that God will take care of us, then we'll realize that we don't need very much to exist happily. We collect (I should talk) and hold on to everything (even what we don't need), but we forget that everything is temporary—after all, we won't be taking anything with us when we go Home.

I've been bankrupt, and also well provided for—and either way, I truly was fine as long as I could provide shelter for my family and put food on the table. But worries such as these, as authentic as we think they are, keep spirituality away. God always provides a way, and sometimes the small things in life—like a "Thank you," a smile, or a meant compliment—are what really count.

My youngest son is like me when it comes to animals, and he has three cats that just show up at his house. A friend was sitting at his table, saw Chris go get food for each of the cats, and asked, "Why would you do that?"

"Because they're hungry," my son replied. It's as simple as that: If there's a need, fill it. We should never turn our backs on a need. For example, I was in Wal-Mart one day when my grandson Willy pointed out an old lady trying to reach a roll of paper towels. I went over and got it down for her. People were walking by in throngs, and no one but a child noticed her plight.

I really don't believe that people are mean; rather, we've all become so focused on our own problems that we really don't see the big picture. It's like we have blinders on and all we see is the road ahead—that is, getting from point A to point B. Time not only flies but seems to be speeding up, and we never seem to have time for anything. We fill our days with useless tasks that will not only wait, but many times won't matter if they ever get done. "If I don't get to that sale today, I'll miss it!" we worry. So we rush around to *not* miss it, and what does that get us? Couldn't we live without it?

I don't mean that we shouldn't enjoy the simple pleasures of life, but all these have-tos are getting to be too much. I mean, lunch *has* to be at noon, dinner at six, and bed at ten (or whatever). We have so many rituals and rules: Monday is wash day, Tuesday is housecleaning day, and so forth. Everything can wait for us, so we really need to try to change our regimen if it's so demanding. As I've mentioned, during my first marriage it was almost as if I had obsessive-compulsive disorder—I was cleaning, scrubbing, cooking, working, and going to school to fill up my outside life so that I wouldn't have to think of what I was missing on the inside.

I was so proud of myself at Christmas last year when I had people over. My table holds 8 but there were 20 people, so the kids and I ate at the coffee table. My granddaughter, Angelia, lit every candle in the house, and there were drippings everywhere. For a moment I got a little crazy, and then I told myself, *Who cares, considering the joy it brought her? What's a little wax, Sylvia?*

Yes, I like cleanliness, but a home is a home and not a showplace. I remember years ago when my first husband and I went to visit a friend. Kansas City is cold in the winter, yet this woman had everything covered with plastic and there were floor runners everywhere. Coming in from the cold, the plastic stuck to me as if I had static electricity, and it was freezing. All I could think of was how long it must have taken her to cover everything in this plastic house.

You see, we get sidetracked by things that don't last anyway, when our time would be better spent performing a good deed, educating ourselves, or even sending a remote healing to someone. However, austerity isn't the way to go either—to spend ten hours in meditation is fine, but it's all inside you and won't help your fellow humans.

We don't have to spend lots of time doing a *great* act of good, just something small at least once a day, such as a telephone call, a card, or a visit; letting someone get ahead of us in line at a store; or just giving a stranger a smile or a kind word can do wonders for a heavy heart. I remember when I was ten years old, for instance, and I attended early Mass every day. I'd be there in the pew before my classmates arrived, and there was an old woman who would come in. She always walked by me, and I always smiled at her.

One day after about a year, she walked over to me and said, "Sweet girl, I love coming to church, but what I treasure is your sweet smile—it brightens my whole day. I hope you never lose it." What seemed natural to me was a bonus to a lonely old lady, and from then on, I never forgot that the smallest kindnesses are sometimes the real gems in life to a soul that thirsts to be recognized or loved.

I don't want to bore you with my Uncle Henry's writings and collections, but this fits so well here. It's called "The Brighter Side."

Someone committed murder last night,
But hundreds of thousands were kind.
For the wrong that is done is forever in sight
To the good that are fearfully blind.

Someone deserted his children today,
But millions of fathers are true.
The bad deeds are not such a fearful array
Compared to the good that men do.

Somebody stole from his brother last night,
But millions of honest men live.
Someone was killed in a murderous fight,
But thousands were glad to forgive . . .

Their brothers, the wrongs that were fancied or real.
The crimes that we hear of each day
Compared in the good deeds that we could reveal,
Make not such a fearful array.

I would answer the men who stand up and declare
That the world is much given to vice,
That the sum of men's crimes every day, everywhere,
Can't compare with man's sweet sacrifice.

That for every black soul there are thousands pure white.
The sum of the sinners hopefully is few,
And I know in my heart that the world is all right,
When I think of the good that hopefully men do.

This is a beautiful and optimistic view of humankind, and it's true that we can steep ourselves in all the bad and never see the good that people do. Yes, I know the world is full of stress, with wars and famine and natural disasters, but we'll survive. And if we don't, what's the worst thing that could happen? We'll all go Home to God together.

It amazes me how many times I've talked to people who've tried to commit suicide and failed, but if you tell them that they have a health problem, they freak out. It all comes down to control: We say, "I want to be in charge of my life, my finances, my family, and my destiny." Well, when will we realize that we're not in control down here? We've made our chart and it's set, so we can choose to live it with dignity or sorrow.

Again, in order to enjoy our very existence, we just need to take one day at a time—enjoy the simple pleasures and quit anticipating what could be or was. If we live as if we have a limited time here on Earth (which, of course, we all have), then we can stand before God and say that we did our best in our existence for Him/Her.

How Can This Tenet Help You?

How many times a day do you think about God? If you don't do so regularly, try to keep Him/Her in your mind. In almost any situation you can ask yourself, "What would our Lord do?" It's easy once you start (we certainly obsess enough about everything else). Just to say affirmations such as "God loves me, and I am full of grace" does wonders for your soul. You can also follow up by saying, "Whatever I go through, You will never abandon me."

Even if you live to be 100 years old, this life is short and transient—it's merely a place to visit and make different, not unlike those who go to Bosnia, Rwanda, or other such places to help others. Now you don't have to join the Peace Corps (although this is truly admirable), but you can certainly go the extra mile to help others in your circle. Sometimes when I'm tired and someone calls me for assistance, I force myself to take the call—and by the time I've helped them, I'm rejuvenated.

I'm reminded of this woman who phoned me the other day, moaning about losing her faith—she felt alone, useless, and abandoned. Yes, we all feel that way at one time or another, but hopefully we don't let despair immobilize us. I said, "I don't have a magic potion to get you out of this," but she wanted some advice anyway. I said, "Just get out and take a class, join a church, or even pray."

"But I'm too tired to do anything," she replied.

"You're depressed because it's all about 'poor you,'" I countered. "You need to get past that. The best way is to volunteer, perhaps at a hospital."

One month later she wrote to say that she was helping out at a hospice and felt better than she ever had. I know that to get out of the hole of despair—hell, to even get dressed and go out some days—is hard, but it isn't as hard as living in the nothingness of your own pains and ills. The old expression that there are always people worse off than you are doesn't work when you feel like hell, but no one can get you out but you.

If you look at life as a trip to complete your mission for God and yourself, so many of these worries go away. Then, as I've said, your existence will mean something. You'll be setting an example for others, which will make your mind, your soul, and even your physical self better. Try to find happy people, because negativity is catching and it's like a terrible flu of the soul. If someone drains you and is always complaining and depressed, get away!

Time may be running out for this negative world, but that doesn't mean that there isn't time to raise its spiritual consciousness. So, regardless of what your lot in life might be, you still can stop and give someone a smile, a shoulder to cry on, or a helping hand to get them through the desert. I promise that no matter how down, tired, or ill you feel, if you give of yourself, God will take care of you (plus, too much of your own self is probably what's making you feel so down).

I know that there's a universal law in which God says, "If you take care of mine, I'll take care of you." Try it like I have, and you'll be living proof that it works.

* * * * * *

TENET XVII

War is profane; defense is compulsory.

We Gnostics do not believe in war, for through the ages it hasn't accomplished much except death and destruction. We do believe that we must protect our lives and homes, but to have most of the world in turmoil is ridiculous. Look at all the battles that we know of throughout history and how useless they were—and the reasons for them often boil down to greed and power. Of course we need defense to protect our loved ones, but there are so many senseless skirmishes over land, the acquisition of power, or conquering others. For example:

— The Crusades started out to be a holy war to take back Jerusalem from the Moors, but they quickly turned into exercises in ravaging and pillaging. So what started out as a noble cause turned to avarice and greed . . . along with the accompanying bloodshed.

— America had a revolutionary war in order to be freed from the strict English rule, but what I find so ironic is that the colonists put far more religious restrictions on themselves (and others) than they'd suffered in England. In addition, we wanted freedom and fought a war to get it—and then turned around and subjected other people to slavery. It's funny how so many times we become what we fight against.

— Adolf Hitler was a maniacal man who fancied himself to be a demigod and attacked countries just so he could conquer and enslave them. Of course he should have been stopped for his atrocities against the Judaic people and others—defense was mandatory. But even today, there are still pockets of people who admire him and believe that the Aryan race is superior.

— None of us will ever know (at least I won't) what the Vietnam War was about. Not only that, but we so shamefully treated the brave people who served in that waste of human life!

From the beginning of time, humankind seems to have used war as their mode to fix whatever wrongs they think exist. Now when we look at Sanskrit texts that are thousands of years old, which describe war and devastation from flying machines; the Romans, Genghis Khan, Alexander the Great, Napoleon, Attila the Hun, and other conquerors; or the marauding Celts and other tribes, it appears that humans have always waged war on each other. In the process, civilizations have disappeared and precious legacies such as the libraries at Alexandria (which contained irreplaceable ancient scrolls and books of human history) have been lost forever. That's the ultimate tragedy of war: It destroys so much of our civilization's art, writings, and buildings, which can never ever be replaced—not to mention the most precious things of all: human lives.

War always seems to start out with a higher purpose, but remember that "he who lives by the sword, dies by the sword." Proponents like to trot out the law of cause and effect, which seems to be more powerful than what we think of as karma. In other words, for every action there will be a reaction that many times has a rebound effect. Yet the motive for war never seems to stay so pure.

To stop the tyranny that threatens our existence is one thing, but to have war just for the sake of conquering and pillaging is morally, spiritually, and ethically wrong. It's like mob violence in that it becomes a senseless trigger effect that leads to the raping and killing of women and the torture and crucifixion of those who don't share the "right" beliefs.

America is a prime example of this. Our country started out with high hopes and a motive to provide freedom for everyone. But we proceeded to take over land that belonged to the Indians, and then relegated them to desert and swampland areas that nobody wanted (which we called "reservations"). Of course when we found something valuable on the reservations, such as gold in the Black Hills of South Dakota, we moved the tribes to even bleaker places.

Americans have murdered, lynched, and debased others; taken over lands that weren't rightfully ours; and gone to Africa to acquire slaves. Why? To make the local gentry feel superior? Because we're lazy? Or to show how well off certain landowners were because they could keep slaves? This was all just a by-product of the greed and power that causes humans to wage war on other humans. Conquering and enslaving has always been about money and power.

Humankind has always been its own worst enemy. The problem lies in not believing in our inner spirituality—so we become so frightened or so controlled by emotion that all intellect goes out the window. Look how Hitler took hold in Germany: It became a mass frenzy for all the wrong reasons (even though they might have seemed noble at the onset), and then the whole thing disintegrated into giving a tyrant too much religious, political, and monetary power, and it affected millions.

Humankind must—and cannot wait any longer to—try to get along. I truly believe that we don't have much time left on this planet to learn for God, so we've got to live together in harmony and not worry about who has what land and who has the most resources. We have to stop the discriminations in this world that are racial, ethnic, sexual, religious, or political . . . after all, we're all made by the same God.

Yes, we Gnostics do believe in defending our country, homes, and loved ones, but we've never been for war for war's sake. When I formed Novus Spiritus, I put us under "conscientious objector" status, with the caveat that if our country was attacked, we'd help to defend it.

True Christians don't believe in starting a fight. The best thing we can do is strive for peace, since the negativity of war just begets more negativity. Now you may wonder, "Don't you want to help others, save the world, and bring about freedom and democracy?" Of course I do! I believe that we should make our voices heard over excessive taxation, inequities, and the like, but in the last 65 years we've had one war after the other.

I remember in the 1940s when they had blackouts and air-raid drills (my dad was an air-raid warden). I was at an age where I thought this was exciting, since my grandmother and I would sit in the dark and listen to the short-wave radio. Later, when it dawned on me how many lives were lost, it really tore me up. It was then that I realized that, regardless of what goes on in the world, we must all strive for peace.

I want to make a very important point here: *In no way am I trying to imply that I don't support our men and women who fight on orders from our government.* It's just that, as I've said for years, after living through World War II—along with the combat in Korea, Vietnam, Kuwait, and Iraq—I strongly feel that we should think about protecting and taking care of our own country first. Even the Bible says that charity begins at home. If everyone kept peace in their own dwellings, their own blocks, their own communities, and their own countries, then we'd certainly cut down on the dissent in the world.

Acts of war have never stopped and are still prevalent today for the same old-as-time reasons. Sometimes they're even infantile in their messages of "If you hurt me, I'll hurt you" or "I want your riches, your women, your slaves, and your land so that I can conquer and feel powerful." Battles fought for these reasons are always futile and useless, for all "empires" crumble eventually under poor rule.

We can even see this in a microcosm of an office or corporation. Take Enron, for instance—the corruption became overwhelming because of greed. What the company's executives did used to be called "cooking the books"; in this case, they put out false income reports that made their stock jump in price, while the CEOs were making themselves rich with stock options and selling them off. Yet when the end came, thousands of hardworking employees were left with a useless and overpriced stock, and the company was basically bankrupt.

In this country, we've seen junk-bond dealers, bad stocks, real estate that went up and then crashed down, and the bursting of the dot-com bubble—all of which has wreaked financial havoc on many. We're currently in a time when we have to tighten our belts and be vigilant about our finances. It's sad but true, but as the world gets greedier, we have to become more careful. That doesn't mean we need to live in a fortress, but being smart and aware has to be our focus now.

* * *

I find it strange that our own homes can become mini war zones. For example, we choose sides; often vie for the affection and attention of one or more members; and experience jealousy, vengeance, and greed. I remember when my second husband's mother died and we went over to see his stepfather. When I walked in, I was appalled: The poor man was sitting in a vacant house—all that was left was a chair, a bed, a TV, and two lamps. My husband's three brothers and their families had descended like locusts before their mother was even cold in the grave, and they'd taken almost all the furniture, dishes, glassware, jewelry, and anything else that wasn't nailed down.

The stepfather was obviously grief-stricken and in shock, yet he looked at me and said, "Mom wanted you to have some of her jewelry, but I don't know where it is."

"That's all right," I assured him. "Don't you worry—I don't need anything because I have my memories of her." (Everyone as a precaution should draft an airtight will, but even then families can become torn apart.)

The other problem that causes so much friction in our lives, whether it's personally, socially, religiously, or politically, is not telling the truth. The problem (or maybe it's a good thing) is that lies always unravel. The lust for power and money can certainly cause trouble, but lies can also insidiously wreck families, for children learn to duplicate this behavior. And no matter how much the populace pleads for truth, governments or heads of state keep on lying. They tell us, "Taxes will go down" (they don't), "There will be work for all" (there isn't), "We want peace" (as they invade another country), and on and on. We see it in our personal lives, too, when our loved ones say, "I won't drink anymore" (they do), "I'll stop spending our money" (they don't), or "I won't ever be unfaithful" (they are), and so on.

If we can't trust our country, our beliefs, or our loved ones, then our life will feel as if it has derailed. We must be vigilant so that we can keep war out of our homes by demanding honesty, loyalty, and commitment (which is our Gnostic motto), because if we have these three, everything else falls into place.

However, we must be aware of the war we often wage

within *ourselves*. In fact, we are the most dangerous adversary we can face. To illustrate, I'd like to share something I wrote in my old Douay Bible in August 1954. I'd forgotten all about these words until I happened to open right to them as I was doing research for this book. Although what I wrote is quite personal, I'm going to share it with you because it's so pertinent to our "inner wars."

> This night, dear God, things have fallen into place, out of my confused and bewildered mind I realize. Things for so long have been chaos, and now I feel I know the answer. I have tried to figure out my life and chart and even lean on others, when it should have just simply been You all the time.
>
> Far have I traveled from Thee, O God, and long were the years I traveled with Thee—happy in your light—and then life and work and time filled in and I no longer turned to You. My faith and beliefs went begging, as if they drifted to a foreign shore. Now this day, kneeling, I saw what I hadn't seen for months . . . a light and a voice in my heart. "I am still here . . . you have only to turn inward and look." And I did and my whole life became clear. The decisions I must make, and the road I must follow—it is all so easy now, when before, when I was so outward it was so hard. How could I have crowded in so many things before You—when for so long I lived so near You? You are my true love, and the answer to all frustrations . . . a complete and perfect outlet. The only Being that never falters or fails. O God, I'm home again and so at peace and so much more in harmony with my public destiny and what You want from me. This road that I have chosen will not be as fearful and lonely as I imagine . . . for You above shall be with me all through my life showing me the way.

This was a plaintive plea—a recognition of a war going on inside of me—that I wrote when I realized that I really had to go public. It has been hard, but never lonely . . . and neither will your road be if you keep peace in your heart, your home, and your community.

How Can This Tenet Help You?

My grandmother used to say, "If you weed your own garden, you won't have to worry, and you're also keeping the weeds' spores from other people's gardens." It's like I've said so often: Take care of your home first, and *then* go out and help others. In other words, don't go next door and feed your neighbor's children if yours are starving—sharing is better.

It can be difficult to have this philosophy when our global community has suffered so much recently. In just a few short years, we've seen the tsunami that struck Indonesia, Sri Lanka, and India; earthquakes in Mexico, Japan, and Turkey; volcanic eruptions, floods, and tornadoes; and hurricanes that destroyed so much of the South—it's almost as if Mother Nature is declaring war on us for what we've done to her. On top of all this, we've lived through the bombing of the federal building in Oklahoma and trains in Madrid and London, the attacks on the World Trade Center and the Pentagon, and the mailing of anthrax—all the work of terrorists. Then we've had to deal with SARS, AIDS, and various types of new flu epidemics that are real biological wars, which have medical technology faltering in the onslaught of the resurgence of illnesses thought to be conquered and new ones that have no cure as yet.

When you look at this big picture, don't your daily worries seem insignificant? If you do what you can for humanity as a whole by giving aid to those who need you and praying that the world will become more spiritual, you'll be elevated above your personal times of stress and strife.

The mother who loses her son to war might be inconsolable in her loss. Yet if she knows that he died for a greater good, then his moral and spiritual intention to make this world a better place will rub off on her. No death is useless, but many times they seem to be senseless. But bless the many young men and women who go to all corners of the earth from Germany to Korea, Vietnam to Iraq, following the life charts they created in order to help make this a better world.

I didn't want my sons to go to war, and I was fortunate that when they came of age, there was no draft. But now my grandsons are growing up, and there doesn't seem to be an end in sight. I'm certain that if we stop these wars, our consciousness and spirituality will be raised and *every* parent's child will be safe. So let's lift our love and spirituality to create a conversion to peace throughout the world, and there will be no more sacrifices of life.

When I was a little girl, we could walk anywhere at any time and no harm would befall us; also, no one locked their doors. But the world pendulum swings wildly, and most of us cannot do that anymore. The good news is that once it swings to the bad, it always goes to a neutral place and then comes back to a better place. Before the end of times, we're going to see peace. In fact, I'm convinced that extraterrestrials will show themselves in the next decade to help us bring peace to this world. We need *some* type of intervention, since we don't seem to be able to do it ourselves. However, each and every one of us still has the power of our God-centeredness to not only pray for peace, but to also ask for God's army of angels to surround this planet.

Any concept that's not built on spiritual motives will come crashing down like a house of cards. If something doesn't feel right—even a cause that seems just, but begins to be run by ego—run! To go and live in a compound and eat rice and give all your money to one person who promises salvation is illogical. This is what leads us to believe in an anti-Christ, which won't actually be one person, but a type of insane ideology that will sweep across the world. We still have years to create a type of harmonious convergence to fight this movement and lift the energy of a sick world.

In fact, Francine says that in the last two decades, angels have surrounded the earth more than ever before. You may wonder why there's been so much horror then, and all I can say is, "Can you even comprehend how bad it would be if they *weren't* here?"

It's like the e-mails I received after 9/11 in which countless people told me about all the angels that were spotted in the sky. And look at how people pulled together in that crisis—I saw more patriotism than I've ever seen in my lifetime, then it sort of dwindled away. Regardless, what we face now or in the future was not only planned in our charts, but the real strength will be reveled in how we handle these situations.

That's why it's so important to raise your spirituality by never forgetting to surround yourself and your loved ones with the white light of the Holy Spirit. And if you keep saying positive affirmations, you can prevent many negative occurrences. Stopping war and creating peace will engender miracles for all of humankind.

✻ ✻ ✻ ✻ ✻ ✻

TENET XVIII

Death is the act of returning Home;
it should be done with grace and dignity.
You may preserve that dignity by refusing
prolonged use of artificial life-support
systems. Let God's will be done.

Human beings, either on their own, or as a result of their religious or spiritual beliefs, seem to either fear death or feel that dying for a cause is noble. And besides love, there's no other subject that's been debated, argued, or eulogized more: "For the wages of sin is death," "Death comes like a thief in the night," "The angel of death has come for you," and on and on. The subject has permeated our poetry and art, along with our social, religious, and commercial sectors.

For many years, death has been viewed as the ultimate punishment for humankind. Consequently, all types of religious doctrine have grown out of trying to escape it or learning to fear it as the ultimate end and not the beginning. The macabre saying "ashes to ashes, dust to dust" has always seemed like such a depressing lie to me because it sounds as if we came from nothing and will go back to nothing . . . which, of course, couldn't be further from the truth.

Death has been around me all my life. I was introduced to it with my grandfather's passing when I was three years old. Later on came the deaths of my grandmother and my Uncle Marcus, and even my own near-death experience at 26. But I think that the passing of my grandmother's son Paul, which happened long before I was born, may have actually impacted me the most. A very spiritual mystic, Paul told my mother before he died that she'd have a daughter with "the gift," and he asked that she call the baby Sylvia, after his favorite song.

Below is an excerpt from the eulogy that Bishop Robert Nelson Spencer gave at Paul's funeral on January 4, 1931, (five years before my birth). I've included it because it's a beautiful tribute, and I'm also very proud of the spirituality that came from those who went before me. Perhaps it will also give you insight into what began to shape my life and chart.

Paul [Coil] did not grow up like his great namesake, the apostle, with frail stature and some mysterious physical defect . . . this Paul grew up [so] like a straight young tree that I have not seen a finer specimen of young manhood than was his. When he was in high school, he swept everything before him in the games and on the track. And for that they gave him a scholarship to the local college.

But Paul Coil had something besides strength in that fine young body—in his throat, there was a golden voice. And Paul valued that gift of song more than he valued the pole vault or the broad jump. So Paul went to the School of Fine Arts at [the University of Kansas in] Lawrence rather than to the local college. Later Paul took that lovely tenor voice of his down through the Southwest, singing in competition on the radio, and there would have been a good contract for Paul to sign if he had lived. For it is true of Paul, as it was of another:

Because I have loved so vainly,
And have sung with such faltering breath,
The Master in mercy gave me
The beautiful boon of Death.

I have always held that of those separating things, written of in the Eighth of Romans—and it was Paul's namesake who wrote them—that of "life and death and principalities and powers," the most separating thing is life. It was life that separated Paul and me. I did not know until the deadly sarcoma had laid that fine young athlete on his bed that he was in Kansas City. I did not know that he had come, when he could get away from his own choir, with the crowds to Grace and Holy Trinity; that he had knelt there when it must have been an agony with that poor afflicted leg of his. . . .

In one respect he was like that other Paul, after whom he was named: Paul Coil was a missionary. He did not go up and down Asia and the half of Europe when society was pagan to the core, but he did move through a society that still has many pagan ideas, and his fine face and fine eyes and handsome young body gave him something of that appeal that has made paganism in every age turn and look. Perhaps the most remarkable thing about Paul Coil was the testimony that came to his mother when he was dead . . . [people called her] and said: "His natural and unaffected goodness changed my life." That is why I am writing about Paul. I think it is worthwhile to write about Paul Coil the missionary!

So vital and clean had been that young manhood that Paul was long to die. Even the doctors in St. Luke's marveled at his hold on life. Again and again I went to see him, thinking it must be time to close those great dark eyes, but there was always in them hope—his hope to live and get well—and never any fear at all.

I saw him last in the evening of his last day. He put up two very thin hands, clasping one of mine. "I am glad to see you, Bishop, but I am very tired tonight . . . I guess I am sleepy, Bishop—won't you wake me up?" And in the wee hours of the morning, God wakened Paul from the dream of life.

Of all the eulogies I've heard Bishop Spencer give, this is one of the best. I also came to love this man who confirmed me in the Episcopalian religion (I later became Catholic), and I loved the way *he* loved God in a deep, poetic way. He believed, long before most people started putting it forth, that death was a celebration of life.

Just as my Uncle Paul did, most individuals know when their time is coming. And if they're aware, the people around them can feel their loved one almost "retract," or pull their soul away. (For example, I saw my father and some of my friends do this.)

Even in the deaths of children or trauma victims, a loved one will many times report, "He said that he wasn't going to live long." For example, a woman I talked to recently said that her granddaughter had told the family that she wanted to be with her grandfather (who'd died a year previously), and he'd even come for her twice. The granddaughter said, "The third time, I'll go." And she did.

Now, I can feel when someone is not only sick, but just gives up. Life just gets too tiring—or their chart says that it's time to graduate. When the brother of Gina, my son Chris's wife at the time, died, it was such a terrible tragedy. He was an incredibly sweet and unassuming young man—kind, caring, and considerate—and he was only in his 20s. He'd had terrible headaches all his life and had started to have seizures, so they had to operate.

Well, we all decided to throw a party for him on the evening before he was to go into the hospital. He had the best time that night—he even came up to me to tell me how much fun he was having. Unfortunately, the surgery came and there was no hope of recovery. I was outside with my granddaughter, Angelia, while the family was with Gina's brother (his name was also Chris). All of a sudden, young Chris appeared to me and said, "Please tell them that I'm all right and they can quit rubbing me. I'm going to play my guitar and have a lot of fun now."

Just then, Gina came down, and I told her what had happened. Sure enough, she said that the nurses were indeed rubbing her brother, and the doctor had confirmed that it was hopeless. Soon after, we held a memorial service for this wonderful young man, who will always be remembered in our hearts as a gentle soul who loved everyone and was loved *by* everyone.

Gina and Chris's mother, Phyllis, will never get over this (who can or does?), but the family has survived and gone on bravely. As a tribute to him, they donated many of his organs after his death, which helped six people to either live or improve their quality of life. As I said at the time, "He did go happy and positively—it's only those of us left behind who are suffering from the loss."

With all the grief I've felt for the people I've loved and lost, I've *never* demanded external means just to keep them alive when their quality of life is gone. When my father was 87 and full of cancer, they wanted him to be on life support. He begged me to have them give him morphine for his pain, yet the doctor told me, "We don't want him to get addicted."

"Huh?!" I retorted. "He's dying, so turn up the drip." I mean, my dad certainly wasn't going to get up and go dancing! Of course it was hard to witness this, but I couldn't stand to see him suffer, no matter how much I wanted him to stay with me.

Medicine is marvelous, but sometimes we keep people alive when there's no *life* left. Yes, miracles happen, but for the terminally ill and the elderly, we need to let God's will be done. We'd all be wise to sign the "Do Not Resuscitate" form, or if we experience brain damage, we'll be on a machine for years while our soul has already vacated our body. (I discussed this subject in detail, especially as it pertained to the Terri Schiavo case, not too long ago in one of my newsletters.)

We spend so much time celebrating a soul coming in, but if he or she is going Home, we don't want to face it. Don't get me wrong, because I've been there—I know this is horribly hard, but the spiritual and unselfish thing to do is to talk the person over to the Other Side. My second husband, Dal, was able to do this for his mother when she lay in a coma due to lymphatic cancer. He related how he spoke in her left ear (which is controlled by the intellect) and explained that she should look for and go toward the white light, and then she'd meet a loved one who would help and go with her to the Other Side.

Dal then told me that he sat back in a chair by her bedside, and within moments he saw his mother come out of her body, as an entity from the Other Side came to stand beside her. He said that they stood there for a few minutes and then proceeded to move away and disappear through a wall. He was so moved by the incident, and the fact that he was able to help his mother pass peacefully. (At the time of her passing, I felt her go, too—moments later Francine confirmed that my dear mother-in-law had passed over and was getting ready to attend a big homecoming party.)

Every one of our Novus Spiritus ministers who has died went peacefully without fear or hesitation. Of course we Gnostics fight for life, but when the time comes, we can just let go with dignity and smile with joy because we're going Home to our loved ones, Jesus, and our blessed Mother and Father God. For us, death is a celebration of life—but now it's over, and we've graduated.

* * *

I know I already covered the concept of hell in this book, but I want to take some time here to discuss death and the afterlife in sacred texts. Death permeates the Christian Bible, and it seems that "sin" is always punished by it.

Well, what then about all the good people who die, including children who couldn't possibly be full of this so-called sin? It's no wonder that after all these centuries of negativity piling upon itself and gaining power, humankind has either been so scared about death or just wishes that it would all be over with. This malaise settles on us, and we become as our Lord says: spiritually poor. There's nothing to look back on, or forward to, because we supposedly even come into life full of sin. The tragedy is that many of us have bought all this hook, line, and sinker.

In addition, Christianity has made so much more of hell than the other religions have (or at least their acknowledgment of the devil seems to have taken front and center). Other religions believe in karma, cause and effect, and forms of retribution, but they don't seem to have the gruesome sword of eternal damnation always hanging over their heads. I'm not criticizing—after all, we in Novus Spritus *are* Gnostic Christians—but rather am simply pointing out a way that so many of us have been reined by fear.

As for purgatory and limbo, this is probably the most confusing part of Christianity (not just Catholicism). Even if there aren't such places, they seem to have infiltrated the collective consciousness of humankind. Before we get into this, let me say that I'm not just picking on one particular religion. So many of the world's faiths have a similar concept as purgatory, and it can vary in interpretation from one sect to another.

Now then, as believed by Catholics, purgatory is a place of temporary punishment for those who die in God's grace, but aren't completely free from venial (minor) sins or haven't entirely paid for their sins. Gnostics believe that some souls get caught in between dimensions because they don't know that they're dead (they're what we think of as ghosts). If we stretch this, we could see this behavior comes from unfinished business or a type of derangement, possibly caused by the type of death the individuals incurred. I've personally seen a holding place where entities who, out of despair, committed suicide. They were waiting to be released back into life, but weren't being punished in any way. So I hope you see here that there's a big difference between what someone decides to do as a reaction to stress, pressure, depression, or mental illness . . . and an outside entity judging where that person is going to spend eternity.

While I can somewhat see the argument for purgatory, limbo, on the other hand, has always been a bone of contention with me. Limbo is considered to be the place where unbaptized souls go, never to get out and see God. If that's true, then limbo is more full of souls than hell is. Think of all the people prior to the advent of Christianity (or even after) who didn't know about baptism.

Gnostics believe that we use baptism as a symbol to rinse away past-life negativities, and it's an optional sacrament. We certainly don't agree that an all-loving God would blame and condemn someone who not only wasn't baptized, but didn't even know He/She existed. What if they belonged to another religion that didn't believe in God? And what about a helpless baby who dies and doesn't get a chance to be baptized—how can that be loving or even rational?

At least the belief in purgatory and limbo isn't as dire as the Calvinistic notion that whether or not a person goes to heaven or hell is already set into stone before they're even born. Other sects such as the Jehovah's Witnesses believe that there will only be a certain number of souls who gain salvation—so even if everyone is good, some folks might not be saved. Then you have those who are certain that you have to believe in and be saved by Jesus Christ to reach heaven (and God pity those who have never heard of him). All of these notions are just ridiculous!

I also don't believe that God needs us to sit on a mountaintop meditating our life away, mutilate our bodies for religious purposes, or perform human sacrifice and murder in the name of what's "holy." This isn't a criticism, but rather a logical intellectual commentary on an all-knowing, all-loving, forgiving, and already-accepting God. I don't need to walk on coals of fire to prove I love Him/Her.

We put human-made dogma before God. God just wants us to live our lives as fully and happily as possible and then simply go Home. He/She doesn't want us to fear where we're going, but to live, do good deeds, and come back after death to the Other Side—which was made for us to live happily in for eternity.

It's so funny that we're afraid to live *and* afraid to die, and that only dogma is supposed to sustain us, when none of this ever came from the mouth of Christ. I had a priest tell me many years ago at a funeral that everyone who wanted to go to heaven got there. What a beautiful, simple concept. . . .

How Can This Tenet Help You?

When the time comes, you don't need to allow artificial means or machines to prolong your life—unless, of course, you choose them to. That doesn't mean that you shouldn't get medical or holistic aid, but you may reach the point when enough is enough. So if the cure becomes worse than the illness, you have the right to say, "Let God's will be done."

You also have every right to preserve life—and it's never okay for you to cause anyone else's death with assisted suicide, like Dr. Jack Kevorkian has done. At the same time, you have the right to remove life support when someone you care about has no chance to recover, would be a vegetable, or would simply be a body without mind and soul kept alive by machines. In these cases, the soul has already departed. I've never seen anyone hang around in a body that has no hope of recovery.

If you're faced with the decision of either keeping life support going or removing it for a loved one, you have my sympathies, because it's not an easy decision (especially if continuing it is financially draining). The first thing you must do is ascertain whether the patient has a chance for recovery. If they do, what quality of life will they have? If they're going to be in a coma forever or live without the benefit of their mind, then I can assure you that they're not there—and they would not want to be kept alive artificially.

Common sense dictates that if a person doesn't have a chance of recovery or living some type of quality existence with artificial support, then it should be removed and God will take it from there. To preserve a life because a machine can keep the heart beating and the lungs breathing isn't always fair to the patient or to the family, especially when the soul has already departed and is looking at the situation from the Other Side.

I remember when my 92-year-old mother was in a coma from pneumonia, and the doctor wanted to perform a thyroid test on her. I said, "Are you crazy?! She's dying."

His reply was, "Well, that *is* a problem," and left the room.

I told everyone to just allow Mother to be comfortable and to let her go. She went within the hour.

Similarly, when Grandma Ada was dying (also of pneumonia), I kept saying, "Grandma, I love you," even though she was unconscious. All of a sudden her pupils, which had been fixed, turned toward me in a moment of love and recognition—and we telepathically said our good-byes. I know in my bones that both my mother and grandmother went the way they would have wanted—peacefully, and without a long, drawn-out struggle to go Home.

So, as hard as it is, know that you must live for today—but also never fear death, which is the ultimate reward for living. After all, death is a celebration of *life*.

* * * * * *

TENET XIX

*We believe in a Mother God, Who is
co-Creator with our all-loving Father God.*

I covered a lot of information about this subject in my book *Mother God,* but there's still so much out there in terms of researching how the matriarchal principle has always raised her head throughout history.

The fact is, pure logic dictates that if there is a male principle, there has to be a female counterpart. So in this tenet I'd like to briefly address this female deity (which we call Azna), and not just from an intellectual and emotional level. Who is She; what purpose does She play; and why do we pray to, petition, and—above all—love Her?

She's been called Theodora, Sophia, Isis, Hera, the Mother Goddess, and a hundred other names by ancient humankind, as well as by many religions. My guide Francine says that Her visage can change to make Her more relatable to all people: She can be African, Asian, Arabian, Latino, Polynesian, or representative of any culture—which, of course, shows that She is all things to all people.

Darren English, one of Novus Spiritus's cardinals and a great researcher, has tracked so much of the Gnostic movement around the world, from Qumran (near the Dead Sea) to France. The information he's discovered (with the aid of Francine's direction) has been truly amazing, and I use much of it in my books where pertinent. Notwithstanding the fact that he's been a great addition to our movement, Darren has also been with me on many trips, particularly to Egypt, France, Greece, and Turkey, where we viewed and explored various temples of the Goddess.

In our travels, Darren and I have had many interactions with the local populace of each country, and we've found that a great number of them believe in the Mother God or Goddess. They generally keep quiet about it, as many of them belong to a religion that doesn't condone the belief in Her, but they believe inwardly. It's strange how it manifested when Darren and I started talking about the Mother God with these people: When they heard our views, they came out in the open and fervently praised Her and extolled Her virtues, especially in answering their prayers to Her.

For years I've noticed that She is alive and well all over the globe. In fact, I was talking to a client in Japan recently who has some of my translated books. She said, "We have always believed in a female deity—the yin and yang, so to speak—and we cannot understand why this concept would be so hard for your country to accept."

The only place in America that really seems to get Azna is Hawaii, where she's referred to as Pele. Native Hawaiians still believe in their ancient religious practices, with *kahunas* (shaman priests) handing down to this day their ancient teachings, which are wonderful and deal so much with nature and its forces. They believe that they're protected by the devas of nature, with Pele controlling volcanoes. Of course, Hawaiians have a long and storied history with gods and goddesses, myths and legends, and heroes and mystical beings, such as the Menehunes, or the little people of Hawaii.

Regardless of the various visages that She takes, when She's seen on the Other Side (which is quite frequently), She tends to be garbed in a golden breastplate; a short, Roman-style tunic and skirt; and golden arm guards—although at times she'll appear in flowing, beautiful dresses, especially if She's in the Rose Garden. She has a voluptuous, Rubenesque type of figure and long, burnished-red hair; and she's tall, with a beautiful face and smile.

Azna always carries a golden sword, which is just a symbol of Her fighting darkness and cutting through evil. We Gnostics use it as a symbol (alongside the three trinity circles of loyalty, gratitude, and commitment) because the sword also makes a cross. I've always believed that you use or make available any symbol that carries positive energy with it, and the cross is certainly that.

Just like Father God, Mother God has always been a Creator. Some believe that She was the *primary* Creator, but that would make our Father fallible and less than She. No, they've both always been in existence, just as all of us have. However, She *is* visually accessible, while He usually chooses not to hold a form for very long, even on the Other Side. She's the activator, the grand interceptor of negativity, and She even has the ability to change charts. She rules over this planet, which makes Her more available to us. Does that make Her more powerful? No, it's just the definite delineation of power.

Azna is like the Heart of this planetary school, while Father God is the Head. We all emulate our Divine Parents: We're emotional *and* intellectual, with the emotional side being Mother God, and the intellectual side being Father God.

Now for eons ancient cultures worshiped the Mother God or Goddess. Religions that practiced polytheism are now considered to be pagan, but the civilizations that did so, such as those in Rome, Greece, Persia, and Egypt, ruled the world for centuries. They brought us art, music, writing, and fundamental truths and laws that still exist today. If you've researched and studied these ancient religions, then you know as I do the beauty and simplicity of their beliefs, which have been submerged and suppressed by the power and wealth of today's modern religions.

In more recent times, Mother God has appeared to look like the pictures we've seen of Mary the Blessed Virgin—which is how she appeared to the children of Fatima, to St. Bernadette at Lourdes, or to the people of Guadalupe. Francine says that She appears like this so that She will be seen in the dress of Christ's time. Yet with the advent of Christianity, Azna was suppressed and almost totally erased. The way they got around the issue was to give us Mary, the mother of Christ, as a substitution for the Mother God, Who is truly our co-Creator.

Although the Christian movement has taken great pains to hide the truth for so many years, little bits and pieces are coming out these days, and the media is taking notice and picking up on the feminine principle. Books such as the aforementioned *Holy Blood, Holy Grail; The Messianic Legacy;* and *The Da Vinci Code* have brought some of these truths out of the proverbial closet and into the public eye. I realize that much of this information addresses Mary and Mary Magdalene, but no one seems to be brave enough to boldly come out and scream, "All right, you have the tail of the elephant—now get the whole thing!"

No one is to blame for this—after all, it's easier for a salmon to swim upstream than it is for us to fly in the face of patriarchal religions. They have their mean and fearful male God and don't want the applecart upset with a loving God, especially if it's a loving *Mother* God. I don't understand why faith has to come into play when logic and plain ol' deductive reasoning show the way.

They used to say when I was in Catholic school that "if God closes the door, Mary will open the window." I'm sure they didn't know how close they were to the ultimate truth. Let's face it, in the early days of the Gnostic Christians (which our Lord was), women were oftentimes the ministers. They'd perform a type of holy religious service, but would also do healings and tell stories of Jesus. When their popularity began to grow, the early apostolic movement decided that this wouldn't work because the Bible says that women are second-class citizens. Apparently they felt that it would go against their own religion—especially the outdated writings of the Old Testament—to elevate women.

Please keep in mind that the Bible wasn't even fully compiled until around A.D. 300, and if it hadn't been for Constantine and his making it the official religion of the Roman empire, I'm sure that Christianity would have gone by the wayside. Its popularity was dwindling because of the Roman persecutions and the splintering off of different sects that often had to meet secretly or be killed. And it had begun to falter because there was no leader and no cohesive organization.

The minute Constantine took over, however, he put in place only the parts of the Bible *he* wanted, and established Christianity to be the patriarchal state religion of the Roman empire . . . and then he declared himself the religion's hero for saving it from extinction. Yet, ironically, Francine says that when Christ was hanging on the cross and said, "Father, forgive them, for they know not what they do," he was speaking to Father God. However, when he said, "Mother, behold thy son," even though everyone assumes that he was talking to his earthly mother, Mary, he was in fact addressing his Mother in heaven.

It seems that the pendulum had to swing to one side (patriarchal religion), and now it's beginning to come back. But please understand that I don't want to see a matriarchal religion—I'd rather that we embrace one that recognizes *both* the Mother and Father from which we all were created.

There are now archaeological theories stating that some of Crete, Egypt, and the Greek Isles was actually part of Atlantis, the long-lost continent located in the Atlantic Ocean that sank many thousands of years ago. There are a number of caves in these regions that have pictographs that show what looks like a female deity or being of power. Francine says that in Atlantis and Lemuria (the lost continent in the Pacific Ocean), the female Goddess was alive and well. Now keep in mind that this would have been thousands of years before Christ was born.

It's interesting to note that we at Novus Spiritus have always been devoted to the Mother God, long before we ever revealed this to the general public through my books. People who came in for regressions would more times than not immediately see the Other Side when taken to a death in a past life. They'd invariably see themselves in the Hall of Wisdom, Hall of Justice, or Hall of Records—places where they viewed their just-lived lives, went over their charts, or met with all their loved ones.

Many of these same people would also see a statue of a beautiful woman dressed in golden armor with a sword at her side. When asked who she was, without hesitation and regardless of what religious beliefs they came from, they'd almost always say, "The Mother God, of course." The replies were so matter-of-fact that it was almost as if we were stupid that we didn't know, or even asked the question at all.

* * *

You know, whether you see me as controversial or not, I'm now at the age where I just try to put forth the truth, and so it is with the Mother God. Whether you believe in Her or not—or if you call Her Sophia, Mary, Theodora, or the Anatole—She is the one in the duality of Creators who performs miracles and eliminates negativity. So if you pray to Her, She will answer.

The stories that have come out of the e-mails my office receives, along with the readings that my son and I do, are numerous and legendary. Not a day goes by that we don't hear of a petition being answered or a miracle being performed by Azna. Most of the missives have the common denominator of being the last hope for help—they often concern near-death concerns, life-threatening illness, calamities of every nature, legal cases, and so on. And in almost every case, whenever our ministers have petitioned Mother God for help or a miracle, the person is healed, custody of a child is won in court, a divorce is reversed, cancer is cured, and on and on it goes. In other words, miracle after miracle occurs.

I personally have no problem petitioning her for any- and everything, from "Please, Mother, don't let the plane be delayed" to the larger problems of my last divorce, which could have been ugly but wasn't (well . . . at least I'll say that it could have been so much more horrific than it was). I petition to protect my loved ones, people I read for, and the planet; my personal health and finances; and so much more. In almost every case, we seem to get right down to the wire, but she always comes through.

I never fail to be amused when I hear someone ask, "Aren't you afraid that you're bothering Her or asking for too much?" No, because we can't . . . for then we'd be putting Her in the same category that we've put Father God into—that is, we make Them aggravated and humanistic like we are. Once and for all, They can't be—*They're perfect, all-loving Beings.*

The only time we human beings get into trouble is when we go into that vanity mode of entitlement—we need something above everything else, or we want something that will hurt another person. In these types of situations, we're not going to get our prayers answered. But trust me, if we're under Her mantle of protection and live a good life, She'll mete out justice.

I always ask Her for protection for myself and others, whether it's verbally or even in writing: I write Her letters or notes and then burn them to request Her help before I do my readings, for example. I encourage people to not only petition Her, but Her army of the phylum of angels called the Thrones as well. This is Her army, the same as the phylum of angels called Principalities is Father God's army.

Every night I petition Her and Her Thrones. But of course, I also call on God the Father and His Principalities, our Lord, and the Holy Spirit (which is really just the love between Mother and Father God that sends grace, strength, protection, and prosperity) to protect my family and loved ones. In addition, I petition Azna for the animals and things that pertain to earthly life.

My devotion to Her has been unwavering. Just to give you what might seem like a mundane example of how I rely on Her help, I had to get to Los Angeles for some important business. At the time there were horrible storms raging in both the San Jose area (about 50 miles south of San Francisco) and in Southern California that included high winds and torrential rains. My assistant, Michael, and I had to go by plane because the highways were closed, but all aircraft was delayed or grounded.

I said, "Please, Mother, get us out." Michael and I went to the airport knowing already that our original flight was delayed a minimum of three hours. As we got to check-in, we found that our flight was indeed pushed back for at least four hours, but the airline had an earlier flight to the same destination. We jumped at the chance to take it, and it left at almost the same time as our original flight had been scheduled to take off. We found out later that right after we took off, all subsequent flights had been grounded and didn't leave until the next day. Now you can say, "Well, Sylvia, that's just coincidence or luck." Yes, I guess you could say that . . . until you try it for yourself.

I'm also reminded of when I was in Houston and got a call that my granddaughter had her lip bitten by a dog. I couldn't get out, so I prayed to Mother God all night. When I got home, I was told that it was a miracle: Angelia's lip, which should have been torn off, was split but inverted on itself, so they pulled it forward and stitched it. She's since had two surgeries to correct it, but the miracle is that when they first looked at it, the lip appeared to be missing. A mistake from two specialists? I think not. . . .

These are just a few of my stories—I could go on and on. The letters my office has received about Mother God are all categorized in our research files, and you start to notice when certain things keep happening. There can't be *that* many coincidences in the world. As I've said, what does it hurt to give it a try? Call Her Mary, Azna, or whatever; but She (like our Lord or Father God) will answer to any call—the point is, just call.

How Can This Tenet Help You?

As I often say, you don't have to believe in any of this—simply take with you what you want—but for the sake of even skepticism, you should just try calling on Mother God. All of my study groups and ministers, who now number in the thousands, pray to Her, and it seems that not a day goes by that I don't hear of a miracle when She's called upon. She's also the spiritual leader of the prayer line that's dedicated to Her—and the results of that line border on the fantastic. (For more information about our prayer line, please visit **www.sylvia.org.**)

If you decide to pray to Azna for help, you can ask Her for your children's sake, your pets, or yourself—even what may seem like petty concerns are never that in Her eyes. By asking, you'll just reinforce the bond you have with Her, and will open the once-closed door for Her to enter your life and show you beyond any doubt what real creative power is. You needn't worry if your prayers are being answered or not.

Of course not *everything* is going to be granted, and praying to Her is not a fix-all or magic bullet. After all, She won't change your chart so drastically that you won't learn, and you're not always going to get your way. But things will get modified, miracles will happen, and things that are negative will turn around faster for the better. She also doles out karma in the sense that She rights wrongs very swiftly.

Ask for proof through your petitions. I don't have any fear that you'll fail to be surprised or convinced (if you're not already). And never forget about our Father, Jesus, the angels, and our guides—if anything, there's so much help available that we don't even utilize it!

* * * * * *

TENET XX

*We believe that our Lord was crucified,
but did not die on the cross. Instead, he went
on to live his life in France with his mother
and Mary Magdalene, his wife.*

Dan Brown's book *The Da Vinci Code* has really piqued the public's interest. Although it's a fictional work that has stayed on the bestseller list for more than two years, the book is actually filled with factual research about secrets that have been kept for years. All of the controversy and curiosity it's provoked will only make researchers delve more deeply into these secrets and come out with the truths that have been suppressed and hidden for centuries.

I personally loved this book, and although some facts may have been embellished a bit, the basic information is entirely true. In fact, we at Novus Spiritus have believed this for many years, and I even covered the subject of Jesus' "death" and lost years in detail in my book *Secrets & Mysteries of the World*. However, in the event that you haven't read either of the above-mentioned books, I'd like to take this opportunity to introduce you to the mystery and phenomenon that is Mary Magdalene, since she was an integral part of Christ's life.

As there are groups and organizations that believe that Jesus Christ was a myth, so are there many who say that the Crucifixion never took place. In my research, I've found that the Crucifixion *did* happen . . . but then I part ways with what many Christians believe (specifically, that Jesus died on the cross).

You see, the scriptures tell us that Pontius Pilate didn't want to crucify Christ. He was even told by his wife that she'd had a dream it would be wrong. He wanted to wash his hands of it, which he literally did, and sent Jesus back from his initial audience, saying that he could find no wrong in what the young prophet had done. Christ was condemned mainly because he was a danger to the traditional Judaic religion, and the Romans didn't want any chance of an uprising to occur. He wasn't against anyone except hypocrites, and he only wanted to put forth the concept of an all-loving God—and for that, he was crucified.

My research, however, unearthed a very plausible plot to save his life. He had many friends, some of whom were fairly wealthy—it's been surmised that a few of them bribed Pontius Pilate in order to save the Messiah's life. Joseph of Arimathea is believed to be the head of this conspiracy; coincidentally, it was his tomb in which Jesus was laid. In fact, coincidence follows coincidence.

Consider the following facts:

1. It normally took several days for people to die on the cross, which was why the Romans preferred it as a form of execution. However, Pontius Pilate made sure that Christ only had to spend a few hours on the cross because he was crucified just before the Jewish Sabbath Day, on which no one could be crucified.

2. Crucifixion victims had their legs broken so
   that they couldn't lift themselves up to breathe.
   (Asphyxiation was the normal cause of death due
   to compression of the lungs while hanging.) Jesus'
   legs were never broken, which allowed him to rest
   his feet and lift himself up.

3. Christ was a healthy young male of 33 and
   would have had a lot of stamina.

4. He was taken down from the cross by friends
   who put him in an above-ground tomb, and he
   was never buried. Therefore, he would have been
   able to get out of the tomb.

Skeptics will point out, "But they pierced his side." Well,
Francine says that this was actually a symbolic scratch—the
vinegar and gall acted as an anesthetic that ended Jesus'
pain and rendered him unconscious in an *assimilated* death.
It's like if you were under anesthesia, you might appear limp
and dead to the uneducated or nonmedical mind.

We have other evidence that relates to Christ's survival,
and ironically it comes from scripture. In Luke 24:5, the
angels in the tomb said to Mary and Mary Magdalene, "Why
do you look for the living among the dead?" Later, Jesus
appeared to his apostles to prove that he was still alive, but
they were startled and panic-stricken, thinking that they saw
a spirit. "And he said to them, 'Why are you disturbed, and
why do doubts arise in your hearts? See my hands and feet,
that it is I myself. Feel me and see; for a spirit does not have
flesh and bones, as you see I have.' And having said this, he
showed them his hands and his feet. But as they still dis-
believed and marveled for joy, he said, 'Have you anything
here to eat?' And they offered him a piece of broiled fish and
a honeycomb. And when he had eaten in their presence, he
took what remained and gave it to them."

Even when Mary Magdalene tried to tell the other

apostles that Christ was alive, they didn't believe her. Not until he showed up at the room where they were hiding did they understand that he wasn't a ghost. Jesus even has Thomas put his hands into his wounds to show he still lived (thus the expression "doubting Thomas"). Now I've had a lot of experience with ghosts, and believe me, they don't eat, you can't feel the solidity of their bodies, and they definitely don't carry healing wounds. These incidents can only be explained by the fact that Jesus had survived the Crucifixion.

Christ fulfilled his chart by going through the trial, scourging, humiliation of carrying his own cross, and of course the Crucifixion—the fact that he didn't die on the cross doesn't take away his divinity or his teachings. In fact, his teachings were so important that he continued them in other parts of the world.

Our Lord was not stupid, and he knew that he had to get away from Jerusalem or risk being caught again. So he left his disciples with instructions and went off with his mother and Mary Magdalene to greener pastures. It's amazing to believe that in his lifetime he was certainly loved, but he was also ridiculed, ostracized, and even called "the evil prince [or king]." It seems that the idea of love just doesn't take too well in this world. It seems to fly in the face of those who would rather have a fearful, vengeful, and humanized God. Of course this concept also has a tendency to keep people in line and thereby under control.

※ ※ ※

The following is from an article that Darren English wrote for our Novus Spiritus newsletter. I think it's really amazing, and even though it's somewhat long, it adds a lot to the issues of this section.

How Do You Know What You Know?
(From *Novus Connection*, January 2005)

We make judgments based on our personal experiences that color our makeup as a person. Sylvia tells us we can judge the action, but not the soul, of the person. We must be careful of making judgments, even if we are just judging the action, because not far from judging the action comes ascribing a motive, which is quickly followed by making a judgment of the soul.

We learn through experience, research, listening, discernment, and infusion; but tradition [also] plays a large part in our learning. As anyone in the office will tell you, I love reading. I especially enjoy reading history, including the history of Gnosticism. However, we can't look at history and suppose we can understand the motivation of the characters involved. . . .

What do we know or think we know about Mary Magdalene? What did Mary Magdalene do for a living before she met Jesus? We've been told that she was a prostitute. It's in the Bible—right? Nowhere does it say in the Bible that Mary Magdalene was a harlot. So how did [she] get labeled a prostitute?

We need to remember that we can't judge history or historical figures from our 21st-century perspective. In A.D. 591, Pope Gregory I gave a sermon that included information about Mary [Magdalene]. In Luke 8, it says that Jesus cast out seven demons from Mary Magdalene. Pope Gregory said that the seven demons represented the seven deadly sins. He also stated that Mary Magdalene was the woman identified in Luke as the woman living a life of sin, who anointed Jesus' feet with perfumed oils. Pope Gregory stated that she used these perfumes in her profession as a prostitute. From 591 on, Mary Magdalene was labeled a harlot. Did you know that in 1969 the Catholic Church repealed the declaration that Mary Magdalene was a prostitute? Unfortunately, once an accusation has been made

[or] once someone has been labeled, even falsely, the stain of that accusation lingers on. . . .

So the traditional teaching of Mary Magdalene wasn't correct. It's easy to start pointing our little Gnostic fingers at Pope Gregory and say that he was motivated by misogyny, that he was trying to squelch the feminine principle by labeling Mary Magdalene a prostitute. I don't know what his motivation was, but the result of this mislabeling and misinformation was used as a powerful illustration of Christ's perfect love, of God's perfect love. The idea that Mary Magdalene was forgiven and embraced by Jesus became a beautiful example of the love that God holds for each of us—no matter how we regard ourselves, no matter how low an opinion others have of us, God is still there, loving us all as His children. Mary became St. Mary Magdalene, the Saint of Repentance; her feast day is July 22.

So who is this woman, Mary Magdalene, if she wasn't the repentant prostitute that we've known her as for so many years? The name *Magdalene* may have denoted her hometown of Magdala on the shore of Galilee, or it may have been a title. In Aramaic, *Magdala* means "Tower." So Mary the Magdalene may have been a title, similar to "Mary the Great," or "Mary of Towering Faith."

In the Gospels, [she] is portrayed as not a primary disciple, but as one of the women who traveled with Jesus and his disciples and supported them monetarily in their ministry. Mary Magdalene, however, was one of the few of Jesus' followers present at the Crucifixion, not his mother, Mary. Most of the male disciples were in hiding, afraid that they might be arrested and crucified [also]. Mary Magdalene was the first to visit the tomb where Christ was placed and witnessed the risen Christ. She is actually known as the "Apostle to the Apostles," because it was she who brought the news to the disciples that Jesus was not dead.

We know Mary not only from the New Testament Gospels but also from the Gnostic Gospels of Mary Magdalene, the Gospel of Phillip, the Gospel of Thomas, the Pistis Sophia, and the Dialogue of the Savior run in. These texts give us a different picture of Mary Magdalene than we see in the New Testament Gospels. Through the[m], we find that she was not only a follower of Jesus, but [his] confidant and closest spiritual companion, his consort, and a primary apostolic figure in the early Christian church. According to the Gospel of Phillip, Mary is the one who Jesus loved the most and "kissed often on the mouth."

In [a] 1979 trance, Francine said that "Christ had a very beautiful love affair with Mary Magdalene, actually like a soul-mate concept. They were very deeply in love with each other." In the Gospel of Mary Magdalene, Peter says, "We know the savior loved you more than any other woman." Peter then asks Mary to tell him and the other disciples what teachings Jesus shared with her in private. . . .

Raheim, a second guide of Sylvia's who also speaks through Sylvia during trance, tells us that when Mary Magdalene anointed Jesus' feet with perfumed oils, it was an anointment of ritual, [but] she was actually [also] using a form of therapeutic massage or reflexology to tend to him. We read over and over in the Bible that Jesus healed and tended to the sick, but Mary Magdalene and Mary, his mother, are the only figures in the Bible to tend to Jesus.

The verse in Luke where we read that Jesus cast out seven demons from Mary Magdalene still bothered me a bit, until I started to think about it from a wider perspective. In the ancient world any illness was seen as being caused not by a virus, but by a demon. During his formative years prior to beginning his ministry, Jesus studied not only Jewish/Hebrew texts, but also studied in India and Tibet and would have certainly have known of chakras and energy healing. I asked Sylvia if this "casting out of demons" wasn't actually a chakra cleansing. [She] said yes, it was a chakra cleansing as opposed to an exorcism that Jesus performed on Mary.

Francine tells us that Jesus was "trying to bring the

female principle forward, whether it was Mary Magda-lene or his mother." Gnostic tradition tells us that Mary Magdalene was a principal figure in the early church. By reading the Gnostic Gospels in conjunction with the New Testament Gospels, we get a much wider picture of Mary Magdalene and her teachings as a woman who was able to "turn the disciple's hearts to the good" to the Christ Con-sciousness within. . . .

So ask yourself, how do you know what you know? Are you holding on to illusions that you've adopted as tradi-tion? Question everything you think you know. But know this: No matter what anyone says about you, no matter what they think of you, our God the Mother and God the Father love you very much, and nothing you do [or] say will ever change that.

For generations the Cathars and the Knights Templar have known all this information, and they fought to the death to keep the secret of Christ's continued life. Yet it's awfully hard for the Catholic Church to accept the fact that Jesus married Mary Magdalene, especially after they'd worked the scripture to make her look like a harlot.

It's strange, though—over the years Mary has not only been canonized, but in France there's the church of "The Magdalene." Why would the Church retract what they've said? Well, there could be a very simple explanation: They know the truth. Maybe they're just covering their tracks, especially when you consider that the Vatican contains thousands of writings that are kept in vaults that no one can see. It would be hard to imagine that the Church doesn't know the truth, especially when they had the wealth and power to get it if they so chose. Certainly the same truth that's been researched lately would have been available to their scholars and researchers.

All of this is a delicate matter for the Church—after all, how do they handle this truth when it goes against what they've been teaching for the last 2,000 years? It would certainly rock their foundations and create utter chaos among the faithful . . . which is probably why they'll never overtly let the truth out. However, we *have* gotten little tidbits of what they know, such as when Pope John XXIII said, "Christ's Crucifixion or his death or life should not affect our belief."

Maybe as time goes by, the Church will try to ease the faithful into the truth—unless, of course, it blows up in their face. And let's be honest here: The Catholic Church is a powerful organization, and past practice has seen them move exceedingly slowly in acknowledging their mistakes. Nevertheless, truth is truth, and whether or not you believe that Jesus lived or died after his crucifixion shouldn't affect Christianity—I've always believed that the *teachings* of Christ are the real cornerstones of Christianity, not whether he died on a cross and was subsequently resurrected. After all, each and every one of us resurrects when we die.

How Can This Tenet Help You?

Before you read on, I'd like you to think about *The Last Supper* by Leonardo da Vinci. (In fact, if you can, please look at the painting for a minute.) Now I defy anyone not to notice that the person sitting to Christ's right is a female, who I believe is Mary Magdalene. Yet for so many years my eyes went directly to our Lord rather than to the other apostles—no matter how many times I looked at and contemplated the meaning of this work of art, I never noticed this female until it was pointed out in *The Da Vinci Code*.

This book has given those of us who've read it pause for thought, and in many cases, a different perspective. It's a known fact that the mind sees what it's been programmed to see, and we bring our own beliefs and agendas with us—so we often miss the things that are right in front of us. I want you to keep that in mind as you ponder this tenet.

Mary Magdalene was the most devoted of any of the apostles (in fact, some theologians have taken to calling her the first real apostle). She washed Jesus' feet, traveled with him, and was by his side during the Crucifixion and afterward. They loved each other and left together after his mission was complete.

If you think it's terrible to even speculate that a true messiah and messenger had a life with a woman who loved him, research it for yourself. Read and peruse the Bible, the Gnostic texts, and the Gnostic Gospels that were found at Nag Hammadi, and you'll find Christ's love for Mary Magdalene. Now if *this* has been swept under the rug, what makes you think that the fear of the feminine principle (which our Lord tried so hard to elevate), wouldn't also be hidden by the patriarchal rule?

If you look at the scriptures closely, Jesus didn't really fulfill what the Judaic religion had prophesied—that he was supposed to come as a king and free the Jews, as Moses did. What they didn't understand or see was that, as he said so often, "My kingdom is not of this world." In other words, he wanted people to know a loving God, not to take this life so seriously, and to look forward to going Home (to the Other Side). Since he was never accepted as their savior, Judaism is still waiting for their prophesied savior to appear.

Christ was truly an Essene and a Gnostic. While the scriptures say that he ascended into heaven, it's interesting to note that the Essene community at Qumran (which was the center of Gnosticism) was called "heaven." Could this have meant that he just went to Qumran? Regardless, since Jesus was a messenger from God, it's not unlikely that he visited heaven and then came back again.

What this boils down to is that we *all* ascend into heaven, both at our death and throughout our lives by means of astral travel—most of us just aren't aware of it. So remember to keep your mind—and your heart—open.

* * * * * *

TENET XXI

*We Gnostics kept the knowledge hidden
that Christ's lineage exists even today,
and the truth long buried is open to research.*

In Dan Brown's book *Angels & Demons,* he writes about a group called "the Illuminati." Although this book is a work of fiction, Brown says that the brotherhood of the Illuminati is not. My spirit guide Francine says that it does indeed exist, as do many other "underground" organizations that have information about Christ's lineage.

Francine says that after Jesus fulfilled his commitment and left his apostles, he took the two Marys (his mother and Magdalene) and went from Jerusalem to Qumran. From there they traveled to Turkey and Kashmir, and finally ended up in France. When I was in Ankara, Turkey, I heard the local oral tradition stating that Christ, Mary, and Mary Magdalene visited there after his supposed death. The strange thing is that the Turks wouldn't have anything to gain, or lose for that matter, by giving out this information. . . .

It was in France that Jesus and Mary Magdalene (whom

he'd married) started a family. Francine goes on to say that they had three children, two boys and a girl; and that our Lord lived to be very old. However, he died before his wife, who spent the rest of her life in his ministry. (Is it a coincidence that in France they have the Church of the Magdalene and honor her as a saint?) Francine also says that she did a lot of writing after Jesus died, but these writings have yet to be found or are hidden and not for public view.

It's interesting to note that one of the largest Gnostic communities was in France. In fact, when I was in southern France one time, I was sitting on a rock, and a vision as clear as a bell came to me. Now I'm not often inclined to have real-life visions, like the ones they depict on TV or in the movies, but this one was incredible. In terms of clarity, it was similar to the one I had when I was at Stonehenge (which I related in my book *Secrets & Mysteries of the World*)—these are the two most vivid visions I've had.

When I see a past murder or crime, I can feel and view it, and I even get names and places, but these two visions were different: It's like I was going back in the records of time and viewing what went on as a third person—and it was so incredibly clear. I believe that we all undergo something similar when we experience déjà vu or a familiarity and longing for certain places, but this is like watching a movie . . . except you're part of it, and the smells and sounds are all around you. It's like a type of conscious trance.

Anyway, what I saw in France began with myself and others winding our way through a forest near dusk. It felt like spring because flowers were beginning to bloom, and we seemed to be on our way toward Montsegur in the Languedoc region, where the Gnostics had a community. Many of those around me were dressed in coarse brown robes, almost like the Franciscans wore, with ropes around their waists. The women's long hair was covered by plain muslin scarves; while the men had their heads shaved, again like the early monks with a tonsure. We all had on rough-hewn sandals with rope straps—I noticed this because my right ankle hurt from the rub of the rope. Some were carrying baskets of fruit, some were carrying grain, and some were pulling goats; while the young ones helped out the elderly—but we all were singing softly.

I'm fairly fluent in French, so I could make out the words *mon dieu* ("my God") as we finally arrived at this type of castle, which didn't seem at all unfamiliar. Other people had already arrived, and seemed to be pulled toward this beautiful man who was standing there with a very attractive dark-haired woman. There was an older lady sitting on a rock, and children were playing nearby. I knew that we were in the presence of the Holy Family, and our allegiance was unquestionable.

We all sat down and listened to what lies beyond this life: the Other Side and the lessons we're all here to learn. It seemed, in fact, as if the whole Gnostic philosophy was unfolding before me. The group I was with then ate and drank, and we returned to our village much later. It seemed that we'd given homage to the Mother God and were now coming back to finish the circle by honoring our Lord—and that we'd made this pilgrimage many times. I remember our Lord saying that it would be many years before the truth would come to the consciousness of humankind. And with that, my vision ended . . . but I will keep it with me for the rest of my life.

No matter if you believe my vision—or this subject—it's absolutely true that information about Christ's survival and his lineage has long been buried and hidden by the Cathars, Knights Templar, and other Gnostic groups that existed in the Middle Ages.

The Cathars were one of the early Gnostic sects of Christianity that believed that the soul goes from body to body until it reaches perfection. Essential acts in their rituals included a kiss on both sides of the cheeks (is this where the typical French greeting came from?) and a blowing on the hands (giving the breath of life and healing and the ability to heal). As such, they were often called the "good men" in their travels. The Cathars were very simplistic and journeyed together, preaching and talking to the people in fields, farmhouses, or barns; and they accepted women gladly into their communities.

While the Cathars seemed to be the teachers, the Knights Templar were the protectors. Formed during the Crusades to protect pilgrims on their way to Jerusalem, the Knights Templar later became the protectors of the secret about Christ's survival and lineage.

The proof that the Cathars and Knights Templar hid is guarded today by such modern-day organizations as the Illuminati, Masons, Rosicrucians, and Priory of Sion. It's also been suggested that these groups hold such treasures as the Ark of the Covenant and the Holy Grail, and they know where Christ's body is buried (among other things). They've kept this knowledge for centuries, building mystery upon mystery behind secret codes, meanings, rituals, and puzzles as a means of shrouding and protecting their knowledge and treasures; and to shield themselves from what they feel is the politically run machine of Christianity.

What is the agenda of these groups? Do they want to bring to power the lineage of Christ, which has been surmised in *Holy Blood, Holy Grail,* or do they have something entirely different planned? In time, I believe that we'll all find out, as researchers by the dozens are investigating these mysteries . . . but in the meantime, little bits and pieces of truth will be let out systematically so as not to unduly shock anyone.

You might wonder why (supposing these underground organizations do exist) they don't just come out with their knowledge. Since I don't belong to any of them, I can't presume to know the answer and can only ask the question. Oh, we can speculate that these groups went underground for fear of persecution, but would that apply today? Having lived for almost 70 years, I can give you my opinion: You bet it would!

Can you imagine the repercussions, which in all likelihood

would be global in proportion? Why invite a glut of media and attacks by Christians all over the world, leave yourself open to ridicule, be accused of being anti-Christ (or of being *the* anti-Christ), make enemies in the millions, and lose the anonymity of your group? It's for these reasons that I believe these organizations from time to time "leak" material or information in the form of new discoveries.

The authors of the books that have stirred up such controversy in recent years discovered so much enlightening information that other seekers have flocked to their sources (including France's Bibliothèque Nationale, which had to limit access to research because of so many requests). These writers have found bits and pieces of information that when put together certainly make a strong case for Christ's having offspring—and that his lineage continues to this day.

❋ ❋ ❋

Since we've gone through the tenets that set the cornerstones for the Gnostic Christian beliefs of Novus Spiritus, I now want to delve further into religion . . . not to criticize or discriminate against anyone, but to show you how we really don't differ that wildly except for our beliefs regarding the Crucifixion and Mother God. But if you research as I have (and I hope you do), you'll see that the truths become overwhelming. Gnostic belief has historically been the *true* Christianity. It's simpler than some of the dogma we've been exposed to, but hopefully like me you'll hear our blessed Lord's words and think of him smiling as he said them. The reason I say this is because it's a shame that all we seem to remember is Christ in his agony on a cross—not the laughing Christ, the healing Christ, the God-loving Christ, Christ the man, Christ the friend, Christ the messenger, and Christ the teacher of the love of a perfect God.

I believe with all my heart that Jesus himself had a hand in the Gnostic Gospels because they were found at Nag Hammadi untarnished by humans. Yes, some previously known works were found—which shows that even then, there was a pecking order as far as what should be kept and what should be destroyed. The manuscripts appear to have been hidden because of a religious purge or a hunt for heretics and heretical material by the mainline Christian church, so they weren't edited, thanks to the morality or control for the day. As **www.religioustolerance.org** states:

> In 1945, Mohammed Ali es Samman, a Muslim camel driver from El Qasr in Egypt, went with his brother to a cliff near Nag Hammadi, a village in northern Egypt. They were digging for nitrate-rich earth that they could use for fertilizer. They came across a large clay jar buried in the ground. They were undecided whether to open it. They feared that it might contain an evil spirit; but they also suspected that it might contain gold or other material of great value. It turns out that their second guess was closer to the truth: the jar contained a library of Gnostic material of immeasurable value. Thirteen volumes survive, comprising 51 different works on 1153 pages. Six were copies of works already known; six others were duplicated within the library, and 41 were new, previously unknown works. Included were the *Gospel of Thomas, Gospel of Truth, Treatise on the Resurrection, Gospel of Phillip, Wisdom of Jesus Christ, Revelation of James, Letter of Peter to Phillip, On the Origin of the World,* and other writings. Of these, the Gospel of Thomas is considered the most important. It was a collection of the sayings of Jesus which were recorded very early in the Christian era. A later Gnostic author edited the Gospel. Some liberal theologians rank it equal in importance to the four Gospels of the Christian Scriptures.

In his book *The Gnostics,* Jaques Lacarriere defines Gnosticism as follows: "[It] is in essence a genesis restoring to man his true birth and overcomes his genetic and mental impurity." Although, as stated earlier, there were many different beliefs in Gnosticism and many different schools of thought, almost all Gnostics have come together on some key points:

1. We believe that mainline Christianity misunderstood Christ's mission on Earth, and Gnostic practices truly understood his message of love. Therefore, Gnostic practitioners are the only ones actually doing and continuing Christ's ministry.

2. Gnostic devotion to the gaining of knowledge is not just intellectual in nature. We believe that knowledge is the key to salvation; consequently, we read countless texts from other religions, garner the bits of truth in each of them as our own, and practice them. We also believe that knowledge is gained from experience, and in doing so, the soul must utilize the truths gained for salvation. All Gnostics believe that knowledge of and for the soul is paramount.

3. We believe in the male and female principles of God—just as there is duality in nature, so is there in God. The Mother God is worshiped as well as the Father God.

4. We believe that the soul or spirit is Divinely good and that the body and the earth are filled with evil and temptation. We believe that there is a spark of God in all of us due to Mother God's putting in the seeds of life.

5. We believe that each of us can attain his or her own personal peace and harmony by realizing that we are a Divine spark of God. Death allows us to escape this earthly plane and ascend and be reunited with God (salvation).

6. We do not look upon the world as having been created perfectly because we need to perfect and gain knowledge for the soul.

Little has been written about how ancient Gnostic groups functioned, but Francine goes along with what some theologians and historians have supposed: For many years, Gnostics who didn't really have a place to practice were solitary practitioners. (You don't realize how many e-mails and letters I got when my *Journey of the Soul* books came out that said, "I always believed this way but felt I was all alone.") Others were probably members of mainline Christian congregations, but they formed their own cliques within each church.

Until recently, there was no consensus on a "canon of Gnostic scripture," although many books that have been circulated over the years prefaced their own rendition. Now, however, thanks to Elaine Pagels and Barbara Thiering and their writings and compilations of Gnostic texts, we have what we've been waiting for. So if you want to research as I have, then a good place to start are their works. In addition, there are so many books coming out that are not only exposing what the original truth was, but comparing it to what has become "truth" politically over time. Once the truth is out, then people can make their own decisions about their belief system in an educated and logical manner, without having to wade through the half-truths and lies that have been perpetuated over the centuries.

Gnostics have always insisted that ignorance, not sin, causes us the mental and physical suffering that then leads to the suffering of the soul. Much like our modern psychotherapy, without self-knowledge, humans are led by compulsions and impulses that we don't understand or know. The truth, whatever that means to you, will set your soul free—your love of an all-loving God will grow, and your soul will find peace in the simple truths.

Just as our Lord said, the one theme that keeps repeating in Gnosticism is: "The kingdom of God is inside of you." This is probably one of the most powerful of Christ's teachings, and he reiterates it many times in many different ways. It tells us that we'll find such a kingdom not only in our intelligence, but in our emotions, and acts of good toward others.

I feel with this enlightened age of search and research that each of us has begun to embark upon our own journey for spirituality, and to find the true Christ Consciousness within our own heart and soul—after all, the words of Jesus were what the Gnostics lived by and still do.

How Can This Tenet Help You?

You'll find your truth if you keep your mind and soul open. You don't need me or anyone else to tell you that things are really simpler than we've made them over the last 2,000 years. And remember that it's not just Christianity that has split off radical and close-minded sects. The fundamentalists of any religion are strict to the point of being prejudicial, judgmental, and lacking in love and compassion. Of course they hide it under the excuse that they're following scripture to the letter, but it's their *interpretation* that's flawed.

Also, many of these individuals' radical actions go against that very same scripture—that's how we get suicide bombers who kill thousands of innocents, or monks who douse themselves with gasoline and burn to death. Church rules and dogma oftentimes directly contradict the original words of the prophets who brought forth simple messages of love, for God and one another.

Even with all the attempts by the world's religious organizations to keep us mired in hate and fear, this feeling and tradition of a loving God has nevertheless crept in. I know this firsthand: When I was in Turkey and Egypt and talked to all the people who came with me on the trips, so many of the local citizens nearby would gather and listen. At first this was a little disconcerting because I never wanted any Muslims to think I was against them. But when I was invited to come on their television shows and had articles on me written in their newspapers, it was just the opposite. People on the street would come up to me and tell me that Mohammed preached love, and they always made me feel very welcome.

Love is the universal language that keeps this world going; unfortunately, the dark side plays its part with greed, ego, hate, and discrimination. So, regardless of what religion you aspire to, always remember that we have a *loving and forgiving God*. If someone tells you that unless you listen to or join them, you won't be saved, run away as fast as you can—or you're going to get caught in the trap of religious control and authority. In addition, if you just take what you're told as gospel and don't research your so-called belief systems, then you're not following Christ's words.

Children used to learn spirituality at home—just as the Judaic faith still ensures that its teachings become a family affair in the celebration of holidays such as Passover and Hanukah. This is as it should be. Spirituality ought to be part and parcel of our everyday lives, no matter what we believe in. In teaching our children, we must at least make them aware of other faiths and, if possible, have enough background in them to answer the kids' inevitable questions. If you do your research, you can be well versed in the different religions and faiths of this world and make a better choice for yourself—and you can also be a veritable well of information for your children, who may have questions about God or religious philosophies.

I personally believe in allowing young people to choose their own belief system when they can discern for themselves (after all, Jesus was only 12 when he was at the Temple teaching, while his mother and father were searching for him). But I also realize that many churches stress bringing kids into their parents' religion. It can cause conflict, but faith is such a personal thing that it shouldn't be chosen by another, for this will just create greater problems in the long run.

Consider this: Jesus himself went to the church of Antioch as a guest speaker and called them hypocrites; later, he took a whip to the money changers at the Temple. Now I'm not saying that you shouldn't go to church . . . it's just that you must go into church *with* God, not to find Him/ Her. You see, God is in our homes and cars; He/She is everywhere we go and everywhere we are (including church, of course).

I'm reminded of the popular movie from several years ago called *Oh, God!* The most interesting parts of this film were when truisms were spouted, albeit tongue-in-cheek. One that hit me right between the eyes was when John Denver's character essentially asked God (played by George Burns) if Jesus Christ is the son of God. And God says something to the effect that yes he is—and so are you, and so is the man over there on the other side of the street, and so are all the others in this world. The point is, we all come from the same Creative Source.

Whatever you believe, be sure to come to know an all-loving Creator Who wants the best for you. We're all God's sons and daughters, and every single one of us has a spark of the Divine within. Never, ever, forget that.

✳ ✳ ✳ ✳ ✳ ✳

CONCLUSIONS

Thanks for coming along with me for another book. I hope it was as much a joy for you to read as it was for me to write. Now, instead of the same old Afterword, I'm going to end this book a little differently: with a list of the services we provide at the Society of Novus Spiritus, and a final discussion on dogmatic religion.

Novus Spiritus Services

Here's what we offer, along with an explanation of each service:

Prayer Groups

Numbering in the thousands, our prayer groups have been a tremendous success story. Here, a group of no more than 20 or 30 gather together to pore over Gnostic texts and philosophy. Such groups provide an atmosphere of fellowship for studying research transcripts and texts, and there's always a liaison with our church to field questions and provide answers. We try to keep the groups small so that study can be intensive and intimate, and this encourages participation by all.

The fees involved are very nominal—maybe costing a

few dollars or less per participant per month, depending on the group's size (fees are $20 per month for the entire group)—and they cover the expenses of paper and the publication of the study materials. Anyone can be a study-group member, or even start their own group.

For additional information, you can look on my Website, **www.sylvia.org**. You can also call (408) 379-7070, ext. 129; or e-mail **studygroup@novus.org**, and one of my ministers will be happy to help you.

Prayer/Crisis Line

The Society of Novus Spiritus also has a prayer/crisis line. This is utilized for those who call in with an illness or a problem (mental, physical, legal, economic, and so on), either for themselves or someone else, and we put their name on the prayer line. Then it begins to roll: The staff member who takes the name calls the study groups, and they in turn call others within the group so that it becomes hundreds of people praying at nine o'clock every night for all those on our list. Again, it doesn't matter if you know these people or even what their problem is . . . God does. We have hundreds of affidavits in our files from people who have been on the prayer line and either been healed or helped in some way.

You can contact our office to put yourself or someone else on the line, and there's no cost for this service. Please call (408) 379-7070, ext. 107; e-mail **office@sylvia.org**; or send a letter to 1700 Winchester Blvd., Suite 100, Campbell, CA 95008.

Letters

Finally, we at Novus Spiritus write letters to Mother God or to the universe (there is something not only powerful, but very cathartic, about writing down your needs). Then we burn or bury them and ask the Holy Spirit and angels to take our petition to Mother God. We also do this at our services, and the petitions we collect are burned by our ministers without anyone ever looking at them.

It's interesting to note that a few of our ministers who have collected the letters (again, without ever reading them), have dug holes in their garden and planted a bush, tree, or flower over them. One minister brought me a picture of the most magnificent rose bush that was planted over some of these petitions. It won a prize in the horticultural entries at the county fair: The roses, I kid you not, were as big as a baby's head!

A Final Word about Religion

To blame God for the suffering of humankind is completely erroneous. We can see how we mortal beings have created our own suffering thanks to our religious teachings, prejudices, morals, dogma, attitudes, intolerance . . . and the list can go on forever it seems.

So I'm going to end this book with an essay that was given to me by one of my followers who wishes to remain anonymous. Some of you might think it's a harsh commentary, but read it as more of a wake-up call so that we don't keep repeating the past. Read it with an open mind, for it applies to *all* religions, and because the trumpet of God will resound in your soul. (Note that it has been edited for clarity.)

Is Religion the Answer?

Religion is both the savior and bane of mankind. How many millions have been comforted by organized religion over the ages, and how many millions have been killed, tortured, raped, and plundered over these same ages? How many religions have not been persecuted? The answer is none. *All* religions have been persecuted at some point in their histories, and that continues to this day. In this modern "civilization," we still have not learned to love and tolerate one another. We have all the problems of economy, racism, ethnic purging, discrimination, hunger, poverty, politics, power, greed, terrorism, and on and on . . . seemingly endless it goes. Isn't this world wonderful? No wonder we're all depressed and tired—we hear about and experience these problems every day. It has got to stop, or the generations that follow us will have nothing.

We must start with organized religion, for it's both part of the problem and the key to the salvation of the world. The major religions of the world have got to band together and not only preach but practice religious tolerance.

Islam, the fastest-growing religion in the world today, has got to go back to its roots of religious tolerance (it is one of the most tolerant of religions) and oust the extremists who practice terrorism in the name of a holy Jihad (holy war) on the "infidels" of other religions or countries. Most of the message from Mohammed was Christlike, teaching love and tolerance for others . . . his teachings have been warped by extremists and conservative clerics who lust for power and greed at any cost of human life. Most Muslims are very devout and loving people who treat others with respect and kindness; but extremists are grabbing the headlines and perpetuating their wars against Israel, India, Europe, and the United States by playing on the emotions of the followers of Islam in their self-proclaimed "holy war."

Peace will never be obtained through terrorism, for it is the method of despicable evil. Peace can only be obtained through tolerance and negotiation in which both sides bend and compromise. Gone is the day when military might could conquer and bring a forced peace—the world will not stand for any country conquering and taking over another (the United States included). Yes, we still have places such as Iraq and Afghanistan that were subdued by military might, but the outrage of the world was heard, and these countries are being given back to the people that inhabit them. The world of Islam must go back to its messenger and practice what he brought forth in love and tolerance to climb that mountain of self.

Christianity also has some major problems that it must face. The Catholic Church has many internal problems that hurt others, and it's on the wane because it's slow to change and make compromises. It has lost the respect of many for its many internal scandals and failure to acknowledge its mistakes both in the past and present. It has trapped itself in its own unbendable traditions and become stagnant, and certainly makes less of an impact on the world today. It must make wholesale changes or it will go down, as so many inflexible dynasties have, and not be the powerful voice it once was.

The Protestant movement is also becoming more inflexible and conservative, with its right-wing politics creating myriad problems in the forms of bigotry, intolerance, and its propensity to try to gain power in the political arena. What's the old adage—religion and politics don't mix well? Christianity is one of the least tolerant toward other religions, which makes the task of bonding with other worldwide religions, in order to accomplish an overall good for the world, seem near to impossible, but it must be done.

Christianity today has become warped in many areas, namely that of preaching and practicing the worship of an all-loving and merciful God. Many churches concentrate more on the "hellfire and brimstone" approach to battling evil, invoking the fear of God and His wrath on those who "sin," or constantly using the Bible to rule their congregations by fear. It seems like a complete contradiction to me, as Christ always preached about an all-loving and merciful God. Some of these so-called Christian churches use the Bible so much that they ought to be named "Bible worshipers" instead of "worshipers of Christ."

If Christ were to come down to the world today, I doubt he'd proclaim himself a Christian. Christianity needs to practice more religious tolerance, get out of the political arena, and really put forth the concept of an all-loving and merciful God—rather than a wrathful, vengeful God Who has all of the imperfect emotions of mankind. In order for Christianity to take its place in saving this world, its followers have got to leave their hidden agendas of politics and getting wealthy behind and put forth the agenda of Christ. They have got to climb that mountain of ego that has been built up with their wealth and power and get down to helping others in the way that Christ would have wanted . . . no matter what their ethnic, racial, religious, or sexual background may be.

If you want people to be a part of your religion, do it with the truth and the love of God, not with your own self-righteous agendas. Concentrate more on the joy, truth, and love of God, not your own human-made truth . . . for you should at least be able to recognize that you may be wrong. Christianity has always been ruled by fear and money: the fear of being wrong and the money to build more churches (to get even more money). Its bloody history and its intolerance toward other faiths and beliefs prove this to be true. The Christian motto seems to be: *If you're threatened in your faith, for God's sake don't tolerate the right of others to believe otherwise. Instead, just destroy them, whether it be from the pulpit, in the political arena, with propaganda, or the sword.*

I know I'm on a soapbox, and I know I'm being tough and harsh in my criticism of some of these major religions, but damn it, someone has got to speak up. The religions of this world have to band together to help the planet, not tear it apart and asunder with their own agendas. I know that there are millions out there who aren't being helped by the faith they're now following, and I know that there are millions out there who have left their faith because it didn't give them the truth and comfort they were seeking. It's such a tragedy that the major religions of this world have messed up the simple act of worshiping God. God created us all in our many different colors and ethnic backgrounds, and He even sent messengers to help us find the way to His all-loving, merciful, and perfect Self. We turn around and disregard or warp all that and make war and commit atrocities on each other. It is the tragedy of tragedies.

We live in a time of exciting spiritual awareness and freedom of thought, so don't waste it in a box of dogma. As the poem goes: "God's in His heaven [and with you] / And all's right with the world" . . . if it isn't, make it all right in *your* world and the world around you.

God love you, I do,
Sylvia

✳ ✳ ✳ ✳ ✳ ✳

Accepting the Psychic Torch

⇥ PREFACE ⇤

This is a story about a woman named Ada Coil and her granddaughter, who happens to be me: Sylvia Browne. We took a journey together for almost 18 years, and it formed who and what I am today. Hopefully this story will help you with your own abilities, and allow you to be brave and put your beliefs out there, no matter who tries to destroy them and no matter what the world says. If you keep your goals and love of God in front of you always, then you will ultimately triumph. Your soul may be a little battered and worn, but it will glow in a world of darkness.

This book also allows me to share my grandmother with all of you, which is something I've wanted to do for decades. You may ask why I'm compelled to do so—well, I'm reminded of the *Reader's Digest* series of articles on "The Most Unforgettable Person in My Life" that used to be a regular part of their publication. If you haven't been lucky enough to have a mentor, as I did, you may not realize how important it is to pattern your life after someone with great grace and knowledge. Perhaps just reading about this incredible woman will bring something worthwhile to your life.

In addition, I've received countless requests from my readers to write about Grandma Ada, who passed the psychic torch on to me and has influenced so much of the work I've done. It's much like how Dr. Wayne Dyer is enamored with, and inspired by, the teachings of Ram Dass. True mentors—people like Ram Dass and my grandmother—are the mission-life entities (that is, people who are very advanced spiritually) who pull the rocks out of our path . . . and if we do happen to step on the stones, they help us deal with the bruises.

I consider writing about my grandmother and what she's done for me to be a great honor, and I only hope I can do her justice in doing so. As you read this book, may all of you gain some insight into this wonderful soul who just happened to be my beloved grandma. If you don't, then that's my fault, for I have not conveyed how this special woman from God affected so many lives . . . especially mine.

⇥ INTRODUCTION ⇤

It was 1882, and a young woman of German nobility lived in Hamburg with her mother, father, brother, and two sisters. Even at her tender age, this girl had already become well known in her hometown and the surrounding areas as a psychic, as had her mother before her. Although Ida Katrina von Banica indeed had the psychic gift, it seemed to be stronger and more prominent in her firstborn son, Henry, and in this girl, who was the youngest of her four children.

However, the young lady in question felt that was all behind her now. Because of political tensions with the Russians and the French, her parents had decided to leave their home and go to the foreign land of America. Being the obedient daughter, she'd elected to go with them and start a new chapter in her life. She was only 17, and all she'd taken with her for the long journey ahead was a little bit of money and two diamond shoe buckles.

As the teenager boarded the ship with her parents and siblings, she noticed how crowded it was, with so many people who also sought a new life in the United States. She instantly took a shine to a young man named Jason . . . unfortunately, not long after they set sail, an epidemic of cholera ran rampant through the ship's passengers and crew. It was probably inevitable that the German girl and both of her parents became ill, as did her new friend. To look at this budding woman with the golden blonde hair, you wouldn't think that she could survive such a ravaging disease, but evidently God had other things in store for her.

The young German woman was lying on a cot in a small cubicle surrounded by curtains, tossing and turning with fever, with her mother and father also ill in cots beside her. All of a sudden she became very lucid and watched the hanging curtain in front of her bed lift up, as if by invisible hands. It revealed the horror of Jason's lifeless body being taken up to the deck on a stretcher . . . he was dead from the cholera. There was no wind below deck that could have moved the young lady's curtains, but she wasn't really surprised at how the curtain was pulled up because she was used to such paranormal events in her life. This was the first time she'd ever experienced such heartache, however, so she let out an anguished cry and buried her head in her pillow as the tears started to flow. As she quickly went back into a fevered stupor, she didn't realize that it wouldn't be the last tragedy she'd experience on this voyage: her father died several days later.

Although the rest of the German girl's family survived the cholera epidemic on board the ship, they were all now in the process of dealing with tremendous pain as they clung to each other in their grief. Frightened, terrified, and alone, they had to face a new life in a new country without a husband or father to help and guide them.

The young woman in this story was named Ada von Banica . . . and she was my dear and loving grandmother.

Thus, in dramatic and movielike fashion, my grandmother and her family arrived in America. When they got to New York, they decided to follow through on the original plan that my great-grandfather had come up with, which was to seek out distant relatives who lived near San Antonio, Texas. So, with the little money they had, the von Banicas made the long and arduous journey from New York to Texas, found their relatives, and stayed with them.

My great-grandmother was quickly introduced to Henri Kaufholz, a prosperous mercantile owner who had a daughter and who had recently been widowed. He was short and heavyset, with bright blue eyes and a great business sense—and, as Ida later stated to my grandmother, he made her laugh. After a short courtship (back then a single woman didn't stay single long), Henri proposed, and he and Ida were married. It was a testament to his love for her that he took in her four grown children from her previous marriage as well; they, in turn, took the Kaufholz name.

As I mentioned, Ida's son, Henry, had a great psychic gift, but her daughters Lena and Annie did not. It was Ida's youngest daughter, Ada, who seemed to have inherited the strongest psychic abilities, which she started demonstrating at an early age. She had contact with her guide, Isabella, and supposedly also had several others because she often talked about her many "voices." (That's something I've never had, as I only have vocal contact with my guide Francine [I do have another guide, Raheim, whom I don't speak to directly—and you'll hear much more about them both later], but Grandma was more like Edgar Cayce, who had many entities speaking to and through him in trance.)

My grandmother wasn't treated differently, since her mother and brother also had the gift and didn't consider it unusual. Just like me, Grandma started giving readings early in life—after all, at that time, Spiritualism, "table tapping" (which just meant that a medium called upon spirits to tap a table once for *yes* and twice for *no*), and séances were very popular.

While in Texas, Ada always knew when there was a possibility of an Indian attack. Since she'd been an expert horsewoman from the time she was small, she'd ride on the underside of her horse's belly and shut the stockade gates whenever such attacks occurred. After a while, Henri got tired of this hazard to his family and took them all to Springfield, Missouri, to enjoy a more refined type of life.

The Kaufholzes loved being together as a family, and they resided happily on Elm Street in a beautiful Victorian house that I believe still stands today. (When I was a girl I got to see it, and I remember that it was immense but gorgeous, with all sorts of turrets and gables.) Aside from being well-to-do, Ada and her two sisters were accomplished musicians and would sing and play all over town, thereby attracting a good deal of male attention. (Bernice, Henri's daughter from his first marriage, was part of the family but very much kept to herself.) Annie, who was tall and willowy, had a number of gentleman callers; while Lena, who was petite and rather frail, had only a few. But Ada—with her striking hourglass figure, not to mention her long blonde hair and large china blue eyes—outdid them all. She kept all of her suitors at bay for years because she loved her home life so much. She even had seven men asking for her hand, and she discouraged every one of them.

Ada's brother, Henry, was a commanding presence—he was a robust man who stood 6'6" tall—and he had many a young woman trying to get him to marry. He was also very famous in his day: as reports have it, he was a great healer who could create *apports* (having objects appear out of thin air). He spent much of his life in Florida in the psychic Chesterfield (Spiritualist) camps, where he built up quite a reputation as a medium and healer.

Henry died at the age of 96 in Pawhuska, Oklahoma, among Indians who looked to him as a shaman, and he was the last to carry the Kaufholz name. I still have his scrapbook, which I cherish. It's full of wonderful paranormal information that he'd written, along with scientific discoveries or other clippings that backed up his predictions. (My grandmother, however, was more like me: feeling that it's nice to be validated, but if you're doing the right thing you'll have all the proof you need. I have hundreds of validations in my files, but I try not to read too many of them because I don't want them to influence me. I do read a lot of my e-mails and appreciate all of the kind words sent my way . . . and I always hope that the individuals sending them know that I truly love them, too.)

One day, a newcomer by the name of Marcus Coil rode into Springfield. He immediately set up his own store and then did a type of banking—offering loans with low interest. The young man's family was from an Irish-Scottish background (although he'd been raised in an orphanage), and he was darkly handsome. Yet he had eyes only for Ada and managed to get introduced to her. During their courtship, Marcus became well aware of Ada's psychic ability and encouraged it, and the two were soon married. My grandmother didn't marry until she was 30 years old, which was quite old for a single woman at that time, but again she'd put off marriage because her home life had been so pleasant.

About a year or so after marrying, my grandparents had their first son, whom they named after his father but called "Brother." Tragically, he was born with cerebral palsy, which often stems from a mishap at birth—my uncle was a "forceps baby," meaning that they used forceps to deliver him, and they damaged his neck and nervous system in the process. He could walk, but his head bent to one side and he couldn't see very well peripherally. He never married, and even though my grandmother took care of him for the rest of her life, she'd often say that he was a gift from God and a joy in her life.

My grandmother then gave birth to my mother, Celeste; and then had her final child, Paul, who inherited the psychic gift. So my mother's immediate family had my grandmother Ada, my great-uncle Henry, and my uncle Paul as those carrying the psychic gift before I even came along.

When Grandma married and had her children, she kept doing her work as much as she could. It truly was a Victorian era of peace and love—and for many, affluence. It was a time when the so-called mom-and-pop businesses flourished. Grandpa had several such businesses and was very busy with his enterprises, and since he and Grandma were quite wealthy, she had lots of help running their home. She would sit in her study, and Esther (the Coils' housekeeper and nanny) would bring people in when they had appointments. My grandmother would then give them a reading or a healing depending upon their need. She became very famous locally, and as her fame spread, she started to see clients who came from far away. Usually, however, she confined herself to local clientele. Even so, at parties she couldn't help herself . . . after giving a few people psychic predictions, she'd be off and running. She told me later that when your ability is there you can try to deny it, but because it's part of you it just naturally comes out.

Although my grandmother and her siblings had only gone though the eighth grade in a convent school in Germany, that was still more education than most people in that time got. My great-grandfather, who was an avid reader, also had a library at their home in Hamburg, with three walls covered from top to bottom with bookshelves. One day Grandma apparently just decided to start in one corner . . . and then she doggedly read every book in that library over the next several years. I found that her retentive memory with respect to poetry, plays, and stories was unequaled. And although I had other influences in my life, it was my grandmother who primarily gave me my love for reading and writing.

One evening when I was about ten, we were sitting on her front porch eating watermelon. Venus seemed to be sitting in the curve of the moon, and Grandma let me know that this was the Islamic symbol, just like Christians have the cross. I'd never seen it before, and I've only spotted it one time since, but I'm sure that astronomers can verify this celestial configuration.

My grandmother loved to read, and when I got into literature myself, I found that you learn history, geography, social and cultural structures, and many other subjects just from books. In fact, Grandma knew more about geography than you might imagine—including where everything was from the Amazon to Europe, and all other parts of the globe. She'd memorized large passages from the volumes she'd read, and they stayed with her until the day she died. I have a good memory, too, but sometimes it's a mixed blessing in that the things you want to forget you can't. Of course, the opposite side to that coin is that information is right there in your head if you need it.

Ada Coil's love for her husband, and his for her, was truly beautiful. He constantly complimented her on her writings (even though they were never published) and appreciated her psychic gift and the help she gave others. Their deep bond never wavered, which was a great blessing, since storm clouds were ahead for both of them.

My grandfather owned a lot of stock, and when the market crashed in 1929, he lost everything. As the Great Depression started, his businesses also went under, as so many of them did at that time. Even though they were now basically broke, Grandpa told Grandma that he'd made a million before and he'd make it again. He decided to move his family to Kansas City, Missouri, since it was more populated and there were more opportunities. So the Coils packed up and left their beautiful home, moving to a modest house in northern Kansas City. Once settled, my grandfather set out to find work; before long, he was able to take care of his family in style again.

As for my grandmother, she thought that her days of doing readings and helping people would come to an end when they left Springfield, but it was not to be. As her children were growing up, she now had more time to put into her gift, as well as to gather herbs for healing (something I'm sorry I didn't learn). Leave her alone in a field and Grandma would come back with an apron full of what looked like a bunch of weeds. She'd then cook them up and make poultices and all kinds of concoctions, and I'm a witness to the fact that they worked on every manner of ailment suffered by the seemingly endless line of people that knocked on her door.

My grandmother had a lovely life, despite the challenges of having a child with cerebral palsy. She always seemed to make good out of bad. Even when she lost her youngest son, Paul, to cancer when he was only 21, she seemed to pull it together. She was then hit with another tragedy eight months after that when her beloved husband died of blood poisoning and she was left destitute (people didn't tend to have life insurance back then). My mother had married my father by this time, and Grandma opened a boardinghouse to help make ends meet. Then, as she so sweetly said, "And God sent you, Sylvia, to replace what I lost."

Grandma and I had a wonderful time together: she taught me to knit, do lace tatting, crochet, make macramé rugs, sew, cook, and do all the things a young woman who was "well bred" should learn to do. (As an aside, I've gone on to teach my own granddaughter needlepoint, knitting, sewing, and the like.) But this book is primarily devoted to Ada Coil's vast philosophy and spirituality, which she wove throughout the short years we spent together.

Please note that I have included correspondence between the two of us whenever appropriate in the chapters ahead. However, these letters have been edited for clarity, since many of them were written in pencil and are hard to decipher—particularly since we're talking about letters that are 60-plus years old. (Even so, a few images of them can be found in the Appendix because I'd like you to be able to see Grandma's handwriting and the way she wrote. Here you'll also find family photographs that supplement those I included in *Adventures of a Psychic*.) I'm sure that as you read my grandmother's letters, you'll see how I formed a lot of my views, especially when it comes to giving people guidance and assistance, along with how many of her sayings have now become my own.

I cut my teeth on Grandma Ada's love of humanity and helping others. She made my life's journey so much easier and gave me signposts that have lasted throughout my entire life. She wanted me to carry the flag, as she used to say, and God knows I've tried.

I hope you enjoy this very personal tribute to the woman who changed my life forever.

Chapter One

FROM ONE
PSYCHIC
TO ANOTHER

My earliest memories are of my grandmother, and I always knew that I was in the presence of greatness. While we obviously had a special relationship because of our shared abilities, she said that she sensed our connection from the moment I was born. I must have known it, too, because I'd cry hysterically whenever I was taken from her.

By the time I came along, my grandmother was already 70 years old, and I used to regret that I only had her in my life for less than 18 years. But now I realize how fortunate I was to have her around for as long as I did, especially during my formative years. And, of course, it isn't how much time we spend with someone but the *quality* of that time that's important. These days I have no regrets about the time Grandma and I spent together on Earth because I know that every moment we had together was precious.

From a very early age I'd know who was coming over, who was going to call on the phone, and who was sick before anyone else did. Unfortunately (or fortunately) I was born with a practical mind—in other words, if you can't prove it, it can't be true—so I'm sure that made things harder for me. I was more interested in acting and literature and found this sixth sense to be a big nuisance, as my best friends from that time will tell you.

My gift wasn't easy to handle; in fact, I could see and feel some terrifying things. When I was five, for instance, I saw my great-grandmothers' faces melt, and I didn't understand why this had happened until Grandma Ada explained that it meant they were going to die. That was a pretty traumatic episode for a little girl, so Grandma told me to just ask God to remove the horrible visuals from me. She said, "You can still know when someone is going to die, but you don't need to see it." Even today I can indeed still know when someone is going to die, but thank God I never got that image of faces melting ever again.

Thanks to my grandmother's help, I was better equipped to deal with my psychic abilities. I often think that if I hadn't had her in my life I would have gone insane . . . Lord knows my mother told me that often enough. I think that since Mama had been around it so much in her life, she hoped that the genetics had died out or at least diminished by the time they got to me. I also have a feeling that she was jealous because I was so close to Grandma and my dad, who was perfectly comfortable with my gift even though he hadn't personally been brought up in that type of family.

My grandmother was very smart about not pushing me into anything psychic, and as I reflect back on those times, I realize that I probably would have completely rebelled against it if she had. She always waited for me to come to *her,* and then she'd explain what was going on and how to handle or enhance it. In those early years, I couldn't always control the manifestation of my gift, and it was my grandmother who guided and helped me to do so, which made life *much* easier.

Grandma didn't mention my abilities too much around other people, but instead kept what she saw and wanted for me between the two of us. Sometimes she'd hand me notes or letters because she didn't want Mama to see and then go into one of her rants about how I'd go crazy if I kept talking to spirits and seeing things. My mother always praised my sister, Sharon, for being "normal," but as one of my grandmother's notes to me states:

Dearest Sweetheart,

Never be afraid of what you see and hear. Everything is from God, and since you have a pure heart, I never worry about you. Keep what we say to each other between us. You'll see as you get older how great this gift will be for you to do God's work. . . .

Faith and Healing

Grandma and I had lots of long talks with each other over the years, which ran the gamut from the lost continent of Atlantis, to spirit guides that watched over us, to ghosts. She always wanted ghosts to be released because she said they were caught between two worlds and should be sent back to God.

My grandmother would often tell me, "You and I are old souls who have spent many lives together." Although I didn't believe in reincarnation back then, it was her thing and I respected it. Whenever she brought it up and saw the blank look in my eyes, she'd just give me that knowing smile of hers and say, "Someday you'll know what I know." She always felt that God was all-loving and merciful and gave us many chances to learn by living more than one life, and she had a real problem with the Old Testament's portrayal of a mean God.

Grandma was the closest thing to a real saint I've ever known. Even Father Keys, who baptized my entire family when I was a young girl, said the same thing. You see, my parents and grandmother all belonged to different faiths, and Grandma felt that all of us becoming Catholic would solve the problem. So she brought Brother, Sharon, my mother, my father (who wasn't even a churchgoing man), and me into Catholicism.

Grandma loved certain aspects of Catholicism—for example, she greatly enjoyed Fulton J. Sheen, a Catholic bishop who used to appear on television and was quite a showman. However, she was a true Gnostic in that she believed that everyone should seek his or her own God center. She was also the first person I knew who actually took what she wanted with her and left the rest behind.

491

In ancient times she probably would have been likened to the Gnostic sect of Essenes; in fact, she was the one who first told me that Jesus was an Essene (a fact later confirmed by my spirit guide Francine). So even though she was a practicing Catholic, she was really more Gnostic in nature. Interestingly enough, if you look in the dictionary, *catholic* means "universal," which I think aptly describes my grandmother in her beliefs.

She wasn't what I would call terribly ritualistic as far as religion is concerned, but she *was* very big on intention and affirmations. Sometimes when I hear Wayne Dyer speak on the subject of intention, so much of it rings true because that's exactly what Grandma believed.

In the time that I was with my grandmother, we only disagreed on three things: reincarnation, fairies, and UFOs. I *wanted* to believe, but before long I had become so steeped in Catholicism that it prevented me from doing so.

This reminds me of the story Grandma told me about how she gained her knowledge of herbal remedies. She said that when she was about 15 years old, her father decided to take the family on a trip to the Black Forest area of Germany, where they stayed with some of my great-grandmother's relatives for about a month. My grandmother liked to go exploring in the forest, and one day she met a little man who sported a green waistcoat with gold buttons and a black top hat. He told her that he lived in the forest, and she wasn't sure if he was a dwarf, midget, or gnome. She said he looked very old with his gnarled and stubby fingers, and he spoke with a slight accent that she couldn't place—it definitely wasn't German or Polish, since she spoke both languages fluently. She also noted that although he was very short and bowlegged, he moved so fast that she had a hard time keeping up with him.

My grandmother asked the man for his name, and he replied that he wanted to be referred to as "Mr. Wickes." But when she inquired as to where he came from, he wouldn't answer her. He just said that she'd eventually need the information he was going to share with her. So every day during her stay, my grandmother would meet this man in the forest at 12 o'clock sharp and stay with him until suppertime. She insisted that Mr. Wickes was the one who taught her all about the different cures plants and trees could provide, and she never forgot his lessons.

I was pretty young when she related this story to me, and I laughed and said something to the effect that this sounded like a fairy tale . . . something I never, ever said again. She gave me a sharp, stern look with those piercing blue eyes of hers, and I knew she was telling the truth. It took me another ten minutes of saying I was sorry before she continued speaking. Now if you knew my grandmother, you'd know without a second thought that she was far too educated to ever concoct a story like this, nor was she given to flights of fancy. I believe that when she was in the Black Forest, she tuned in to one of the lower levels of creation where the fairies and gnomes live. It was almost like a small Bermuda Triangle, or an opening in time that God allowed her to experience. (For more on these levels, please see my book *Exploring the Levels of Creation.*)

In my mind's eye, I can just see Grandma following this little man around and committing to that remarkable memory of hers every herb, leaf, and flower he told her about. Fast-forwarding to a later time, I remember sitting in the car while she'd go out in a field in Kansas City with her skirt up and proceed to gather all types of wild plants to make poultices, folk medicines, and other concoctions to treat boils, pleurisy, stomach problems, and even arthritis. She always told me that someday cures for cancer, diabetes, and all the ills of humankind would be discovered in the Amazon.

Like me, my grandmother believed in doctors—she'd often say that God gave us everything in nature to cure us, but God made doctors, too. A great deal of medical knowledge has come to me psychically, but I also have an excellent physician-referral list because a psychic should never take the place of a medical professional. But where did my medical knowledge come from? I'm sure primarily from God, but I actually had an ancestor who was a doctor in Germany, which was almost unheard of for a woman at that time. According to the stories about her that have been handed down over the years, everyone consulted her for her psychic diagnostic skills—so I also feel that my medical knowledge is somewhat genetic. In addition, Grandma once told me that besides being from a long line of psychics in *this* life, we were psychics or alchemists in others as well. *Oh great,* I thought, *we never get a break.* I don't feel that way now; I'm so grateful and thankful for my gift.

My grandmother said that people basically know their charts better than you think they do, and I've found this to be so true. (Our charts are like a blueprint of our life, which we plot out before we incarnate.) I've had to tell people that they need to seek medical help for a deadly disease, and they've nodded their heads in agreement—I've never had anyone say, "How dare you?!" I've received countless letters from people who have thanked me for sending them to a doctor or for steering them clear of riding in a car with someone who wound up getting into a terrible accident. Grandma used to impress upon me that we psychics are here to prevent mishaps because God may have put us in others' charts to warn them. Of course, there are lots of things that are hidden from us for individuals' own development . . . and then there are some folks who I know won't listen at all, and that's their choice, too.

Meeting Francine

I've never explained in detail just how frightened I was when I first started to hear my spirit guide Francine. Yes, I'd already been manifesting all sorts of psychic abilities, such as predicting who was going to call or come by, as I've already mentioned. I'd even finish the sentences of my parents and family friends and notice the knowing looks that passed between them, but hearing this voice was another thing altogether.

I was almost eight years old and was brushing my hair in front of a mirror when I sensed a presence on my right. I'd always felt this so I thought it was normal, but what came next wasn't exactly something I'd planned on. In a very high-pitched voice, I heard these words: "I come from God, so don't be afraid." It's funny because over the years, people who first hear their guides have reported this same high and hollow-sounding voice to me. I'm convinced that such a sound is necessary to traverse the dimensions—spirit guides have to come from an elevated environment into a "very thick, gravity-bound, pea-soup environment," as Francine calls it.

The voice contact bothered me immensely. I already had enough to deal with, particularly since at night I had a lot of spirit activity surrounding me as I tried to go to sleep. My grandmother had given me a flashlight, which helped quite a bit. I still sleep with a night-light, not because I'm afraid of the dark, but because it diffuses all the images in my busy bedroom that can be so distracting. I see all these spirits coming and going in glowing color—they seem to come in almost like infrared forms or images, but our artificial light blocks it out, thank God. I've always said that the dead can't hurt you, but if you can see them like I do, you don't want to watch them walking around when you're trying to get some rest.

This doesn't mean that spirits are haunting us; we simply occupy the same space but in different dimensions. I see them going about their business, really paying no attention to us on Earth. As crazy as this sounds, *we* are spirits in *their* world, and that world (the Other Side) is the one that is real and true.

Anyway, when I first heard Francine, I was scared to death and ran screaming to my grandmother. She immediately calmed me down and proceeded to set me straight, telling me about the history of our family and how we'd both come from a long line of psychics. Then she explained that for more than 300 years, all of my psychic forebearers had voice contact with their spirit guides, including my uncle Henry, who was working as a trance medium in Florida and had a guide named Alexander. She also reminded me about her own voices, pointing out that she functioned perfectly well with them. She helped me a great deal at that time in understanding this manifestation of my psychic ability, as I knew that while Grandma heard voices, she certainly wasn't mentally ill in any way.

My grandmother always encouraged me to investigate all of this further, so years later I decided once and for all to consult with others to put my fears to rest. As I grew older, I began to wonder whether my ancestors may have all been prone to some genetic fault that had come down through the generations to me, and that's when I began what I call my "skeptical search." I talked to professors, priests, psychiatrists, and psychologists, each of whom said that I was a normal person who had some kind of paranormal ability. Later on I was observed and tested by Drs. Rennick, Blatner, Weras, and Yabroff—all eminent psychiatrists and psychologists—and they all came up with the same conclusion: I simply possessed psychic or paranormal abilities. Other doctors, including the very dear Melvin Morse, have also tested me, but in the 1940s and '50s paranormal abilities certainly weren't a focal point of psychiatry. And even today, many doctors still can't explain how or why such abilities show up in certain individuals.

Grandma always felt that words healed, but so did being a conduit for God's grace to come through. Thus, she talked to her voices all day long and lived her life like a prayer. She'd never say that her "voices said such and such." Her favorite expression was "I heard," which meant that she'd gotten voice contact that was relevant to whatever subject she was discussing. I do the same thing, really. I use Francine more for researching theology, religion, and my books than for personal interests. Oh sure, she's a dear friend and confidante and I discuss some of my personal problems with her, but I've never asked her to give me lottery numbers or anything like that. Francine once told me that if I ever misquoted her or used her for my own personal gain, she'd still stay with me because she's my guide, but she'd never speak another word to me, ever. That's why I'm so conscientious about quoting her accurately.

Although Grandma was psychic on her own, like me she was saved many times by the guides and angels who seemed to surround her. I once saw a Native American beside her who was wearing a full chieftain's headdress, and she just matter-of-factly said, "That's Running Bear," and didn't elaborate. She had at least three more guides but usually didn't refer to them by name but rather as "them."

Here's another interesting story she told me: Because she was such a horsewoman all her life, right after she was married she would go out and saddle up the family horse, Bill, to go to church every Sunday. One morning it seems that Bill, who was normally the model of gentle behavior, started to buck and rear back. She kept trying to pull him closer to the barn to saddle him up, but the harder she pulled on the reins, the more he pulled back. She was strong and held on to him, though, and just as he gave her a huge pull, a giant beam gave way from the barn and crashed to the ground. Had Bill not pulled Grandma away, it would have killed her. She always had a special love for this horse, but this endeared him to her even more.

Grandma was a great advocate and admirer of psychic Edgar Cayce and hoped that we'd meet him, but he died when I was around nine. I think one of the reasons why she admired him so much was because he heard many voices, just as she did. I, on the other hand, have only heard Francine's voice. (Later on in life I found that I had another guide, Raheim, who aided Francine, but Francine has always been my primary guide and the only one I have voice contact with. That is, Raheim doesn't speak to me directly.)

Looking back, it must have been hard for my grandmother to have so many voices contact her because I know how challenging it was just to deal with hearing the voice of *one* spirit guide. Yet I learned to not only handle Francine's voice but to welcome it and love her as my closest friend . . . and that, like so many other things in my life, is thanks to my grandmother.

Chapter Two

COMING TO TERMS WITH MY GIFT

I'm so lucky that my grandmother helped me make sense of the extremely unconventional things that were happening to me. For example, when I began to see spirits and ghosts, she explained what they were—spirits have made it to the Other Side, while ghosts haven't gotten there yet and need to be helped Home—and gave me a great deal of guidance in understanding and dealing with them. When I saw the movie *The Sixth Sense* so many years after my childhood, it really rang some bells for me, specifically when the young boy revealed that he saw dead people. The movie *Ghost* did, too, especially when Oda Mae Brown (Whoopi Goldberg) would hear the deceased Sam Wheat (Patrick Swayze) and tell his girlfriend, Molly (Demi Moore), what he was saying. It's too bad that these kinds of movies weren't out when I was young, but at least I was able to bounce things of this nature off of Grandma.

I remember one time when we were making cookies in her kitchen, and I saw her son Paul standing beside her and watching what she was doing. He was very tall, and as he looked over at me and smiled, I noticed that he had the most gorgeous soft brown eyes. He put his finger to his lips, as if to say, "Be quiet about seeing me," and my grandmother shivered and looked behind her several times. I didn't say a word; it was like Paul and I were sharing a private joke. He then moved the saltshaker, and Grandma looked at it and then at me. "Sylvia," she said, "you see him, don't you?"

"Who?" I asked innocently.

"Paul. He's behind me, isn't he?"

I couldn't lie, so I just nodded.

She then asked if he was "playing" with her, and I said yes. She smiled and told me that this was so much like him: often when she was cooking he'd come up and untie her apron or kiss her on the cheek.

I really felt like I knew Paul, even though he'd been dead for years by the time I came along. (Of course we all know each other on the Other Side, but I felt a particularly strong connection to him.) When I told my grandmother this, she informed me that we were brother and sister in Istanbul in a past life. That explained why I felt so close to him . . . after all, he'd foreseen my birth and told my mother that he wanted me to be named Sylvia after his favorite song. Interestingly enough, I've only heard that song once in my entire life.

After my encounter with Paul, I picked up the presence of a fellow named Jim. I had no idea who he might be, but when I described him to Grandma, she got very excited—apparently this was Jim Coil, her husband's brother and a man of great moral fiber. My grandmother told me that Jim was a physician practicing in Springfield, Kansas, and he helped out during the First World War by determining the health status of recruits. One man came in and motioned to Jim that he was deaf, but my great-uncle was convinced that he wasn't. Of course, back then they certainly didn't have the medical equipment we have now to back up such hunches, so as he dismissed the man, Jim threw a silver dollar on the floor as he was walking out. The man wouldn't have been able to see my great-uncle do this, yet he immediately reached toward the sound to pick up the money. Needless to say, this man was deemed fit enough to be enlisted in the Army.

Jim Coil was also a hero in the family. When he heard about the devastating influenza epidemic that was spreading throughout the U.S., especially New York, he decided to go there to see if he could help. When his loved ones protested that it was too dangerous and tried to keep him from going, he just said, "Well, that's why I became a doctor: to help where needed." Unfortunately he contracted the virus himself and died not long after arriving in New York.

Grandma was thrilled because no one had been able to get in touch with Jim after he passed. But now he told me that he was fine—he said the hardest part was feeling helpless as a doctor, especially when it came to watching children suffer, yet he felt that he was actually able to come to the aid of many people before he was stricken by the flu himself. As for me, I felt incredibly proud that I could be in contact with someone who meant so much to my grandmother.

Confidence and Encouragement

My ability seemed to accelerate as I got older, and the more I tried to hold it down, the more it pushed hard on me. Grandma said, "Stop fighting it and let it come, or it will rage on inside of you."

My mother certainly didn't help during this time, often reprimanding me, "If you keep this spook stuff up, they're going to lock you up!" This attitude seems so strange for a woman who grew up with a psychic mother. I've tried to rationalize her behavior over the years, but when I was a little girl it really affected me. I used to lie in bed and feel so anxious that I could see my heart beating through the blankets. That's why I encourage families to help nurture children's psychic ability. Never force it . . . just let it be and evolve with your support, like my grandmother did with me.

When I was very young, times were tough. Americans were going through a Depression and then a war, and we used to have to stand in line for bread, sugar, and other staples. (Gas was also rationed.) My grandmother liked to frequent a grocery store called Milgram's, and every Friday they had a drawing for a basketful of groceries. Grandma had made friends with everyone, so they let me pluck out the winning ticket, and I swear I drew hers. She and

I were ecstatic. The next week I was chosen to draw again . . . and again I picked her ticket. Needless to say, that was the end of my "psychic drawing" career.

Around that time, Grandma would cut out figures from the Sunday funny papers and put them in eggshells, which she'd place in a huge pan full of water. We'd line up the shells on one side of the pan, and she'd move the water a little bit and ask, "Sylvia, which one of these will win by getting to the other side of the pan first?" I'd usually guess right, and with that little nod of her head, she'd say, "You can absolutely see who will win." This may not sound like much, but it gave me so much confidence.

Over the years my grandmother helped me hone my psychic ability in all sorts of ways. At first she'd do simple things like go in the other room and pick out a picture in a book and ask me to draw it, which today is one of the tests involved in what they call "remote viewing."

She'd also ask me to tell her what she was holding behind her back, with the explicit direction of "No guessing!" We'd use playing cards, and I'd tell her if she was holding a particular card, such as the king of diamonds. (We hadn't heard of the Zener cards being used by Dr. J.B. Rhine in his parapsychology experiments at Duke University at that time.) Most of the time I'd get eight or nine out of every ten cards right, and it made me so frustrated that I couldn't get all of them. That's when she'd say, "Stop that— you're not God. Besides, this keeps you humble and knowing you're human." Even with the occasional admonishment, she was always pleased, and she complimented me whenever we played these psychic games.

Needless to say, my grandmother and I had a great psychic connection, but her theory was that if you have the gift, you should keep using it because it will become stronger. I'm not a mentalist by any means, but my family, friends, and employees frequently tell me, "You read my mind—I was just going to say that!" I'm convinced that the more you're around that energy, the more connected you become. That's why I like to use games, much like the ones my grandmother and I played, in the psychic-development classes I hold. One of my favorites to use with students is to get a coffee can, put an object in it, and have them tell me what it is . . . which was an Ada Coil specialty.

Sometimes she'd tell me, "This next week I will think of you very hard and send you a code word, and when we see each other again, you'll tell me what it is." I remember in particular one Wednesday at 9 P.M., I kept getting a picture of her in her chair and the word was *blue*. I immediately wrote down the time and the word, and I saw her seal the "code word" in an envelope. The next time I saw her, she told me to open the envelope I'd envisioned, and there it was: the word *blue*. We'd also do it the other way: I'd sit and send her a message, and she always seemed to get it.

My grandmother and I started out with very basic exercises, such as predicting what color car would show up at a stoplight first, but then they got more elaborate. Once we were in a restaurant eating lunch when Grandma noticed a woman drinking tomato juice all alone. (When I was in college I went on to write a short story about this lonely woman.) She asked, "Sylvia, what's going on with that woman?" As she had taught me to do, without thinking about it first I said, "She's waiting for a man who isn't coming. I think that he's married and trying to break it off. . . . In a few minutes she'll look at the clock, throw her napkin on the table, and say, 'I never liked tomato juice anyway.'"

Sure enough, the words were just out of my mouth when this woman did exactly what I said she would. Grandma merely smiled and ate her food.

Incidents like this more or less had me convinced that I could see into the present, but what about the past and future? To me, seeing into the future or way back in the past seemed like insurmountable tasks. I told myself that things that were immediate were easier and more predictable, but to go out and tap into the ethers of time seemed impossible. When I told Grandma all this, she didn't respond immediately. However, I received this letter soon afterward:

May 9, 1950
Dearest Sugar Lamb,

Don't let it get you down; just let it come. If you can tell the present, the past and future will come. God has everything on a wheel of time. Just think or say in your mind, "I want to turn the wheel backward or forward." Remember, darling, you have the gift . . . the gift doesn't have you. It is an addition to the soul that God gave you, blessed girl, and you'll carry on where generations have built upon this time for you to shine.

You won't always be right, but if you keep your motives clear and have God in front of you, you'll be more right than wrong. Don't fret or obsess, since this only clogs you up . . . just open your mouth and let the records from God come in. Never soften the truth; always tell it as it is. You are only the messenger, not the editor. Only God is the Supreme Editor. . . .

I've kept these words written in my heart, along with so many more from this mentor who possessed knowledge far beyond time and space. Sometimes I sit and think about all of the psychic women in my family who came before me and the rejection they must have faced. Here I was dealing with it in the 20th century, but what kinds of hardships did they have to deal with in the previous two centuries? Any strife I went through just made me stronger and gave me a feeling that I wanted my ancestors to be proud of me.

I have vowed that even though life gets hard at times, I won't let that psychic torch go out . . . no matter what mental crucifixion I have to go through.

Dipping My Toe in the Pool of Readings

My grandmother never stopped telling me how smart I was or how strong I'd grow up to be. As she was fond of reminding me: "Don't you ever forget who you are and where you came from and what your purpose in life will be." I'm reminded of these words whenever I come in contact with people who have no idea who they are, where they've been, or where they're going. Grandma Ada's philosophy was: "Do for others, and in that way, you'll find *you.*"

Grandma would always tell me to think with my solar plexus (she never would have said "gut") and rely on my own psychic ability. She kept encouraging me to talk to Francine; however, she said that while spirit guides can certainly be helpers, we should use our own channels as much as possible instead of exclusively depending upon our guides. She also stressed that I should never let my heart rule my head whenever I'd tell people things about themselves. She said that I must always ask myself questions, for the answers will come. The more I did this with my classmates, the more it worked.

From time to time I'd walk up to Grandma when she was cooking or gardening, and I'd hear her talking out loud to her voices. I'd ask her what they said, and most of the time she'd answer vaguely. But one time she announced that she'd been told I'd have two boys, go to California, and teach and write; and before too long, my name would be known. She didn't see me do it, but I just rolled my eyes. As I started to walk away, she added, "Sylvia, don't let your sons go into the service or play football. They won't come back if they go to war, and they'll get hurt if they play football."

Needless to say, I did come to California and teach and write—and I never did let my boys play football or enter the service. They played soccer and basketball, ran track, and wrestled, but there was no football. While there wasn't a war going on when they became young men, they still could have enlisted in the service but chose not to. Since I was a fairly permissive mother, when I asked them not to do those two things, they listened . . . especially when I told them that their psychic great-grandmother had told me not to allow it.

Grandma's psychic advice and healings were so powerful that she usually had a long line of folks waiting to see her. In fact, not too long ago I met a woman who'd had a reading with my grandmother when she was a young girl. Her mother had taken her to Grandma because of seizures and, as she proudly told me, after that visit she never had another one.

I was overjoyed that here was an actual person who had been touched by my grandmother. I asked this woman to send in a validation if she could—of course in those days there weren't tape recorders like there are now, so people relied on their memory or took notes. I remember this Jesuit priest who used to come to Grandma and the black journal he had in which he wrote down everything she said. I wish I could read that journal now, as it would be fascinating.

My grandmother would usually work with people from nine in the morning to around noon, but if there was a serious case, she'd go till later in the afternoon. When she finished, she'd hang out a sign she'd crocheted that said No More Business Today—Come Back Tomorrow at 9 O'clock. I remember feeling so relieved when I saw this sign, because that meant we could play or she'd tell me stories.

Grandma didn't use crystals, tarot cards, or astrology in her readings . . . it wasn't that she was against these things, but she felt that different people had different ways of using their ability. She was more for using yourself as a tube from God to bring information through. It's strange because she did grow up in a Victorian world of Spiritualism, table tapping, and séances; along with the Fox sisters, Madame Blavatsky, and so many other famous physical and spiritual mediums. She was very much into phrenology (the study of the face and head for mental faculties and character and personality traits) because she felt that who we were was etched on our faces. According to phrenology, people with small mouths and ears aren't generous; people with beady eyes are prone to lying; people with large eyes and lips are very sensuous; and on and on it went. No, it isn't an exact science, but many times I've found all of the above to be true, I'm afraid.

Grandma knew that I was going to be a trance medium and kept telling me that her voices told her so, as well as that I would be afraid at first but would get used to it. She herself never went into trance, but her brother and mother did. My grandmother was like Chris, my psychic son, in that she didn't want to let go. If Francine hadn't come into my body during a hypnosis class, I don't think that I would have wanted to let go either. Of course if I have to listen to that high-pitched voice for too long, I'd just as soon get out of my body and let my guide handle the questions and impart her knowledge.

Having someone coming in and talking with my voice box really repulsed me at first, and even today when I hear my office staff playing a tape of Francine, I ask that they turn it off. Nor can I stand to see myself in trance on video . . . it's just too weird because I have no memory of what transpires during these sessions, and I feel as if everyone else is having a party and I have to go to bed.

Francine used to come in for my ministers and research groups, but now she appears during my salons. Everyone remarks at the change on my face and how her demeanor is so different from mine. It's funny that when she first started to come into my body, she didn't understand our slang and would get confused. Once someone asked her how they'd do in a garage sale, for instance, and she replied, "Why would you want to sell your garage?" She used to be very literal, but as time has passed, she's apparently become more adept at speaking the way we in 21st-century America do.

I'd like to add here that in the 65 years since Francine first contacted me, I've never known her to frighten anyone or become too esoteric, or to give orders as to what to do. She, more than I, is the model of diplomacy. And when I went into trance for Montel Williams, he told me that it was one of the most spiritual experiences he'd been through in his life (bless his sweet heart).

Grandma and I didn't sit around and do readings on each other, but when I got older, she broke me in with her own clients. She'd have me stand beside her, and when someone asked her something, she'd look at me and say, "You take this one." At first I hated that . . . I can still see myself standing next to her chair so nervous that I thought I'd die. But then I'd just go for it when it was my turn, and her assurances gave me courage. She'd always squeeze my hand or look up and wink and smile to make me feel better. I wanted to please everyone, but I never wanted to embarrass her . . . if I ever did, I certainly didn't know about it.

As I got more validation, I became more confident, but my grandmother kept telling me, "Keep yourself out of it—if you're wrong, you're wrong. It's just God's way of letting us know that He is the only source that is always right." She also impressed upon me that under God's law, we could *never* divulge what went on between us and our clients, no matter what penalty might be hanging over our heads. I personally have heard so much in my life that could blow the lid off a lot of things, but I cannot and will not ever reveal them. A priest once told me that I was like him in that we'd never disclose who we talked to or what they talked about. People have offered me a fortune for my list of clients, particularly to find out about the celebrities I've read for. I won't even give them a single name.

Thank God I started doing readings before Grandma died, or I don't know if I would have had the courage. When she'd see the long line of folks waiting for her, she'd say, "Now we'll have fun!" When we were done, we'd celebrate by having a Coke. Then we'd play cards, sing, tell stories, talk about the day, and make dinner; and she'd invariably remark, "This was a good day, darling, a very good day—and tomorrow will be even better."

My grandmother was a teacher of parables . . . she was forever telling me stories with a moral ending, much like the ones Jesus himself taught. She believed that you had to be true to yourself, and although she wanted me to pursue a higher education, she wanted me to keep my psychic ability as well. But she *really* wanted me to focus on healing people's hearts—telling the truth the best I could and keeping a pure motive to rescue a soul's lost virtues.

Dealing with the Dead

While I couldn't help my grandmother with readings all
the time, I did try to do so after school, in the summer, and on
holidays. Whenever she came to stay at our house, she'd feel so
guilty because her clients needed her, so after a few days she tended
to go home.

Speaking of our house, my parents, sister, and I lived on
Charlotte Street in Kansas City, right next door to a house that
had once been owned by Diamond Jim Brady. Ours was a Queen
Anne–style home that had previously belonged to an old sea
captain, and it was 75 years old when my father bought it.

Grandma was so ahead of her time and a real "ghost whisperer."
She and I were both aware that the sea captain kept coming in and
out of the house and then ended up in the basement. After she
told me that he was trying to show me something, I followed him
down to the basement (with great trepidation) the next time he
appeared. He pointed to a smooth stone that stood out from all
the other rough ones, looking more like a drawer. I took a hammer
and cracked the mortar around the stone, and sure enough, there
was a cubbyhole with lots of papers in it. Yet as soon as air hit
them, they simply crumbled into dust. The captain must have
hidden some important documents in there, but unfortunately
time had destroyed them.

My grandmother and I later found a place in the attic where,
if you dropped anything down, it took well over a minute to hear
it hit bottom. Now I'm not a scientist, but that's a long way down.
And hidden in the rafters, we found books on the Ku Klux Klan that
we subsequently burned. But even with all of its idiosyncrasies, I
loved that house—and as crazy as it sounds, it loved me back.
I've lived in many places, but none of them have been home like
this one was. When I get down, my mind goes back to the attic;
my bedroom; the butler's pantry, where I used to write and hide;
and under the back porch, where I made a little fort, and I feel so
much better. Maybe it had a lot to do with Grandma Ada and her
blessings and energy, but whatever it was, that house on Charlotte
Street was my sanctuary.

Grandma and I went on to investigate the hauntings and paranormal activity in several other homes. She made sure that we both had a notebook in hand, and we'd walk through and not say a word to each other in order to prevent suggestibility from entering our psychic impressions. We'd write down what we felt, heard, or saw and then compare notes when we were done. We'd then try to corroborate our psychic insights through county records or old maps. For example, we once went to the Meyers residence and discovered an older woman haunting it. I immediately got her name—Edna Hamilton—and Grandma was so proud of me for picking this up. When we later researched information about the property, we found that indeed an Edna Hamilton and her family had lived in the house previously. Grandma and I were able to talk her over to the Other Side, and the haunting of the Meyers' place ceased.

I also remember going to the Scanlon residence, where objects moved around by themselves and loud thumping noises were routinely heard. The Scanlons had two children: a teenage son, and a daughter with Down syndrome. When my grandmother and I walked in, we sensed a deep depression and quickly found its source: the parents. They were convinced that their daughter was cursed, and their anxiety was causing an implant of similar energy. Grandma and I explained what an advanced spirit their daughter was and that their worry and negativity was creating a depressive atmosphere. We didn't feel that there was a ghost causing the movement of objects and thumping noises; rather, their teenage son was unconsciously causing these events.

Thanks to my research over the years, I've discovered that much of the activity attributed to poltergeists actually happens around teenagers and menopausal women. It turns out that their increased hormonal energy floods the atmosphere with estrogen or testosterone in an uncontrolled manner, which can manifest in what appears to be ghostly or paranormal activity.

I also have personal experience where this matter is concerned. When I was a pubescent girl, I used to fill journals (that I still have) with poems, many of which were downright depressing.

I even got an honorary box in *The Atlantic Monthly* magazine with this one:

> *Out of a night torn with a black, pitiless storm,*
> *A lark of sunlight and early morn was strangled in the wind;*
> *Where shall morning go without the lark's heralding cry,*
> *It will lock its small shafts of light and die.*

I'm sure a psychological study could make a lot out of that little ditty, but I really think I just felt confused and trapped. I'd started to see dead people in earnest now; whereas before the images had been vague and cloudy, at this point in my life they'd become crystal clear. I didn't mind so much at first, but then it seemed that the more I talked to these souls, the more others came to me. It was like, "Hey, we all have a telephone now, so let's chat!"

When I shared this with Grandma, she told me to tell any ghosts to go toward the white light to find God, and that really helped. (Again, "spirits" are those who have passed and made it to the Other Side, which most of us do without any problem. "Ghosts," on the other hand, have passed but haven't made it to the Other Side yet, which is the reason for most hauntings.) This ability came in handy later on when I'd investigate hauntings or when people asked me about their dead loved ones, because I could see and talk to them, thereby helping both the living and the dead.

Death used to be the hardest thing for me to deal with. As I've already related, I saw the faces of my two great-grandmothers run when I was very young, and I've always taken the deaths of my loved ones hard. Grandma tried to soothe me with literature, asking, "Do you remember the famous lines that say when you're born, you cry, because you've come to this hard learning place; but when you die, you smile and are young and healthy again, but everyone else weeps?" But she also confided to me her feeling of loss when her brother, Henry, died at the age of 96. She said, "It was a shock [at 96?], and I had a good cry when I got to my studio." (This is what she called her meditation place.)

Below is a letter she wrote me right before she and Brother went to Oklahoma to bury Henry, and it talks about a good friend of hers, Mr. Barker:

> *March 26, 1950*
> *Sylvia Celeste Shoemaker*
> *My Darling,*
>
> *It has been said that a student gathered knowledge but not wisdom—but you, my heart's love, are gathering <u>both</u>. Something of sweetness, something of God, dear one, is better for thee!*
>
> *The death of Uncle Henry was a shock to us all, yet not unexpected. When your mother told me, I would not allow myself to cry until I reached my "studio," and then Brother tried to comfort me. Rest in peace, Henry—awake in joy. How often we have heard people say, "Poor Jane (or Joe) is dead—the poor thing died"? Well, why pity them? They should rejoice that the dead are free from suffering.*
>
> *I think I will have to get a private secretary—it seems like I write as much as three letters a day. Now I have something funny to tell you about Mr. Barker. He is in my studio <u>every day</u> one to three times. He is very respectful—while I was sick but not in bed, he found out and came in with a 1/2 gallon or more of something with gilt labels, seals, etc. He placed it at my feet, and I asked what it was. He paused and said, "Beer." I said, "No . . . all those gilt labels, seals, etc., say that is expensive <u>wine</u>!" He did not deny it, so I said, "No! I do <u>not</u> want it—take it back and get yourself a new hat and clothes with it." I <u>made</u> him take it; after all, how could I preach temperance to him if I drank anything? No matter if I was sick, I would still refuse—it might encourage others to drink.*

For some reason, probably because she was very busy, the letter ends there and she forgot to sign it. I replied to her with the letter below—I was taking care of her birds while she was away, and as you'll read, I tended to be overly conscientious about ever hurting her feelings:

> *Dear Grandma,*
>
> *I miss you every day of my life. You are the most precious thing in life to me. I love you with all my heart. I miss you, but we will meet next Saturday. I will be lonesome till then, but you will come back and we will have the same fun again. Well, I hope you are fine. I liked your dinner. Tell Brother I think he is handsome and I love him very much. I love you, too, do you love me? I know you do. I'm sorry if I said anything to hurt your feelings—if I did, I'm sorry. Please write me a long, long letter because I'm lonesome to see you. Won't you call sometime?*
>
> *God bless you both and protect you, and I pray for you every night. I will take care of your birds and feed and bathe them and change their cages, so don't worry about them. I will go get that box from Mrs. Hopper, and it will be ready for you next Saturday. I had a pleasant time when you were here. I love to have you here—you bring happiness into our home. I love it just the minute you come in the house, you are both darlings. Tell Elmer hello and all your friends. Do get in touch with us, will you? Well, till then I hope you are all fine. I must go now, but take care of yourself and God Bless and keep you.*
>
> *Love,*
> *Sylvia*

As you can see, even as I entered my teenage years, I was as close as ever to my grandmother!

Chapter Three

THE MOTHER
I NEVER HAD

As Grandma Ada got older, her golden blonde hair turned snow white, but she still kept it long and swept up into the Gibson-girl style she'd favored much of her life. She moved with a slightly off-center step, and as I watch myself go on or off the stage when I'm on TV, I notice that I do the same thing. Yet although she couldn't walk for long distances, she was ambulatory until the day she died and never used a walker or cane.

When my grandmother was younger, she was 5'8" and slender; after she had her three children, her figure started to become more rounded. I'm built just like her . . . except that she stuffed her bra even into her 80s, which I have never had to do. It wasn't just Grandma's stature, though—her *presence* was larger than life, and when she entered a room, you knew she was there. She had such a striking demeanor that heads would unfailingly turn toward her. And, of course, her engaging personality always came out, especially in the stories she told and in her sense of humor that she never lost.

I used to ask her endlessly if I was going to be like her when I grew up. She'd simply smile and say, "You'll see." She said that so many people throughout the world would know me, and all I could do was laugh, since at that time I was merely a young schoolgirl in Kansas City.

But when I was little, Grandma *had* told me that I'd go to the West Coast, and I thought that this psychic prediction had already come true (my parents, Sharon, and I spent almost every summer in the Los Angeles area from the time I was 9 until I was 21). I do remember sitting at Nickodell's restaurant on Melrose (which is no longer there) and informing my father, "Someday I'll come here and people will know me." He smiled, patted my hand, and said, "Pumpkin, you can do anything you put your mind to." As I'd come to find out, life and our charts take strange twists and turns to get us all where we need to be. . . .

My grandmother loved to write children's stories that unfortunately never got published. But she didn't write for fame and fortune—she just loved all of life for the experience of it. As she used to tell me, "Enjoy the present because that's what it is: a *present*. The past is behind us, so it's to be learned from and nothing else. The future is also an adventure to get us closer to God." What a wonderful way to live: I try to be the same way and maintain a positive attitude, but I don't always succeed. Even though as I get older it does get easier, I know that I still haven't reached Grandma's level of evolvement.

If my grandmother made up her mind about something, she could be as stubborn as a bull, which would make sense if she were a Taurus; but while she did exhibit some traits of this astrological sign, her birthday was July 4, which is in Cancer. Her tenacity, loyalty, and love of home were decidedly Cancerian. Montel's birthday is July 3, and being a Libra, I seem to do well with water signs—Libra is fortunate to rise above a lot of the pettiness.

My grandmother loved religions, even the obscure ones. She said that all human beings should be free to worship God in their own way. And, of course, she pointed out that God loved everyone and understood everything about them, including their heritage, education, history, and culture—not to mention their charts. She read the Koran, the Bhagavad Gita, both the Tibetan and Egyptian Books of the Dead, and so on, but thought (as I do) that they made death too complicated. Birth can be such a traumatic experience that it's usually harder to get *in* to life than *out* of it.

Grandma Ada was very much into Leonardo da Vinci, long before author Dan Brown or the like was. She used to tell me that one day the information would come out regarding what a genius da Vinci was and how many secrets he held. When I'd press her for more, she'd just say, "You'll live long enough to see it" . . . and so I have. While my grandmother wasn't into conspiracy theories, she did feel that there were so many factions in our world that were organized by a hidden power. Now this was in the early 1950s, so she really could see far ahead. Grandma also believed that the world was on its last go-around, so to speak, and she could tell this by the plants, the climates, and the way the winds blew. While I didn't understand, I felt that she knew what she was talking about. It turns out that Grandma was right—as time has gone by, almost everything she predicted has come to pass.

My grandmother's thoughts and quotes are so profound, and it's amazing how her words echo in my soul at dark times. Through the letters that I'm sharing with you, may you also be touched by her wisdom and love.

Here, Grandma also mentions some simple treats like fresh watermelon and her famous hamburger hash. Now this may sound repulsive to you, but everyone who had her hash went crazy over it—I watched and even helped her make it so many times over the years, yet whenever I've tried to make it without her, it just hasn't turned out the same.

> *Aug. 28, 1950*
>
> *My Darling Treasure—My Sweetheart, Sylvia,*
>
> *Well, you certainly can write a fine descriptive letter. Dear heart, as you stood near to nature's heart, you had a keen sense of the beautiful. Do you remember I told you once about something that happened when I was out walking with my sister Lena? She and I were admiring a rainbow and the hurrying clouds heaped up in their immensity. We were thrilled—awed—by this beauty that belongs to God. When a neighbor came by and spoke to us, we called her attention to the clouds, etc. She looked critically upward and anxiously said, "It looks like rain and not a good wash day." How narrow . . . how down to earth.*

"Materialistic" souls can be so disgusting. Brother and I are up a little after 5 A.M. to watch the sun rise in all its splendor—oh, how beautiful it is. We also watched a lovely rainbow Sunday. You know that they are placed there after rains as a promise from God to us all that the earth will not be destroyed by water again. I saw every color but white and black in the rainbow—how wonderful the works of God are, yet we often see as through a glass darkly.

Barker was telling me of that grocery man here who can hardly see. He said, "If there is a God, why—why—did He make me half blind?" It was the cry of an unbelieving soul who wants to believe. But he is too earthbound, thinking of himself, to realize that we are the victims of our own carelessness or of the circumstances that surround us.

I admire your artistic love of nature—God's works are so uplifting that they make one realize He is behind it all, watching over those who love and obey Him. There is nothing so soothing or comforting to a disturbed mind than just to relax, watch the clouds, listen to the song of birds, or look at the flowers as they glisten with the morning dewdrops shining like jewels. Yes, love, your soul was in tune with the beautiful as you stood on the mountaintops admiring God's work—and I know He was pleased, as was the blessed Mary. They felt the door of your heart was open to Them and all that was pure, good, and uplifting. May it always be so, love—and while your arm is around the cross, reach down and help some other person reach the heights. It is not always easy to do this. A Christian life is a constant watchful struggle, but the good reward you get in every way is worth it when the end comes, and the soul passes through the door leading to heaven. Yes, I know if I stood on the mountaintops, I too would feel like an ant or sparrow—and God says He watches over them as well. To admire nature and all of God's work speaks so well of you, darling. Keep Sharon that way, too—talk to her and teach her to observe what is beautiful in life. If you aim high, you can't fall low; if you keep the laws of God, you will keep the laws of man.

Brother and I thank you so much for your sweet, beautiful words of love. But, darling, Brother has earned love—suffering as he has done all his life—yet I feel so <u>very</u> unworthy of anyone's love. It is love alone that rules the world, as we know, yet one can do wonderful things with kind comforting words. Men especially need this appreciation, as a rule. I think the whole trouble with my many lovers is that I grew spoiled. I had too many lovers, like going into a store and seeing too much of the articles there—you become bewildered and tired and do not know what to take or love, so you lose the man you <u>did</u> love.

I was not fickle or a flirt. I like to be loved, and I was delighted to have them say that they loved me. I suppose you think I was very hard-hearted—no, I was all the time gentle and ladylike. "She attended to her own affairs," they said of me. I never thought of flirting or trying to torture men's hearts, yet somehow I felt uncertain.

When I was in the hospital, I told a nun about my life and she said, "God has let you have these troubles in order to lead you into the Church." Strange but true. I once loved the Episcopal Church and worked hard for it, but my loved one was a Catholic and loved his Church. I lost my lover, and now I see where I was wrong: I was spoiled. Well, we are blind at times.

Do you know what I am going to do? I am going to order some ground beef and some homegrown watermelon, big and sweet, for you, and have it brought to your house. We will come over the next day and make hash and eat fine watermelon. How does that sound, my darling, my angel girl, love of my life? I did not get to see you much this year but hope to later. Kiss your dear parents and Sharon for us.

From Grandma Coil and Brother

As you can see, my grandmother was very spiritual. She'd been Episcopalian before converting to Catholicism, but she always kept her Gnostic ideals. She believed in a Mother God as well as a Father in heaven, which is certainly a modern Gnostic belief. She referred to our Mother as "Mary" instead of "Azna" (which is what my spirit guide Francine says is the Mother God's name on the Other Side) because she said that she was too old to change. She also felt that no matter what you called Mother and Father God, They still were who They were.

Grandma once briefly stated that she'd been visited by Mother God twice—once just after Paul had died of cancer and once around Christmas 1936, about two months after I was born. I say "briefly" because she wouldn't go into any details about either incident. In retrospect, I'd have to say that meeting our Creator would probably be an intimate and private event that few of us would share with anybody, especially if it was meant for our eyes and ears only. I do wonder if that second incident had something to do with me, since my grandmother became my beloved mentor—and the mother figure in my life—for the rest of her days.

Grandma and Brother would often stay over at our house, and I was thrilled when they were there. I was always aware that I might not have her long and wanted to soak up all her knowledge and love while I could. I was so afraid she was going to die, and she'd wave me off and say, "I'll be with you until you don't need me anymore." I railed against the fates that she had to be 70 when I was born. I thank God every day that I was only in my early 50s when I had grandchildren.

My grandmother was close to 89 when she died, and she never heard an ambulance without making the sign of the cross. You see, spirituality wasn't like a coat she'd put on and then take off; it was a living, breathing part of every aspect of her life. If things were good, she thanked God for the blessings. If things were bad, she thanked God for the lesson. Aside from the loss of her son Paul, I think that my mother was the greatest tragedy of her life. Since she was the middle child in her family, Mama always seemed to be moody and into herself growing up, or so Grandma Ada told me. She knew that earthly life was a test, so she thought that having a child like my mother taught her patience and tolerance. Grandma couldn't seem to make Mama be a better mother; even so, she never wanted me to be disrespectful or cruel. I wasn't, but I'd go in my room and punch my teddy bear to pieces. And when I wrote in my diary, I sure did vent.

My grandmother was very big on keeping journals and diaries, and I have a long shelf full of them that date back to when I was seven. I haven't kept up with my journaling in the last few years because my public writing has taken over in its place—and in a way, this has been a journal of my spirituality and research, along with the knowledge that I've garnered from talking to countless people for more than 50 years.

Life with Brother

I know that my grandmother spent a lot of time dealing with Brother, her eldest son. While he could eat and walk unassisted, his cerebral palsy made it so that his head would bob uncontrollably and he couldn't dress himself. When asked once if he was a problem, Grandma answered with some irritation that if it wasn't for him, she never would have experienced the wonderful talks (he had a brilliant mind) and fun they had together. There's where you turn lemons not just into lemonade but lemon *pie*. I never knew her to express anything other than the belief that everything could eventually be fixed or worked out. I've personally lived long enough to realize that even the tragedies in my life made me better or more spiritual, and that goodness often comes on the tail of the bad-luck dragon.

I was the apple of Brother's eye, and we often chatted for hours. He had a daily ritual of reading every single article in the newspaper. He also listened to all of the news broadcasts on the radio and loved the band concerts that they held at Troost Park each Saturday. One of my earliest memories, in fact, is going to these concerts with Grandma and Brother when I was around three or four. We'd get there, and Grandma would say, "Get up and dance, Sylvia." Can you imagine a three-year-old dancing down the aisle and even getting onstage . . . much to the chagrin of the band director? I'm sure that on the Saturdays we didn't show up, he thanked God.

I often went shopping with Grandma and Brother, too. Her favorite place was Woolworth's, which was a five-and-ten store that was very popular in the 1940s. She was always looking for thread and yarn and had no trouble arguing the sales clerk down in price. She was never cheap, because she'd come from wealth—but in these days of World War II, everything was tight. She told me that businesses always made enough or they wouldn't be in business, and coming from a mercantile background, she knew the markups.

Looking back, I see how if we'd just remember the little things we come into contact with every day, it would help us deal with the big things in life—particularly when it comes to being more understanding with each other. People would stare at Brother, for instance, and I'd stare back or ask them what they were looking at. Grandma told me that folks don't tend to look beyond the physical to the soul that resides within. These experiences with Brother gave me great respect for those who have any type of disability—after all, as I tell people today, only the very advanced soul picks a life with such a challenge, since a soul that isn't advanced would never be able to handle it. Think about all of the individuals you see who are gifted with great abilities and have everything, yet they flush it all down the drain of excesses in life.

I used to play checkers and cards with Brother until I thought my head would fall off, but I kept doing it because he loved it so much. He didn't get much enjoyment in life because he didn't get out much, and he was just terrified of stairs. The doctor said it was because his equilibrium was thrown off, and high places disoriented him. I was the only one he trusted to take him up and down the stairs, even though I talked 90 miles an hour. He'd squeeze my arm so hard I'd be bruised, and I could feel his fear of being out of control.

When I was younger, I was running with a curtain rod one day, and it caught on a rock and cut up half my palate. There I was, bleeding and screaming, but Grandma immediately consoled me and brought me inside to rinse out my mouth with salt water. But then I looked over at Brother and saw that he was shaking all over and his head was bobbing violently. From that time on, I tried my best not to upset him by getting sick or hurt.

As frail as my uncle seemed to be, his strength was there when needed. Before we moved to our wonderful home on Charlotte Street, we lived for a while next to a family that had a certifiably insane daughter. Unlike now, many families at that time took care of their own and didn't put their mentally ill in institutions. This girl, for example, had two nurses with her and was kept on the second floor of this house. However, there were bars on the window of her room, and at night, I could hear my neighbor howl.

I was just a little girl at the time, and one day I was sitting under a huge apple tree in the front yard, making a daisy chain like Grandma had taught me to do. All of a sudden Brother came rushing out the door toward me, and I'd never seen him move so fast. At that moment, I looked to the right and noticed that the crazy daughter, who had somehow gotten away from her nurses, was advancing upon me. Her fingernails were bared like claws, and I could see that her eyes were squinty and hard. Brother grabbed me, ran to the house, and closed the screen door behind me—and then he turned and stood in front of the door. Before the nurses were able to get her under control, she'd scratched up Brother pretty good, but she never got to me.

I loved my uncle's sweet soul. In fact, I remember when I was little and had to go upstairs to the bathroom. It was dark because there was no light on the stairs, and he stood down there at the bottom and talked to me the whole time so I wouldn't be afraid. You might think that this is such a little thing it's not even worth mentioning in this book, but it's a big, wonderful memory to me.

Always There for Me

Grandma and Brother both adored animals, and she actually had what I called the "St. Francis of Assisi ability." Even when my grandmother was gardening, which she loved to do (and I swear she could put a dead stick in the ground and it would grow!), animals would just flock to her: butterflies and hummingbirds would hover around her, and rabbits would be hopping at her feet. I have some of that, too, but it's nothing compared to Grandma.

My grandmother also raised canaries: she'd mate them, put the babies in handmade nests, and then sell them (yet she was always sad to see them go). Hartz Mountain even gave her a year's supply of birdseed, although they didn't understand how someone with "no knowledge of raising canaries" could indeed do just that, and so successfully.

Grandma had a favorite canary named Choo Choo who would sing its little heart out. And when she came to stay with us, she wouldn't let our cat, Lady, into the dining room because that's where Choo Choo would be. One day about noon, I heard Lady meowing at the back door. I closed off the door from the kitchen to the dining room and gave her some milk, not realizing that Lady could go from the kitchen into the hall and across the front room to the dining room. I went about playing until I heard a moan come from the dining room. When I opened the door, I saw Lady sitting next to my grandmother, who was holding a dead Choo Choo. She looked inconsolable, and I cried out, "Oh Grandma, I'm so sorry!"

She merely said, "I know, sweetheart." She never scolded me or anything like that, which I think actually made me feel worse. And although I saved for four weeks and bought her another canary, I'm sure it never took Choo Choo's place.

Grandma used to say that if you find anyone who hates animals, children, or music—run. She absolutely adored music— her favorite pieces were "Clair de Lune" and "Ave Maria"—and she had a beautiful singing voice all her life. (As I stated earlier, she and her two sisters were the toast of Springfield for their beautiful voices and harmony.) However, I remember once when I was about eight, I asked her why her voice cracked in the middle of the song she was singing. She looked at me with those china blue eyes and said, "Maybe it did, but it hurts people's feelings to point out defects, Sylvia." Yet another well-made point that has stayed with me over the years.

My grandmother really wanted me to become a performer. While she knew I couldn't sing that well, she hoped I'd make up for it in other ways. So every Saturday, much to my chagrin, we'd get on the bus or streetcar and go to Mrs. Gold's studio for an hour of tap dancing . . . and then get on another bus or streetcar to go see Mrs. Borserini for drama lessons. Then, of course, there were the annual recitals. Grandma would make my costumes and help me with my lines, and when I'd go onstage, I couldn't help but look for her eyes and the glow around her. I never felt that I needed her approval, since she gave me unconditional love, but I certainly wanted to show her that her investment in me wasn't for nothing.

I kept thinking that I'd be in plays (which I was all through college) or perhaps movies when I grew up. Of course I've been performing in a different way for many years: before live audiences offering spiritual insights. So my grandmother was right to insist that I have that training when I was younger, which I'm sure she knew.

Grandma Ada had no prejudices against race, color, religion, or people's sexuality; but being raised in the Victorian age, she felt that a woman should keep herself pure until married. In fact, Grandma's home life was Victorian through and through, with all the manners and etiquette that went with it. While she became very modern as time went by, social amenities were never forgotten. Nevertheless, I used to wear short shorts and tube tops when I was young, and her remarks were along the lines of "If you have a beautiful body, show it off." This may seem like a paradox, but I'm sure she loved me so much that she knew without a doubt that I had social graces and morals.

My grandmother helped me with so much when I was growing up, and not just psychic issues. When I started my period for the first time, for instance, I thought that I'd really hurt myself. I was frantic because Mama had never told me anything about menstruation or a woman's cycles. Thank God Grandma was around—she made it a proud thing by saying that now I was a woman and had come through a rite of passage in life. If she hadn't been there, I probably would have gone into a full-blown anxiety attack and been convinced that I was bleeding to death.

It seems that the pendulum of morality can't hang straight: it either has to swing wildly to the right or the left. Nowadays it's clear over to the left, but I have a feeling that it will eventually center itself with increased spirituality. That era of the late 1940s and the 1950s was wonderful and innocent on the one hand, but the pendulum was also all the way over to the right in that many of us who were young at the time were kept in the dark. Whether it was ejaculation, menstrual periods, or the growth of hair in new places, we really didn't understand what was happening to our bodies . . . and we weren't supposed to, since none of this was ever talked about in class or at home. My mother viewed the subject of sex as especially distasteful, calling genitalia our "nasty parts."

I don't remember much of my mother growing up except for her cruelty—but luckily I had Grandma, Brother, and my dear father, so she receded into the background like a bad dream. My grandmother never would have allowed Mama to be cruel when she was around, and if they would have had a confrontation, my money would have been on Grandma because she could have eaten my mother for breakfast.

Grandma stayed close to her sister Annie, who was two years older than she was and lived in Hays, Kansas. (Lena, the eldest sister, had remained in Springfield, but she had arthritis and was confined to a wheelchair.) Strangely enough, Annie's son had also died at the age of 21, like my uncle Paul had, but from a burst appendix. She now lived with her daughter, who took such good care of her. We visited them from time to time, and I even occasionally helped out at their Western Auto store. While Annie was sort of haughty and not as warm as Grandma, she was still very kind to me.

Looking back, it must have been hard for Grandma: her sisters were quite a distance away; her husband had died; and she had one son with cerebral palsy, a dark soul for a daughter, and a psychic and spiritual son who died so young. She didn't talk about Paul too much, except to relate how he helped everyone and talked to God all the time.

Many years later, I went through her brown box that I'd inherited, and I found a folded piece of paper that she'd written on. It read:

> *There is a hole in my heart that will never be filled. You were so pure of heart, my sweet son, and I ache to hold you one more time. I know it was our chart and you are happy, but I am human and in a frail human form. Only my pillow at night knows my uncontrollable tears. I know that it was God's will, and may His will above all be done. . . .*
> *Your mother,*
> *Ada*

You wouldn't see such raw suffering to look at her, and if I ever brought up the subject, Grandma would say, "But look—God sent you, and when I look in your big brown eyes, I see Paul. So God gives back what we feel we've lost."

While she always felt that I was there for her, I don't ever remember a single moment that she wasn't there for me. Take the time I had my tonsils removed. When my mother and Grandma came to pick me up from the hospital, a nurse told them that I'd been up all night consoling a scared little girl named Katherine who was in the room next to mine. When I got home, I slept on my grandmother's lap for six hours—I'm told that when I finally woke up, she could hardly move. Imagine sitting still for six hours with a kid on your lap!

Grandma Ada just always seemed to have a sense of whatever I was going through. For example, when I was in second grade, it was my first year of school—I'd skipped kindergarten and first grade because Grandma had already taught me my colors and to read, print, and do math. But this is by no means an ego booster because I hadn't been acclimated to school or the social dynamics of it. I had to drop out midyear anyway because of an epidemic of diphtheria, although I didn't actually contract the disease. My grandmother had made an asafidity bag (which is used in folk medicine and stinks to high heaven) and hung it around my neck.

Clearly, the reason I never got diphtheria was because no one could stand to come near me!

Anyway, when I was in the second grade, there was a series of books involving the characters of "Dick and Jane" that the nun wanted to test me on one day after school. The page I was shown said, "Run, Jane, run," and I read it aloud. The next page also said, "Run, Jane, run," but I wouldn't say it this time. I don't know what happened, but nothing she could do would make me read the second page. The only thing I can think of as I've pondered it over the years is that I didn't want to read what I'd already read. In my mind, whether it was stubbornness or simply feeling that it was silly to repeat something, I absolutely would *not* read it.

The nun got her ruler out and cracked my knuckles, and then she pulled on one of my pigtails. (That was in the days when there was no prohibition against abusing a child in class, and I'm sure that many of you who went to Catholic school years ago will confirm what I say.) Even though it hurt and tears were streaming down my face, I still wouldn't read it. Rosie, our maid who was with us until I was 20, came to walk me home, and I cried all the way, holding my red and bruised knuckles.

I walked into the house with a red face and teary eyes, and Grandma instantly asked me what had happened. I said that I didn't want to talk about it, because I believed that in some way I had done something really wrong. When Rosie finally told her what the nun had done, my grandmother got a really tight-lipped type of look and put on her coat, gloves, hat (she always wore a hat when she went out), and of course a hat pin to hold it on. With me in tow, we walked back to the Our Lady of Good Counsel school in Kansas City (which is still there, by the way).

The nun was getting ready to lock up when my grandmother caught her by the arm. Looking like an avenging angel, she asked the nun why she had hit me like that. The nun said someone had to break my stubborn spirit . . . well, that did it. I caught only bits and pieces of their talk, since Grandma's voice was very low, steely, and determined. I did hear her tell the nun that she wouldn't see genius if it hit her in the face and that if she ever touched me again, she would report her to Bishop O'Hare, whom Grandma knew very well. The nun turned white, apologized to me, and indeed never hit me again. In fact, she acted as if I didn't exist most of the time.

Not only was Grandma protective of me, but if I was ever concerned about anything, she'd immediately say, "Sylvia, there's a question on your mind—do you want to talk about it?" I'd say no, but before the day was over I'd end up telling her. I knew that she was psychically aware of what I was going through, but she didn't want to interfere. (I'm like that now with my staff or the people I meet—as a psychic, there are things I could tell them, but I have to maintain an ethical stance of not infringing on their lives. Of course, if I see some trauma or tragedy that I can warn them about, I certainly will.)

I remember one day I came home from school so distressed because I wanted the part of Becky Thatcher in *The Adventures of Tom Sawyer.* Unfortunately, the nun in charge, Sister Frances, had said that while I was excellent, I was too tall. The second I walked in the door, Grandma asked me what was on my mind. When I mumbled that it didn't matter, she replied, "Maybe not to you, sweetheart, but it does to me." So I told her and she said, "Never mind now. I know you'll get the part—I just feel it." I went up to my room and thought that she was trying to appease me . . . no sooner was the thought out of my head than I heard the phone ring. It turned out to be Sister Frances calling to tell me that Maureen, the girl who was going to play Becky Thatcher, found out that she was moving so I now had the part. Grandma and I had a celebration that night with her famous hash, and she even gave me a little glass of Mogen David wine. I hate that stuff because it tastes like maple syrup, but she used to tell me that it was good for the blood once in a while.

Then there was the time that Grandma made me this leopard-skin-print blouse that was so lovely I wore it to a sock hop. This bitchy girl came up to me and made a snide remark about my blouse, and I ignored her. She came up to me again and said, "Whoever made that for you or sold it to you should be shot."

That was it! I took her by her ponytail and wheeled her around while she shrieked. Father Hicks, who had witnessed the whole episode, didn't do anything to me except smile and say, "I will never worry about you, Sylvia. No one will ever get the best of you." Later I heard that four other students beat the hell out of this girl for her mouth; and when I saw her at my 50-year class reunion, I noted that she had become an old, broken, and mean woman. Like Grandma always said, leopards don't change their spots (pun intended!).

Giving Me Life's Building Blocks

Even though my grandmother has been gone now for 55 years, sometimes it still seems like she was here just yesterday. She was such a force of nature that you'd have to lose your mind to forget her. So although I didn't have what I would consider a "real" mother, I did have the best female role model by my side for almost 18 years. No, that wasn't enough time for me, but I'm sure that she stayed long enough to give me the building blocks of my life. It's hard to ever find that kind of selfless love, so no matter how long it lasts, hold it fast because it's as close to the Other Side as we'll get here on this hellhole of a planet.

Grandma believed that Earth was hell, too, but she also believed that you could make anything bad better. As she used to say, "Keep your eyes upward, not down. Stand tall and look up—that's where the sky and trees and birds reside, not down in the rocks and mud. This applies to all of life . . . there's the promise in the sky of another day that could bring happiness and joy." Grandma was always telling me to be brave and keep my focus on what was real. She must have known—both psychically and from experience—what a tough road it is, but she'd add that it would bring me great joy, and so it has. We all have to experience sorrow to appreciate joy.

In the fall I remember Grandma showing me leaves; in the spring, it was the birds; in the winter, the shape of snowflakes; and in the summer, the wavy mirages of heat. There was nothing in nature that escaped her. If she'd been born in another place and time, she would have been a shaman, fakir, or avatar; but because she lived in Missouri in the middle of the 20th century, she was an anonymous lady who had a great gift that helped lots of people.

I missed her so much when she went home that I'd count the days until I saw her. We wrote each other a lot, and I liked sending her cards and handmade valentines. Here are a few of them that she saved from when I was about five or six:

It would be smooth sailing
If you were my Valentine

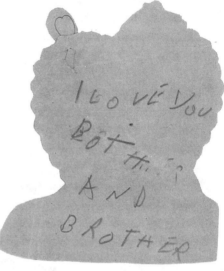

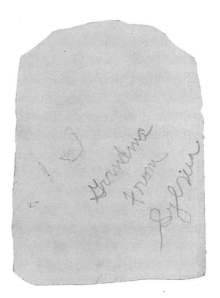

It was very common in those days to cut off pieces of hair as a remembrance, and Grandma kept this card as a keepsake:

The problem I often ran into when I wrote my grandmother was that my mother wouldn't give me a stamp. (Thankfully, Rosie would mail them for me.) Mama was so dark that she often went through my things and felt no compunction about stealing. That's why to this day, my sister and I never leave our purses anywhere— our mother would constantly go through them and take anything she wanted. She would deny doing so, of course, but we caught her several times, and she remained amoral all of her life.

Here is a Christmas card I sent Grandma, which speaks for itself. As you can see, I was very young at the time:

This is just a small indicator of what life was like with my mother. I only bring it here to show everyone the paradox of dark and light, which I'll cover in more detail in the next chapter.

❀ ❀ ❀

⇥ *Chapter Four* ⇤

CUTTING THROUGH THE DARKNESS

My grandmother was highly attuned to negative energy, which tends to be brought on by a lot of dissension or fighting. You see, things that are traumatic in nature—such as murder, suicide, and abuse—can leave an energy imprint so strong that it makes you sick. So before you buy a house, thoroughly explore how you feel about this potential residence. Similarly, when you're looking to purchase *any* object (especially if it's an antique), note how you feel when you touch it. If you find that you can't breathe well, you become nauseated or faint, or you get an immediate sensation of apprehension or depression, then it doesn't matter how beautiful the item is . . . don't bring it into your home.

Grandma also believed, as I do, that other people can drain you and cause you to become ill. It's a medical fact that some folks who have cancer or other severe diseases have found that when they get out of a negative environment, they're cured more often than those who go back to such a place. I remember this friend of mine who owned the famous Norfolk Hotel (where Ernest Hemingway, Teddy Roosevelt, and other notable men and women have stayed) in Nairobi, Kenya. He was married to a very unpleasant woman and under unbelievable stress. He contracted lymphoma, which is usually deadly—yet soon after divorcing his wife and turning his business over to his son, he made a complete recovery. I hear hundreds of stories like these in my readings, so I know that getting rid of negativity has definite merit.

My grandmother said that negativity was deflected by living things such as animals and plants because they're God's pure creations. She was always quick to tell her clients who were experiencing abnormal activity to bless their homes at least once a month. Like me, she felt that if you clean your house and yourself, why not do a *spiritual* cleaning as well, since negativity can come in from everywhere. I remember Grandma going through every room in our home with a crucifix, but I go further than she ever did.

I bless everyone in my own home with virgin olive oil, making the sign of the cross and telling them to surround themselves with the white light of the Holy Spirit and to call on all the angels (especially the Thrones, Principalities, and Archangels), as well as Jesus and Mother and Father God. Next, I go through each room and sprinkle it with holy water, while making the sign of the cross with a crucifix. (You can make your own holy water: place a bowl of water outside in the sun for three hours, and every hour go out and make the sign of the cross over the bowl—you now have holy water.) Finally, I go around the whole outside perimeter of my house and sprinkle salt, again making the sign of the cross with a crucifix.

I also have the Star of David in my home, a mezuzah at the front door, a statue of Buddha in my family room, and a cross in every room; in fact, I have a collection of crosses from all over the world. I'll also burn a white candle on the third hours (12, 3, 6, and 9) of the day because these are the trinity hours. Of course I don't do these rituals every day, but I do them from time to time to protect and bless my house and its visitors. Over the years I've discovered that I know when the negativity has built up to the point where a cleansing is needed.

My grandmother believed that water dispelled negativity, which is why I have a small fountain in my home. She, bless her, made her own in her one-room tenement, with some help from a friend of hers who lived down the hall. It would splatter sometimes, but it did work and was quite soothing. (If I ever get enough time, I'd like to have a Chinese garden with running water.)

But going beyond our possessions and surroundings, Grandma liked to stress to me that we should always try to *be* as positive as possible, since thoughts are things. To illustrate her point, she told me a dramatic story about a husband and wife who lived next door to her in Springfield when she was first married. The wife was very spiritual and had hung a beautiful crucifix over the bed she shared with her husband. He, however, was an adamant atheist and wanted the cross to come down. Even though women didn't often stand up to their husbands in that day and age, this lady wouldn't give in. When she later got pregnant, the couple began to fight about how their child should be raised. The husband wanted no word of God spoken and became even more rabid about the crucifix, screaming out at one point, "I hope our child never sees any religious artifacts!" Their daughter was born blind, which was most likely a coincidence . . . or was it?

The husband ended up converting to Christianity, and he even went on to become an esteemed bishop in the Anglican Church. Grandma said that God works in mysterious ways—while He didn't cause the blindness, maybe the entity that came in as this couple's daughter chose to be blind in order to wake the father up. The girl did go on to become a teacher to the blind, and she married and had three children who could all see just fine.

Now I don't mean to scare you and have you be overly concerned about every thought you have. Even if your spouse leaves you and you're so despondent that you wish a truck would hit him or her, that's just a human reaction to pain, and it's temporary in nature. But if you consciously try to direct evil and negativity to another person with the intent of inflicting harm, you're in trouble. Always remember that what you send out in your thoughts will come back to you a hundredfold.

Grandma used to say, "Send out good thoughts" and told me that the more we concentrated on emitting our healing energy, the more effective it would become. Sending out these types of thoughts wouldn't interfere with anyone's charts (including our own), because if it wasn't in our charts to do this, we wouldn't think of it . . . just like a fashion model wouldn't all of a sudden decide to become a lumberjack.

Taking on the Skeptics and Naysayers

Once when I was young, Grandma was having a hard time with Brother. (Every so often his nerves just went, causing his head to bob uncontrollably, and she'd give him herbs and rub his neck.) I, for some reason, was really sick to my stomach that day, but I didn't want to cause her more stress. So I crawled under the porch to lie on the floor of the little refuge I'd fixed up there. I liked this spot because no one knew where I was—I'd never told anyone about my secret place—and when I went there I could really listen to Francine, whom I was somewhat getting used to. I was lying there for about 30 minutes hoping that I wasn't going to throw up, when I saw Grandma's head poke in. She said, "Come out of there and I'll make you feel better."

She took me inside and mixed up some nasty-tasting stuff that I dutifully drank, and sure enough, in a few minutes I was better. I asked, "Grandma, how did you know where I was?" She just looked at me and calmly replied, "I followed the trail of your spirit." It took me years to figure out what that meant, but I understood it when I started helping police with crimes or looking for missing persons. I'd zoom in on the individuals' soul or essence, and I'd start to get a feel for their tracks or how they died. Have I always been right? No, but as many detectives will tell you, I've been more right than wrong—yet I never want my work with law enforcement publicized, and it's always pro bono.

Grandma used to tell me, "You will go through skepticism and cruelty as you do your good works, but the world will turn around if you just stand tall and weather it. Look only to the good you do and your motives; if you do this, you'll make it through any verbal crucifixion." God knows there has been some of that, but my faith truly sustains me, as do the people who write me letters or e-mail me to say that I saved their life or that of a loved one.

Grandma wouldn't put up with skeptics: if someone tried to test her, she'd just shut them down. She'd tell me, "You won't convert them, and you'll end up wearing yourself out for nothing. Besides, there are too many people who really need you."

Even so, she did have her detractors, a group of religious zealots called "the Way." While they weren't atheists like some of mine are—I believe they were Protestants, but I don't know for sure—they might as well have been for the judgment they passed out. (Whatever happened to Christ's words: "Judge not, lest ye be judged"?) Members of this organization would go to the people in line to be read or healed by Grandma and tell them that she was just in it for the glory, or that she was a witch and in league with the devil. She ignored them, but I knew it hurt her very deeply at times . . . particularly since she was trying to do something for God and humankind and certainly not for material gain.

Grandma also once had a problem with a Catholic monsignor who threatened to denounce her. When he came to tell her that she was doing the devil's work, she reached over and touched his shoulder. He asked why she'd done that, and she replied, "Your shoulder is torn in the muscle." He stared at her and then exclaimed, "It doesn't hurt anymore!" This monsignor later demanded that all his priests visit Ada Coil if they had any sort of malady.

My grandmother would often tell people to beware of storefront fortune-tellers. She'd say that all they did was take innocent folks' money and scare them by insisting that they were cursed. That's good advice even today—always be wary of any psychic who says that you're cursed but they'll gladly remove that curse for a price. I've cooperated with several police departments and district attorneys who have exposed scam artists who were actually using my name to bilk the public; unfortunately, many times when you catch and convict one, another crops up. But I will keep fighting . . . just as I will always try to point as many people as I can to the bright light of our all-loving Mother and Father until the day I die, like my grandmother before me.

❧

I once wrote Grandma Ada to confess how nervous I was to one day go public with my psychic gift. I was afraid to be wrong, I felt unworthy, and I didn't want to be a spectacle. Why couldn't I just live a normal life rather than be subjected to naysayers and branded crazy? I have read and reread her response to me many times, and if you've attended my lectures, you'll hear some familiar statements and instantly understand where my whole philosophy came from. Of course you can hear words in this life but not live by them, so I felt fortunate that no matter how afraid I was, I not only heard my grandmother's advice, but I fully embraced it, too.

The underlying message here is that no matter what you go through, if you give your life to others and forget your own sorrows, God will always see you through. If you forget yourself and take care of others, that is the way to spirituality, love, and health. And having lived for almost 73 years, I can tell you that this really works.

When you read this letter, you can see that Grandma really spells out the strife that I'd endure, as well as how I'd get through it. It may be somewhat cryptic, but you can still see how much she was trying to encourage me to get out and expand my gift:

> *September 7, 1951*
>
> *Miss Sylvia Celeste Shoemaker, my heart, loved one,*
>
> *You have no birthday as yet, but these lines are running through my head: "What shall I wish for thee: Ask for thee sweet skies that are brightest and best? In life for you, honey, with lots of fun and money? But you will find at the end of your childhood's days, something of sweetness, something of strife at times, dear one, was better for thee."*
>
> *You may ask, "What kind of strife?" Well, to remain good and avoid evil. In life, we rush from one thing to another like a child trying to catch a butterfly—when it has caught the butterfly, it just tries to catch another. There is but one way to happiness, and that is forgetfulness of self—to cultivate an unselfish disposition and try to make others happy. There is one thing above all: lay your burden upon the Lord; pray and <u>trust</u>*

God to answer your prayer for your nervous, timid habit of being afraid. Why, darling, should you fear anything when your (and our) prayers wing themselves out to the throne of God and are answered? But, love, you must have <u>faith</u>—heaped up, pressed down, and running over, as it is said—and then all these fears will pass away like dark clouds. When they part, revealing the glorious light of heaven, the sun—and the Son—will come into your sweet pure life and heart.

And soon you will look back to these storm-tossed days and tangled threads of life and note that things are so calm and placid. Just know that with God's help and your prayers (and ours), you can win and control your fears. In life we stand and fight our battles alone if we ignore the hand of Christ stretched out to help us. To try to fight our nerves and fears alone cannot be done well without prayers. If we are to avoid our physical, mental, and spiritual ailments, we must be <u>nearer</u> to God—in our thoughts, words, and deeds. We must have forgetfulness of self.

When anything frightens or disturbs you, love, just say, "Why, what have I to fear? I am the child of God—did He not promise to protect and guide me always, even to the end of the world and life?" Pray to God every time you are nervous or afraid: "Help me, God, to know that You will guide and protect me—help me. I know that You will keep Your promise to those who love and worship You, but please help my disbelief and make me strong, fearless, and safe—<u>guide</u> me and mine always." And Sylvia, when you pray at night, be sure to pray for your loved ones at home as well as those who govern your country— Christians and our blessed Church. We must remember to say that we worship God, trusting and loving the Lord always.

Now this is as true as God's stars or world above us. When our nerves are disturbed, there is just one reason for this: we are holding too fast to earthly, material things. We are too self-centered and think too much of gloomy thoughts. We must cast dull care aside and help some other sorrowing heart to be happy and comforted, and then we will find the peace that the world cannot give or understand. Then when we look back to the sad days that have gone, we will know that it was all for the best, in some way and some time. That is why we have prayer—so that God will guide and help us.

We will just trust Him—love Him above all else. It is a strong thought of mine that every living soul wants to be appreciated and noticed, but as the poet says, "For our own we use the harshest word, yet we love our own the best." Why, I wonder, do we speak harshly to, let's say, our mothers. Did you ever notice the sad pleading look in a mother's eyes when a harsh word is spoken to her, a woman who is a living sacrifice for her children? Oh, those harsh words . . . in later years, memory will hurt us awfully and we will long for her when she has passed on. And, oh, the peace it brings us when we think of the sweet and encouraging words and deeds—and the kind, thoughtful, unselfish acts of help we gave her to keep her from worry and trouble. God sends His blessing and help to us to do our best and learn the rest.

Now, darling, forgive this letter if it sounds dull and sad. I try not to be, and I wish for you to avoid troubles that come. Dear God has blessed you with all of the gifts—beauty, wit, wisdom, grace, tact, etc.—that are good, true, pure, and honorable. He has given you a father who is a good provider and an angelic mother of noble birth. You have all of this—and they have given you a chance to get a good education, lucky girl—and a lovable sister, too.

Now what is it that troubles you and causes you to be so nervous or sad? Be careful, because these thoughts are chiseling themselves upon your face and manners. Each day will stay there if you continue to have this troubled look on your face. The face is the mirror of the heart and soul, and you cannot be beautiful when frowning or sad. What you cultivate of yourself in your younger days will stay with you. When you are older, it can cause you to win love or lose it—along with the respect of others. No wife can hold the love of her husband if she lets her words be wreathed with complaints and her face be subject to

angry or sad looks day in and day out—and it certainly would
not bring sunshine to those who love her.
   God bless you, darling, we love you dearly—
   Ada Coil

In one of her last letters to me, Grandma said that there will always be those who hate who I am and what I do. If these individuals don't have the hatred of races, creeds, heritages, or beliefs to focus on, then they'll turn their attention to other subjects, such as psychics. She told me that we have to be patient with those who condemn, but I'm not patient with people who judge.

My grandmother could spot dark or gray-souled entities better than anyone I have ever known—certainly better than I can, or I wouldn't have made so many mistakes in my marriages. Yet she always told me that "those who love you always will, and those who don't, won't—but the world will see your heart." I've tried to keep her words in my mind, but whenever I'm attacked, it hurts. When someone tries to do good in any field and then becomes a target for negativity, you wonder why that is. I must admit that in many cases, it's beyond me—but then if you think about it, it's a learning experience. I look at Montel, who is one of the best people I know, yet he also has mean and spiteful things written or said about him. We've been friends for almost 20 years, and I've never known him to hurt anyone. He gives freely of his own money to help so many with his good works, and while the press may not know about it, I know—and so does God.

Similarly, you may be aware that Shirley MacLaine and I are friends because she tells people and has even contributed to my newsletter. What a fantastic, spiritual, moral, and brave woman she is! She stepped out in the forefront of the New Age field at the same time I did, and like me, she's borne the brunt for those who came after us. This isn't because we're so great; it was just in our charts. Shirley has had some fantastic adventures, such as going to Tibet in her search for spirituality. What a wonderfully bright light she is in this sometimes dark world, and God knows that she is psychic herself—she doesn't come out and admit it, but she even blows me away. And boy is she tough . . . she doesn't suffer fools and won't put up with anyone making fun of her beliefs. She is one gutsy broad, and time just makes her more beautiful.

Then there was Bob Williams, my professor who encouraged me to open up a foundation. After he died of AIDS in the 1970s, I did just that, in memory of him. And other kindred spirits such as Montel and my dear publisher Reid Tracy at Hay House came along years later. I'm convinced that so many wonderful people have come into my life because of Grandma, whose chart was so closely wound into mine. In this way, she ensured that opportunities abounded for me and I received encouragement long after she was gone.

Nobody's Perfect

Now I don't want you to get the idea that my grandmother was perfect or even that I thought she was. She did have a temper— which no one would ever forget if they talked down to her as if she were dim-witted or stupid. I once saw what she called her "naughty fault" in action when Daddy came home one evening and said, "Hi Ada, are you still here?" Without a word, she got up, put her coat and hat on, and was out the door.

I'd learned to drive by that time, so I went out and jumped in the car. I found her walking toward the streetcar, and I pulled up next to her and said, "Grandma, please get in. He didn't mean anything by that." I knew that my father had just made a throwaway observation, but she felt that he was saying she'd stayed too long, which was something she never wanted to do. She wouldn't be reasonable; it must have taken me a good 30 minutes to convince her to get in the car with the promise that my dad would apologize.

When we finally got back to the house, I told my father why she'd left and explained that he'd have to tell her he was sorry. He replied, "I will . . . but for God's sake, it was just a remark." Daddy did apologize, and all went well. Grandma told me later that she didn't know if it was her disposition or her pride, which she said she fought, but she'd always been like that. I hadn't seen it before, but I certainly saw the royal von Banica bloodline rear its head that day.

Yet I have to say there is some of that in me, too. If I'm out with you and you look at your watch a few times, I'm gone. I feel that if you're looking at your watch that much, you're either bored or you have another appointment, so there's no point in my sticking around.

Even though my grandmother and I were so close, there was a time or two when we had a misunderstanding. These letters explain one such rough patch we hit when I was 14, and my parents, Sharon, and I were spending the summer in California:

Thursday, July 26, 1951

My beautiful mistaken darling—Paul's "alter ego"—Sylvia,

Well, of all things, my sweetheart, I want to remind you that no pain, burden, care, or even death itself could control or make me cease loving <u>you</u>, Sharon, your mother, or Brother. If you all even brought a disgrace on your mother's ancestors—who never had a skeleton or disgrace in the family—if you brought the first disgrace on our family name, even <u>then</u> I would love you <u>better than anything next to God.</u>

Now I want you to stand before the judge of a woman's soul—me—in the case of a young lovely girl and her grandmother. Once upon a time, an old lady and her son happened to have the luck of being grandmother and uncle to this sweet maiden, who at times acted cold and bored when they were at her lovely home. The grandmother found the maiden deeply interested in the girlfriends who were in her home, and she felt as lonely as a wallflower at a dance or a wet hen after a rain. The grandmother thought her usual decision when those she loves are happy: <u>I am happy, I want each one to enjoy themselves as they think best.</u>

Then the last time this tiresome old-fogy grandma was at this beloved maiden's house, she came downstairs, her lovely face distorted with a frown of boredom and displeasure that took all the beauty out of her face—and made the grandmother feel like she was talking to a very unhappy girl. She thought of the poem "Beauty like the morning rose vanishes—with angry thoughts, the hot sun scorches the rose." The grandmother wondered why must she be greeted so—was it true that old, aged people grow tiresome?

I know that young folks would rather be alone, and it is natural. I was not irritated or angry in any way—but it has been my life's habit to be careful not to annoy, or become "too numerous" or tiresome to people. If I think that they're tired of me, I simply try to be tactful and stay in my place until I'm shown that I'm not in the way . . . your letter made me so glad, darling. I may not show any of you how much I love you—perhaps you will never know or understand me or my great undying love for you all and God. I would gladly lay down my life to make you happy or save you in any way. I hope you will never doubt my love "Till the sun grows cold / And the stars grow old / And the leaves of the Judgment Book unfold."

Oh dear, the children downstairs are bothering me as I write and try to think—they are fussing here wanting me to make them each an apron out of their cloth. If there is anything they need—from a penny to a dollar or a pin to a thresher—they come to me, even with my sore fingers, etc. I will write again when alone. These children are tiresome at times. I love you— love you always.

Love,

Grandma Coil and Brother

Sunday, July 29, 1951
Dear Sylvia,

As I have four letters to write, I will write just a short one this time, love—my love—my sweetheart. Dream girl, I am sending you, Sharon, and your mother each money to spend and have a good time. My prayers (and Brother's) in church and at home, night and day, is for all of your safety and pleasure. Stay out there as long as you can, dear, as things here are in a dreadful condition. [There had been a terrible flood in the area right at the time of her writing me this letter.] *The ones who lost their homes—one thousand families—want to use the schoolhouses here for their apartments. Of course we think they won't get them, but I doubt if the schools will open soon, as there is so much confusion here now and water, etc., on the streets. Barker said that the drains are doing better, but the boxes, etc., are stacked up high. So many people have been out of work, but it is gradually getting normal again.*

Sweetheart, I am so ashamed of that last letter I wrote to you. Destroy it—forget it—I had so much to bother and go wrong with us, especially when I think of how unselfish you have been—taking so much of your time to take care of Brother and help us have such a good time. I think in my last letter you might think that I was greedy—selfish—jealous of your attention . . . well, I think we are so when we love anyone as dearly as I love you and your mother and sister. God bless you all. You will never know how Brother misses you all and talks and dreams of the happy moments you have given us. Thank you, darling, and forgive us if we hurt you in any way—I will write you a nice letter later. Love—my love—good night.

Grandma and Brother Coil

❄

Wednesday, August 1, 1951
Sylvia, my precious darling,

Words cannot describe my great sorrow when I began to read your sweet letter. I would gladly take a hard kicking if it could remedy the deed my ugly letter made—bringing tears and trouble to your beautiful eyes. I never did doubt your love for <u>us</u>, darling. For the first time—the <u>first time,</u> mind you, <u>in my life</u>—I woke up to the knowledge that the green-eyed monster—jealousy of your attention to your sweet girlfriends—had taken possession of your letter from me. Yes, I had myself "on the carpet" and found out that your grandmother Coil was jealous—yes, <u>jealous</u>—of our beautiful Sylvia and your attention to others. Now I guess this will seem ridiculous and silly—maybe you will think that it was caused by old age, but that is not true.

My intense love for you has made me so jealous of you and followed me all through the years. I have never doubted your regard for us, but even Christ said that our God was a jealous God. I hate to confess this fault of mine, and I know not what to do about it—this jealous feeling—I must confess it to the priest, perhaps he can recommend a <u>severe</u> punishment.

I have an idea that trouble has taken possession of all of you even though the lips are silent and grow white with the heart's despair about your father's unfaithfulness to all of you. Sylvia dear, do not worry about anything, especially the wrongdoings of someone else—Dad—which all of you are trying to keep from me. The watchful eyes of those who love you can read between the lines and can read the sorrow in your and your mother's eyes—which for so many years you have tried to shield. Forgive the wrongdoings of your father—it is like a constant drop of water that wears away even a stone.

Always remember: in every heart, there is a sorrow; in every sweet rosebud, there is a worm, as the Scottish poet said. The wrongdoer, God help him, will suffer more than you, for the mills of God grind slow but exceedingly fine. Someday, when the home scenes change—when children's voices have gone to make homes for themselves, as is natural, and only memories greet *him in the lonely home that once echoed the voices of fun and frolic to greet him—all will be silent and lonely. Even his wife, like a silent angel or saint, will be a constant reproach to him— silence speaks louder than words. Conscience, ye gods, makes cowards—restless human beings. A lifelong remorse—misery, regret, sorrow—nothing can ever erase that. The punishment will come, and God help him—this person needs pity then as well as now, for what will come in his thoughts and conscience speaks louder than words to all for what he has done. Every tear or sorrow to others will land like a millstone around his neck. I hope it will not ruin his life.*

God must be the great judge—we must have pity; patience; and a sweet, kind, forgiving attitude for those who have been hurting us. One person can be like a pebble or rock thrown into a stream—how it stirs the water—circles go 'round, and where it stops, no one knows. This person's evil deeds hurt others around him, but eventually the result will return to him and he will reap the results in a whirlwind harvest of despair and all the emotion of a sin-sick soul. God alone can comfort him, but the suffering will be there as long as life lasts him. For all this we make ourselves sick and wrinkled—we have no right to seek revenge and punishment for the wrongdoer. If we could look into the hearts of sinners or those who wound us, we'd see more to pity than to punish or condemn.

In a way, your father has tried to atone for his conduct— sin—by giving you a lovely home, clothes, etc., but the heart wants something more. A true, pure life; faithful and devoted alone to his God, family, and country; is above reproach to be sure. But, darling, life is not a bed of roses—every family and every heart will know its own bitterness. If life were a bed of roses, we might forget God. Now, dear, you are so young for life's burdens. While you must always expect them, darling one, pick up the tangled threads of life and weave them into a God-like pattern of love and forgiveness. Be a comfort to your suffering mother, who endures more in silence for the sake of her beloved children—ease her burden and so prolong her valuable life. A crippled mother can be more to you than a walking father, but as he works to support you, never allow him to know you do not love him—that will drive him farther away from you. Show him a glad delight, kiss of forgiveness, and fond word of love, and regret when he goes away to work for you all.

Bill lacks self-control—firmness. You can never keep him, or make him repent with anger—scorn, angry looks, or words of hatred or reproachful coals of fire. Use kind words and show him that you know he will be true and faithful. As our sainted boy Paul said lovingly to me once, "Mother, we can't do or go wrong because Sister and I know you <u>trust</u> us when we go out."

Show love—trust, faith, devotion—no matter how hard it is to do so, for you will have your reward of all that is good. There is so much good even in the worst of people, especially when they love as your father does you. He might make an immediate change in his life—ashamed of himself and his conduct—if he thinks you all trust, love, and care for him. Do not nag or reprove—a silent example of a Christian life will do more to reform than spite, etc. Give that hag of Satan's agent—that woman who has tried to win him from his family—plenty of rope and she will hang <u>herself,</u> not him or you. And remember, what is in your heart, let no one know—not to a friend a secret show, for when your friend becomes your foe, then all the world your secret knows. We are all players of the day, as on life's stage we play—what lies hidden behind your mask, yourself may only know.

All men as a rule sow their wild oats, late or early, but passion will burn itself out in time. When your dad sees the constant difference between a woman he found to be angelic, good, and sweet tempered and a lewd, vulgar whore who is generally a gold digger and avoids men who cannot give her the good things of life—he'll see that a woman like her is lower than a beast and worse than one, and the doors of hell will open for her. Do your best and leave the rest to God. Your dad has many good traits of character: he's tenderhearted, provides for his family, etc. And remember, this you need: love.

Grandma Coil

While Grandma obviously knew that my father had a mistress, she never seemed to judge except for cruelty and injustice. She was also very conscious of the fact that Mama would read my letters and have a fit if there was anything that remotely addressed the psychic, so she was very careful to almost write in code.

Grandma gave me the strength to know what my purpose in life was and what I was here for, but she also taught me not to get overly involved with myself or take myself too seriously because acclaim and fame are fleeting. She used to say, "When all else fails, you have your family and loved ones," and that is so true. I've never lost the people who were there for me, from a cameraman to a producer; from an understanding principal to a janitor. Like my grandmother said, all of these people have made up my life.

Although I didn't believe it at the time, she said that we've all had lives in which we were low and high, rich and poor, healthy and sick, and so forth—and this gives us all learning for God. Then she'd take me out at night when the stars were so big and bright and ask, "Don't you think that it's possible that we might not be the only life created? Look at the billions of stars up there, and realize that other life exists."

To be a good psychic, you not only have to have the ability but you also need to love people—and I truly do. I believe that humanity is made of all types of individuals: some are good, and some are very bad, but everyone makes up a montage of existence. Then we are like woolgatherers who can weave a tapestry of our life from the beautiful pieces and let the other parts fall away.

When people tell me they love me, I say from my heart, "I love you, too." I do what I do out of love, and I'm sure that if I didn't, you'd feel it. Even if I could somehow fool you all, the eye of the camera or my stage presence at a lecture would ferret me out. But absolutely nothing in the world can compare with the love I have for you. The light you all shine on me, and the world, truly cuts right through the darkness—for there is nothing more powerful than love.

≫ Chapter Five ≪

A VICTORIAN YET MODERN-THINKING WOMAN

As I go through Grandma Ada's letters now, I can see that they're like a manual for morals and correct behavior. Yes, she was concerned with encouraging my psychic gift, but this almost seemed secondary to her insistence that I become a lady and respect myself.

To that end, I just got through reading a letter dated March 17, 1952, in which she reminded me of the purity of the great and royal bloodline I came from, as she did so many times. She wasn't haughty; rather, she was very proud of our lineage . . . when at that time, I honestly couldn't have cared less. She also went on to tell me to enjoy my family and my youth because it was fleeting—such sentiments made me realize even then that I must try to live my life so that I wouldn't have any regrets. And she included this warning:

> *Don't get yourself involved too early, sweet girl. Marriage has its sweetness, but a career that means something to you and helps people and makes your forebearers proud is very important. It is noble to have a family, but, my angel, you are destined for great things, and a husband and children can stop your own desires. The saddest thing by word or pen is "it might have been."*

In rereading much of my grandmother's correspondence, I've found it a little amusing to see how formally she'd end her letters, even after she'd just poured out her love for pages at a stretch. Once in a while (and more so later on in life) she might end one to me with "Grandma Coil" or "Brother and Grandma Coil," but she usually signed off with "Ada Coil" or "Marcus and Ada Coil." I think this was her upbringing coming out subconsciously, since she was always aware of the nobility that she came from, and nobility tends to be very formal in nature.

In many ways, Grandma Ada was a paradox: caught between a Victorian lady and a modern-thinking woman. The only respectable things for ladies of that time to do were needlepoint and have babies, yet she discouraged me from getting married too soon. Still, Grandma was so pure . . . which reminds me of something that happened when I went with a boyfriend of mine, Warren, to get a haircut. Afterward, we stopped to get a Coke, and I decided to call home to check in. When my grandmother asked if I was having a good time, I said, "Oh yes. I went to the barbershop with Warren so he could get a haircut."

There was dead silence on the other end.

"Grandma, are you there?" I asked. When I still didn't hear anything coming through the receiver, I got a little worried and almost screamed, "What's wrong?!" All she said was, "We'll talk when you get home." This was so unlike her that I told Warren I wanted to go home right away. He was confused—and so was I —but I knew that something definitely wasn't right with my grandmother. I got home as fast as I could, full of dread as I ran up the steps of our house, wondering what I could have possibly done wrong.

I found Grandma in the kitchen making her famous hamburger hash. I'd always accuse her of putting some magical herb in it that I didn't see and she'd just laugh . . . but she was in no laughing mood just then. After I again asked her what was wrong, she turned and looked at me. Finally, in a quiet, measured tone, she asked, "Sylvia, how could you go into a male barbershop?"

I was aghast. "What's wrong with a barbershop?"

She replied, "It is the domain of men, and no young lady should let herself stoop to go into such a place."

I was dumbfounded, but told her that I was sorry and would never do it again. Since Grandma got over things immediately, she patted me on the cheek and said, "You didn't know, darling, and now you do." And that was the end of it.

I later learned that in her day, barbershops were where men smoked cigars and told jokes, many of which were off-color, and women were never allowed in this male sanctuary unless they were of ill repute. To try to explain to my grandmother that it wasn't like that anymore would have been useless. (Yet even today, believe it or not, when I take my grandsons to get their hair cut, I still feel a slight clutch in my stomach.)

I think that Grandma's strong reaction also stemmed from the fact that she didn't like Warren. She thought he was too loud and often crude, but she never said anything to me about it until I broke up with him—and, honestly, his loudness and crudeness (not to mention his drinking) got to me, too, especially at our young age.

Similarly, my grandmother didn't care for a certain friend of mine who lived down the street. She was always polite to this girl, but Grandma's mouth had a tight look whenever she was around her. When I asked her one evening why she didn't like our neighbor, she looked me in the eye and said, "Because she doesn't respect her own body, especially when it comes to boys." I didn't see that; in fact, I commented that if I was so psychic, why couldn't I pick up that information about my friend myself? I knew that she liked boys and parties, but I didn't think she was "loose."

That's when Grandma said, "Remember this all your life: You can tune your senses to feel good and bad, but you can't be psychic about yourself. Sure, your guide will give you messages, but you're here to learn like everyone else." I was irritated . . . but not two months later, I heard rumors that this friend of mine was pregnant and had been sent away to a convent in Colorado. Grandma was right again, as she almost always was. Yet she never lectured or talked down to me; rather, she'd give me stories that applied to the situation and then leave it alone.

For example, she used to tell me that when she was a girl, she was out jumping rope one day with a strap holding her books in hand. When she finished, Jimmy Hawk (funny how you remember names) came up to her, holding a stick to his crotch, and said, "Ada, do you know what's this long?" Her response was to take her book strap and hit him in the head with her books. She made it a point to tell me that she didn't really hurt him that badly, but he never did anything like that to her again.

This brings to mind a memory of my own, when I was standing in line in third grade and a boy named David put his arm around me. I turned around and with a resounding slap asked him, "What kind of girl do you think I am?" He just stared at me with his mouth agape. I got in trouble, but when I told Sister Stephanie what had happened, I could see that she was stifling a smile as she told me she'd handle it.

Grandma said that girls didn't necessarily have to resort to violence, but boys should never take "liberties" with us because they wouldn't respect us. As old-fashioned as that may seem, I've found that this still holds true today. That's why I say that my grandmother was so ahead of her time, and yet just timeless in other ways.

Nostalgia for a Simpler Time

Grandma Ada had a great sense of humor, although at times it was a little bizarre (and I think I'm the same way). For example, she was endlessly amused by this story about Ruth, an older woman who lived a few doors down from her when she was a girl. One day my grandmother paid Ruth a visit and saw that she was baking a pie. She also noticed that after Ruth put the top crust on, she'd take out her dentures, wash them off (thank God), and use them to make the crimped edge around the whole pie. This woman, bless her heart, often sent pies down for my grandmother's family to enjoy . . . and no one ever understood why Grandma would refuse to eat them and then collapse into spasms of laughter.

The next letter shows her sense of humor. It may seem silly to you, but it *was* a different time:

> One of my naughty tricks . . .
> Darling Sylvia,
> While looking at the small thermometer this morning, it reminded me of my childhood days—we had one large one everyone went to look at it as it was so accurate. Well, one day it was quite cold, and for some reason I could not go out to play—I wanted that thermometer to say the weather was warm, so I could play. I held a match under it, and the needle flew up about 100 degrees. My! Oh! My, the puzzled looks of all—what was the matter with the thermometer? Well, I did the trick once too often because it broke—I suppose I must have done it, since I was always going out to play no matter how cold it was. Such a naughty girl . . . and funny.
> Grandma Coil

Speaking of a sign of the times, Grandma would often send me a dollar with her letters, usually on my birthday or at Christmas. Now in those days, a dollar was nothing to be sneezed at, especially when you consider that she supported both herself and Brother on a very limited income.

It's been bittersweet remembering the times my grandmother and I spent together . . . not to mention all of the stories, the information, and the help she gave me. It also makes me very nostalgic to write about those days when life was so much simpler. When I look back, it feels like another lifetime, not just another era—it almost seems like it couldn't have existed because everything was so innocent.

Take, for example, what my grandmother wrote to me on my tenth birthday:

Sylvia Shoemaker,

Our darling birthday girl—we wish you joy, good health, love, happiness, and all the God-given blessings of success. You will get love and comfort from others if you love and trust God and keep His commandments. The only way to get happiness is to make others happy, in a considerate and unselfish way, for happiness lies <u>within</u> ourselves. Keep your mind free from worry or impure thoughts. Keep your feet on the ground but your eyes and thoughts on heavenly things.

Ten long years of your life God has given to us. You children have been a comfort, a blessing, and happiness to us all, especially your dear parents—so self-sacrificing and noble to you both. Again, we wish you many happy returns of the day, and always remember that Brother and I love you more than life, and the only way to get a friend to love you is to be a friend and love all good people. We send you one dollar.

Love from Brother and Grandma

The following letter, which was written almost exactly three years later (it was two days before my 13th birthday), is chock-full of literature references, and spells out all that Grandma Ada wanted for me. You can see how much confidence she had in me . . . and, of course, all the love she felt for me:

Sunday, October 17, 1949
My Dear Darling Sylvia,

Brother and I are sending you $1.00, a small token of our sincere love and regards—congratulations and well wishes for you and yours for a long, long, happy life; good health; peace; prosperity; and, as the Greeks say, "And all the gifts that God can provide" and has given you. I think of the time 13 years ago when that "blessed event" happened, and they placed you in my arms. As memory turns the pages of time, I think I can see a certain dainty girl come flying down Troost Park, her little lovely dress fluctuating in the breeze. Lively and sweet, you were a good baby—my, how quick you would go to sleep when I held

you in my arms and sang "Way down yonder in the cornfields"
and imitated the horn they blew. You would look sleepy eyed at
me and wonder what a silly grandma you had, but it put you
to sleep. Sure, one has to be silly—I imagine that a professor
could not easily be a babysitter or croon a baby to sleep. To
interest children one has to become <u>one</u> *of them, "reverse" the*
mind—do what will amuse them.

Then the years drifted by—the happy play days we have all
had, with you as leader in games. And yet, "Into each life some
rain must fall / some days must be dark and dreary"—but we
must look for the silver lining to our clouds, for God watches
there, ready to help us. You have been so interesting as a child—
Brother claims he taught you how to crawl, as you decided to
crawl backward and learned to crawl toward him—quick to
learn. You were stormy at times, but in a moment you had self-
control and were all tears, smiles, and kind words—our darling
was her sweet self again—God bless you.

Then how bravely you have watched, and prayed for,
Sharon—given her a mother's care while your own saintlike
mother was working—God will reward you for it. And how your
dear father would kiss you and amuse you when you were a
baby. I heard him say once when he bent over you, "You have
mighty good blood in you, Sylvia." Then I can see your mother,
like an angel from heaven, bending over you when you were
sick and when you broke your arm—what love shines in her
eyes as she watches over you. Never think that your parents
are unreasonable or cruel—they are doing all they can to help
you become educated in fine arts, and I hope you can be well
trained in what you have talents for. They are trying to make
you happy—help them to be so, too.

Study hard, loved one. Show the world they need you and
that your brains, talent, and ambition can help others upward
in life's struggles. You deserve great praise and credit for not
being boy crazy—no, you are not. Beauty fades—leaves us in
face or form—as we grow older. As the poet says, "Old age leaves
only a rag and a bone," but if we cultivate our minds and have

good behavior—fill or store our minds with only that which is good, kind, and beautiful—it will not only be a virtue but a great pleasure to us and others when old.

I had a woman tell me the other day that when she first saw me move in, she thought, <u>Oh, she might be as cross and mean as some other old lady,</u> but then, as she told me, "It is like my son said—he lived to hear you talk to him and be near you." Well, I can never understand when anyone compliments me, as I have myself "on the carpet" to see my many faults. I am a severe critic of myself—to get a habit of self-control, it becomes habitual to us, and that habit will control us.

You have great dramatic talent—a love for harmony and song, poetry and music—cultivate these gifts, and your parents will help you. Also, you have fine intellect, charm, beauty, grace, and tact; but beauty of mind and heart and manners—<u>these</u> last. Our tomorrows will soon be our todays, so make good use of every flying moment. They never return, and we must give an account of them when we see God.

Children are here as I write—and they dress up in adult clothes. Reminds me of how you and Sharon would dress up and act the part of nuns, ladies, etc. You were so talented. I am glad to see you have fine grades in school, and I hope that you can get an AB [that is, a Bachelor of Arts] degree. I read of Mrs. Hadley, who I think will soon be married to Vice President Barkley, and she said that after her husband died, she brushed up on her education, which helped her get her own two children educated. So be prepared for the "struggle with trouble."

I see the change there is between you and other children— you are so talented, ambitious, and capable. A boy age 13 came to see me here, and I asked him what his talents and desires for the future were. He was nearly 14, and he said, "None. I am going to do <u>nothing</u> but fish—my mother will have to support me the <u>rest of my life</u>." I said, "You don't care to be independent or earn your money when old?" He said, "No, never. I don't care about going to school either."

May life be one grand sweet song, as President Cleveland said of his married life—and Sylvia, may your life be as brilliant as the stars above and as pure as the beautiful white snow. And successful—if you aim very high you can't fall low. Chasing after happiness, etc., is like chasing butterflies—when caught, you have nothing of any value. Sinful souls are restless and unhappy—they tire of all the rubbish they thought was gold and worth striving for. When they are older, they have only gained scorn—forsaken by even God, if they do not repent. A Christian life is not a bed of roses, but the <u>reward</u> we get in heaven is worth the struggle. Do you remember the lines that say: "When you were born you cried, and all around you rejoiced / live so that when you die you smile and all around you weep"? Every rose has its thorns, and everything has something given it to protect its self-worth.

May your life be a shining example to Sharon—she behaves, acts, and at times copies your manners, I notice—love her as deeply as she loves you. You are her criterion—copy—so, darling, help her to be as perfect as you want her to be. Both of you are darlings and we love you, even though you two may be as the poet says—"Many a flower is born to blush unseen / And waste its sweetness on the desert air"—but don't be discouraged. You have too many gifts to go, as the poet says, "unwept, unhonor'd, and unsung" to the grave. No, this will not happen to any of you—even though, as the poet said, "We all are players for our day / On the stage of life we fare / Each with his little part to play / Each with his mask to wear . . . for what lies hidden behind the mask / Only ourselves may know."

As I told you, you have beauty of face, and it is said that "beauty [of face and form] is like the morning rose that withers in its bloom." But Sylvia, darling, I have watched you carefully over the happy hours I have been with you, and I have <u>seen</u> you have a wealth of beautiful thoughts. You do not like disorder; you are neat and perfect and have good taste in selecting things to wear, etc.; you hate what in life is trashy, vulgar, impure, or flashy/sensual; and you like the fine, noble things of life—

thank God for this—due to your disposition, home training, and the Church. Cultivate all of this, and hold fast to what is good. Please do not think that I am preaching—I am just writing thoughts and do not mean to hurt. Our loved ones tell us the truth; our enemies flatter and harm us.

This is Monday afternoon; how I miss all of you. Come when you can, and I will have something good to eat—just let me know when you can come. I am making rugs for your home and would like to have these two sacks Mrs. Kline sent me and the twine. . . . I hope your mother is better. Help her all you can, love—when Rosie is not there, this will save your mother's life or at least prolong it—you can have but one good mother. This rest at home will be just what cured her from a nervous breakdown.

I have had great trouble finishing this letter, with company every moment. I will make mistakes, I know—I must "run between the raindrops." Well, Karen was here, but I got rid of her. She was upset and locked the door on the outside with the clasp, so I had to call until others came and let me out. Mrs. Bourd was so angry (Karen locks them in, too) that she told the manager. He went to Karen's folks, and they had a big fuss. The manager told them to pay more rent or get out.

Brother and I went to a parade with four small children. We walked six blocks and waited three hours—quite a task, but a happy one, too. I have been eating so many grapes (dark ones, fine) that I have some hives now, just like when I eat strawberries—I never have them at any other time. I ate more grapes today—for spite I will fight it—this allergic business does not please me.

Love and best wishes to all of you from
Brother and Grandma Coil

Through my grandmother's writing, I hope that you not only see her philosophy, but you also note her great knowledge of poetry and literature. I'm sure you can't miss her morals, along with the messages about spirituality regarding God and all humankind that were a big part of her tutelage. As you've probably noticed, she gave advice in almost every letter she wrote me. Although she often apologized for seeming preachy, I never took it like that. I knew what she wanted for me—she was truly my blessed mentor, and I loved her so much. (Notice her reference in the preceding letter to Mama's nervous breakdown. My mother was always having some issue and locking herself in her bedroom, making poor Rosie the maid wait on her.)

It's funny how life takes its twists and turns. . . . As I sit here looking back on these days, I realize how full they were of basic joys, and it makes me happy and sad at the same time. Take the holidays, for instance, which were the best of times when I was young (despite my mother's antics). Daddy would get the tree, and Grandma and I would glue strips of colored paper together to make a chain for it. We'd also string popcorn and use tinsel, and she loved those bubble lights.

On Christmas Eve, my family and I would sit around and sing songs, read *The Night Before Christmas,* and listen as Grandma Ada told us what the real meaning of Christmas was. Then we'd take a new Bible, close our eyes, and randomly tear a page out of it. We'd then put our selections under our pillows and read them aloud the next morning, since Grandma always said that this would give us a message for the upcoming year. No matter how many times I did this, I always got the 91st Psalm, which is still my favorite Bible verse to this day. It's also favored by our Gnostic movement, because it relays protection. I thought it was weird that, no matter where in the Bible I tore out my page, I always got the same psalm, but my grandmother told me that God really wanted me to be protected.

As I've previously mentioned, in these days of the Depression and a world war, no one had any money. We had to wait in line for everything, yet Grandma never seemed to fail at charming a turkey out of Mr. Milgram, who ran his own grocery store (and, of course, she'd always fix her famous hamburger hash). My grandmother would knit us all mittens, hats, and lace doilies for presents; I'd crochet blankets for her legs, lost stitches and all, and make her Christmas cards. The world outside may have seemed frightening, but we enjoyed our simple blessings to the fullest. As Grandma used to say on Christmas Eve, "Let's not forget what we have tonight, and carry this feeling with us all through the year." My family was so grateful to have each other and to be healthy and together. These Christmases were almost like something out of Dickens; it's such a shame that the holiday now is all glitzy and shiny.

Last year I decided to venture out for my Christmas shopping at a nearby mall. What a horrible nightmare! Traffic was backed up for three miles; when I finally reached my destination, there wasn't anyplace to park. People were honking for other folks to move, but nobody *could* move because they were blocked in by other cars waiting. Right then and there, I said, "If I get out of this, I'm never putting myself through this hell again," and I haven't. I order from catalogs now, but my sons and I just buy for the children anyway—our Christmas is spent eating and talking and laughing, and no one cares who got what from whom or how much it cost. I don't care what state the economy is in; *no one* has enough money to go into debt all year for one day.

Even Jesus himself wasn't into celebrating Christmas, but he did observe Passover and the other Jewish holidays. Yet it doesn't matter what religion you are—just give thanks that you have your loved ones around you. And whether you believe it or not, all those who are living *or* have passed on celebrate with you. Forget the commercialism and get back to the basics of gratitude, loyalty, and commitment.

A Fountain of Wisdom

Grandma Ada certainly always stressed loyalty, gratitude, and commitment; and she absolutely despised it when anyone felt entitled. As she used to say, "If you've done a good job, it will be its own reward—and other than that, you're not entitled to anything." I find it sad how often we see people who have a sense of entitlement in the world today. I was so fortunate, with God's grace, to have let my grandmother's words take root in the thirsty soil of my mind. They're just as important to me now as they were then . . . maybe even more so.

These next few letters are incomplete, since I've lost some of the pages, but I think you'll be able to see how Grandma imparted these wonderful little pearls of insight from time to time:

Do today's duty and fight today's temptations—do not weaken—tomorrow is not ours until it comes. We can say that today was well lived and today's work was well done—we lived to carry life's burden till nightfall bravely and sweetly, no matter how hard the day—patiently, lovingly, purely, making others smile and helping them carry their work or burdens. God gives us nights to shut down our little days. We cannot see beyond, so we should not look for things we cannot see or understand. Short horizons make life easier and give us the blessed secrets of being brave and true—holy living is a blessing to others, bringing hope, joy, and smiles to those who are sad. God permits all of our sorrows—if we glorify Him as He desires, walk after Him, and trust Him, we will be happy. Chaining down some emotions or passions is not good for us.

Doing some generous deed—like teaching ignorance to see what is good, turning grief to a smile, or helping someone befriend their greatest foe—with a warm heart and confidence is divine. And lay a strong hold on God, Who made you and gave you all. 'Tis virtue and good deeds and words that make the bliss wherever we dwell. Life is all a void if our selfish thoughts and deeds are employed.

[Here are some sayings Grandma included in the letter; while some of them are quotes that she remembered, many are her own thoughts about life, God, and helping others:]

— *Translated from the German:*
Bear your own burdens.
No true help but God's—
It is the eternal song—
For each one loves to learn or cling to another.
Be brave. For self is the man—self-knowledge,
self-control, self-reverence to God, self-help—
leads us to power to win.

— *All who joy would win / must share it,*
Happiness was born a twin.

— *There is so much bad in the best of us and so*
much good in the worst of us that it ill behooves
any of us to rail at the faults of the rest of us.

— *I shall pass through this world but once. Any*
good therefore that I can do, or any kindness
that I can show to any human being, let me
do it now. Let me not defer nor neglect it, for
I shall not pass this way again.

— *Know then this truth (enough for man to know)*
"Virtue alone is happiness below."

— *There can be no harmony in our being, except*
our happiness coincide with our duty.

— *Life brings us—and means—self-denial and*
self-sacrifices, if we want peace and happiness.

In the next letter, my grandmother goes a little overboard about my looks and disposition, but then that was her way of showing me her love:

My Sylvia—the dream girl of all who know you—

Graceful as a fairy . . . voice soft and low . . . a lover of the nice, beautiful, soulful things of heaven and earth . . . whose soul is as pure and white as a new snowflake . . . whose features—eyes, ears, mouth, and nose—are perfect. A fine artist would be delighted to paint the faces of calm peace, intellect, and refinement that Sylvia and Sharon have—their form is as perfect as the Venus de Milo or something Rembrandt would produce. Sylvia (and Sharon, too) is a beautiful picture of grace and refinement, but above all this beauty is the fact that her mental ability is greater than most adults—her soft, low pronunciation, correct in every detail, is splendid—as are her manners. And her great artistic abilities are the perfection of her mind, soul, and heart. All fade away, but these gifts from God live forever and are priceless—above beauty of form or face, which fade and are soon forgotten.

True beauty is in a loving disposition, a spotless character, the little kind acts, the forgetfulness of self, the art of making friends—and keeping them by avoiding all those little pinpricks that cause people's feelings to feel like they are coals being heaped on a fire. When alone, try to think of how you have spent your time and what you have said when you talked. When you are out, let your eyes rest on everyone, showing no partiality. Never show anger or ridicule in company—of anyone—never repeat what in any way would hurt anyone's character or secret they told you. Be a friend—treat all alike with kind words and smiles. Never complain to your friends—they no more pity you than birds of prey pity the wounded dove. When your friend becomes your foe, then all the world your secret knows. . . .

Here, Grandma shows a bit of her psychic ability, which she hardly ever wrote about, and then goes on to relate a funny incident. Of course, just like most of her other letters, she ends with advice—she was a fountain of wisdom, and I have carried much of it with me always:

July 28, 1952
Darling Sylvia,

Well, I hope you are having a good time and that Sharon has found her purse. Poor child . . . I feel that it was stolen by one of her friends. I suppose God has many thieves and purse snatchers—they are so deft and quick—tell Sharon that the girl with blonde hair stole it but will not admit it. I think it is a wise plan to wear those large pocketbooks with straps that come over the shoulder, and it is such a comfort you can wear and know it is safe, unlike those small purses that I see so many using.

It is quite cool here now; we had three blankets over us last night, and the wind is quite fierce. We were at the breakfast table eating when a tin pie pan flew off the table by the window and landed on top of Brother's head—how comical it did look, and I laughed heartily. But lo and behold, a large one then hit me and bounced into my lap.

I am glad you are enjoying yourself, and I hope that you will take Sharon with you. It is wonderful that your father is there . . . I know you love your parents and are grateful to them.

We miss you so much, every one of you. "'Tis better to have loved and lost / Than never to have loved at all," and at times it is better to be loved than to love—or be a young man's slave and an older man's darling. How many found that they have made a mistake but the Church held them to their vows when married—in later years, if we ask God with faith, He will show us that it was all for our good. Where there is no trust in God, there is no love. In love there is trust, but when love and trust in God are absent, the song of the soul is silent, and hope is depressed, destroyed, lifeless. Love is our great test; without faith, we deny there is a God—we cannot love or believe in what He said or love Him. Jesus had faith in God; faith brings trust, and this brings love—for God or man. Remember that prayer can help us always have faith.

Looking back over my life, I have found out how wicked it was to let myself encourage a man's love for me. I did not mean to do it—you may call it a gift, but it is a cruel one for a man.

Sylvia, sometimes I am so worried that you have inherited that fateful gift—winning hearts and casting them aside as a child would a toy, never satisfied—loving a little in return for a man's sincere love and then growing tired (innocently, of course). One is never completely satisfied until one has a family—I loved my children, and there my heart found its resting place—but the misery I have created with hearts.

In my home life there was no love talk or love kisses. All was stern but kind and noble, a religious atmosphere to love life, virtue, and culture—and all the fine things of life that were pure and honest, such as a love of country and to defend your honor with your life—upward, onward, near to God. But earthly love was not mentioned to us girls. . . .

Grandma admitted to being what we would now refer to as a "tease," and since I had many boyfriends, I'm sure that she thought I'd turn out the same way. She often referred to these teasing ways as "wicked," and I know she regretted the many hearts she broke. However, as you can see from the above letter, her home life with her family was very Victorian and formal in nature. She wrote to me a couple of times about not being very "demonstrative" in her love, but I never had any problem getting hugs and kisses from her—although as I look back on it now, I realize that she didn't do much of that with other people around. Oh sure, I used to sit in her lap even with others present, but the hugs and kisses were given to me much more in private than when in the company of others. I just think it was her upbringing and the staid nature of her family; they didn't reveal much emotion or love in private or in public. Again, it was a different time.

Yet even through my teen years, I could go to my grandmother with anything, without fear of criticism or reprisal. She was a wonderful sounding board, and she was always careful to remind me of the importance of education, as you'll see in the next chapter.

Chapter Six

POINTING THE
WAY TOWARD
MY DESTINY

During my teenage years, I got caught up with "the two Joes."
Joe Tschirhart was a friend whom I married in the hopes of keeping
my parents together (there will be more about this in just a little
bit). He's still alive—after working for years on the railroad, he
retired and now makes wine—and we've remained close. Joe Behm
was a mechanic who was employed at his father's body shop and
then went to work for my father at the Riss & Co. truckline. We
dated on and off for five years, and sadly, he passed away a few
years ago.

Both Joes loved Grandma Ada and Brother and would do
anything for them, and she thought that they were upstanding
young men. She was big on backgrounds and bloodlines, which
was very Victorian, but was my grandmother ever discriminatory?
No, never. She loved all cultures and held them in high esteem,
and she loathed the Ku Klux Klan and the Japanese-American
internment camps of World War II. What was most important to
Grandma was that I get a college degree and not marry too young.
She was adamant that I get an education, but that's because she
knew how important it would be as I went about my life. Her
feelings are made very clear in this letter, which was sent to me
when I was only 13:

May 23, 1950

To our beloved, beautiful Sylvia C. Shoemaker—

Please allow your grandmother and "Brother" to send you their sincere love and well wishes with a <u>small</u> token of their <u>great</u> regard. I wish this one dollar could be one million. I would gladly give it to you, sweetheart—girl of my sweet dreams, and always a pleasure to meet you then or when I am awake.

You have won your first graduation day with the help of your noble parents—God will surely reward them for it. This is the first day you have graduated, and I hope it won't be the last. May you win your AB degree from St. Teresa's College and step into a new life, surrounded by culture, refinement, and happiness; in an atmosphere of all that is good, beautiful, and educated; leading you onward, upward, and nearer to God. Make hay while the sun shines. Study, store your mind with all that is worthy to know—and when you are old, your thoughts will be so good and well informed that they will entertain and comfort you and keep you from being lonely.

Your parents will be rewarded for this grand gift of education. They are noble; be a good, faithful, and helpful daughter to them, and all your kindness will return to you, dear heart. "Give every flying moment something to keep in store." Be helpful to others intellectually and financially—with your duty to God first—then get as much joy in life as you can <u>all the time</u> without neglecting your duties at home. Your education now is most important, and later it will be a happy home with children. Now the serious question before you is education—never before has there been such a demand as there is now, in any position in life. It may be a hard hill to climb, but it will be worth it. An educated mind is ready to meet the obstacles that ignorance brings before us in life—calm, serene, kind, and self-controlled, we can win life's battles.

You, darling, will have many temptations to do wrong, but you have noble blood in your veins, so take the advice my mother gave my sisters and me: defend your honor with your life. You will always remain God's pure and good child, but do not be in a hurry to marry, love. Man and wife tire of each other if tied down—when you have children, your social pleasures must be given up. Babysitters, I am told, are cruel and neglectful—I could write a book or a long article about their treatments . . . someday I will.

Let your older judgment be your guide. When you get in your 20s or 30s, you will look critically at the man you are taking as your mate for life—you will make him stand before the throne of a woman's soul and find out if he is worthy of your love and devotion. You will look at his character and habits— if he is industrious and has all the good traits, such as being a good provider or manager, and is faithful to you and God. Now you look for the gifts of grace and manners, a handsome face, wit, charm, and other outward personal attractions . . . oh, sweetheart, be careful. Your charming self can and should be careful of your choice that is for life—and life seems long when unhappy. And for God's sake, don't try to win the love of a man you can never come to marry. Be kind, that is all—a serious man will destroy the girl he cannot win if she encourages him in any way. May your footsteps leave a mark of honor, never a stain.

God bless and guide you always is the wish of—
Grandmother Coil and Marcus

When it came to men, my grandmother liked to say, "Look at their eyes, which are the windows of the soul. If they're hard and expressionless, beware. And don't listen to what their mouths say—watch how they treat their family members and friends, as well as strangers and even animals." If I had only heeded that advice, I wouldn't have married my last husband, who abandoned his mother, his sister, and every relationship he had—if something wasn't good for him, he left.

As I mentioned at the beginning of the chapter, Joe Tschirhart was my first husband (although the marriage was never consummated). I told the story of what happened in detail in *Adventures of a Psychic*, so here I'll just say that this was something I did when I was 16 to keep my parents from divorcing. My plan actually worked, and my father had my marriage annulled a week later. Joe really saved me a lot of grief with my parents, and I'm so happy that he found true love with a wonderful woman. He still lives in Kansas City and we've remained dear friends—I try to see him and his wife whenever I return for visits.

Even though I knew how my grandmother felt about my marrying too early, I went to her after I eloped with Joe. Through tears, and with my head on her lap, I told her everything. As she was consoling me, Mama asked Grandma what they were going to do with me. Grandma gave her a look like I had never seen and coldly replied, "No, Celeste, what are we going to do with *you?*" As mean as my mother was, she never bucked her mother. I think that somewhere in her soul was the knowledge that Grandma Ada's light would just extinguish her darkness.

My grandmother and I never discussed what I'd done again, and she went out of her way to make me feel better. And that's when I first heard the phrase that I've used and written about so many times in my life: "Within your weakness lies your strength sleeping." God, how that one phrase has carried me from the bowels of hell back to a reality that is rational and sane.

Grandma wouldn't directly interfere with my choice of boyfriends—she didn't tend to comment much on them at all—but she always managed to get her point across. This next letter, which was written around the time of my annulment and during my family's summer vacation, underscored Grandma's feelings about marrying too young. Although she was a very religious and devout person, you can see that she also had some firm opinions and didn't hesitate to write them down:

> *Darling Love of my Heart*
> *Well, well, Sylvia—Sweetheart—*
> *So, you are very happy. Well, perhaps the two or three dollars I send you, dear, will help you to be this way, as it takes money to go places. I am sending five dollars to your mother, since I thought that to send money to each of you may not be*

safe. One dollar goes to Sharon, and some to your mother. Is your dear sweet dad with you? If so, I will send one to him next time—but the five dollars go to your mother, and she can give you two or three as she likes.

Please tell Joe that I pray for him, and I thank him for helping you to be so happy. I am deeply grateful to him for opening your eyes and finding out that it is safer to have just a friendship with a boy until you are older and know what real love is. A youthful love like yours often leads to an early marriage, and I have found out they nearly always lead to a divorce, which means the loss of our blessed Church benefits.

Oh, look before you leap. Youth loves too hastily, not wisely or too well. Youth loves <u>glamour</u>—nice attention, good looks, praise, good behavior, gifts, nice dates—all of these fascinate and arouse the emotions of love. Life is long, and changeable youth grows tired of being chained down, even with your lover— you grow tired of each other. Then if you divorce and have children, what a life for them. It is a sure fact that the children raised in divided hearts and homes never do well or learn to be fine citizens. They go astray, as a child needs a father's tender care and support, and love and advice—as well as a mother's. God help a child who lives with a pants-wearing, smoking, whiskey-drinking, "chasing" mother who is out playing cards or sports—it is better that such a mother had never been born.

All children need a religious atmosphere with prayer— a "pious" home of everything that is good. Here they will grow up and learn how to be good parents by helping their own parents with the work at home, relieving them as much as possible of work and worry. As they greet each other with cheerfulness and a smile, they so prolong their parents' life and love—for as children treat their parents, so they will be treated when they have their own children.

Sylvia, I want to tell you something—please do not grow angry, but your smile and your beautiful eyes like twin stars did not lighten up but have had an angry, moody, and sullen look that was in danger of spoiling your lovely face. Such a *hard and resentful look would never cause others to love you. Now when you said you had been "weaned" from your great love for Warren, I knew that my prayers were answered. Daily, Brother and I would tell (or as some say "<u>count</u>") our beads— rosary—that God, helped by the Blessed Mother, should show you the right path of love and guide you on it. We asked that you be a grateful child, help your parents, and be a loving pal to them and your sister—take Sharon with you—and above all, keep away from evil influences or companions that lead to destruction and ruin. May all the good that is in you never be destroyed by evil.*

Barker will send this letter to you and your dear ones by special delivery—I hope you are all well and happy and can stay until August sometime. I have such hopes that you will be happy and that your good father can stay with you—God bless him and all of you. We are well and contented. So is the terrible breeze—it blows towels, daily papers, flowerpots, etc., out of the window. The janitor is taking all of the windows out of the room and painting them. Well, God bless all of you—we are praying for all your safety.

Love,

Ada and Marcus Coil

A Brief Commentary on Technology

Time passed and I met Joe Behm, who accepted my psychic gift and championed what I saw and felt until the day he died. Grandma absolutely loved Joe—especially since he'd often bring her and Brother along when he and I went out for rides.

I tried to do everything to entertain my grandmother and uncle, yet as I look back now, I can see how foolish this was. The two of them seemed to have a great time just listening to the radio, going to band concerts, and talking about everything from religion to world affairs and politics. As I often tell my audiences, we put sweaters on other people when we're cold. . . .

To deviate for a moment, in those days there wasn't so much technology to eat up our time, so we just had each other. We'd really *talk* and share ideas, and we got to know each other and our friends quite well and had very strong ties.

I remember when I took Grandma and Brother to see the movie *The Robe* with Richard Burton, and while they were both grateful for the outing, they agreed that the picture was too long. They said that the evening was pleasant, but we had no time to talk, tell stories, or really communicate with one another. Don't get me wrong—they loved watching Bishop Sheen and a few other TV programs, but then they turned off the tube and talked.

I clearly remember Grandma telling me, "Someday it will all be pictures, either on the movie screen or on television. People will quit eating together and just watch pictures, living through what they saw rather than what they experienced." Well, that someday is now. We all seem to have lost our conversation skills: instead of asking each other how we're doing, we so often jump in with, "Did you see that show on TV the other night?" I have a friend who relates every single thing in life to something he's seen in a movie . . . what a waste of a mind.

Try for one week to go without television and see how you feel. I have, and the first few nights I kept hearing, "Tonight's the night! You can't miss when such and such happens!"—and then I remembered that they announced the same thing last week.

When it comes to TV programming, I find news broadcasts to be very depressing, and so many of the programs about the legal system or solving crimes are filled with death and violence. I prefer to watch A&E, TLC, the National Geographic Channel, the Discovery Channel, History, and History International for their educational programs on different animals, history, and cultures; but even that can be infrequent. When I'm traveling, I barely watch TV at all, since it isn't exactly conducive to experiencing life.

I was on a cruise not long ago, and while waiting in line to disembark, I heard several people comment on how much they loved the lectures I'd given, the new friends they'd made, and the spiritual atmosphere they'd discovered; but I also inevitably heard that "at least back in the States, we have decent TV shows" or "I sure do miss my favorite program." I'm not trying to be too critical, but it's a shame that we live through what's on a screen. To be surrounded by people and ideas is so much more interesting.

I met a woman on that cruise who had stage IV cancer, yet rather than wait out her days in a hospital, she decided that she wanted to see as much of the world as possible. She even took the more strenuous climbing and walking trips to places like Ephesus in Turkey, and she said that she was so grateful God had given her this time to experience life before she went. She also related to me that she might want to incarnate one more time to help other people during the end of times. Now *that* is a soul!

If I'd been in my room watching TV during this trip, I would have missed out on so many stories about how people found our Christian movement and now saw their lives very differently. Most of us don't know where we're going or where we've been—and the technology that was supposed to have made life easier has instead robbed us of ourselves.

Getting back to *The Robe*, Grandma made a comment after the movie that while it might have been interesting, it wasn't true. She really stressed the importance of truth, and not just when it came to our psychic readings, but where history and religion were concerned as well. She had such a hard time (as I do) with the disparity between what human beings have written and what really happened. For example, although she read the Bible and had great respect for it, she also felt that a lot of the stories were just analogies to show God's power, not actual facts.

My grandmother wasn't able to do research, as I've been able to—since I have access to a lot of different resources that she didn't have, and I'm also able to go into trance to receive information from Francine and the Other Side—so I've been able to carry on where she left off. As I've gone deeper and deeper into exploring the Bible and other religious works, I've found it depressing that what the messengers and avatars said and what really happened were often very different.

I think that both Grandma and I were well served as psychics by not having so much technology around us. It seems that this made us more empathetic and understanding to the needs of people, and we cultivated relationships more. I know several friends who have devoted their lives to helping others and they're the same way . . . it seems that the soul becomes uplifted and closer to God when our lives are more filled with actual experiences of life rather than anything done vicariously.

The Importance of Being Educated

As I got older, my grandmother became much more vehement about my getting an education and a career. I look back now and am convinced that she psychically knew I'd never have a man to support me, because she wouldn't have come off that strong unless she was dead-center right. As it turns out, in all of my almost-73 years, I've never had a man take care of me. My first husband demanded that I work even as I was raising our two boys. My second husband supported me for about three years, but as soon as I started making money as a psychic, he quit his job—and while he did so to try to help me and our business, that situation deteriorated over time. My third husband acted as my manager, alienated many, was unfaithful, and stole from me. Throughout all of this, I was lucky enough to work as a teacher and make my own money, which then turned into a way of life. Now I can't imagine putting up with anyone who tries to tell me what to do.

Even though I began to get pretty serious about Joe Behm, I also planned on going to college. In the letter that follows, you'll see how Grandma—in her psychic, ethereal way—tried to steer me toward a career as well. This is mind-boggling when you realize that she came from a time when a woman's only job was to be a dutiful, proper wife and mother.

Darling Sylvia von Banica Shoemaker,

I was so glad to hear from you all I just cried. Yes, Ada Banica cried, as I was afraid that one or all of my darlings was sick—and then Mr. Sharp hurried down to bring me three precious letters. I am sending you one dollar—tell your mother that I am sending her not less than five dollars and you two precious kids some money each.

Now, sweetheart, I did think you had forgotten me. Brother said, "I believe Sylvia is tired of lugging me up and down the stairway" and felt you just left him to get rid of the trouble—but I read the letters three times to him, and he was so happy. I inserted his name whenever you said something nice to both of us.

I do not know if Joe will come to see Brother and me again. I have only seen him two times—once to call a little while, and once to take us to the drive-in show. We enjoyed the show and his polite attention so very much, but I had a stubborn spell and insisted on footing all expenses. Oh, my pen is so very tearful— it is worth throwing away—yes, Joe is very much in love. He wrote you a letter he said was on the backs of his father's work orders, in the car. If you do not think you are ready to marry him, then do not let him think you are. Why not wait until you are older and both of you have a finished education? Above all, I beg and plead of you to finish your education.

Get a master's degree or even an AB degree, sweetheart, beloved darling. I am telling you the truth, ask any older person—even your father—and he will say sorrowfully, "I wish my parents could have sent me to a college or university and let me finish my education." I have heard this cry many times, and it has come from those who worked with their hands and remained poor. An educated mind for the "worthwhile" good is what the world wants—an educated mind brings money for ease and comfort of life and helps the Church grow. Many children have worked their way to finish their education, like your uncle Jim Coil—and he was an orphan. God's pure, good, cultured, handsome man—ah, Celeste looks like him, as do you children. And my last request to you, beloved one, when I am ready to throw off this mortal "Coil" would be: Sylvia, love of my life, get your degree and finish your education.

See that the man you want to marry has the same good education, too. Brains, not brawn or muscle, is what pays for the comforts we want. Money may be the root of all evil, as they say, but one has to have it honestly, if he does not want to run to hard manual work with a paper bag or a tin-bucket lunch box. That does not pay for all the things needed when married— the world needs <u>educated minds</u>, not laboring men who are deprived of the comforts or pleasures of life. If a laboring man has asbestos sickness and a loss of work, then what? He can't work when sick or old. One cannot climb the ladder of fame or fortune without a finished education.

A girl here aged 15 got married last week—her husband has a little job, but what a pity. Uneducated minds = poverty-stricken children and broken homes. Children's lack of opportunities on account of their parents' poverty at times makes them ignorant criminals. People say that when poverty darkens the window, "love flies out of the door." I do not care for you to think that one must have riches to be happy. No, but I want you and yours to have the educated minds that the world needs, enabling you to keep from this poverty. Love in a co-mate is the sweetest, truest happiness if they have money to spend for things they need and want.

Joe told me he was going for you—he did think he might come to California, but I may be mistaken. I would not hurry home, since you can learn so much, darling one. Joe could help out your mother, as she is not strong and needs his help. He is so much in love with you, go slow—if you have any doubts and let him live in a fool's paradise of love, it will be a sad blow to him and at times lead to serious trouble. Hell hath no fury like one who is scorned, so tell him to be sure of nothing but death and taxes. Joe is a fine boy.

Darling, I suppose you think I am money mad or overly ambitious, and trying to tell you not to marry any man even if his every hair were shining with diamonds. Just marry a man

*who is good, pure, and ambitious for a university education—
who has a love for the higher things of life. Joe told me that he
loves classic music and that speaks well for him. He is German
and industrious, but is he strong enough to endure physical
work all his life? If he had a finished education, he could avoid
hard manual work always.*

*Now, darling, I am not ready yet to have my funeral notice
printed—not as long as I can eat a lot of salami sandwiches, as
Brother and I are doing now. May God answer all of our prayers
for all of you—you can get Him to answer a marvelous prayer
for anything. Stay as long as you can and forget all that will
worry you, for God will attend to everything if you have faith.*

Love, and I pray God blesses you all,
Ada Coil

In this next letter, Grandma shares her worries that I will move
with Joe to a farm in the country. By this point, I was getting a lot
of pressure from him to get married, and Grandma knew that if I
did, I'd never get a college degree. She loved Joe, and this had less
to do with him than it did with me not getting the education that
she so wanted for me.

Here you'll see some of the many arguments she used to try to
discourage me from going down the wrong path in life:

Darling Sylvia,

*I have often wondered why our dainty, charming, graceful,
beautiful girl did not write to her old grandma. Of course I know
that you are busy in school—I sincerely, prayerfully hope you
will be in school until you have won a finished education. This
is your parents' greatest desire, next to your being God's child—
it is their and our wish. We pray to God and His Holy Mother
to help you get an AB degree. I am not going to write to you
about this because nothing stands in your way. I am sure you
can now get your policy, as you are 17, but save it, dear. Never
let anything cause you to lose the seven hundred dollars you
will perhaps get by this time. [Grandma had set aside some*

money for me over the years that she wanted me to use for my education.]

Your parents will be only too delighted to pay for schooling— if you don't want it, it will break their hearts. I hope that your memories will be sweet, kind, and peaceful when you are old— and you have no regrets that you missed their offer of a fine education they would pay for. Other children at times have not had such a chance. Jim Coil, Marcus's brother, <u>worked</u> his way through two schools—<u>fine</u> man. I do not know your plans for the future, love, and it is none of my affairs—yet there is nothing but great and lasting love for our baby girl Sylvia, our beautiful darling, so wise, so good.

I thought that the reason you avoided me was because you did not want me to ask you to go to school—that you had made other plans and wished to get married. Heaven protect you until you are older and through college—or university—and not let you marry so soon. When you are so young the children are never strong or wise as they would be if you were 20 or so. You are not strong—you are nervous, being so young and pregnant . . . oh, God help you then. If you were in a cottage or rooms in a little town, there would be no sewer or bath—you would have to use well water and a cistern. You would also burn oil lamps and carry your own coal in for heat—and Joe's back, I am sorry to say, may cause him to suffer all his life, poor boy, as his daddy did.

Then there is so much danger of polio in drinking impure water or of typhoid fever, which comes, like all our diseases, from the country. At night there is the lonely hooting of an owl, as all small country places have . . . and the lonely, silent nights. There are so <u>many</u> women raped in the small or country towns that papers speak so of men coming in their homes to rob and kill them. You would also miss all the comforts of home: as you look at a snowy, wet ground; a bathroom outdoors in a tin tub; and a toilet in a dirty shed, oh, it will be a jolt to you and your dainty ways.

Now I know something about the country. I have visited there, and we had to go behind the barn and use corncobs on two different farms—and these were wealthy farmers. Well, the uneducated farmers who dig and work in the soil are as a rule kindhearted, but not all are wise. A man gets impatient when a woman complains—she must be silent. Even when she feels oh so sick, there stand the dirty dishes and a tub of dirty diapers and the family wash—there is nowhere to do laundry there in the country.

You would look at the fine dresses your parents got you: Where can you wear them? What can you do with them— make the curtains for the windows? In a month's time you would be sick of it all and come home free from such misery and trouble—but if you were divorced, you could never wed a prominent, well-to-do man, no matter how you really loved as only a woman's heart can love. You would regret it—regret it so much—and then you would have to work for a living, but without any education or training. Sharon will have a career and a place in the world—she can expect it, as she is learning what she has talent for. God gave you talent, but you still need to be taught to write well, for a critical public, before you can get fame, position, or praise.

Now do you care to bury the golden days of youth in the sticks—this lonely, forsaken place? No. Save the seven hundred dollars you have for yourself; do not let him touch it. If Joe's back improves, know that they are going to draft a lot of boys for training—India is giving us trouble, she has to fight communism—and he might go if called. Then you will have your money spent, be all alone and trying to make a living, even though you have not been trained for journalism. You are so talented—cultivate it—wait until you are out of school before you get married. You cannot have strong children when you are nervous and not strong yourself—they will be like mice and might be cross—you can whip the devil into a child but you cannot whip it out. Look before you leap and wait until you are older to make decisions.

God bless and guide you—
Ada Coil

This is a pretty strong letter, isn't it? Grandma, as you can see, had great hopes for me and seemed to drill them into my head, as if she thought that they would eventually make their way in.

When I graduated from high school, Joe gave me a beautiful engagement ring—and even though I got busy with my plans, Grandma never gave up with her gentle prodding. I know now that she psychically knew what my life would be like.

The Calling at St. Teresa's

My grandmother's advice about the importance of an education, as well as how I should never depend on anyone, haunted me. So one Sunday afternoon I was coming back from seeing a movie with a girlfriend, and I decided to ride the streetcar to the College of St. Teresa (now Avila University). *It can't hurt to look around,* I told myself. *This will be fun.*

Although it was August and the semester had already begun, I set off to explore the campus, which looked more like a Victorian estate than a college. The first building I entered was all dark mahogany and marble floors, and it almost took my breath away. Before I could venture any farther, a nun asked if she could help me. I replied, "Oh, I don't think so . . . I was just curious."

She said, "Well, let me show you around." As she took me to the labs, the old library, the chapel, the meeting halls, and the classrooms, it all seemed to call to me. When we were done with the tour, I commented, "Sister, it's so beautiful here, but it's too late for me to enroll now."

"Nonsense," she insisted. "We still have two openings." When I asked how much tuition was and was told that it was $3,000 a year, I almost fainted. In the 1950s, that was a fortune. She went on to explain that St. Teresa's girls turned out to be the best nurses and teachers, and the school's name carried much weight in Kansas City—yet even as she spoke, I kept thinking, *Dear God! It's so expensive!* While my father made great money then, he wouldn't exactly be jumping up and down to take on this additional expense.

As if reading my mind, the nun patted my hand. "We can work something out," she assured me. "There is library and cafeteria work." *I could do that,* I thought. *Besides, I'd feel independent.* Aloud, I said, "I'll call you tomorrow, Sister." I then ran out the door and gave a kiss to the statue of Mary that was in the center of the drive.

At dinner that evening, I broached the subject with my father. When he heard what it cost, he dropped his fork on his plate in shock and exclaimed, "I don't want to buy the place!"

"It's all right, Daddy," I said. "I can work in the library and cafeteria." Suddenly, his expression changed and his eyes got a faraway look. I could read my father so well, and his thoughts were something along the lines of: *William Shoemaker's daughter working for tuition when her father is vice president of the second-largest truck company in Kansas City . . . how would that look?*

Needless to say, even though it was a little late in the semester, I became a student at St. Teresa's, due in large part to my father's need to maintain his social status, but also because this would keep me close to home. Yet my father loved me so much, and giving me a college education must have been a great source of pride for him. And as for Grandma—well, when she learned that I was going to college, she would have danced on the roof if she could have.

The College of St. Teresa was operated by the Sisters of Carondelet, and I can't say enough about those days. My psychic abilities were getting stronger, and I decided to major in English literature and education and minor in theology. The more I read, the more I found books that had either mysticism or Victorian table tapping in them. And when I confided my abilities to Sister Marcelle Marie and Father Nadeux, they didn't douse me with holy water; instead, they encouraged me, as did my classmates.

I was still somewhat torn, often wondering, *Where will this gift lead me? It certainly isn't acceptable.* When I took psychology,

I learned that hearing voices was a sign of schizophrenia, so I immediately thought that I belonged in a psychiatric ward at the nearest hospital. Doubt and fear regarding my sanity crept in and reared its ugly head. Grandma seemed to be accepted by the various clergy and laypeople, but if *I* put myself out there publicly, what would happen? Of course I knew that our lives are charted by us, but more than anything I wanted to live a "normal" life. I'd already made up my mind to be a teacher, but I wondered how my abilities would fit in. And then there was Joe waiting to get married . . . and that engagement ring began to feel heavier and heavier. He wanted to look at houses, furniture, and so on, but I kept putting him off. When I told Grandma about this, I gave her the excuse that I needed time to think about things. She didn't say a word, but just gave me a knowing smile. Even though she was getting older and weaker by this time, she still had her incredibly sharp mind.

My Grandmother's Foresight

Grandma was happy about my becoming a teacher, but she also kept pushing for me to be a writer, a journalist, or anything that would allow me to put pen to paper. This next letter, which was written only about two months before she died, clearly notes her relief that I was pursuing my education, along with her pride that I had won an award at school. Even so, you can sense her fear that I might drop out, so she reiterated some of those points she'd made so many times before:

> *May 1, 1954*
> *Darling love, Sylvia—*
> *Words cannot permit me to tell you how proud and happy I am, with the knowledge that you are climbing the ladder of fame and fortune in your winning the honor and money you did at school. The way we pray for you, I knew you would. God and Mary have answered our prayers—there is yet one more prayer*

for them to answer, and that is that you can and will finish journalism. Without that, you can never be a great success. You know, darling, the heights have never been reached unless the ones who climbed had all that was needed and patiently waited to make their journey up the mountains safe and well. As a man said, youth is inexperienced and paints life with hopes and beautiful dreams. But when your mother was reading your composition, I <u>cried freely</u>—with joy—that you had such God-given talents. Make the best of your opportunity—grasp it and hold fast to that which is good, as the Bible tells us to do.

I know it is the wish and great <u>heartfelt desire</u> of your parents that you go to St. Teresa's and finish your education. I see the look in your mother's eyes when she tells me that she will let you decide when it comes to their dreams of seeing you win your AB degree—let you do as you wish—but her sad look tells me there is an aching heart behind her words and look.

An education is a weapon by which you can have a life free from want, a life that brings you in good society. The life of a journalist is respected, and when older you may marry the man of your choosing: a Catholic man with a good position; you won't have to ask him for a penny and can have a good woman help you with the housework and take care of the children. A poorly paid laboring man cannot afford to do this—with strikes and days of accidents for those who labor, young men should finish their education to be better fitted as good providers. Why don't young folks think of this? I know that it is love's sweet dream to be together—but the stern realities are forgotten, and they cannot wait until they are really ready for married life.

If you can sit down by the typewriter when you have finished journalism in school—and can know just how to write on your typewriter—your ideas will come to you perfectly. Without a finished course, you cannot be a good writer, no matter how brilliant your mind is—your writings will be imperfect and unacceptable. You can save yourself a life of drudgery, be independent, and have the money you earn—not what is given to you with the remark, "What did you do with the 25 cents

I gave you last week?" It is so hard and causes fussing to be asking your husband for money.

I know you think a lot of your Joe, and he does of you, of course, but why not wait a few years until you are ready to face life's burdens and are fitted for the work and worry that married life brings? Sorry to say so, but to a woman it brings an untold lot of self-sacrifices and trouble of all kinds, but when older she can learn to endure them better, and then she can be happy with the man she loves. Married life is desirable when you have a home; a good provider; good, obedient children who are sweet tempered and will behave and help you all they can, all the time—that is a great, great comfort and reward to the poor, tired mother who lives to make them happy. Life has its problems—but there are rewards if you prepare yourself when young.

I congratulate you, dear, from the bottom of my heart—so does Brother, who loves you with all of his heart. As soon as your saintlike mother finished reading the composition of yours and left, Brother and I got our rosary and how we did (and do) pray that you finish your education and be fitted to be a good writer—you have the gift. Pray, and God will help you do right. He has given you a father who is a good provider; a lovely home; a fine, darling sister; and a saintlike mother—you have much to be thankful for.

God bless you, loved one—
Grandma Coil

I know that the reader may find my grandmother's letters to be overly preachy at times, and increasingly on one track: that I get my education and wait to get married. But you must understand that she was very psychic and knew these were the areas of my life that could really affect my development. Being that she was so determined, her influence played no small part in my getting an education and becoming a writer (although it took me a while—I taught for many years and didn't write my first book until I was 50 years old).

No one will ever convince me that Grandma Ada didn't know I'd have to provide for myself and my family essentially on my own. As I said, a woman coming from her day and age would have wanted me to be a lady of leisure and enjoy all the attendant comforts of wealth. Even when I had a devoted boyfriend like Joe who wanted to marry and take care of me, she still would not budge from her vision of me being independent and taking care of *myself.*

I'm sure she knew that I was the only hope of keeping the family's psychic torch lit. The letters she wrote to my sister, Sharon, were just filled with "Be a good girl and mind your family," and so on. There were no directives given to her about pursuing her education—but Grandma hammered me about going to college constantly.

One of the reasons I wanted to share my grandmother's letters with you was so you could truly understand how farseeing she was—it should be obvious that if I hadn't followed her direction, I wouldn't be where I am today. Even the performing-arts training I had as a child led to my being able to get up in front of thousands of people to teach and lecture without feeling afraid or out of place. Thanks to all of those lessons Grandma made me take, being in front of a crowd came naturally to me.

Without her I'm sure I would have tried to bury my psychic gift. People never believe that I am really shy and only wanted a home and family, but part of it was not to be. Yes, I have two wonderful boys, but I certainly haven't had a conventional home life, with a husband who took care of me or was an example to the boys. For years I felt bad about how this affected my sons until I released it to them one day when they were with me in my office. They both got wide-eyed and said in unison: "Are you crazy, Mom? We were fine because we had you." So I let that drop, but once in a while a little thought of *What if?* does creep in. And then I remember that all I could do was follow my chart . . . and my destiny.

Chapter Seven

GRANDMA GOES HOME

Grandma Ada didn't seem to get frail as she got older, but she did have a heart condition. I could also see her becoming a little more "remote," for lack of a better word. Looking back, I realize that perhaps she recognized that she'd done all she could in this life, and it was time for me to find my own way.

I've written about some of this before, but not in depth. Even today, the emotions this subject brings up are raw, but if I'm to truly honor my grandmother, it's important that I tell her *whole* story. . . .

It was July 1954, and the temperature in Kansas City had risen to 115 degrees—the hottest on record—when my grandmother came down with pneumonia and had to be taken to the hospital. I was attending a summer class, but I rushed to Grandma's side as soon as I heard the news. I arrived at her bedside to find her sitting up, rosary in hand. When she smiled at me, I thought, *Oh, thank God! She's going to be all right.*

That's when the doctor motioned me out in the hall and let me know that they couldn't seem to drain the liquid out of my grandmother's lungs. "She probably won't live through the pneumonia," he told me. Then he added something that I'll never forget: "Pneumonia is the old person's friend."

"It's no friend of mine," I retorted. "Doctor, she's my life." He just smiled, patted me on the shoulder, and walked away.

"Grandma," I said when I walked back in, "you're going to be fine." She just gave me that smile I knew so well—the one that indicated she knew more than I did. Then the smile disappeared when she brought up Brother and what would become of him if something were to happen to her.

"First of all, you're going to be all right," I said. "And second of all, Brother will *always* be all right. We would take care of him if anything happened—but it won't."

"No," my grandmother insisted, vehemently shaking her head. "Your mother will put him away." I didn't answer because I knew it was true. She turned her face to the window, and the jingling beads on her rosary was the only sound in the room except for her labored breathing. I came over and held her hand, and I prayed like crazy.

Even at her age, her china blue eyes had never dimmed. She turned those beautiful eyes to me now and said, "Sylvia, my heart would hear you and beat if it lay for a century dead. We'll always be together because our souls are locked for eternity, and we've been here many times before. Since this is my last time on Earth—and yours, too—I'll wait for you."

Now by this time I was weeping almost uncontrollably and whispered, "Please, *please* don't talk like this. I really couldn't bear a world that didn't have you in it. No one knows what we know . . . how we can read each other's thoughts. No one sees or hears what you and I do . . . no one understands except you and me!"

"The world will keep turning on its axis," Grandma Ada replied so plainly. "I won't lie to you, though—you're going to go through some very hard trials, but you'll find the strength. After all, it's in your blood and your genes."

I thought, *The hell with my heritage, the von Banicas, and the psychics . . . there's more to the two of us than that. Yes, she's my mentor and my confidante, but she's also the one human being who gives me unconditional love, like I give her.*

She lapsed into talking about Brother again and kept insisting that no one would know how to take care of him except her. No matter how much I tried to allay her fears, it didn't work—she just kept saying, "I can't leave him."

Suddenly my mother came in, screaming that she wanted to pinch off Grandma's intravenous tube. Thank God she was removed immediately.

"Why would she want the tube pinched off?" I asked the nurse.

She replied, "Is your mother all right?"

Knowing what she meant, I responded with my own question: "Can you keep her out of here?"

"We're going to have to," she said.

I hated to leave my grandmother that night, but I was forced to. (In those days you couldn't stay in a patient's room like you can now, so when visiting hours were over, they were over and you had to go.) I went home and agonized about her.

The next day, however, my hopes soared. Although Grandma was in a wheelchair and had a bone-rattling cough, she looked like she had some color in her cheeks (silly me, it was a high temperature). I asked the nurse why she was in the chair, and she told me that it was for two reasons: to reduce the threat of bedsores, and because my grandmother couldn't breathe lying down. Then the nurse pulled me aside and said, "She was up all night talking to a mother, and she kept saying something about helping a brother." I said that she was probably talking to her own mother—I didn't feel like going into an explanation of the Mother God or that Grandma actually called her son "Brother." Again, I stayed the whole day, holding my grandmother's hand and praying, until I was forced to leave.

When I got to the hospital the next day, Grandma Ada wasn't in her room. I tore down the hall to the nurse's station and was told that she was in intensive care. Usually they didn't let anyone but hospital staff in that area, but luckily our family physician, Dr. Skinner, was there, and he made an exception for me.

Grandma was unconscious and in an oxygen tent. In between sobs, I told her, "I love you so much, and I don't want you to leave me . . . but if you have to, I'll be all right." That may have been what came out of my mouth, but my mind was screaming, *No! I won't be all right, and I may never be all right again!* I was losing my true mother, my friend, my mentor, and the only person who would ever love me like that. All I could do was repeat "I love you," over and over again.

Dr. Skinner said, "She can't hear you, Sylvia."

I replied, "Oh yes, she can"—and just then, her eyes fluttered open. At first she only had a blank stare, but then her eyes moved and focused on me for maybe 30 seconds. Even Dr. Skinner said, "Well, I'll be damned." In that brief window of time, I was able to read everything she felt and couldn't say. And then she closed her eyes and was gone.

I was so wild with grief that I felt as if all the lights in the world had gone out. I don't remember driving home, but I do remember lots of people telling me that I shouldn't cry—I needed to hold up for my mother. *My mother,* I thought, *just died.*

When Brother asked me, "How's Mom?" I answered, "Fine." I didn't have the energy to tell him what had happened just yet, so I helped him upstairs to his room (my mother had deigned to let him stay with us while Grandma was in the hospital) and went in the bathroom to wash my face. I then popped in to check on him. I noticed that he looked different, and I asked, "What is it, sweetheart?"

"Nothing," he said in a small voice. "Would you say the rosary with me tonight?"

"Of course I will . . . and then we'll find a band concert on the radio." He simply looked past me and began to start the rosary. I said it with him, and this seemed to soothe him somewhat.

Joe, bless his heart, came over that evening and suggested that we take Brother for a ride. I really wasn't up for doing anything, particularly since the rosary service for Grandma was the next day—but then I thought of Brother upstairs, all alone for the first time in his life. I immediately went up and helped my uncle down the stairs and out to the car.

Even though it was late in the evening, it was still very hot, with no hope of cooling off; thanks to the humidity, it felt like 120 degrees out there. Nevertheless, we drove around for about two hours with John Philip Sousa on the radio. Joe kept trying to engage Brother in conversation, but he'd just give short answers. I whispered to Joe that there was something wrong with Brother, for he was usually a veritable magpie whenever we went out, and Joe whispered back that he was probably just worried about Grandma Ada. A sickening dread washed over me, as I wondered how in God's name I could tell him that his mother was dead—and would Mama let him stay with us and not put him in a home? I worried so much that I literally made myself sick.

When we got home, I asked Brother if he wanted to watch TV. He said no, since he was very tired, and I helped him up to his room. If I hadn't been so caught up in my own grief, I would have been more aware that he was deeply depressed.

That night, Joe stayed over, and everyone except Brother slept downstairs, or at least tried to. The next morning I was so sick that I looked like I had the mumps: my glands were incredibly swollen, and I was running a high fever. I didn't sleep and I couldn't eat, but I did make some breakfast for Brother. When I took it up to him, I saw that he still wasn't himself—he didn't want anything to eat and said that he just wanted to rest—but I left him alone. My teenage mind was just beginning to process the fact that I would never see my beloved grandmother again in this life, and that was all I could handle at the moment.

The rosary service for Grandma was held in the late afternoon. Joe and I sat in the back, although he kept feeling my forehead and saying that I should go home. When I finally mustered up the courage to go view Grandma in her coffin, I saw that she looked like wax.

Mama made her grand entrance: Daddy and Jim Gay, a friend of the family, carried her down the aisle, with her screaming all the way, and then she threw herself on the coffin. I know it sounds hateful, but I really wanted to smack her. My father kept shooting me looks, as if to say, "Keep it together for your mother." This despite the fact that Celeste Shoemaker hadn't shown any real signs of grief about the death of her mother up to that point—unless you want to count her saying that she was going to take a hot bath as grief.

We could hardly hear the priest for my mother's keening. I couldn't help it, my mind kept repeating the word *hypocrite*. Then I told myself that maybe in some strange way she did care . . . maybe she was just crazy and not evil. Finally, the service was over, and we had to stand there as the throng of people came by and made clucking noises about how sorry they were. (Of course Grandma Ada *was* loved and respected by countless men and women.) Only my godmother noticed that I looked really bad, saying, "Someone should pay attention to the fact that she's very sick." Joe took me home right away.

As soon as I walked in the door, I yelled, "I'm home!" When there wasn't an answer, I ran up the stairs two at a time—it didn't matter how sick I was. I found Brother lying on the bed with his T-shirt and boxer shorts on, and his whole body was flailing about in a violent seizure. Now if you've never seen anyone in a full-blown seizure, I don't recommend that you go out of your way to do so, because it's very upsetting.

There are times when you really don't think you can take any more, but then life drops another bomb on you. That's how I felt—I just hit the proverbial wall. Somehow I went on automatic, and everything became a blur. In those days, we didn't have 911; we called an ambulance in an emergency. One was called for Brother, who was rushed to the hospital, with my family in pursuit. My mother, however, was useless in this new crisis, deciding that she wouldn't accompany us but would take another bath. She showed no outward signs of alarm or concern . . . but then again, she'd always been ashamed of her brother and his plight.

When we reached the hospital, the doctor came out and told us that they'd dumped Brother in ice because his temperature had hit 108 degrees. Even at my young age, I knew that if my uncle did survive, his brain would be burned out. We weren't allowed to see him, and we were instructed to go home and wait for them to call us.

Before I knew it, it was time to go to Grandma's Mass and then to the cemetery for her burial. While we were in the limousine, my father kept mouthing something to me, but I was in such a fog of pain that I didn't get it. I found out later that he was trying to tell me that the hospital had called and Brother had died. I shouldn't have been surprised, since the one thing that was going through my mind was the way Grandma kept saying, over and over, "I can't leave without him." Over the years, I've often thought of how stupid I was not to realize that she was powerful enough to take her son with her, and that God would have granted her this wish. For all she did for the world, this would have been a significant payment.

I don't mean to imply that God plays games of *If you do this, I'll do that*. Rather, I just feel that the charts of Grandma and Brother were so intertwined that one couldn't have gone through life without the other. Dr. Skinner echoed my thoughts the next time I saw him. "Sylvia," he said, "now your grandmother and uncle are together, because he couldn't have lived without her. They were joined at the hip."

My beloved uncle Marcus Coil had only lived to 52 years of age.

We buried Grandma, and again, so many people showed up to pay their respects. We went to the rosary service for Brother the next night and then back out to the cemetery the following day to bury him right next to her. I thought, *Grandma, you weren't even in the ground yet and he was gone*. On her death certificate, the cause of death was listed as "pneumonia"; his, on the other hand, reads "unknown causes."

The most amazing thing happened when we got home after burying Brother. We found that every piece of his clothing was folded, and so were his newspapers—even though he'd never done this before. His clothes tended to be where he dropped them after taking them off, and his papers were usually all over the room. Also, before we buried him, I noticed that he was mysteriously clean-shaven and his hair had been neatly trimmed. Just as Grandma always picked up after him, she also shaved him and cut his hair, since his head would bob too much for him to do these things himself.

But the one thing that made me stop dead in my tracks was the sight of my grandmother's black crucifix, which the nurses at the hospital had given to me and I'd then passed on to my uncle. Here it was on top of his clothes, along with this note, written in his shaky hand: *I don't need this anymore.* I absolutely know that Grandma came for Brother in a real way, not in a dream or astral state—she got him ready to go and then let us all know that she was there and that both of them were all right.

A couple of years before dear Joe died, I was back in Kansas City for a visit, and several of us were out to dinner. I was absolutely delighted when my old friend told my son and everyone at our table what he and I had been privileged to witness after Brother's burial. We'd gone out for another drive that evening, when we noticed a light on in the backseat . . . and there was Grandma, smiling and sitting there with her hat on. Joe and I both saw it, and he was so shocked that he almost wrecked the car. We drove to Sydney's Drive-In and talked endlessly about what we'd both independently seen, a sighting that had personally given me some relief. Even so, I was still consumed by grief; after all, I'd lost two of the most important people in my life within days of each other.

Yet that wasn't the end of these extraordinary events. After we left the drive-in, Joe and I went back to my house, making small talk with the various well-wishers who had gathered there. Once everyone had left, Joe decided to stay over again. And again, we all slept downstairs, as if none of us could stand to be alone.

In the middle of the night, something woke up my sister and me simultaneously. When we looked over at the rocking chair in the front room that our grandmother had always sat in, we saw that she was sitting there now, except she was dressed in white and looked so much younger and healthier than we'd ever known her. She must have sat there for a full minute, as Sharon and I were holding hands so tight we were hurting each other. I had the presence to say, "I love you, Grandma," and then she was gone.

Daddy, Mama, and Joe all woke up and commented on how cold the room was (remember that it had been excruciatingly hot that summer, even at night). Sharon and I both began to talk at once about what we'd just seen.

I noticed that Joe was shaking his head, so I asked him what was wrong. He responded, "I thought it was a dream. . . . I was in a field, and your grandmother was walking with Brother—he looked sturdy and strong, and she looked young and happy. Then there was a very tall, dark-haired, dark-eyed young man; along with a husky, gray-haired older male. They all linked arms and walked away together." Now Joe had never seen a picture of my uncle Paul or my grandfather, yet he described them to a tee. It was obvious that they had reunited with Grandma and Brother on the Other Side, which made me so happy to hear. It's just like I tell people at my lectures when they ask me how we get total closure after a loved one's passing: We don't! We only get it when we meet up with our loved ones on the Other Side.

Joe and I talked about these events off and on for some 40 years before he died. Although he wasn't psychic, he was so supportive of me and loved my grandmother and uncle, just as they loved him. I'm so glad that they're all together now.

While I'm glad that my old friend is enjoying our blissful Home, I miss him as I talk about these times. As the years go by, it's bittersweet because I seem to be one of the last soldiers standing. As my father told me before he passed on, "You lose all those who remember what you remember."

It's no wonder that as we get older, we all become increasingly ready to rejoin our loved ones and go over old times and the silly things we did. Passing over is truly a great party, as well as a joy that can't be expressed on this plane.

It was strange because so many things that Grandma Ada had told me didn't actually connect with me until she was gone. For example, although I hadn't been afraid of seeing or talking to spirits for a long time, seeing the manifestations of Grandma made the afterlife more real and understandable to me.

And then there was cell memory, which she called "past-life memory." This is what happens when we carry phobias and the like with us from life to life. I've written about this in detail in my book *Past Lives, Future Healing*.

In fact, when I was writing that book, I remembered this one time when my parents were out of town and Grandma and Brother were staying with Sharon and me for the weekend. My grandmother used to make me nightgowns that tied around the neck. I hated the confining feeling, but I never told her because I didn't want to hurt her feelings. Anyway, on this particular weekend, I woke up in the middle of the night and sat straight up in bed gasping for air. When I finally caught my breath, I screamed for Grandma, who came right in to comfort me. I told her that I'd had a dream I couldn't remember, but it left me struggling to breathe. She gently said that it was because I'd been strangled in a past life, and she volunteered that she'd been silly to make the openings on my nightgowns so tight.

I never had another dream about being strangled, nor have I ever woken up fighting for breath again. (I *have* had a few astral-projection episodes, though.) Even so, I'm still not thrilled about tight things around my neck, such as chokers, turtlenecks, and so forth. If you're like that, too, it shouldn't bother you—just don't wear anything tight. It only becomes a problem when it affects your life or interferes with your daily functioning.

So, even though Grandma Ada may have been gone from my life physically, she has continued to be a guiding force in my life, as you'll see in the final chapters of this book.

→⊣ *Chapter Eight* ⊢←

FORGING
ON AHEAD

The days that followed the deaths of Grandma and Brother were a blur. I threw myself into school and was so glad that my grandmother had lived long enough to see me become a college student. I went on to take 22 units a semester and attended summer sessions. I took lots of literature, education, theology, and art classes; I also loved drama and was in several plays. Once I even dressed up as Whistler's mother from the famous painting, fooling my father when I picked him up at the airport after a business trip. Now that's good makeup, if I do say so myself!

These were the golden years of my life, and I look back on them with such fondness. The nuns were very progressive and kind, and I made friends for a lifetime. I loved college life and tried to back off of this whole paranormal business, but I couldn't because it was in the very fiber of my being. And as it turned out, I didn't marry Joe Behm. Of course if I would have chosen that particular path in life, I never would have met the people I've known or had the career I've enjoyed. As my dear ex-fiancé told me many years later, "Your grandma was right, Sylvia: the world called you, and I couldn't compete with that."

Speaking of Grandma, the grief of her death was forever with me. Sure, I felt her presence and even saw her now and again, and my spiritual guide Francine would deliver messages to me—but

I just plain missed her and our talks. Yet it seemed that after my grandmother passed on, Francine really stepped in to provide me with guidance and comfort. She became more vocal and imparted a lot more information to me—not that I didn't know about the Other Side, past lives, God, and other related subjects of a spiritual nature, but my guide filled in the blanks.

My parents and sister were used to Francine by now, and the way they talked about her, you would have thought that she was part of the family . . . which she actually became. They had their own guides, but because Francine was able to talk to them through me, she became like the patron of our family (something that has now transferred over to my ministers and study groups).

Out of the Darkness and into the Light

Even though I thoroughly enjoyed my time at St. Teresa's, there were some dark clouds on the horizon. After breaking my engagement to Joe, I met Ski. He was handsome and charming and made everyone else in my life at that time pale in comparison, and I fell hopelessly in love with him. Unfortunately, I found out about three or four months into our relationship that he was married (although separated). Since I was Catholic, and divorce was not recognized by the Church, I was counseled by the priests and nuns I consulted to end the relationship. I eventually did exactly that, but it was a very painful and heartrending experience.

After that debilitating love affair with Ski, I dated several men, and then I met Gary Dufresne, who was everything that everyone I'd dated before was not. I had some wild idea that settling down with him would ease the pain and fill the void that Ski's departure had left. Gary and I met in October 1958, and on April 2 the following year, we were married. While I didn't love him, he was a responsible police officer, and the one thing really driving me was that I wanted children. Why it didn't dawn on me that I could have married someone else and still have had kids is beyond me. I can only say that after the deaths of Grandma and Brother, the breakup with Joe (which was completely my fault), and the star-crossed affair with a married man, I was really tilted sideways.

The night before my wedding was quite eventful. My closest friend, Mary Margaret, spent much of it trying to talk me out of marrying Gary, but to no avail. Like so many brides, I felt that since the date was set, the church was booked, and the presents were bought and wrapped, I didn't have it in me to cancel all of that and disappoint everyone.

My mother also decided that this was the time to announce, "I hope you're happy—your father will probably leave me now," as if I was the one factor that kept them together. Even though this *was* partly true, my mother was heartless for saying it. And then my sister and I both saw Grandma, and she put her hands gently on our backs, as if to say, "It's all right."

After we were married, I got to see the true Gary, and I wished I would have listened to Mary Margaret and called off the wedding. He didn't turn out to be responsible after all; in fact, he inexplicably left the police department one day. Looking back on it now, I can see that he was fired. When he took the psychology test to get back in, he was turned down, and I always wondered whether they picked up on his violent nature and strange behavior.

His physical cruelty was beyond anything I've ever experienced, and his constant put-downs were devastating. So after having my first son, Paul, I went to see a priest about my marriage—and he told me to get out and take my son with me. For the next month or so I made plans to do just that, and then Gary announced that we were moving to California. Grandma's words came back to me loud and clear: "You'll have two boys and end up on the West Coast."

Even though I'd spent so many summers in California, the idea of leaving my friends, my teaching job, and all that I'd ever known was overwhelming. And it felt like I'd be leaving Grandma and Brother behind, too. Although I always tell people that their deceased loved ones don't actually reside in cemeteries, I felt so disrupted that I wanted to go somewhere, anywhere, where I could feel closer to my grandmother and uncle. So I went to the cemetery and sat between their graves.

It was June 1964. I'd felt, dreamed about, and even seen Grandma Ada, but it wasn't enough. (It never is enough, is it? Encountering your loved ones after they've died may bring you some solace, but it's not like having them with you. Although they see and hear everything you do, it's certainly not like sitting down and having a conversation over lunch.) I was crying and wishing that I could turn back time, obsessing about all the things I could have asked her but didn't. Of course I now know that no matter how many years I would have had with her, there was always going to be "one more thing" I didn't get the chance to say.

As Francine and my grandmother were so fond of telling me, out of every bad thing comes some good. We don't believe that when we're in the middle of darkness, but it's true. Thanks to that miserable, violent marriage to Gary Dufresne, I was given two beautiful sons . . . and I was brought to California to fulfill my destiny.

Gary wouldn't listen to any of my objections about moving, of course, so before I knew it we were living in a town I'd never heard of called Sunnyvale, which is just outside of San Jose. Gary told me that he was going to get a job with the local police force—this never happened, and he was out of work for more than eight months. Luckily, I'd gotten a job teaching almost immediately, but we were living on my meager salary alone. I felt like a ship without a rudder or even sails to take me anywhere, and I was miserably unhappy. I talked to Francine a lot and asked for her guidance, and I also prayed to God and Grandma for patience and the strength to go on.

We'd only been in California for about six weeks when all of a sudden my father, mother, and sister showed up on our doorstep. My father said that he couldn't stand our being apart, so he'd quit his job to be near me. *Near* proved to be a great understatement—Daddy ended up buying the duplex that Gary, Paul, and I were living in and moved right into the unit next door. I was happy to have my dad and sister so close, but I also thought, *I'm never going to be free of my mother.*

Over the next several years I tried to get away from Gary, and we separated a number of times. But like so many abused women, I went back, hoping that things would be better. And then there were my parents: my father wanted me to stay close, and Gary convinced him that we'd never move away; and my mother was always on Gary's side during the separations.

Forced to endure my unhappy marriage and Gary's cruelty, I threw myself into teaching and even went back to school for postgraduate work. I also gave birth to my second son, Christopher, in 1966. Yet when Gary threatened our children, that was it. I took Paul and Chris and got out of there, once and for all. Although divorce was unheard of in my family (and, of course, in my religion), nothing was going to stand in the way of my protecting my children.

Oh well, time heals all wounds. . . . Gary is now a lonely old man, and his children don't want anything to do with him, which is something they came up with on their own. I worked very hard not to bad-mouth their father in front of them, but my boys have always been strong, intuitive men who make up their own minds about everything.

Time to Go for It!

After my divorce from Gary, I had a dream in which Grandma asked me whether or not I was going to start using my God-given ability. I'd given readings for some of the nuns and priests at the school where I taught, and word had spread about my psychic insight. I'd also met Bob Williams when I was pursuing my master's degree, and while he started out as one of my professors, he ultimately became a close friend and confidant. Bob was so impressed with my abilities that he booked me to give lectures and readings for several different groups of people.

I'd also begun to trance-channel more and more for family and friends, because Francine knew more about topics such as history, cell memory, and the Other Side than I did. Little did I know that these trances would lead to the books that Grandma predicted I'd write so many years before. That's why I tell clients who are impatient that something they really want hasn't happened yet, "When you're meant to do it, you will. Life slaps you down and then turns around and pulls you up. If it's in your chart, it's going to happen, and nothing will stop that."

Now even though my grandmother knew I *was* psychic, she'd never mentioned that I'd make any kind of living *being* a psychic. The only one in our family who'd done anything close to that was Uncle Henry—and of course Grandma herself had always had her clients—but it certainly wasn't looked upon as a career. She wanted me to get into journalism, performing arts, or teaching, but the big thing that kept rearing its head in my life had always been my psychic ability.

I finally decided to go for it in the early '70s, even though I was filled with great trepidation. It all started when my second husband, Dal, and I went to a lecture given by a so-called psychic. During the presentation I became infuriated because of the false information she was giving to the audience. I raised my hand to ask some questions, but she never called on me. Afterward, Dal and I went to get a cup of coffee. Noticing how frustrated I was, he said, "You're much better than that lady is . . . why don't you go public with your ability?" We decided then and there to put a small ad in the local newspaper advertising "psychic classes," and we included our telephone number.

Twenty-two people attended that first class at our house in Campbell, California. It took a lot of grassroots effort on the part of countless volunteers and friends to help us build from there— we'd put up fliers on cars and doorknobs and even had dogs chase us. (Oh, the "good ol' days!") It certainly worked, though: it got to the point where we had to rent a hall every Tuesday night at the First Congregational Church to hold all the people. In those days it often seemed like a circus, which made me wonder if this was what God wanted.

My schedule doing readings became so heavy that our burgeoning company could afford to lease a small two-room office in an old business building in downtown Campbell, with my father fielding my calls. Since the office was located in the back of the building, I still don't know how anyone found me, but they did. Demand kept growing: we moved down the street to bigger offices, and I hired my sister, along with a secretary and another girl, Tia. Then we took over the whole building, hired more people, and started giving classes four nights a week. I felt like the newest barbecue pit on the block.

It seemed that I'd completed what Grandma wanted, and her words came back to me often. For example, she once told me that I'd be interviewed on TV by a blonde woman. I remember scoffing at the time, since there really weren't any talk shows back then. Even when Merv Griffin and Mike Douglas came along later, they were obviously men, and why would they want to talk to me? Francine confirmed my grandmother's words, but it wasn't until my career as a psychic started to take off that I appeared on a talk show in San Francisco called *People Are Talking* . . . which was hosted by a delightful, petite blonde named Ann Fraser, who is still a friend to this day.

Grandma's Eternal Protection

Long after she died, Grandma still managed to let me know that she was watching out for me. I have one particularly vivid recollection of her protecting me that gives me the chills to think about even to this day. One evening, Dal had gone to the store, the kids were out playing, and I was cooking dinner. For some reason a fire started in the oven, which was old and had never worked right anyway. The smoke came billowing out like nothing I'd ever seen, immediately filling the house. I kept trying to put the fire out, not realizing that in my panic, I was inhaling the acrid smoke. It wasn't long before I began to feel faint.

I was trying to get from the kitchen to the sliding glass door that led outside, but I hit the floor with a thud. Yet before I blacked out, I felt someone pushing on my diaphragm—and as I was losing consciousness, I saw blonde hair hanging over my face.

It must have been right at that time when Dal, who was a firefighter, got me outside and made sure that I was breathing. He then put out the fire and aired out the house.

When it was all over, all I could do was stare at my husband. Finally, he asked, "Honey, what is it?"

In my still-woozy state, I said, "You don't have long blonde hair!"

Looking at me with concern, he asked, "What do you mean?"

I told him about the blonde hair and the person pushing on my diaphragm, and that's when Francine told me, "That was your grandmother."

"How can that be?" I wanted to know. "She was old with white hair."

"Yes, that's what she looked like when she died, but now she's 30 years of age. She didn't have the time to convert to an 88-year-old woman, and besides, someone that old wouldn't have had the strength to save your life, so she kept her real glorified body."

And years before that, while we were still living in Kansas City, my son Paul had contracted a terrible staph infection when he was five months old. My baby was burning up, and when I called the doctor, he told me that this infection was tearing through the city, and the hospitals were full of people who had it. He said that I should try to keep Paul comfortable with cold baths and lots of liquids, and he'd let me know when space opened up.

For hours, I tended to my son, yet nothing seemed to help him. Finally, all I could think to do was rock him and ask Grandma to help me. Before I knew it, Paul, who'd been really listless and groggy with fever, focused his eyes above me and began to smile and coo. At that moment, a card that I'd wedged in my dressing-table mirror flew out and landed upside down at my feet. I picked it up to discover that it was Ada Coil's funeral card. Within two hours, Paul began to get better, but I got him to the hospital anyway. The doctor admitted that it was miraculous that a baby his age and weight hadn't died from dehydration—as so many babies in Missouri in 1961 didn't survive this virulent infection. So no one can tell me that we don't get help from our loved ones who have died . . . death doesn't stop love, because God *is* love.

Now I have written about this incident before, but it bears repeating. My first full-time job was as a teacher at an elementary school in Kansas City. My father had gotten me a little Chevrolet coupe that I could drive back and forth to my new job. My own car and my first job! As I drove to work that first day, I couldn't help but exclaim, "I'm on my way, Grandma—and it's not in California, but right here in Missouri!"

I absolutely loved teaching, and I adored my principal, Sister Regina Mary, who was tall and beautiful and wore her habit like a medieval princess. I'm sure she knew that I was scared silly when I first started, particularly when I had close to 50 kids in my class (in those days there were no rules on class size), but she was always full of praise and encouragement.

I'd been teaching at Sister Regina Mary's school for a few months when she called me at home one Saturday. She sounded very strange, as if her voice had been constricted. "I don't mean to bother you on the weekend, Sylvia . . . ," she started hesitantly.

Thinking that she was going to ask me some school business, I replied, "Sister, you can call me anytime."

She was silent for a few moments before finally saying, "I don't know how to tell you this."

Now I was getting worried—had I done something wrong, or was she sorry that she'd hired me? With my heart in my throat, I beseeched her, "Please, whatever it is, just tell me."

"Well . . . okay. Earlier today, I was in my office grading some papers and making my lesson plans for the week when I heard a noise downstairs. Since it would have been impossible for anyone to get in without tripping the alarm, I didn't think much of it. But after hearing more noises coming from down there, I realized that I had to investigate."

Sister Regina Mary told me that she went downstairs, where I had my classroom. Apparently, the door to my room was wide open, and there, in the middle of my festively decorated walls, stood a tall lady in a blue dress, with her white hair piled on top of her head.

I could barely breathe. "Then what happened?" I finally managed.

"This woman, who may have been old but had such a youthful look about her, gave me the most beautiful smile and told me that she'd come to see your room. She said, 'You can tell Sylvia that I was here,' and when I asked who she was, she just responded, 'She'll know.'"

Sister Regina Mary then said that she wasn't sure what else to do, so she told the woman that when she was finished looking around, she should come upstairs so that the principal could let her out. Sister Regina Mary went back to her office and resumed her work, but she still had an uneasy feeling. She decided after about 40 minutes to go down to my room to check on the old lady . . . and there was no one there.

I could tell that Sister Regina Mary was beside herself because the old woman couldn't have gotten past her without her knowing it, since the only way out was the door next to her office, and it would have set off the alarm. I knew she was expecting some type of explanation from me, and I wasn't exactly sure what to say to her. Finally, I said, "Sister, that was my grandmother."

"Well, at least she could have told me," she replied. "Did she come back to your house?"

"I don't think so. You see, she's been dead since 1954."

There was silence on the other end of the phone. *Now I've done it,* I thought. *I'll be fired for being a crazy person who teaches children.*

Sister Regina stammered that she was sorry to have bothered me and quickly hung up, and we never talked about this again. I did notice, however, that she occasionally sent kids to me to check if they were having problems at home or were eating properly. And right before I left her school to go teach at another, she did tell me, "You know, of course we Catholics all believe in the afterlife, but that episode with your grandmother has increased my faith a hundredfold."

"I'm glad, Sister," I replied. I then went on to tell her how close I felt to her and how she'd helped me with my abilities.

As I've said so many times before, the Catholic Church and the various parochial schools where I taught never once made me feel evil or different in any way, and for that I will be eternally grateful. Wherever I went, everyone knew about my abilities, but no one made a big deal out of them—if anything, they were very protective of me.

In fact, I want to take a moment here to single out Sister Marian, who was the principal at Presentation High School in San Jose, California. When I first met her, she'd just left the convent to work in Catholic schools, and now she's the head of the entire Catholic-school system in San Jose. I called her last year about getting my granddaughter, Angelia, into a particular school, and during our conversation, she said, "Sylvia, we all knew you were very psychic." Bless her heart, she was the best principal (and boss) I've ever had, and a marvelous and brilliant woman.

My work keeps me so busy now that I don't get to spend much time with wonderful people like Sister Marian, who cheered me on through some of the negativity and skepticism I've encountered, but I want these people to always know how much they mean to me.

Chapter Nine

THE BEAT
GOES ON

I've always been extremely interested in human behavior, and for a time I even entertained the idea of becoming a therapist. Of course being a psychic has brought me a great deal of experience with human beings and their behavior. I've been around long enough to spot a sociopath, narcissist, or paranoid schizophrenic; to see when someone's having a nervous breakdown; and even to sense an impending psychotic break. I don't feel that I'm qualified to give such individuals the kind of help they need, so I do what I can and then refer them to a medical professional. What's interesting is that I've also had a lot of doctors and therapists send *their* clients to me.

The problem with most mediums is that their egos tell them they can handle everything, and that's just wrong. We certainly help society, but we're not medical practitioners. Just because we may know that something is physically or mentally wrong with a person doesn't ever mean that we're qualified to treat it. Some psychics also want their clients to give up their medication and rely solely on their "cures," but what if these individuals have heart problems or diabetes? They could die without their medication, and that's just criminal. I've always recommended that people get second opinions, especially for serious conditions. Look at

Montel—he went years before his multiple sclerosis was correctly diagnosed. He kept being told that he had the flu, was stressed out, and so on, but he wouldn't give up trying to figure out what was wrong. I think that people always know when something is just not right with them, and they shouldn't rest until they find the answer that truly helps them.

Grandma Ada believed in healing—period. She used to tell me that I could do this myself, but I always shied away from it, feeling that I had quite enough on my plate. Running a large company and a church, doing readings, helping the police with cases, talking to the dead, taking part in salons and research trances, answering letters and e-mails, writing, lecturing, appearing on TV shows, putting together my newsletter, and having a weekly radio show have kept me plenty busy . . . I didn't know where I could possibly fit in healing. Yet even though I've pushed it back for so many years, I find that as I get older, it keeps coming to me.

For example, I was recently in Las Vegas lecturing about healing, when I asked two people to come up and sit in my chair, which is something I rarely do. The first person who volunteered was a woman who'd suffered from migraines for 20 years, and the second was a man with a bad back. I put my hands on top of each of their heads, and before long, I felt as if an electrical current had gone through me. When I finished, the woman ecstatically told me that she'd lost her headache, but the man said that, while his back felt better, he could still feel a dull pain. I thought, *Well, Sylvia, it's like the psychic gift—you can't be right all of the time.*

The next night, during a book signing after my lecture at the Excalibur Hotel and Casino, this same man approached me. This time he said, "I don't know if you remember me, but I was the guy you did a healing on last night. I wanted to tell you that at about midnight, all that pain I'd been living with for years up and went away!" So maybe I will do it some more . . . Grandma strikes again!

I remember how red my grandmother's palms used to become after she'd give her healing sessions. I'll never forget the first time I noticed this: I was sitting on her bed and I happened to look over and see that her hands were blood red. She heard me gasp and immediately folded her hands together so as not to scare me further.

"Grandma, let me look," I said. She tried to assure me that it was nothing to worry about, but being stubborn, I wouldn't let it go. Finally, she gave in and let me see her hands. I asked her if she was in pain, and she answered no, but her palms were very hot.

I could feel the heat as I put one to my face, and I asked, "Grandma, why?"

She just said, "I've always had it, and it's something that God has given to me." As the evening wore on, the color faded a little from her hands, but they still remained red.

A couple of years ago I was having dinner with my psychic son, Chris, and he suddenly exclaimed, "Mom, what's wrong with your hands?!" He was so alarmed that I looked at my palms right away and almost fainted—they were incredibly red. I'd just finished doing my readings, so I thought that this was the reason. I was 70 at the time and thought that maybe the redness came on then, but Grandma said that she'd always had it happen to her. Why would it come on for me now?

I feel the same way about healing—I'm very grateful to God, of course, but I honestly don't understand why it's come about so strongly at this point in my life. I've always felt that words heal, but apparently God decided to give that notion an addendum. I still believe that if you can heal the mind, the body will follow suit, but maybe there are some people out there who just need a physical healing. I'm reluctant to broadcast this (even though I've just done so in this book), since I'm not sure how I'll have the time to fit such services into my already-packed schedule. I'm sure that my grandmother wants me to go out with a bang for God and go further than she did in life. What's helped me out there is that the planet feels so much smaller now than it did when she was around—the information we have instant access to nowadays makes it seem as if the whole world can come right into our living rooms.

I'm ready to go wherever, and do whatever, God wants me to, but I always pray for the stamina and blessed energy to do it all!

Oh, I notice that I don't move as fast as I used to, but my energy and stamina are still high, and my physicals every October come out great. We'll see what the future brings. . . .

Passing the Psychic Torch to My Own Family

Grandma had told me that I'd have two sons who would stay with me always. It's true, I've never had the empty-nest feeling with my children. Of course those who know me will laugh because they'll point out that my sons didn't really leave me. Even when my boys were teenagers, they'd have their friends in the garage playing Ping-Pong or foosball, but they loved to ask me to "come out and play," too. And although they're now in their 40s, they still live three minutes from me: Chris bought me a home several years ago so that I'd be close, and Paul moved up to my area of San Jose. So while they have their own families, I see them all the time.

I've never believed the old saying that "a son is a son till he takes a wife, but a daughter is a daughter all of her life." That certainly hasn't been true in my case. I don't take sides when my sons have problems in their relationships, nor do I give them advice. When they ask for it, I turn it around and ask what *they* want to do. I've always loved the women my sons have loved, and they've loved me, which certainly helps. But if my boys had married monkeys, I'd still love them (or at least make an attempt).

If you're a parent who's having trouble with the person your child is in a relationship with, why cause friction because you "don't approve"? Why set yourself up for alienation? I know that there are some individuals who are just dark and can't be loved—if that's the case, stay away and keep your mouth shut! Grandma used to say that kind words turn away wrath, and unless something or someone is simply too evil or unjust, it's best to keep your opinions to yourself.

My grandmother also told me that one of my boys would be psychic. I thought it would be my eldest, Paul, because he could astrally project, but then along came Chris, and boom—he started with a bang! He had a spirit guide he could talk to, was constantly seeing spirits and ghosts (especially lost children), knew who was coming over and would be calling on the phone, and liked to astrally project even more than Paul did. He projected so much as a child, in fact, that Francine told me to ask him to stay off the steps of the Other Side's Hall of Justice (I go into great detail about this magnificent edifice in my book *Temples on the Other Side*). It seems that Chris liked to go there to play with other boys and girls . . . and although I did pass along Francine's request, I don't think it worked.

The same thing happened with my grandchildren. Angelia's psychic abilities came out right away, but as she hit her teen years, she put them on the back burner; however, I do still see them rise up in full force when she's asked a question. Yet just like with Paul, it's Angelia's younger brother who is demonstrating a stunning psychic gift. Willy, my youngest grandchild, can tell you what's going to happen and who's bad or good—he's like a barometer for dark entities, which is priceless.

Several years ago Chris and I were trying to talk about what we'd seen in France. Willy was just two years old at the time, and he up and said, "Eiffel Tower," before Chris or I could get the words out of our mouths. My son and I just stared at each other, since no way does a two-year-old know about something like that, much less pronounce it correctly. Yet that's nothing compared to the things he comes up with every day now that he's older. You can't surprise him in any way—not with presents, a party, or the like. He even picked up something in the background of one of Chris's friends, which no one else knew, and it turned out to be true.

I'm not saying this because they belong to me, but Willy and Angelia's mother and father are spectacular parents. Even though they're divorced now, they still consult each other on everything and stick together where their kids are concerned. They both talk to their children constantly, and there is never any semblance of discord because of the divorce. They have joint custody, and both kids are fine with the arrangement. As Willy told me the other day, "Staying with one parent for a couple of weeks is no problem because just when I'm getting tired of one of them, I get to go visit the other one." I had to hide my mouth and bite my hand to keep from laughing at that one. The whole situation truly makes my heart glad.

And then there's Paul's precious, kind son, Jeffrey, who loves to watch my lectures. When he was young, he told his dad that when he grew up, he wanted to be a "psycho" like his grandma. We still laugh about that—especially since Paul didn't correct his choice of words. Jeffrey is a teenager now, and he's very intuitive as well, telling his mother what time his dad will be home and so forth.

So this just shows that there's obviously a genetic component to mediumship that is not diminishing with time; indeed, sometimes I think it's actually getting stronger. Thank God we live in a time when the world is more prepared for psychics. (It makes sense that with the way things are going on this planet, we're going to need these advanced spiritual beings before the end to help people see the light of the soul's survival.) I'm especially grateful that my grandchildren have grown up in such an accepting environment—none of them has to hide his or her light under a bushel.

It was so strange when I became a grandmother, though: it seemed that one minute I was a granddaughter myself, and the next I had a sapphire-eyed little girl with curly black hair sitting on my lap, listening to the same stories I was told by my own grandmother.

In fact, I feel there is a distinct possibility that Grandma Ada came back into life as Angelia, my eldest grandchild. I say this even though Grandma told me that she was on her last life. After all, if I got talked into living more lives than I intended, why wouldn't she? When Angelia was small, she'd freak me out by telling me things that only Grandma and I knew. And when she was two years old, she pointed at Grandma's picture and then pointed to herself and said, "Me." My granddaughter has the same mannerisms and likes and dislikes that my grandmother did, such as her love of writing and performing, as well as an aptitude for seeing ghosts.

I also believe that she is Ada because I don't feel Grandma as much as I did before Angelia was born; it's strange to think that while I miss her presence behind me, I might have her in the flesh. Angelia's family isn't too keen on this notion, but if she isn't Ada, she's certainly getting my grandmother's knowledge from somewhere . . . but then Willy's getting it, too, so I guess we'll see how this ultimately plays out.

I look back at how Grandma used to point out the good and bad friends around me—for all of her humanitarianism, she did not suffer fools—as well as how she admitted to being jealous of the time I spent with my friends. Now that I'm 72 and Angelia is 16, I can see all too well how my grandmother felt. Since Angelia has a psychic father and grandmother, the family gift just seems to be normal to her, and she's now focusing on other things. I've encouraged her to go into the performing arts, and she's taking acting lessons and going on auditions and loves the whole thing. She's also attending Notre Dame High School, and is enrolled in college-prep classes.

Unlike Grandma, I don't feel any jealousy toward my own granddaughter . . . it's more of a heartfelt sadness when I remember the little girl who would hang on me, wanting to hear stories, do crafts, and cuddle with me at night. All that went away, and now she has her own drama classes, sleepovers and other activities with her friends, her iPod and computer, and so on. I've receded to the background of memory—I may have lost her to time, but not to love. It's funny how I had to get there myself before I could understand how my grandmother felt.

The other day I asked Angelia, "Remember when you would travel with me?" She, with her teenage mouth, retorted, "Is that all you want to talk about, Bagdah [her name for me]—the past?" I stared her square in the eye and said, "Well, Eya [her nickname],

I don't have the present or the future of the two of us to refer to, so what else can I talk to you about?" She got really quiet after that.

The next day she came to me and said, "I'm sorry, Bagdah, I don't mean to be a butt."

I replied, "It's fine, sweetheart. I'm not so old that I don't remember what it's like to be a teenager, but honestly, this all really hit me because I've been reading Grandma's letters." I went on to read her the one in which my grandmother admitted being bitten by the green-eyed monster of jealousy.

"But Bagdah, you know I love you," Angelia said when I finished.

"I know, darling, and it's all part of life. It's like replacing the guard—the younger ones come in, and the older ones have to retreat to let them come forward."

"Well, I go through people hurting me, too," she admitted, looking at me with her large sapphire eyes.

"Yes, of course you do," I assured her. "If you love as deeply as I know you can, you'll feel that grab at your heart." It was then that I remembered that Angelia and I had both seen an Indian girl who lives near my home, and she gave each of us the name "Raining Tears," independently of one another. I'm sure that my granddaughter will return to her psychic abilities in time.

Just as Grandma Ada had predictions for me, there are a few things I can see for my grandchildren, and someday they'll read it here first. Jeffrey will get married early—by early, I mean in his 20s—and have a boy and a girl. Angelia will not get married for many, many years, if at all, and she won't have children. She'll write books like mad and take over my church and foundation after Chris dies, so the heritage will go on. Willy will marry and have three children, two of which will be twins. One of his girls will be psychic and will be able to trance, so she'll carry on the psychic tradition in the family, which will take us to almost 400 years of genetic psychics.

Mama's Grip, Grandma's Love

You hear people ask, "Where did the time go?" but you don't fully comprehend this question in its totality until you take a second to look back on your life and the people who have made the biggest impact on it. My grandmother used to say that cleaning and work will wait, but children wouldn't. How true that is—when I was with her, she'd drop everything if I needed her, knowing that whatever she was doing would keep until later. I feel very fortunate because few people in this life (family or not) are of one mind and understand another person completely, especially when they barely understand themselves, but my grandmother certainly understood me.

The final letter I'd like to share with you was written during one of the many summers my parents, sister, and I spent away from Kansas City. I'm sure that those times were hard on both Grandma and Brother, as our only communication was through letters, and the two of them didn't get to see the rest of us very much. It's a sad thing, but when kids are having fun, they don't often think about their grandparents. Even so, it was hard for me to be away from Grandma and Brother, too, and I wrote them often. I want you to see, once again, how loving her letters could be:

> *Darling Kiddies,*
>
> *I'm sending you some yarn, you blessed babies. I bought this bunch from Mrs. Board for 15 cents—it was all matted together, and I stuffed it in my pocketbook and straightened it out. I had bought two bunches from her before for the quilt, for 5 cents each—hope you like them. If you have no use for the thread, give it to someone else.*
>
> *Tell Mother to wash the inside of the dresser with Clorox or some disinfectant—as the poor McManuses who had it before were very clean, but the man had what they were afraid of—the pneumonia that was developing into TB (consumption) before he was admitted two months ago to the Leeds Sanitarium, for TB patients. He varnished it and put new knobs on it. You can*

have the dresser—I told them it was yours, so you are welcome to it.

Sylvia, I am going to give you and Sharon some money when I see you—I would send it today but am afraid it will be stolen. How are you, my precious little sweetheart, the love of our hearts? I miss you so much, darling beauty heart—honey, baby love, precious love—we will always love and look for you both. You both are always in our prayers and thoughts. I may not show my love, darling, but the stillest water runs deepest, and even though I am not as demonstrative as I would like to be, my heart is thrilled when I see any of you and your parents. I love you all—and how we pray and hope that only the good that God can send will all be yours forever.

Love,

Grandma Coil and Brother

P.S. As the pest man is coming, I want to mail this to my wonderful sweetheart—our lovely, kind, pure Sylvia—from Grandma.

Please phone the laundry man to come for my laundry soon as he can.

And I must see you often, love, either at my house or at yours. Brother got a lot of funny papers just now from Aunt Annie—will save them and bring them to you when I see you— let me know when you need us.

Grandma Ada didn't have much of a relationship with my sister; in fact, I don't remember Sharon being affectionate with her at all. It could have been her age, but Sharon was so bonded with Mama that *no one* could get in. When Mama would come to pick us up from our grandmother's house, I'd cry because I had to leave Grandma, but Sharon would run to Mama happily. Even though I raised my sister (by that I mean doing all the perfunctory things like dressing her, fixing her hair, feeding her, and taking her with me—even on dates, if you can believe that), she was still tied to whatever Mama said. My father just gave up, and nothing Grandma said had any effect.

Mama got a firm grip on my sister, particularly in the way she used to tell Sharon that she was sickly and frail. Mama would say to her, "If you don't want to go to school, you don't have to," so she'd lie in her room while our mother brought her sandwiches. Sharon later got into alcohol—something that I was saved from, thank God—and Mama gave her uppers even though she was still very young. I tried for years to get my sister into teaching, art, or any number of constructive things, but nothing worked. She's now suffering with the effects of what is tantamount to drug and alcohol abuse, God bless her. I call her, but it's like talking to a stranger. She's an old, feeble woman who has simply given up.

Life is so full of everything, but it doesn't come to your door— you have to go out and find it. It's so sad, but you know you can't beat the odds when it comes to what another person decides to do with his or her life, so sometimes you have to walk away. I can't truly blame my mother for everything that happened to my sister, since Sharon could have fought against it. I guess it was just easier for her to float along on the surface of life. You may look at this as a waste, but my grandmother and I always knew that Sharon had a few other lives to live yet, and we didn't. Now I know why . . . this life has been no life for her at all.

Still Influencing My Life

Once in a while Grandma used to say that if something hit you squarely in the solar plexus, that was a psychic hit, so you had to make a fast decision. By the same token, when you meet someone, your first impression is usually right because your intellect hasn't gotten in there to mess it up yet. But if you do something blindly for all the wrong reasons, then your haste will make waste.

My grandmother was so ahead of her time. For example, she ingrained in my soul that this world was just a temporary place to learn and do good. She also used to say that being psychic is only part of a bigger picture, which was to show people that God's consciousness is all around us, and that His and Her helpers are always there for us, as long as we don't get caught up in our own "stuff" and ego. I've personally been defamed, gone broke, been divorced, and lost loved ones; yet I keep getting up and trying again, knowing that those who love me always will, and those who don't love me aren't going to, and that's all right, too.

Even now when I'm in the throes of helping someone and it gets to be too hard, I hear Grandma's words: "If you keep carrying someone, his legs won't work anymore." I think it's amazing that so many decades after she went Home, her words are still influencing my life, but that's bound to happen with someone as full of insight, wisdom, and greatness as she was.

My grandmother had a saying for everything, and one of my favorites was: "Lazy people take the most pains." It's true—if you try to do something as a shortcut, for some reason it will actually take you more time to get it done. Another one she liked was: "Do something in haste and repent in leisure," and I've found that to be spot-on as well.

Grandma used to say that there was a time for everything, and if you just stayed on a good course, God would present you with opportunities. She told me to expect nothing, accept everything that was good on my path, and negate the bad. I wish I'd listened to that more, but then again I wouldn't have learned some of my life's most important lessons.

Here are some more of Grandma's favorite sayings:

- "Kind words turn away wrath."

- "Smile, and the world smiles with you; cry, and you'll weep alone."

- "Within your weakness lies your strength sleeping."

- "Love can overcome any problem."

- "You can shatter the vase if you will, but the scent of the roses clings to it still." [Meaning that you never forget good things, no matter how "broken" life becomes.]

- If asked how she was, she'd say, "Fine as silk and a yard wide." [This is an old sewing phrase.]

- "Let's get down to brass tacks." [This was a way of getting to the problem, but also a way of measuring a yard between two brass tacks.]

- "God's mill grinds slow, but exceedingly fine." [A reference to karma and how you reap what you sow.]

- "Don't let negativity fill your heart . . . it will show in your eyes and on your face."

- "Don't just dream what you'll do—do it!"

- "That person looked like a pot full of mice." [Said about someone who had a mean face.]

- "If your family fails you, surround yourself with people who take their place."

- "To obsess over riches is meaningless because all that glitters is not gold."

- "If you lose something precious, God will replace it with something good." [She thought that I was God's gift to her after losing her son Paul.]

- "In your sorrow, lift up your eyes and see the hand of God."

- "God lets us see ghosts and spirits to show us that we live on beyond this life."

- "People who are born disabled show us the patience and greatness of spirit."

- "Ignorance is the worst thing you can let your mind entertain."

- "If you have a secret, keep it to yourself, or else the whole world will know it."

- "Unkind words are like opening a feather pillow in the wind and then picking up all the feathers." [You can't actually do this, just as you can't take unkind words back.]

- "The more you cry, the less you'll pee." [This was just another way of her looking on the bright side of everything.]

- "He is so stingy that he squeaks when he walks."

- "Out of the mouth of babes come gems and ditties and stories with morals."

- "Write a letter at night, and read it in the morning."

- "When children are little, they step on your feet; when they are older, they step on your heart."

- "Don't put sweaters on your children when *you* are cold."

- "Dirt will wait, but your children won't."

- "If you lie, you weave a web that you become imprisoned in."

- "Love puts curtains on the windows."

- "God only knows love."

- "Love falls before pride."

- "If you wish or pray for something, be prepared for the consequences."

- "They look like they've been ridden hard and put away wet."

- "A woman never uses profanity, and a woman never smokes in public if at all."

- "You can't make a silk purse out of a sow's ear."

- "Pretty is as pretty does."

- "True love is like gold . . . it never tarnishes."

- "God answers prayers. He just sometimes says no."

- "What you are becomes written on your face and in your eyes."

- "You have to be respectful to be respected."

There are so many more, and some of them are included in the letters I've shared with you throughout this book. I know that several of these sayings come from literature or the Bible and have been around for a long time, but it takes a good mind to know when to apply them so that they pack the greatest punch.

I treasure Grandma Ada's words—I have dozens of her letters, which are crumbling and yellowed with age, but they're absolutely priceless to me. She wanted to write in her life, and I hope that in a way, she now has. Tragically, it can take so long for greatness to be realized in this world, and my grandmother is a perfect example of this. She was a German woman who came to the U.S. and settled in the Midwest to raise her family—she was never on the radio or television, but she gave help to thousands of people, and isn't that ultimately what really matters? I'm sure that all of the souls who watched her from the Other Side learned from her and cheered.

So if you feel that you toil along in life without anyone knowing your name or recognizing what you've done, please remember Ada von Banica Coil, who gave her granddaughter the courage to not only explore her own gift, but to give hope and knowledge to the world as well. I hope I've done her justice—it's important that I pay tribute to my blessed mentor, the person who brought me so much love and knowledge, which has filled every single day of my life.

As the song goes, when things go bad, I remember a few of my favorite things; and there's Grandma, head and shoulders above everyone and everything in my thoughts. I wish I could have seen her with my boys—yes, I know she can see them and my grandchildren from the Other Side, but I don't get to enjoy seeing her with them . . . but that's the way things go.

She was my guiding light, my mother, my friend, and the love of my life. I learned more from her in close to 18 years than I have in the remaining decades of my life. Do I miss her? Yes, of course I do, but every time I see Angelia, I see Grandma: the blue eyes; the toss of the head; the love of babies, animals, and people; the caring and the tender heart. When I first held that precious baby girl in my arms, I said, "Well, now we've come full circle." Today I find myself giving Angelia the same encouraging words my grandmother gave me, such as: "Know that you are good, beautiful, and smart; love others, but don't let anything keep you from your goal."

So the beat goes on . . . and hopefully, it will still go on long after I'm gone and not get lost in the dust of fear, bigotry, and injustice. I do pray daily for that because I don't want everything that Grandma and I (not to mention our forebearers) accomplished to have been in vain; that is, we didn't experience the highest joys and the depths of despair for nothing. Of course I know that no life is ever lost, but words do get trampled under the fundamentalist righteousness of prejudice; and until we come to truly care for and love one another, nothing will change.

I have so much to be thankful for. I've always been grateful, but as life goes on it seems that I've become even more so. I'm grateful for my precious staff (some of whom have been with me for more than 30 years), my study groups and members of my church, and the philosophy that keeps pressing onward and upward and spreading to all countries. I'm grateful for my wonderful sons and my God-given grandchildren, who are the joys of my life. I'm grateful for Ben, who travels with me and unselfishly helps me and anticipates my needs; Michael, Ben's partner, who patiently lets him travel with me; Linda, whom I could give my life to for safekeeping and never blink an eye; Vera, Jen, Darren, Sheila, Pam, Gene, John, Gloria, Tom, Brooke, Susan, Loren, Virginia, Mary, and so many more. And I'm grateful for all of you, my dear loved ones, who come to see me, read my books, watch me on TV, or have me read for you . . . where would I be without you?

I know in my heart that although my grandmother told me I'd reach her level of spirituality, I haven't done so yet, but I keep trying. Maybe with God's help, by the time I'm 89, I will finally get there. After all, the journey may be trying, but it's also joyous and fascinating—and it's all part of the learning process.

→ AFTERWORD ←

As I end this book, I'd like to share some personal thoughts that I'm addressing directly to my grandmother. First, here's a poem I wrote that doesn't have a title—but for the purposes of convention, let's just say it's called "Grandma"—and then I have some words of thanks for her:

Out of the mists of my memory in time,
Your words come back, but your image is fine.
Fine as gossamer wings that whisper in my ear,
That even not seeing you, I know you are near.
There is no closure for those we love in our soul,
To meet them again is our ultimate goal.
I lost my mentor, my queen, and my mother,
And in 72 years there has been no other.
So this is a love story that I wanted to write,
Before you and I faded from this earthly plight.
You gave me the courage to see life through,
And every day I pray I will be more like you.
So what I wish for is for everyone to have your wisdom and wit,
If we did, our souls would be surely fit.
With optimism, love, and a God full of love,
You are my Holy Spirit, as white as a dove.
I'll embrace you and hold you and see your beautiful eyes,
I have more to do, but time rapidly flies.
So I'll wait, as we all do, to see your face,
And rejoice in the fact that we finished God's final race.

Last but not least, I want to thank you, Grandma, for teaching me . . .

. . . that life isn't always "rainbows and lollipops."

. . . that life is full of strife, but with God's help, I could overcome it.

. . . that I could never be bored, since smart people can always find something to do.

. . . that tolerance should be given to everyone in the world.

. . . what unconditional love really means.

. . . that I could be better than I ever dreamed I could be.

. . . that I could be educated and rely on myself.

. . . that I should never be ashamed of my gift and to use it wisely.

. . . not to be afraid to be wrong, because only God is always right.

. . . to suffer the slings and arrows of skeptics but to get up and keep on going.

. . . to never use my gift for my own gain.

. . . to never misquote my guide.

. . . not to expect my life to be charmed, since I have to learn, too.

. . . to live by example as well as words.

. . . to never look down on anyone, no matter what their station in life may be.

. . . to become a writer and speak from my heart.

. . . that the law of the universe is: whatever you put out comes back to you.

. . . to share what I have with others.

. . . not to depend on others to hold me up—to stand on my own two feet.

. . . to be there for my family and friends and the people who need me.

. . . that giving to others is the way to health and happiness.

Thank you, sweet soul, for gracing my life and others' lives, too. I can see you in the Rose Garden on the Other Side, walking with Brother, who is now tall and strong, without cerebral palsy—when I'm down, that image gives me strength. I love life, but I'll be glad to see you again. As you said, "My heart would hear you and beat if it lay for a century dead."

And most of all, Grandma, thank you for just being you . . . which would fill volumes.

Finally, to you, my wonderful readers, please understand that even though I may not be lecturing and traveling so much anymore, I will always love you. If I have touched *you*, it's nothing compared to the way you have touched *my* heart. God bless all of you. Whenever I've had my moments of "What if?" they instantly fade away when I hear your encouraging voices and see your sweet, smiling faces. Know that, while this book is a love letter to my grandmother, it's certainly one for you as well.

God love you. I do.
Sylvia

❖ ❖ ❖

⋇ APPENDIX ⋇

Letters from Ada Coil to Sylvia (Shoemaker) Browne:

> Darling Sylvia – One of my naughty Tricks
>   While looking at the
> small thermometer this morning
> reminded me of my childhood
> days – we had one large one every one
> went to look at it as it was so
> accurate, well one day it seems
> it was quite cold – and for some
> reason I could not go out to play –
> well I wanted the Thermometer to
> say the weather was warm, so
> I could play – I held a Match
> under it and the needle flew up
> about 1 hund deg – my, oh, my, the
> puzzled looks of all – what was the
> matter with the Thermometer – well, I
> did the trick once too often, it
> broke – I suppose I must have done
> it – I was always going out to play
> no matter how cold it could – such a naughty
> girl – and funny
>   Grandma Coil

Sylvia Shoemaker,
Our Darling Birthday
girl — we wish you all the joy
good health long life, happiness
and all the God given blessings
of success — love and comfort
you will get from others if you
love and trust God and keep
his command ments. — The only way
to get happiness is to make others
happy. in a considerate — and
unselfish way. — for happiness
lies within ourselves. keep your
mind free from worry or impure
thoughts. Keep your feet on the ground
but your eyes and thoughts on
heavenly things. and live so. —
Ten long years of your life God
has given to us. — Your children
have been a comfort — blessing
and happiness to us all. especially
your dear parents. so self
sacrificing. and noble — to you
both. — Again we wish you

Many happy returns of
the day. and always remember
Brother and I love you
more then life our life and the
only way to keep or get a
friend to love you is to be
a friend and love all good
people - We send you one
dollar.

Love from
Brother and
Youndma

Wed - May 23 - 1950,

To our Beloved - Beautiful
Sylvia C. Shoemaker -
Please Allow your grandmother
and "Brother" to send you their
sincere love and well wishes with
a small token of their great regard
1⁰⁰ . I wish it was one million $
I would would gladly give it to
you - Sweetheart - give of my sweet
dreams, - and always a pleasure
to meet you all ᵒ⁄₁ when we are awake
you have now your first -
graduation day - with the help of
your noble parents - God will sure
reward them for it - your first day
you graduate I hope it wont be the
last - that you will win your
A - B - degree - in St Theresa - you
will step into a new life - surrounded
with culture refinement - happiness
and an atmosphere of all that is good
beautiful and educated leading you
onward - upward nearer to God -

Make hay while the Sun shines 2ᵈ study. Store your mind with all that is worthy to know — and when old your thoughts will be so good and well informed they will entertain you — comfort and keep you from being lonely — Your first graduation day — I hope it wont be the last — day that would deprive you of your A. B - degree. Your parents will be rewarded for this grand gift of education. They are noble — be to them a good faithful helpful daughter. all your kindness to them will return to you dear heart — give every flying moment something to lay in store. intellectually — financ — financially — helpful to others, your duty to God first then get as much joy in life — as you can all the time with out neglecting your duties, — at home your education now is the most — later is happy home, with children — now the

My Sylvia - The Dream Girl - of all who know you - Graceful as a fairy - Voice soft and low - a lover of the nice beautiful soulful things of Heaven and earth, - whose soul - is as pure and white as a new snow flake - whose features, - eyes - ears mouth nose are perfect, a fine Artist would be delighted to paint the faces of calm peace - intellect and refinement that Sylvia and Sharon have, - their form is like as perfect as the Venice DeMilo - the beautiful statue, a Rembrant (artist,) would produce Sylvia and Sharon - a beautiful picture of grace - and refinement - but above all this love of beauty and grace is the fact - her soft low pronunciation, correct in every detail - her Mental ability is greater then most adults, splendid - but above all beauty of form face and manners and her great artistic abilities is the perfection of her mind - Soul and heart, all fade away but these gifts form you live forever - a priceless gift above beauty of form or face this fades and soon forgotten,

2

the beauty of loving disposition
a spotless character – the little kind
acts, the forgetfulness of self the art
of making friends – and keeping them
by avoiding all those little pin
pricks that one gets to their feelings
heaping coals of fire – when alone
try to think of how you have spent
your time – and what you have said
did you even when you talked.
let your eyes rest on every one
showing no partiality – never show
anger or ridicule in company –
of any one – never repeat what in
any way would hurt any ones
character or secret they told you –
be a friend – treat all alike – with
kind words and smiles – never complain
to your friends – they no more pity
you then birds of prey pity the
wounded dove – when your friend
becomes your foe then all the
world your secret knows –

Family Photographs:

A young Ada Coil.

Another photo of Grandma Ada when she was a young woman.

My grandfather Marcus Coil, Grandma Ada, their son Paul, and Uncle Henry.

My great-grandfather Henri Kaufholz.

Aunt Annie Kaufholz.

Grandpa Marcus Coil.

My uncle Marcus Coil (also known as "Brother") when he was a baby.

A very young Brother.

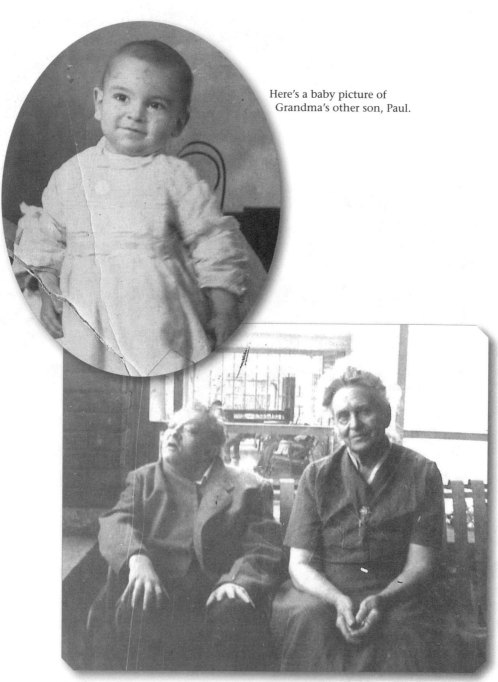

Here's a baby picture of Grandma's other son, Paul.

Brother and Grandma.

Here I am at age two, with
my mother, Celeste.

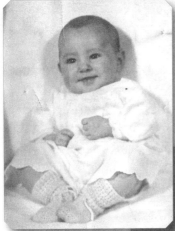

Me at six weeks
of age.

Me at age 18.

⟩≫ ABOUT THE AUTHOR ≪⟨

Sylvia Browne is the #1 *New York Times* best-selling author and world-famous psychic medium who has appeared regularly on *The Montel Williams Show* and *Larry King Live,* as well as making countless other media and public appearances. With her down-to-earth personality and great sense of humor, Sylvia thrills audiences on her lecture tours and still has time to write numerous immensely popular books. She has a master's degree in English literature and plans to write as long as she can hold a pen.

Sylvia is the president of the Sylvia Browne Corporation; and is the founder of her church, the Society of Novus Spiritus, located in Campbell, California. Please contact her at: **www.sylvia.org,** or call **(408) 379-7070** for further information about her work. Sylvia is also featured on an additional Website: **www.SpiritNow.com.**

HAY HOUSE TITLES OF RELATED INTEREST

YOU CAN HEAL YOUR LIFE, the movie,
starring Louise L. Hay & Friends
(available as a 1-DVD program and an expanded 2-DVD set)
Watch the trailer at: **www.LouiseHayMovie.com**

THE SHIFT, the movie,
starring Dr. Wayne W. Dyer
(available as a 1-DVD program and an expanded 2-DVD set)
Watch the trailer at: **www.DyerMovie.com**

DIARY OF A PSYCHIC: Shattering the Myths, by Sonia Choquette

EXCUSES BEGONE! How to Change Lifelong,
Self-Defeating Thinking Habits, by Dr. Wayne W. Dyer

THE LIGHTWORKER'S WAY: Awakening Your Spiritual
Power to Know and Heal, by Doreen Virtue

THE LIVES OUR MOTHERS LEAVE US: Prominent Women
Discuss the Complex, Humorous, and Ultimately Loving
Relationships They Have with Their Mothers, by Patti Davis

MESSAGES FROM SPIRIT: The Extraordinary Power
of Oracles, Omens, and Signs, by Colette Baron-Reid

OUR LADY OF KIBEHO: Mary Speaks to the World from
the Heart of Africa, by Immaculée Ilibagiza, with Steve Erwin

PRACTICAL PRAYING: Using the Rosary to Enhance Your Life,
by John Edward (book-with-CD)

SPIRIT MESSENGER: The Remarkable Story of a Seventh
Son of a Seventh Son, by Gordon Smith

THE SPIRIT WHISPERER: Chronicles of a Medium, by John Holland
(available February 2010)

All of the above are available at your local bookstore,
or may be ordered by contacting Hay House (see next page).

We hope you enjoyed this Hay House book.
If you'd like to receive our online catalog featuring additional
information on Hay House books and products, or
if you'd like to find out more about the
Hay Foundation, please contact:

Hay House, Inc.
P.O. Box 5100
Carlsbad, CA 92018-5100

(760) 431-7695 or **(800) 654-5126**
(760) 431-6948 (fax) or **(800) 650-5115 (fax)**
www.hayhouse.com® • **www.hayfoundation.org**

Published and distributed in Australia by: Hay House Australia Pty. Ltd.,
18/36 Ralph St., Alexandria NSW 2015 • *Phone:* 612-9669-4299
Fax: 612-9669-4144 • www.hayhouse.com.au

Published and distributed in the United Kingdom by: Hay House UK, Ltd.,
292B Kensal Rd., London W10 5BE • *Phone:* 44-20-8962-1230
Fax: 44-20-8962-1239 • www.hayhouse.co.uk

Published and distributed in the Republic of South Africa by: Hay House SA
(Pty), Ltd., P.O. Box 990, Witkoppen 2068 • *Phone/Fax:* 27-11-467-8904
info@hayhouse.co.za • www.hayhouse.co.za

Published in India by: Hay House Publishers India, Muskaan Complex,
Plot No. 3, B-2, Vasant Kunj, New Delhi 110 070 • *Phone:* 91-11-4176-1620
Fax: 91-11-4176-1630 • www.hayhouse.co.in

Distributed in Canada by: Raincoast, 9050 Shaughnessy St., Vancouver, B.C.
V6P 6E5 • *Phone:* (604) 323-7100 • *Fax:* (604) 323-2600 • www.raincoast.com

<u>**Take Your Soul on a Vacation**</u>

Visit **www.HealYourLife.com®** to regroup, recharge,
and reconnect with your own magnificence.
Featuring blogs, mind-body-spirit news, and life-changing
wisdom from Louise Hay and friends.

Visit **www.HealYourLife.com** today!

HEAL YOUR LIFE ♥

Take Your Soul on a Vacation

Get your daily dose of inspiration today at **www.HealYourLife.com®**. Brimming with all of the necessary elements to ease your mind and educate your soul, this Website will become the foundation from which you'll start each day. This essential site delivers the latest in mind, body, and spirit news and real-time content from your favorite Hay House authors.

Make It Your Home Page Today!

www.HealYourLife.com®